CW01184252

NOT HEAVY ENOUGH TO WIN A PRIZE?

MEMOIRS

Keith Diggle

[signature]
8 Sept 2011

GREENFIELD HOUSE

First published 1997
by Greenfield House
27 Old Gloucester Street, London W1N 3XX

ISBN 0 9531086 0 0

© 1997 Keith Diggle

The right of Keith Diggle to be identified as the author of this work has been asserted by him in accordance with the Copyright, Designs and Patents Act 1988.

All rights reserved. No part of this book may be reprinted or reproduced, stored in or introduced into any form of retrieval system, or transmitted in any form, or by any electronic, mechanical, or other means, including photocopying and recording, now known or devised hereafter, without permission in writing from the publisher.

A CIP catalogue record for this book is available from the British Library

Printed in Great Britain by Perfectaprint (UK) Limited, Byfleet, Surrey, KT14 7JG

This book is sold subject to the condition that it shall not, by way of trade or otherwise, be lent, re-sold, hired out, or otherwise circulated without the publisher's prior consent in any form of binding or cover other than that in which it is published.

BIG ROACH CAUGHT AT BATH

But Not Heavy Enough to Win a Prize

Mr. G. E. Diggle, fishing in the Avon at Bath, landed a fine roach weighing one ounce short of 3lbs.

He entered his catch in a competiton run by a London newspaper, but the prize was won by another competitor, who grassed a roach which turned the scale at 3lbs. 1oz! This was caught by Mr. T. Jackson fishing in Mapperley (Nottingham) Reservoir.

From a Bath newspaper, July 1934

Dedication

I dedicate this history of the first 40 years or so of my life to my wife Heather, known here and there in this text as 'The Lit', to my two sons, Marcus and Julian, and to the memory of my Father and Mother, my Father in Law, Charles Henry Ellis and our firstborn, Piers Winfield, who was with us for such a short time.

Thanks

I wish to express my thanks to designer Sarah Davies, who has worked hard to create for us all a good-looking book (which I hope the reader will agree that this is) and my eternal gratitude to two kind and helpful colleagues who have assisted me most ably in bringing this book to the point where it was fit to be designed: Felicity Rich and Sarah Williams – without them my words have remained but electrons swimming around within the innards of my Toshiba T2130CS.

CONTENTS

Preface		xi
Chapter 1	For Marcus And Julian	1
Chapter 2	He With His Genteel Background And Intellectual Pretensions; She With Neither	5
Chapter 3	Life Was Full Of Jewels *Number 8, Pembroke Road, Kingswood, Bristol (1937-1945)*	14
Chapter 4	Who Says There Isn't A Good Fairy? *Pauntley Court (1945-1946)*	31
Chapter 5	Oh How I Feared Miscellaneous *Gotherington Fields Farm (1946-1949)*	42
Chapter 6	I Must Ameliorate My Q List Average *Honington, Leasingham, Billingborough (1949-1951)*	49
Chapter 7	One Minute He Was Up In The Air And Then He Crashed To Earth *Polebrooke Aerodrome (September 1951 – July 1953)*	59
Chapter 8	Not Heavy Enough To Win A Prize *Living in Oundle (1953-1955)*	75
Chapter 9	There He Stands, This Fine British Youth, Facing An Exciting Future *Atomic Energy Research Establishment, Harwell (September 1955 – August 1956)*	86
Chapter 10	She Wrote Her Name And Her Telephone Number On The Back Of A Small Brown Envelope and Gave It To Me *Finding a Vocation (Summer 1956 – Summer 1957)*	91

CHAPTER 11 We Young Men Accepted This Form Of
Sexual Discrimination Without Question
The Royal Air Force (August 1957 – September 1958)   99

CHAPTER 12 'Oi 'Ave To 'Ave 'Im For Moi Own!'
*Saltley College, Birmingham
(September 1958 – July 1960)*   108

CHAPTER 13 Heather Would Have To Do The Bedrooms
On The Morning Of Her Wedding So That
Mr Maxwell Could Make A Proper Job
Of Polishing The Car
Getting Married (September 1960 – September 1961)   123

CHAPTER 14 They Were Such Sweet And Simple People
First Year of Marriage (September 1961 – August 1962)   129

CHAPTER 15 No More Maths! No More Maths!!
Corby (September 1962 – December 1966)   133

~

A RESORT RUNS THROUGH IT   149
*This book within the book is a romantic recollection of two seaside
resorts – one in England, one in France – that in the author's
memory become inextricably and fondly linked*

~

CHAPTER 16 'Give Him The Money, Godfrey,
For Heaven's Sake Give Him The Money!'
The Midland Sinfonia, Nottingham (1967-1968)   181

CHAPTER 17 I Remember Darkness . . . But There Was
To Be Light As Well
*Merseyside Arts Association (December 1968 –
September 1973) and The First Great Sea Adventure*   190

CHAPTER 18 We Were At The Mercy Of A Tide That
Was Steadily Carrying Us Backwards Into The Maelstrom.
Oh, The Horror!
*John Player & Sons, Nottingham (September 1973 –
September 1974) and The Second Great Sea Adventure*   208

CHAPTER 19	No Problem With Snakes, Signor; The Wild Boar Eat Them	
	A Freelance Life (September 1974 – April 1976)	219
CHAPTER 20	We Ate A Lot of *Questo* In Those Days	
	Life in Italy (April 1976 – August 1976)	226
CHAPTER 21	It Was The Great Disappearing And Diving Light Show Being Played in Reverse	
	The Third Great Sea Adventure (August 1976 – October 1976)	240
CHAPTER 22	They Were, It Transpired, Members Of The Red Brigade, Urban Terrorists	
	(October 1976 – July 1977)	266
CHAPTER 23	Large Wads Of Money Secured By Elastic Bands Are Passed Over To Disappear Into Capacious Pockets	
	The Fourth Great Sea Adventure (August 1977)	281
CHAPTER 24	No More Would We Need to Ask 'Where The Hell Are We?'	
	Back to England (September 1977 – December 1978)	286
CHAPTER 25	A Whistle-Stop Tour Of The Past 20 Years Or So	
	Life in Gravesend and Oundle and the Growth of Rhinegold (1978 – Present Day)	292

UNSERIOUS POEMS   304

For Julian After A Creative Dream
Anagrammatic Poem For Peter Palumbo
Christmas Time In The West Indies
Religious Experience
The Black Death
The Gypsy's Warning
Exercise 94
Welsh Mantra
For Adrian Henri
Not Dorking Dworkin

News Report
Pillow Talk
The Arts Manager's Prayer
Changing My Mind
Holiday Advice

SERIOUS POEMS   309

Watch Your Language
Dreaming Of Illegal Elderberries
The Overclass
Dresden
Ancient Dosser
The Earth Loves You
Souvenir of War
Sniper
Nursing Home
Reasons Why We Killed You

NAMES DROPPED   319

Preface

In the tattered slim manila file of memorabilia that I found amongst my Father's few possessions after his death I found something that struck me as being particularly appropriate to his life and to mine. It is a newspaper cutting from a Bath newspaper recording that in July 1934 my Father caught a 2lb 15oz roach in the River Avon. The headline reads BIG ROACH CAUGHT AT BATH. The sub-heading says **But not heavy enough to win a prize**.

Those who write autobiographies often search for quotations or figures of speech that contain within them a metaphor for the life they have led, from which they may fashion a title. When I saw this cutting I knew that in the sub-heading lay my title. It made me laugh out loud when I saw it. There have been so many times when I was judged to be not heavy enough, not *quite* heavy enough to win whatever prize it was upon which I had set my sights. My choice of title should not be taken to mean that what follows is a miserable catalogue of all the wrongs that life has wrought upon me – far from it – but it should reassure the reader that this book is not one of those extended boasts that the great and successful frequently launch upon an undeserving public.

'Why should I not publish my diary? I have often seen reminiscences of people I have never heard of, and I fail to see – because I do not happen to be a 'Somebody' – why my diary should not be interesting.'
Mr Pooter muses in *The Diary of a Nobody* by George and Weedon Grossmith.

Chapter 1

For Marcus and Julian

Dear Sons, when my Father, George Ernest Diggle, died he left me nothing at all; that is to say he left nothing tangible as a conscious act. He willed me nothing. He willed my Mother nothing. He did not, I believe, ever consider what effect his death would have on my Mother or on me – and, if he ever did, he certainly took no action on the matter. I had always known not to expect anything in the way of wealth but when he died I was surprised to find that he had left almost nothing at all. For my Mother there were 600 one pound notes neatly laid beneath the mattress of the bed in the caravan where he died but this was not really a bequest as such, for they were in the middle of their annual eight or nine month sojourn at Brean Sands, near Burnham-on-Sea, Somerset and this would have been the housekeeping money to be doled out to my Mother every week. Even then, 1972, £600 was not very much money – it was, perhaps, the equivalent of six weeks after-tax salary for me at the time.

For me there was nothing of monetary value but far worse, nothing of *any* kind of value. It was as if I had been ruled out of his life altogether. I had hoped for a letter, a simple note, but there was nothing except one handkerchief with the initial 'G' that I managed to salvage before what few clothes and possessions he had were given to nearby caravan dwellers by my Mother. The handkerchief stayed around for many years at the back of a drawer until someone decided it was too old and too ragged to be of any possible value and threw it out.

I still have a few things that I later recovered from my Mother, such as an ashtray made out of a hard aluminium alloy called 'Duralumin', used in aircraft, that my Father made in the factory where he worked during the war, Aero Engines Limited in Kingswood, Bristol. (The production of what were – and probably still are – known as 'foreigners', items for private use made from company owned materials and in company time on company machines has always been one of the perks of the factory worker.) There was a toy, that I think was an invention of my Father, a little man with flapping arms and legs that was suspended by the top of his head from a device that made him dance when a small lever was tapped; he was named by my Father, 'Willy Flapdoodle', and he was very much appreciated by a little boy in wartime Britain where toys, as sold in toyshops, were almost non-existent.

There were masses of photographs of him, family, friends that were his mementoes and became mine. No neat sorting out into albums, just a small suitcase made from cardboard stuffed with them. There wasn't much more.

So nothing that I could hold and say to myself, 'This was intended for me by my Father, this was something he wanted me to have'. Not even the time taken to drop me a line, and that was odd, because if my Father had one ambition in life it was to have been a writer. I don't count his manuscripts as being a legacy for they were certainly not written for me. I acquired them when my Mother died on 18 August 1994, along with the ashtray; four novels, unpublished, showing signs of repeated postings to and from the publishers and literary agents, the final rejection letter being posted to him the day after his death. And his typewriter, a portable from Boots the Chemists, that he typed to death. Once he had settled down in his caravan in his retirement, with thoughts of work far behind him, he typed his way through his days at Brean Sands and I'm sure he was happy at it.

He surely could have written something for me. Even something straightforward like what to do after his death or even whether he wanted his body to be buried or cremated. Or something to show he cared. I am sure he did care but it was the sort of caring that was, once I had become an adult, only implicit in our relationship; it was never openly stated or demonstrated. As you will soon see he was a wonderfully caring father when I was a child. We found each other less attractive during my later teenage years and circumstances kept us apart when I became adult. In his later years we got on very well together, we became quite close. He died in 1972 on 4 July at the age of 71 years when I was 34 years old.

There was a legacy, of course; there always is a legacy of some kind. It was a legacy of memories and to this day my Father lives in my memory as a sweet and gentle, totally self-centred, humorously inclined, very musical man, a failure in material terms, who lied about himself in order to obtain work and to give me someone to be proud of, and never once even allowed himself the thought that I might have loved him for what he was and that I might have valued him simply for what he brought to our family life. He was a man who, perhaps, towards the end of his life, thought so little of what he had achieved that it seemed better simply to slip out of it quietly without even saying goodbye. I wish that I could have had the opportunity of telling him how much I valued the life he gave me and I wish that he had thought to leave me some words from his heart.

My intentions in writing this book are several but the most important is that you should not be left, as I was left, without a word or two from your Father. Whether or not you inherit money and things of monetary value is very much in the balance as I write this (don't count any chickens on this score!) but you will possess, in this book, something that will, I hope, add a different sort of value to your lives. I hope you will find the story interesting and illuminating and that it helps you put your own lives into context. You will see the influences that made me the sort of person I became and you will see, perhaps, some of the influences – whether hereditary or environmental – that made you become the sort of people you are.

My other intentions? The main one is simply a desire to examine and put on record my own story for my own sake. Memory is an odd faculty that omits awkwardnesses and embarrassments and enhances the part one plays in episodes of life. The principal device used to record the main events of one's life is the anecdote, the story one tells over and over again to describe an incident or a person or a state of mind, and the anecdote is, above all, an entertainment. Mostly one tells stories in order to amuse people and so the facts of one's history must be shaped, altered and given a 'punchline', so that one's audience is held and amused. I have found that in re-telling aspects of my life I unwittingly change facts in order to make them more interesting, amusing and even, on occasion, thrilling. I believe that we all do this to an extent; it is harmless enough – provided that *you* do not believe the fictions you recount – but it is not appropriate to a book like this. The anecdotes you will read here are true to the detail, I shall embroider hardly at all. What I shall do in the writing of this book is to examine everything I record to ensure that it is as true as I can make it and trust in the facts and my skill as a writer to keep you reading. For me the benefit is that I shall have, for once and for all, examined the first 40 years or so of my life in detail, winnowed out the fictions, and established for myself what is the story of my life.

Why only the first 40 years or so? The period 1977 to 1979 is a convenient time to end what must be seen by me as Volume One (all autobiographies are in a sense Volume One, of course) and 1977 is when I began a new phase of my life, when I decided to knuckle down to the harder challenges of life, when I chose to take my responsibilities to the two of you more seriously . . . when I started to grow up, if you like. 1978 is when the decision started to pay dividends. 1979 is when things started to move very quickly. By ending the detailed account at this point I also save from embarrassment those good people whose lives have been interwoven with mine since that time and still are in many cases. This means that I should not lose myself too many friends when this book is published.

When thinking about writing this book I also simply wanted to make better use of time that would otherwise be wasted. Every working day I travel on Great North Eastern Railway trains from Peterborough to London, King's Cross, to go to my business and then travel back again. I thus spend some two hours of every one of those days sitting in a comfortable seat in a first-class compartment watching the same world flash by. It would be perfect, I thought, to spend that time in writing. I bought myself a little computer and on Monday 29 April 1996 I set to work to write a commutative autobiography, a North to South and South to North autobiography, something written while 780 miles flash by each week that will, if this work occupies me for rather more than a year as I think it will, have spanned nearly 40,000 miles. I have promised myself that not a word will be written either at home or in the office of Rhinegold Publishing Limited, the company that I helped to start after the significant year of 1977. A year or so allowed for the writing and I intend to have this book in print well before my 60th birthday which falls on 19 December 1997. As a publisher I should be able to meet these deadlines, but only time will tell.

So this is your legacy from me. As you get older you will add to it and qualify it with your own memories. You will relate it to your memories of Heather, your Mother, who plays an essential part in this story but who will appear only in outline, as it were. You know that we, your Mother and I, have always had a wonderfully close, mutually supportive relationship. Not only do we love each other very much, we depend on each other in a host of different ways and we have always been each other's best friends. Our backgrounds are so very similar that neither of us believes that we could have made any progress in life without the other. But this is my story; I cannot tell Heather's story for her and she must inevitably appear in a 'supporting rôle' as they say in the movies. In the same way my reference to Cathie and Charles Ellis, your maternal grandparents, will be scant in relation to what I can tell you of my parents; I can only write what I know and they are part of Heather's story, not mine.

Chapter 2

He With His Genteel Background and Intellectual Pretentions; She With Neither

In my early life there were few material advantages over the rest of our world. When my memories begin, that is when I remember detail rather than broad impressions, we seemed to be quite poor. My Mother told me long afterwards that when my Father became unemployed due to ill-health we lived for quite a long time on £1 a week which her Mother gave her; the rent of Number 8, Pembroke Road, Kingswood, Bristol where we went to live soon after I was born was half that, ten shillings a week (this was the mid forties). £1 a week was the barest minimum for survival. In the family spoken history this period of deprivation was said to have lasted for years but Father's papers show that it was much shorter, only four months – from February to June 1945. My Father was frequently off work due to ill-health (and in the custom of those days would not have been paid) and when he was at work and being paid he was paid very little; losing his job because of ill-health found him with no savings and left him with no income. It was a tragedy, the impact of which was magnified in terms of the time it lasted because there was no other way of magnifying it; the impact was as awful as it could be and like many other awful things seemed to last for a long, long time.

Father never said much about this time in his life and the documentation that exists is unreliable because he had a tendency to alter the dates of documents such as personal testimonials (that were absolutely vital to gaining employment). The impression I get from looking through the very small file of personal papers that I acquired following the death of my Mother is of a person with something to hide, someone who tried to create for himself a convincing *curriculum vitae* that was not altogether supported by the facts. Nothing sinister has been concealed, I am sure, but there was, without doubt, a very long period in his life when he had no work, and, probably along with hundreds of thousands of men of his generation who suffered in the Great Depression from the mid-Twenties to the mid-Thirties, he later took steps to conceal the fact. The end result is, however, confusing to someone who is trying to find out the truth.

Father was born on 25 January 1901 in Stalybridge, Cheshire. From the original indenture, which I possess, I know that on 8 June 1917, when he was 16 and a half, he signed up for a five-year apprenticeship in Marine and General Engineering with the Southampton firm of Hemsley Bell, Turner and Co Limited, and I also know from the testimonial the firm produced for him that he left them on 21 June 1920. The date of this document has been changed, inexpertly, almost certainly by my Father, to read 1923.

I think it highly likely that he joined the Royal Air Force in 1920, having given up the apprenticeship, and he remained a serviceman until 1926, serving for most of the time in the part of India that is now Pakistan. There is no documentation to authenticate his claim to have achieved the rank of Flight Lieutenant when in the RAF. The wealth of the anecdotes told to me and the large amount of photographs in the cardboard suitcase confirm beyond any doubt that he was in the RAF, that his work involved aeroplanes (and flying in them) and that he was in India – but there is nothing official to prove this and certainly nothing convincing to show that he achieved officer status. The photographs show pictures of Father in a flying suit but never in an officer's uniform. There are pictures of him dressed for public performance in a dance band ('The Syncopated Six' – he played the one-stringed fiddle) when in India and I am not at all sure that in that class-conscious age an officer would have been seen playing in a dance band. He was probably what was called an Airframe Fitter and his rank would not have been any more senior than Senior Aircraftsman.

There is a letter in the file dated 26 June 1933 addressed to one Flt/Lt. Diggle, G. E. at C Flight Office, No 2 F. T. School, Digby, Lincs confirming that his resignation was accepted and was to take effect from the date of the letter. The letter ends 'I am desired by the Air Marshall (*sic,* the second 'l' is crossed out by hand) to tender his regrets that repeated attacks of malaria have compelled you to relinquish your commission. He authorises you to use, in civilian life, the rank and style of Flight Lieutenant'. The letter is signed by one Walter Padleigh, Squadron Leader i/c Postings. The signature has clearly been executed by my Father and the whole is rather badly typed on a vaguely official looking piece of paper with a crest that might have come from any government office, with all identifying information having been typed rather than printed. This is very unreliable evidence and is best ignored I think. It is a fake.

I know that in 1930 he acquired a passport, applied for and was granted an immigration visa to enter the USA and the visa application (upon which I doubt if he would have lied) which required him to list his places of residence over the previous five years shows him to have lived in Southampton from 1926. He did not, however, travel to the USA. He stayed in England.

There is one document, a testimonial that appears to be authentic, from the company Aero Engines Limited of Kingswood, Bristol, which describes him in glowing terms and says he was a Chargehand there from 3 December 1935 to 23 February 1945. (The several copies of this letter that accompany the original in the file have him elevated to the status of Supervisor.)

Another reliable document, from the National Council of YMCAs that was later to employ him, has him working for the YMCA from 18 June 1945 to 24 November 1951.

So from the documentary evidence we have a young man who served three years of an engineering apprenticeship (until 1920, when he was 19 years old), who was in the RAF (until 1926, when he was 25 years old), who was unemployed (until the end of 1935, when he was 34 years old – a period of nine years), who worked as an engineer (achieving the position of Chargehand) until the early part of 1945 when he fell ill. After four months of unemployment arising from his ill-health and having suffered severe financial hardship he found another job, a very different kind of job, with the YMCA.

Apart from his work and unemployment record, what else do I know of my Father? He had been a member of the Independent Labour Party in Southampton where he had known the socialist pioneer James Maxted (he was intensely proud of this). He was well read and well spoken with just a touch of a Lancashire accent. He possessed many books (predominantly Penguin books which had started to become available in 1935) and amongst his collection there was the ubiquitous Fitzgerald's *Rubaiyat of Omar Khayyam* (which many young people with intellectual pretensions in the Thirties owned and committed to memory and would then recite when slightly drunk), large parts of which he had memorised. He would have loved to have been called a 'left wing intellectual'.

I have already referred to his ambition to be a successful writer; the manuscripts I inherited bear witness to the fact that he tried to be one. Cousin Kenneth Poolman, son of Father's sister Monica (known to all as Mona), tells me that during the part of his nine-year period of unemployment when he lived in Bath my Father, who had quasi-parental influence over him, spoke constantly of wanting to live a writer's life and, says Ken who achieved that ambition, was largely responsible for setting him on that path. My Father told him stories and showed him the imagination at work. Sadly, apart from a few letters published in newspapers, my Father never saw a word of his own in print, although during my early life he claimed to me to have had a book published in Russia; this is supported only by a letter in the file of documents from the 'Co-operative Publishing Society of Foreign Workers in the USSR' dated 20 December 1933 acknowledging receipt of the manuscript of his book called *The Life Chain;* I believe its publication is mythical.

~

Notwithstanding his modest achievements in life my Father always believed that he was superior to the common herd and his family background encouraged him in this. Ken Poolman told me that my paternal grandmother, born Isabella

Winfield, had been a cotton heiress from Lancashire who had fallen for a ne'er-do-well, Samuel Diggle. He had married her and given her eight children; my Father being the youngest. His brothers were Albert, Samuel and Harold and his sisters were Hilda, Monica, Marjorie and Dora, who died at the age of 19 when my Father was nine. Grandfather Samuel ran through Grandmother Isabella's fortune in various ill-conceived business ventures and then decamped for the USA in the company of a young lady assistant from the confectionery shop he then owned in Southampton.

Before the shop there were other ventures, including a business in Liverpool and the transportation of the entire family (prior to my Father's birth) to South Africa where, the story goes, my Aunt Mona was presented with a prize for running by Cecil Rhodes. After Grandfather's departure the fortunes of the remaining family suffered badly and whereas the older children had gone to private fee-paying schools, young George Ernest was sent to a state school and, I understand, felt the deprivation keenly. Certainly my Father would not have been 'put to' the engineering trade as an apprentice had the family remained together and its fortunes maintained.

When Grandfather went to the USA his two eldest sons tried to make contact with him. Eventually Albert decided to go out to the USA to find him and try to persuade him to return. He arrived in the USA but failed to find their Father; he stayed on. Samuel decided to go out to join Albert in the search for their Father and they were both unsuccessful. Grandfather's eventual end is a family mystery but, on his track record, it was probably a sticky one.

The family remaining in England was thus also deprived of the two eldest sons who did not show themselves again until 1917 when they returned to England wearing the uniforms of the American Expeditionary Force prior to its moving into France towards the end of the First World War. Ken Poolman, who told me this story, added the snippet that my Uncle Albert was the pastrycook to General Pershing (it would be nice if I could include a war hero in our family but we shall have to settle for a military patissier). Both my uncles survived the war and returned to the USA where they married, raised children and lived happily ever after. In 1918 or 1919 my Aunt Hilda went to live in the USA (it is thought she married one of those American soldiers – perhaps a friend of my two uncles?) and in 1920 Grandmother Diggle went to live with her in Seattle. Presumably my Father's intention, when he applied for his immigration visa to the USA in 1930, was to join them. Nothing is known of my Aunt Hilda's first marriage but presumably it ended because later on she married a nautical man, a quartermaster who worked on cruise ships, called Jack Flattum who, from the snaps I found in the cardboard suitcase, looked like a very jolly fellow. There were thus five members of our family on my Father's side who lived and died in the USA.

There was a distinct, but not necessarily major, musical talent running through this side of the family. Grandmother Diggle played the piano and composed music; I have a copy of a piano piece she wrote called *The Cranleigh*

Polka and it is rather good. My cousin Sheila, daughter of Aunt Marjorie, told me that at one stage in her early life Grandmother Diggle played the organ in Winchester Cathedral and she and Grandfather Diggle actually lived in the Cathedral Close for a while. Uncle Sam played the 'cello and at the time of his death owned an instrument that was sufficiently good to be willed to the music department of Seattle University. My Father had the ability to play a variety of instruments well enough to give pleasure to others and once wrote a rather pleasant little song, called *You Came To Me Like An Angel,* which, in the course of writing this book, I was able to recall (having heard it last in 1945) and 'dictate', as it were, all of the melody and most of the words to my colleague Sarah Williams, who took it down on manuscript paper as I sang it and attempted to pick out the tune on a child's battery-powered keyboard. I then had the song properly set and reproduce it overleaf.

Uncle Harold, who stayed in England, married Alice (they had no children) and set up home in Southampton was, in his early years at least – and I base this upon one of his paintings that I now own – a painter of talent. The little seascape, signed and dated 1904, is a confident and convincing piece and I love it. Uncle Harold was also a patissier, working on the grand ocean-going liners out of Southampton, and from the cookery books that accompanied him around the world countless times, I have found, lodged within the pages along with his handwritten special recipes, photographs of his confectionary creations made as set pieces for grand dinners. Uncle Harold was an artistic chap, no doubt about it.

Grandfather Diggle obviously included confectionary skills amongst his talents for he did run that shop in Southampton and it would be from him and from the experience of working in the shop that Uncles Albert and Harold discovered and developed their own skills. Cooking, like music, runs, albeit erratically, in the family and emerges in your generation, my sons, for you both love to cook and are, in your different ways, not at all bad at it.

There is much more to be discovered and perhaps written about this branch of the family and all I can offer you here is a taster, a sample, so that you may see something of your roots. From the other lines, from my Mother's side and from your Mother's side, far less is known nor will it be known, I suspect. I remain intrigued by that Victorian Diggle family and, no doubt, when this book is finished I will start to dig deeper into that history.

~

My Mother was born Lilian Margaret Staddon in Chipping Sodbury, Gloucestershire on 18 August 1914, a daughter of John Staddon, a farmer, and his wife, my maternal Grandmother whose name was never known to me; she was always called 'Gran Staddon' and that was that. Mother had two sisters, Florence and Marie, and three brothers; James, who went to live in New Zealand after the Second World War; Thomas, who emigrated to South Africa at about the same time; and the youngest, Benjamin, an Able Seaman in the Royal Navy, who died

YOU CAME TO ME LIKE AN ANGEL

Words and music by George Ernest Diggle

You came to me like an an-gel when I was sad and a-lone. You gave me a glimpse of hea-ven at a time when my heart was like stone. Just for a while you'll be with me hel-ping me with your smile. Then you must go and then I know there'll be ma-ny a wea-ry mile. What shall I do when you leave me how shall I pass my time? How can I face life with-out you once I have known the sub-lime?

© Copyright 1997: GREENFIELD HOUSE

My Father's Song

during the war when his ship the *Jarvis Bay* was sunk – he was 19 years old. Mother left school at 14 years to be a children's nanny and met my Father in Bath, probably in 1933 or 1934, where she was then 'in service' with a well-off family. Father, having left Southampton, had moved to Bath where he eventually took up rent-free residence in a boat-house on the banks of the River Avon.

Mother was and remained throughout her life a country girl, unsophisticated and undemanding, whose greatest pleasure in life lay in looking after other people. She was warm and cuddly. She could cook very well – an attribute that would stand the family in good stead when things got rougher; indeed she eventually became the family breadwinner. Her cooking was of what might be termed the 'old-fashioned' style and I regard it as being significant that both my Father and the man she married after my Father died, have as Cause of Death on their Death Certificates the words 'Myocardial infarction due to Coronary atheroma' – indication of a very high fat diet. She also had a violent temper that was terrifying when it emerged. Of education she had but little but she could read perfectly well, she could write simply and clearly and she was, although not at all well educated, much more intelligent than people took her to be. My Father and I owed her a great deal.

Father and Mother were married on 22 February 1936 and I, Keith Winfield Diggle, was born on 19 December 1937.

How they came to marry I cannot say. They were in almost every way an ill-matched couple. He with his genteel background and intellectual pretentions; she with neither. He with his rather thin, very slightly posh voice; she with a Gloucester burr that became Bristolian (an accent I always thought ugly even when a very young child – I acquired a West Country accent but never once took on a hint of Bristol although I lived there for the first seven years of my life) whenever she was in the company of her sisters, both of whom were living in Bristol when I was born. He talked left-wing politics, possessed and played a ukelele banjo and a one-stringed fiddle, could play the piano but didn't have one, read extensively and saw himself as a thinking, cultured man. She only ever concerned herself with looking after her family and she was well occupied at that.

Father's ill-health ran throughout our lives. He had come out of the RAF with malaria and sandfly fever, contracted during the six-year period in India and suffered from recurring bouts of ill health derived from these diseases. On his return to England in 1926 he had been given a dire prognosis by a doctor, a verdict that my Mother took a strange pleasure in recounting to all she met. My Father had been told that 'he would never walk or work again' and Mother trotted this out regularly, partly (I have always thought) because she liked the alliteration, to account for the nine-year gap in his employment history and for his recurrent absences from work at Aero Engines Limited. The very fact of my Father working and earning a living thus became a considerable triumph over dire odds (which it may very well have been).

Father was not a robust man. He seemed to exist in a constant paroxism of bronchitic coughing during the early part of my life and to his state of health was ascribed all the misfortunes of his life. I do not now believe, however, that he was inordinately fond of work – or at least the work that was available to him at that time, or indeed later on, when he effectively withdrew from the unequal struggle. Now I think of it I do believe that I never once heard him say anything that could be construed as a career ambition. To win the football pools, yes – that was a definite ambition; to have a book published and to make a fortune therefrom, yes – that would do very well. To work for it? I don't think he ever entertained the idea seriously.

Working to earn a living was something he accepted as a regrettable necessity. He would rather be employed and have some money than not and, during the prolonged period when he was out of work, I am sure that he felt his situation keenly. It was simply that he appeared to have no ambition beyond scraping by. To be wealthy could only be brought about by fortune not endeavour. I suppose that in those hard times that was a view shared by most.

Two good things in particular characterised my Father's contribution to our life then and to my life today: the 'language' and a seemingly infinite supply of the most inconsequential, bizarre, silly but always tuneful popular songs that derived from his youth – he was born in 1901 – and from his Mother, Isabella Winfield Diggle, who was born in 1861. The nature of the 'language', which is absolutely part of me and was eagerly taken on by your Mother, Heather, also known as 'the Lit' (which is in itself part of the language and was contributed by you Marcus) and which you both know well – or should – is a sort of degeneration of normal speech along baby-talk lines combined with arcane associations the origins of which are long lost or is made up on the spur of the moment according to a few very simple rules. A new addition to the language is best if it is obscure and challenges the other members of the family.

The best example of the language that I can give you is one which I know derives from the earliest days of my parents' marriage. My Father would put his arm around my Mother (always known by him as 'the Mums') and he would say that he was providing her with a 'protective arm'. My Mother, when she wanted him to put his arm around her would ask for a 'Tec Tec Arm'. Later, when my Father slipped his arm around Mother's shoulder, he would say 'Tec Tec Arm' and she would then say, in a comfortable way, 'er', turning the 'arm' into 'armour' as in 'protective armour'. Today we still have this ritual when arms are put around shoulders but the Lit has taken it to a ridiculous length. There is an American TV hospital series called 'ER' (Emergency Room). The Lit refers to the show as 'Tec Tec Arm'. This may sound very peculiar but my Father would have been proud of her.

The songs poured forth from my Father, sometimes accompanied on the ukelele banjo, sometimes the one-stringed fiddle, but as often as not without their benefit. My Mother would sing popular songs of the day ('Any umb-er-ellas, any umb-er-ellas to mend today?' 'There'll be bluebirds over the white cliffs of Dover') but my Father eschewed such modern rubbish; he preferred old rubbish. I loved it all. It sometimes seems to me today that he never sang a line that I didn't take into my memory instantly. It all went in and stayed there so that even today a strain, a line or so, will return. I try it out on the Lit. 'Have I ever given you this one?' I ask, and sing out the words. These days she usually says that I have but perhaps once a month something comes back that she has never heard from me before.

CHAPTER 3

LIFE WAS FULL OF JEWELS

Number 8, Pembroke Road, Kingswood, Bristol (1937-1945)

I was born at 11, Alexandra Gardens, Staple Hill, Bristol on 19 December 1937. Part of our family history has it that when my Mother went into labour my Father occupied himself by fitting a new goatskin membrane to the front of his ukelele banjo. The birth took place in the bedroom with the assistance of a midwife. Family history does not hold me responsible for any particular difficulty in the process and this can be relied upon, for families are generally unremitting in their allocation of lifelong guilt for troubles caused during one's entrance into the world; the matter has never been raised. Early in 1938 my parents moved to Number 8, Pembroke Road, Kingswood, Bristol and it is there I lived until June 1945.

~

Number 8, which we rented, was a semi-detached, two-bedroomed house, with a 'front room' with the best furniture (that one entered only when someone came to call and that was infrequently), a 'living room' (at the back but it was never called a 'back room' as working class folk might have called it), a kitchen, a bathroom on the first floor with no WC and a WC on the ground floor contained within a small brick extension at the rear that also contained a coal store. It was a very cold WC but it was better than my Gran Staddon's; she lived in Chipping Sodbury where she owned a tumbledown village shop called Staddon's Stores and she didn't have a WC at all; she had a two seater in a hut in the garden which had buckets beneath the seats, torn up newspapers on a nail and a disposal system called Bill. I was always fascinated by the amount of woodworm infestation in the wooden seats and used to wonder if eventually the bugs would win the day and someone would be dropped into the dark mystery below.

There was no central heating in the house and during the winter there was only one small fire in the living room. My Father, having spent so long in India, felt cold acutely and so wore 'combinations' to keep warm – horrid woollen garments that with age took on an unpleasant shade of pinky yellow; they covered the body from wrist to ankle and were changed (Heavens, the thought of it!) weekly. After their consignment to the wash (which took place in a copper boiler in the kitchen) they appeared on the washing line and, on frosty days, froze.

I once stood in awe in the garden, staring at one of these garments, solid as a board, which when caught by the wind hit me smartly in the face.

Kingswood is a suburb of Bristol. You had to take the bus to go into what my Mother always called 'the Centre', a journey of perhaps twenty minutes or more. Our house faced a piece of open land and beyond that were the railings of the large red brick Primary School, a school that catered for Infants and Juniors. Long before I started at the Infant school I was familiar with the sight of long rows of children waiting to be marched into the building first thing in the morning, after the midday break and after the morning and afternoon 'playtimes'. In the morning the children were required to do a sort of marching on the spot before going into their classrooms and were helped along in this with a pretty little tune that was played on an upright piano. I never knew how the sound of a piano could have been projected so loudly that not only the children in the playground could hear it but so could I in the front garden of Number 8. The tune stayed with me as did almost every tune I ever heard at this time in my life and I can whistle it on demand (not that anyone ever does demand it).

Of our neighbours I remember only a few details. None possessed cars. Television, although it had been invented, was an unknown thing; not only did no-one possess a television set, no-one ever expressed a desire for one – they were as equally likely to have wished for a personal computer. Most had radios – 'wireless sets' – vital for following the progress of the war and for the songs that went straight into my head and never left it. All of us were by today's standards poor but by standards of that time definitely superior to the class *we* thought of as poor. Our economic situation then was such that new clothes were so rare that I cannot remember ever having seeing my parents have any. Being ill was serious if it involved visiting a doctor because one had to pay unless one was prepared to experience the indignity of 'going on the panel', a sort of means-tested charity scheme that people like my parents would have died rather than apply for.

The strange thing for me about this period is that for all what now seem to be deprivations I remember it as being a blissfully happy time. There were one or two fairly nasty incidents, including a caning on the hand, four strokes 'for talking' during my first week in Junior school, when I was about six years old which has always seemed rather harsh treatment. The constant presence of Adolf Hitler – the wretched man never seemed to go away – and the solemn tones of wartime News on the wireless adds a dark shadow to my recollections. Other than a few things like that it was all rather good with plenty of love and attention from parents who clearly wanted me. I was born some 22 months after they were married and this fact was later used by my Father to explain to me somewhat obliquely, what he meant when he told me that I was 'wanted'; I had always taken this for granted, of course.

I lived here until June 1945 when we left so that my Father and Mother could take up a new job, a wonderfully exciting new job that would mean a whole new life for us. During our time at Number 8 the Second World War had started and ended as far as Europe was concerned and a few weeks after we left for our new home the Allies ended it as far as Japan was concerned.

From my Mother

On eating well:
The Lord be praised
My belly be raised
One inch about the table.
For I'll be damned
If I ain't crammed
As much as I be able.

On humour:
Theece make oi laugh
Theece make oi cry
Theece make I pee myself

On hunger:
My stomach thinks my throat is cut

On sorrow:
Stop crying
Thy peebag's too near thy eyes

Of rather weak tea:
That's tea bewitched and water bebuggered

On breaking wind:
Wherever you be
Let your wind go free
For keeping it back
Was the death of me

~

The sound of sirens: the Alert and the All Clear. The sound of waves of German bombers overhead going to bomb Filton aeroplane factory and the factory where my Father worked (they succeeded, frequently). Anti-aircraft balloons, 'Wimpies' or 'Barrage Balloons', clearly visible every day suspended high in the sky, their wires invisible to me. The distinct odour of damp clay detected in public air-raid shelters. My Father's ARP (Air Raid Precautions) helmet, bucket of sand and long handled scoop left in the porch to use against incendiary bombs. Collecting bomb shrapnel from the streets after a raid, a commodity that had considerable swap value and was part of school currency.

~

We had a grey tom cat called 'Joe', named after Joseph Stalin, who, during the war was something of a hero because of the courageous Russian resistance to the Hun. I don't think my Father ever came to know the awful truth about this mass-murderer.

~

Cinema-going seemed to be occasionally affordable and my parents were enthusiastic about films. The first film I saw in the company of my Mother and Father was at the Ambassador cinema in Kingswood which, during wartime, was completely shrouded in thick camouflage made of heavy netting adorned with pieces of hessian, and involved Edward G. Robinson killing someone with a pair of scissors. Joan Taylor was also in the film the title of which was *Woman in the Picture*. My Mother watched films sitting on the edge of her seat, a picture of concentration, making audible comments such as 'Look behind you!' and 'Oh No! Oh No!'.

There was children's cinema at the Regal in Staple Hill and when I was old enough my parents found the necessary few pence for me to go in the company of an older child who lived nearby. Apart from Tarzan, Abbot and Costello, Laurel and Hardy, The Three Stooges, The Marx Brothers and a serial involving someone possessing some of the characteristics of Superman (mask and tights), what I remember most is the incredible atmosphere of a vast auditorium filled with children who yelled and stamped their feet before the programme started and made so much noise that the manager had to go on stage and demand silence before he would start the show. Being in the company of so many I found quite disturbing; there was something in the air that wasn't simply the result of the spray that usherettes blasted in our directions as they moved up and down the aisles (bug control, you see; children had bugs in those days). I was part of a *mob* and I didn't like it.

I also remember seeing a film about Zorro (wonderful swordfighting) and *The Desert Song;* I had fantastic dreams after seeing this musical film in which I was the sheik galloping across the desert – I think this was my first experience of *yearning* for something. I would wake up yearning to be this character.

(My Father told me that once he shared a room with a man who used to imitate playing the xylophone. There is an exciting sort of horse galloping tune in *The Desert*

Song, very fast and furious, and the man would stand, holding imaginary sticks and would run them up and down an imaginary key board at high speed, hitting imaginary notes, while singing, 'Oh, Jesus Christ Almighty How D'You Do?'.)

The two great occasions of my early film-going were *Bambi* which reduced all of us, children and adults alike, to tears upon tears, and *The Wizard of Oz* the sheer genius of which more than made up for the nightmares those bloody Munchkins gave me.

Songs my Father taught me

Four and Nine – I took her to the Cecil
Four and Nine – I couldn't get inside.
I took her to Lockhart's and ordered wine
And bang went fourpence of my Four and Nine.

I gave her an apple, she let me hold her hand.
I gave her an orange we kissed to beat the band.
I gave her a grapefruit she let me hold her tight.
I'm going to take a water melon to my girl tonight!

A gallant young Airman lay dying
And as in the wreckage he lay
To the other young Airmen around him
These last dying words he did say . . .
'Take the camshaft from out of my kidneys
Take the piston from out of my brain
From the small of my back take the joystick
And assemble the old crate again.'

To be sung when a little boy yawns without covering his mouth; the index finger is pointed at the chasm and then is sung
That reminds me where I left my umb-er-ella!
Left me umb-er-ella last night!!

~

My emergence into full up-and-running childhood was a process of veils being slowly lifted so that over a long period reality was revealed to me. It still seems that I started by looking at the world through a small misty hole which gradually expanded as I got older and as I was able to relate what I saw to what I had seen. So, at first, my family defined normality to me. Later, as my experience widened, I became aware of neighbours, people in the street and children at school who were, in some way, physically different from what I had come to see as normal and they frightened me. There was a street character, a man with Down's Syndrome (then called Mongolism), who was known as Big Bob and who only uttered frightening roars and bellows. Another, often seen when shopping with my Mother in Staple Hill, had had both legs amputated and wheeled himself around on a low trolley that put him only a few inches from the ground so that his head, a dirty, violent looking head with livid face, was almost level with mine. I was terrified by these men.

At school there were children who had had 'mastoid' operations. I still do not know exactly what the procedure involved but it left a large jagged scar behind the ear and when the children returned to school after the necessary time at home and the dressings were removed this horrifying wound could be clearly seen, one's attention drawn to it by the purple stain of some kind of antiseptic.

At the end of Pembroke Road there lived a couple who would occasionally be seen taking their son out in a wheelchair, a teenage boy suffering from hydrocephaly, a disorder that makes the head swell to a vast size from birth. And next door there was Brenda Painter's sister Vera. Brenda was a normal girl but Vera had one eye that was quite white and sightless and an air of not being long for this world – which proved to be the case for she died before we left Number 8.

At the age of five I was taken into hospital to have my tonsils and adenoids removed – it was generally held that young people could not progress into adulthood in possession of these organs. As I slowly awoke from the operation my eyes fell on the bed next to me where a man lay, a victim of a bomber raid the night before. Almost the whole side of his face was gone. For some reason – perhaps because he had only just been brought in – there was no dressing on the wound and I was left to stare at this awful sight as I drifted in and out of consciousness.

Imagine the effect on me when in 1945 I was taken into a cinema – it would have been a 'News Theatre', an establishment given over to the showing of British Movietone News ('The Eyes and Ears of the World') and other news programmes plus lots of cartoon films – by my Mother and the first of the news reports on the Nazi concentration camps were shown. To this day I cannot imagine how a child of this age, I was then just seven, could have been allowed to see scenes that were so terrible that they still came into my mind twenty or thirty years later and have their influence upon me today. Then it was the sight of the emaciated bodies, rather than an appreciation of the ghastly suffering experienced or the cosmic implication of what had been going on in those places, that burned itself into my memory. When you are a child you perceive things only in terms of the impact they have on you; the vicarious sense takes time to develop.

And yet the suffering of others did have an impact. Early on at school I found the hymn that starts 'There is a green hill far away' almost overwhelmingly sad. The combination of the tune and the words that said 'We do not know, we cannot tell, what pains he suffered there' brought tears to my eyes when I was only five years old. (In common with almost every other child, of course, the green hill without a city wall caused some confusion – 'why did a hill need a city wall in the first place?', I mused.)

~

When I was ill and in bed my Mother once bought me a comic – the Beano. It is the smell that I remember most, it was as good as the smell of freshly baked bread. Comics became a vital part of boyhood life. They were one's principal source of reading material. Given the range of comics that was available your choice of comic could quickly define you to others in some strange way. I would, for example, borrow a Knockout but would never buy one. I would buy or borrow a Radio Fun but would not been seen, under any circumstances, with a Film Fun. I had nothing but contempt for readers of Mickey Mouse.

One's ambition, of course, was to progress on to the comics that required one to read fluently, the comics that weren't really comics at all, but were a collection of stories plus features aimed at the older child. My cousin Roy (on my Mother's side), older than me, read the Hotspur and the Wizard and so defined himself as being almost grown up. One of those two featured the indefatigable 'Wilson', a super athlete, man of steel and terribly brave fellow, who usually stripped down to what looked like black combinations before taking on the challenge of a Zulu chieftain to jump over a 100-foot barrier made up of warriors holding their assegais above their heads. He was a sort of British equivalent to Superman (whom you will know because he is still current) or Captain Marvell (whom you will probably not know). All were required to change their clothing before they could perform.

As time went by – and here I go ahead of myself chronologically – comics from America became available and I was seduced by them. Not only Superman and Captain Marvell but females too. There was Superwoman, naturally, but it is less well known that Captain Marvell had a sister, Mary Marvell, who, like her brother, had only to say the word SHAZAM to be converted into something rather more athletic and shapely than her normal self. SHAZAM was an acronym made up from the initial letters of six greek gods (for the good Captain) and six greek goddesses (for his sister). I don't think I ever knew the male version but Mary's Marvell's transformation formula was something like Selena, Hippolyta, Ariadne, Zena, Aphrodite and Minerva.

There was Little Orphan Annie with her round glasses and no eyes and a dog that went 'Arf, arf' and L'il Abner from Dogpatch, USA with a cast of wonderful characters like Daisy Mae, Stoopefying Johnson, Evil Eye Flugel and many more; later the strip was made into a stage musical and then into a really good movie musical which I adore.

My parents read the Daily Mirror newspaper and this had a whole page of different syndicated comic strips once a week. There was Garth, Belinda, Captain Reilly ffoul, the very famous Jane who nearly always ended *almost* naked and was a favourite with the armed forces, and Popeye – very occasionally the paper would give over the entire page to the spinach guzzling sailor and to me, a devoted fan, this was a very paradise. I was told that at a very early age I would take the paper to see if there was 'a nun-nun (ie another) page of Popeye'. Without wishing to embarrass you in front of all your friends, dear sons, I will confess that the Lit has taken this expression to her heart and will use it to express her delight at something truly wonderful that happens by chance and, on occasion, when moved, I have used it too.

~

There were, nearby, places of adventure, places where older children would go: a shop in Staple Hill where glasses of fizzy drinks could be bought for a penny (you did not have to buy a whole bottle) and towards the end of the war a shop in Kingswood let it be known that it had *ice-cream* for sale and the attraction of this made me more adventurous than ever before and I made the trip, deep into foreign territory to try something I had only heard about. Imagine, being six years old and never having tasted ice-cream! It was poor homemade stuff I suppose but I had had an adventure in the finding of it and I was well satisfied when I got myself safely home.

Rodway Common was a place where adults went for walks, young children went with their parents to play and slightly older children went bird-nesting. It was on one of my first visits, in the company of some older and responsible children, that I came across some boys who had found a hedge-sparrow's nest and had all its eggs in a tobacco tin lined with grass. I did not know the ethics of bird- nesting at the time, namely that only one egg is ever taken and the location of a nest is always kept a close secret to stop others, even one's closest friends, from taking more. Today those unwritten rules are sadly redundant as bird-nesting is now firmly outside of the law – sadly, I say, because the pursuit as followed by my childhood friends and me brought us into such close contact with the natural world and encouraged us to develop what were almost curatorial skills in keeping our collections well displayed with neat labels, that I do believe it caused more good than harm.

The boys showed me the six bright blue eggs in the tin. They were exquisite. They were jewels. I begged and begged and they gave me one for myself and with it instructions for its blowing so that the shell could be kept forever. I took it proudly home and innocently sought my parents' help in the blowing. What followed reduced me to helpless tears for hours. They were shocked. These boys had robbed a mother bird of her babies. What would she feel when she got back home and found her babies gone? And I was an accomplice! How could I make amends? I couldn't take it back. I didn't know where the nest was. I gave the egg to my Father and begged forgiveness, from him, from my Mother and from the mother hedge sparrow. Father disposed of the egg well out of my sight and the matter was never discussed again. Later, when we lived in the country, bird nesting became my all consuming passion; I respected the ethics of the business and built a fine collection.

~

Small, beautiful things proved fascinating – and still do. My Mother once showed me how to make an antirrhinum blossom, the snapdragon, open and close its mouth by pinching its sides. The opening and closing was interesting, even amusing, but I had never looked really closely at a flower before. I was very struck by it. It was like looking at the bird's eggs. It was another jewel.

One Autumn, when I had been kept away from school because of some minor ailment, I took some leaves from a nearby hawthorn hedge. They were yellow and the fine tracery of their veins could be clearly seen. I spent several hours drawing them in an exercise book and then colouring them. They too were jewels. I loved them as I loved the flower and the bird's egg.

Butterflies too. Perhaps more than birds' eggs, flowers and autumnal leaves. Intricate, tiny, delicate, brightly coloured. Irresistible!

Now, dear sons, consider the Lit. Is she not small and beautiful? Is she not a jewel? And do I not shower her with small beautiful things? As the bough is bent so the tree will grow.

~

Living in Bristol and not acquiring the bizarre manner of speech of that city was an accomplishment for which I deserve some credit. All around me, apart from my Father and Mother, had it but I somehow resisted it. There were three components to Bristol speech. The first derived from the puritan influences on the city and this took the form of using 'thee' and 'thou' when addressing others and words like 'bide' to mean 'stay'. The second was based upon an eccentric use of the letter 'l'. The third was a strange rising inflection that made every statement into a question.

'Bide where thee bidst' was a commonly used way of telling children to stay where they were.

'This' was often replaced by 'thick', pronounced very . . . thickly. 'Thee sit on thick chair' was the sort of speech commonly heard.

The omission of the 'l' sound at the end of words ending in 'l' and the addition of 'l' to every word possible with a particular inclination towards words ending with vowels was and is peculiar to the speech of Bristolians. The way of demonstrating the strange 'l' phenomenon is to ask a Bristolian to read the following:

Dame Eva Turner
Prima Donna
Of the Carl Rosa Opera Company
Is coming to Bristol

One then hears:

Dame Eval Turnal
Primal Donnal

Of the Car Rosal Operal Company
Is coming to Bristo

Now say this out loud and make the voice rise as though asking a question at the end of each line. Now you have it. Strange isn't it?

The accent I do have was acquired later, when we moved towards our bright and happy future with my Father's new job.

~

Pantomimes – we seemed to find enough money for my Mother to take me to pantomimes at the Empire or the Hippodrome – and wasn't Aladdin's cave superb! All the shammery flim-flam of phoney jewels, all the glitter, I bought the lot. I believed it. That cave into which Aladdin was lowered by his wicked uncle Abanazer existed for me.

The wonder of all wonders was the zoo. Bristol Zoo was totally beyond the limit of what a child had any right to expect. You didn't have to wait until nightfall or until the lights were dimmed to appreciate the miracles of Bristol Zoo! There could not have been many children in Bristol who did not get to spend a day there. There was a definite pattern to the perfect Bristol Zoo day. It started with the fearful thought as my eyes opened that today it might rain and the whole business would be called off. The perfect day, I worked out, started with a touch of frost on the ground (don't ask me how I arrived at this – I'm simply reporting what I believed at the time) and then the sun appeared and bathed us in warmth and bright light for the rest of the day. A picnic would be prepared and packed: thermos flask of tea, little bottle of milk, a paper screw of sugar, cheese and tomato sandwiches, biscuits and then off on the bus to 'the Centre', change to another bus to Clifton and you were there.

At the zoo you paid extra for the aquarium (I called it the *um*quarium and to this day such a wondrous place is called by me an 'um') but it was worth it. Dark, damp tunnels with glass windows and behind the windows . . . small, brightly coloured, intricately designed . . . jewels.

Life was full of jewels.

Getting a ride on Rosie the elephant could not be taken for granted because Rosie was very popular and there was always a queue to pay your sixpence and climb up the ladder to take your place in the *howdah*. You waited and you hoped that nothing would happen to deny you the pleasure and when you got there, up so high with the rank odour of Rosie's hide swirling about you, you wondered how this contraption, filled with children, could remain secure as the vast beast lumbered and swayed you over her established path. A little fear, a lot of excitement. Could there be any better combination?

All of it, the big cats, the snake pit, the chimpanzees, the aquarium, even Rosie, were but a prelude to a visit to he who was Bristol's most famous resident. Alfred, the biggest, oldest silverback male gorilla in captivity, was the star of the whole show. He didn't do much. He mainly sat in his cage and gave audiences. He was awe-inspiring. There was something seriously deficient in your life if, as a Bristol child, you did not spend at least five or ten minutes a year staring into the deep eyes of this epitome of gentle, powerful masculinity. Some years later Alfred died of heart failure brought on, local history has it, by the terror inspired by the noise from the ten engines of the Bristol Brabazon, the largest passenger carrying aircraft ever built in Britain and probably in the world up to that time. The project was rapidly abandoned soon after – no Bristolian could have found it in his heart to have continued after causing such a tragedy.

When I was five or so I had three pictures on my bedroom wall. My Father had made for them little frames out of cardboard and brown sticky tape and they hung where I could see them easily from my bed. There was Field Marshal Montgomery. There was Winston Churchill. There was Alfred. Winston Churchill was my hero; I thought of him as something distinctly superior to God, I thought of him as my good, kind saviour – and I still do. I put Alfred up there with him. Physically they did have very similar characteristics.

~

What did they look like, these parents of mine? My Mother, although quite short, was substantial, there was plenty of her. She had dark brown hair which held its colour right through to the final few years of her life. Her complexion was country girl clear. She had her own teeth, very strong teeth, slightly protruding so that she had to make an effort to cover them with her lips and when in repose her strong incisors were always visible. If she was going out then she would apply face powder with a powder puff (her round face often showed the sheen of perspiration) and, occasionally, a lick of lipstick. At night she would apply Pond's Vanishing Cream. She washed her hair with Drene ('The Shampoo of the Stars' as endorsed by Margaret Lockwood and Patricia Roc, famous film star beauties of the time – and still to be seen on late night TV in films like *The Wicked Lady*) and cleaned her teeth with Kolynos toothpaste. She also reddened our porch floor with Red Cardinal and used Mansion Polish on the floors indoors – the manufacturers of all these cosmetic products appeared to have almost a clear field in terms of competition in those days.

In those final months at Number 8, for which my memory is most clear, when Father was unemployed and poverty was biting, she pined for new clothes. She had never been a great beauty but she must have had the appeal of health, with clear eyes and good skin, and in those few years before she was married she would surely have felt that what money she earned was there to be spent on personal adornment. A photograph I have of her, taken at the time she met my Father, shows her to be as fashionably dressed as any young woman of her time and of her social position could have been. I think my Father must have been very physically attracted to this farmer's daughter he met in Bath.

In the early days of marriage I am sure she set to building a home and accepted the inevitable resulting personal sacrifices as young women and men have always done but later, when there was simply no money and I was there to be fed and clothed *and* there was a War On, it must have been hard for her. She never complained, of course, but she did sing frequently and with feeling the song, *Try A Little Tenderness.*

~

My Father did not have his own teeth. So many people of his generation, a generation that quite rightly regarded dentistry as being both painful and costly, opted for total extraction. They would summon up their courage, walk into the surgery and (one hopes, after anaesthetic) emerge with no teeth and bloody gums. It seems that it needed there to be only a couple of bad teeth for this radical approach to be employed. If this seems almost beyond belief remember that newspapers in those days regularly carried advertisements for false teeth that made them appear to be an enhancement of one's personal appearance; line drawings of handsome men and beautiful women with flashing teeth adorned these advertisements and millions of people must have been seduced into parting with their own in return for these ghastly imitations.

My Father fell for it and made the painful swap. I don't know when he did it but I cannot remember him without these things that were taken out at night and placed in a small jar to soak in some form of cleansing substance. The teeth were small and uniform and given to slippage during difficult eating operations.

Consider the teeth. Consider the woollen combinations. Consider the chamber pot kept beneath his side of the double bed (this receptacle, the *vase de nuit* or the 'po', was used in most households – remember, the WC was downstairs and in an uninsulated brick annexe). Do you not have here a formidable form of contraception?

But these considerations aside, Father was not an unattractive man. He liked to think he looked a little like the film actors David Niven and Trevor Howard and in a way he did. He was not tall, he was around five feet nine inches, and I think he would have preferred to have been taller. His hair was greying when he first appears in my memory and a little later he would experiment with substances to hide the grey. There was one product he used called Morgan's Pomade which changed the grey to the sort of yellow one occasionally sees on the hair of old people who smoke habitually.

Photographs of him as a young man show him to have been slender with wispy hair and no evidence of any 'brilliantine' (a widely favoured way of making hair lie flat and shiny). A very distinctive double-dimple can be seen in his cheeks (a feature which you, Julian, have inherited) which had mysteriously disappeared by the time I knew him.

I do not know if he had always been indifferent to clothes but, as it was with my Mother during the latter period of the war when he was unemployed or off work due to sickness, it did not matter much whether he wanted new clothes or not; new clothes were not affordable. I got used to him being shabby. Even when our bright and happy future dawned he rarely went beyond a pair of corduroy trousers and a sports jacket with leather patches at the elbow. There was a suit later on; I know there was a suit because he wore one when the Lit and I got married. It didn't fit too well as the wedding photographs bear witness.

~

What of moral influences? There were plenty but they were definitely secular in their origin. My Mother did not go to church but she was comfortable there and if she had married a religious man she would happily have attended every Sunday with him. My Father, being a socialist, was an atheist. He never used the term but he was a humanist and his influence has helped to made me one. He had a very strong moral sense; not on sexual matters to which he wisely never ever made reference but on the simple issue of what was right and what was wrong, what was good and what was bad, what was acceptable for a person to do and what was not. Think of the case of the hedge-sparrow's egg and you have an idea of the influence my parents had on me.

My Father based his view of morality on what a 'gentleman' would do, should do, would not do and should not do. Although the word gentleman, with its implications of class, may seem quaint and archaic to many today – perhaps even to you, my sons – the idea behind it, the concept of someone who is driven by an inner compulsion to be honest, fair, kind, and brave, is something I personally find attractive and which has had a definite influence upon me. I may not have achieved the desired state but it has been a goal, it has definitely been a goal; it still is.

Another favourite idea of my Father, closely associated with the gentleman idea, was that of 'honour' as contained within the phrase 'word of honour'. The dear man used this term when he was telling the absolute truth as in, 'I give you my word of honour that this is so'; it did mean that you had to be quick to notice the omission of the term, as in 'I was a Flight Lieutenant in the RAF'. A promise made 'on my word of honour' was a promise that would be kept and he could be relied upon to do this.

Throughout this time, when my own sense of what I could and should do and what I could not and should not do was developing, there were outside influences as well. School laid on the Christian ethic thickly and it did not conflict with what I was being taught at home – apart from the underlying justification for it, of course; at school one was taught to behave well because it was someone else's will, whilst at home one behaved well because something inside you made you behave well.

Overlaying all of this there was the ever present demonstration that Good and Evil existed in tangible form in our world and belief in this was wholly compatible with atheism. There was Hitler and the whole satanic machinery of Nazism; dark, terrible, merciless, as bad as anything conceived by Hieronymous Bosch – and there was us; decent, noble, brave unto death, and led by Winnie the very picture of whom, with his smiling face, his waving hand, his striking tones in broadcast speeches and his contempt, his limitless contempt, for the murderous gangsters of Germany, stirred us, brought out the best in us, made us believe in our own nobility. It is much easier to develop one's own morality when the extremes are before you every day and are thus not abstract ideas.

My only problem lay in the fear of being a bit too good for this world. I have only come to realise this in recent years but at the back of my mind there has always been a feeling that too much good is rather dangerous for one. Does this sound strange? It comes, you see, from one of the songs my Father used to sing, called *Sonny Boy,* made famous by Al Jolson, which says that when the 'Angels are lonely, want you 'cos they're lonely' they really rather fancy snatching this perfect child, Sonny Boy, to keep them company. From quite an early age, I now realise, I have been genuinely fearful of putting myself into the little friend for the angels category and I have always tried to season my undoubted goodness with a little spice. Nothing extreme, you understand, just enough to keep me second in line.

Poetry remnants – from my Father

Sir Ralph the Rover tore his hair
And gnashed his teeth in his despair.
Oh, Christ. It is the Inchcape Rock!
(In the book of verse he had, which had once belonged to a very prim school teacher, the word 'Christ' had been crossed out in pencil and the word 'Heavens' substituted.)

A dear little girl sat under a tree
Sewing as hard as her eyes could see.
Then folding her work and patting it right,
She said, Dear work, Goodnight. Goodnight.
(My Mother loved this poem and had memorised this verse. In the family language 'Goodnight' became 'A'Night' and so has remained to this day. The Lit never says Goodnight, neither do I. It is always A'Night.)

He was known as Mad Carew to the subs of Katmandhu.
He was hotter than I feel inclined to tell,
But for all his foolish pranks
He was worshipped by the ranks
And the Colonel's daughter smiled on him as well.
. . . eventually Mad Carew came to a sticky end:
One dark and gloomy night
When the ball was at its height
She thought of him and hastened to his room.

. . . I always found the description of the atmosphere in the room fearful. The 'floor was wet and slipp'ry where she trod'. It ends thus:
And an ugly knife lay buried in the heart of Mad Carew.
'Twas the vengeance of the little yellow god.

~

When I joined the school that lay across the open land in front of Number 8 I was, perhaps, four or five years old. I joined the Infants and very quickly learned an interesting fact about my personality. On the Friday afternoon of my very first week there the teacher, Miss Davies, gave out small pictures, line drawings of children at play that had been produced by Oxo for free distribution to schools, and we were instructed to colour them in with crayons. (Lovely small pictures – jewels!) I adored it. Then, every Friday afternoon for weeks and weeks, I waited and waited, without result, for the delightful experience to be repeated, which it wasn't. I still incline to this optimistic view of life; if something nice happens to me I go on expecting something nice to happen, regularly – until I twig that it won't.

There was one distinct benefit that arose from my Father's ill-health and his resultant availability in the home during the normal working day; I was prepared for school in an important way by my Father who had laboriously cut out all the letters of the alphabet from some old printed cards and had stuck them to a piece of plywood which he had then varnished. He then set about teaching me the alphabet and how to read, which he did phonetically, a method which has been questioned by educational meddlers, but, as far as I was concerned, worked very well. I was able to read before I set foot in the school. My first book had, as a frontispiece, a picture of HRH Princess Alexandra who was, I believe, a daughter of Queen Victoria; the book was old even then but I worked my way through it with comparative ease. Writing came along quite well although a report on me said that I was 'Slow', which I conveyed to my parents as 'Slough' which showed that there was still some way to go before my reading out loud was truly up to scratch.

I moved through the schools with reasonable tranquillity apart from the caning incident that I have already told you about. Of course I chattered away and to some teachers that was a fearful crime but . . . well, I still think I got a raw deal in that case as I still think I got a raw deal on the only other time I took official corporal punishment. Neither incident turned me into a supporter of this approach to discipline.

It was at the time when my Father became unemployed that I felt most disadvantaged at school. In those days children were expected to drink one third of a pint of milk each morning and afternoon; there was a charge of one penny a day for this essential nourishment (remember, there was a War On, and in the cities some foods were in very short supply). In addition all parents were expected to make through their children a contribution to National Savings, a wartime fundraiser, by buying savings stamps that were priced at six pence each. At the beginning of each week the child was expected to come to school with five pence for milk and six pence as a minimum savings stamp purchase. You took home the sixpenny stamp and stuck it into an oblong savings book and you aimed to fill it up after which it was supposed to be used to buy a £1 savings certificate at the post office.

At this difficult time my parents coached me in remembering my Monday morning duties: I would be given one shilling and asked to recite, 'Six pence savings, five pence milk, and a penny change'. The penny had to come back with the savings stamp. It was an important penny and it was not to be lost. And we never seemed to complete those savings stamp books. It was very strange how I went on sticking in the stamps and then suddenly I was faced with an empty book again and had to start all over. I was a trusting child and never questioned this phenomenon or, if I did, I must have received a satisfactory explanation. My Mother told me many years later that every five weeks she took it to the post office and cashed the two shillings and sixpence worth of stamps that had accumulated. The household economy could not tolerate a loan of six pence to the government every week any more than it could afford the loss of that one penny which the teacher knotted into the corner of my handkerchief.

~

I have no recollection of the build up to the end of the war in Europe. There had always been a War On. There had always been the impedimenta of ARP membership cluttering up the porch, the droning of German bombers overhead, sirens, the earthy smell of public air-raid shelters, BBC news broadcasts with their Beethoven Fifth Symphony beginnings – da da da *dah* (morse code for 'V' our symbol for victory), the smalmy tones of Lord Haw Haw the traitor, the news of parts of Bristol and even nearby Bath being blown apart by bombs, the warnings of booby-trapped gadgets dropped to attract and then maim or kill children (there was one painted to look like a butterfly I was told), the sad the oh-so-sad street-side sales of items salvaged from bombed houses, the absence of toys and food, and the rationing system that made every small shopkeeper a king – all the things that everyone remembers from that time.

The defeat of Germany came as a surprise. One day there was a war and the next day there wasn't – the date was 8 May 1945 and our world took to the streets in celebration on 13 May. My Father cut from an envelope the stamps bearing a VE Day franking and put them aside for me; a little piece of history. There was a neighbourhood party in the hut where I used to go to Sunday School (we won't go into why my atheist Father permitted this); we watched Charlie Chaplin films (he *wasn't* funny – Laurel and Hardy and Abbott and Costello were *funny)* and we came away each with an orange and a bright and shining threepenny piece.

There was still Japan to be dealt with.

~

And then one day there was excitement in the house. One of the letters that my Father had been writing so very carefully, using the special blue paper (without lines – the pad came with a sheet of heavily printed lines on white paper that you put beneath the sheet of blue paper to guide your writing) and special blue envelopes, a distinct cut above the white, lined paper we usually used – scored a hit. We, the three of us, would be travelling by train to *London* within a few days. My Father and Mother would be going to discuss *a job* – and I would be accompanying them. We would be going on (or in) *the tube* and going up and down *escalators*.

It was the beginning of our bright and happy future.

Chapter 4

Who Says There Isn't A Good Fairy?

Pauntley Court (1945-1946)

Long after my work in London began and after the Lit, you two boys and I, had moved to Oundle (in 1986) I began to find the daily travel from Peterborough wearying. I was developing diabetes, and feeling tired most of the time comes with that particular medical territory. However, I did not know this then and so I took steps to compensate for the symptoms of what I thought was simply advancing age; I rented a studio flat very close to my office and announced that I would be travelling from Peterborough on Monday mornings and returning on Friday evenings. I then sought to improve my state of health through exercise and joined the YMCA Club (the organisation proudly states that one need be neither young, male, nor Christian to be a member which does seem to be an abnegation of its original principles – but no matter) in Great Russell Street, London WC2 so that I might swim regularly. Every morning I went to a rather ugly building made of concrete – a modern building – and went down into its bowels to the swimming pool.

One morning, after months of making the brief journey from the northernmost end of Shaftesbury Avenue, where my flat was, to the YMCA, for some reason I stopped in Great Russell Street and looked down to where it meets Tottenham Court Road. I experienced a sudden feeling of *déja vû*. I had been here before. Of course I had – every day for months. No, it was long before, years before, decades before.

I remembered how I had once sat waiting in a room in an elegant house of three or four storeys, in the presence of a young woman seated before a typewriter. I was waiting for my Mother and Father who were in another room being interviewed for . . . *the job*. I was seven. I had walked over to the window and looked out, down onto the street and then over to the right, to where there was a slot machine arcade. This palace of pleasure lay at the junction of Tottenham Court Road and Great Russell Street. The arcade is no longer there (there is now a pub of sorts, called 'The Blue Post') but its location had jogged my memory and so established that the YMCA I was regularly visiting was on the site of the original YMCA building where the imminent future of the Diggle family was decided by the impressive gentleman who escorted my parents from the interview room and who greeted me; Mr Bernard Brain, then General-Secretary of the YMCA.

In those days the YMCA held a wider brief than it does today and one of its functions was to help the war effort by providing hostel accommodation for young people who volunteered to 'Lend A Hand On The Land'; one saw posters and advertisements bearing this exhortation. At that time most workers were in the armed forces but there were still universities and there were still students and these were encouraged to devote their vacations to agricultural work. Whether they were paid or not I cannot say but they certainly received their board and lodgings free and it became the job of my parents to provide this.

(Later on the student scheme was phased out and workers were recruited from the non-combatant Irish Republic and after this, when the war had ended, from the people of Central Europe who, through war and/or the fearful acts of vengeance perpetrated by Joseph Stalin, had lost their homes, had lost everything, and who ended up in Britain as 'displaced persons', being generally known as 'DPs'.)

As we three stepped from the building there was a definite sense that the bad times were over. Over on the right, from the direction of the amusement arcade, came music; it was a record, very popular at the time and still regarded with pleasure by me and many, *Java Jive* sung by The Mills Brothers.

~

A few days later the good news came by post. My parents had got the job. They were to open a new YMCA hostel in Gloucestershire, in an old mansion house called Pauntley Court which was, I was soon to discover, the birthplace of Dick Whittington. My faith in pantomimes was justified; surely this was the next best thing to Aladdin's cave!

~

From the railway station at Gloucester, where we were met by the lorry driver, to Newent and on to Pauntley Court; we tore through leafy lanes, past the deep red soil, the *marl*, of the ploughed fields, down the steep hill, up the other side, noted the church standing all alone looking as though a congregation would never be assembled, and there we were in the courtyard of a fine Elizabethan house in red brick. It was devoid of human presence. No-one came out to greet us, to wave hello, to beam a welcome from ruddy-cheeked peasant faces. My Father had the key in his pocket.

Father, Mother and I had arrived at Pauntley Court all squashed together in the cab of a canvas-topped lorry painted in camouflage green. In the back were the supplies, all the gear necessary to the successful accommodation of some fifty students – apart from beds and bedding that would be arriving later. The students would be coming in a week's time. This imposed something of a serious deadline upon the arrival time of the beds and bedding. Pans and pots, sacks and boxes of food, and our beds and bedding were unloaded onto the yard and the lorry driver made his escape.

~

The place had no electricity. There were light fittings and switches but no power. My parents hunted for a mains switch, found one, switched on the power but of power was there none. We made our beds in the gathering gloom and took to them by candlelight, candles being provided in the YMCA instant hostel manager kit. Next morning Father discovered the secret of Pauntley Court's electricity supply; there in a single-storey building was a vast diesel engine and hundreds of lead acid batteries. The engine, once started, drove a generator which charged the batteries and from this roomful of cells came sufficient power to provide lighting for the whole house. Father, having fairly decent engineering credentials, worked out how to set the beast in motion and there we were. *Fiat lux!* From then on one of Father's principal jobs was to keep us ever supplied with diesel fuel and distilled water with which to top up the batteries.

~

Waking up in my small bedroom for the first time, then furnished only with a bed, and running to look from the window down onto the grounds of Pauntley Court, set in deepest, darkest Gloucestershire, was one of the magic times of my life. A large open area of grass, too big and too unkempt to be called a lawn, stretched out before my eyes. Rabbits were playing on the grass. The only rabbits I had ever seen up to that time had been in hutches, pets of friends, pets that became food when the meat ration coupons ran out. The field ended with a row of trees and beyond the trees another field stretched into the distance ending only when it met a river. Beyond the river there was to the left a wood on rising ground that became a hill. If I were to add now to this picture what I was to discover as the next twelve months unfolded I would put bluebells in the wood, wild daffodils on the hill and in the river, real speckled trout and mythical Irish eels. I will explain the eels later.

After Number 8 Pembroke Road this was like walking into one of the fairy stories of Enid Blyton, then much adored by me and still somewhat respected notwithstanding all the criticism she now receives. Little boy becomes a Prince! Or at least a Man of Property. Who says there isn't a Good Fairy?

~

A year later, when we moved on to another large house converted into a hostel, my parents were offered the chance to buy Pauntley Court for £600. They hadn't the money. They did not own Number 8 Pembroke Road – it was rented – and there was no capital. There never had been any capital and there never would be any. And what would they have done with a vast pile, ever hungry for maintenance, stuck out in the middle of deepest, darkest Gloucestershire? About ten years ago Lit and I made what was for me a sentimental journey and we visited the place. I had written to 'The Owner' explaining my connection and asked if we might call in. David Ayshford Sanford replied saying that he would be delighted to meet us. Pauntley Court had changed sufficiently to make it a modern place to live in; it had mains electricity, a clean bright kitchen and there were all the trappings of a wealthy person living deep in the country but it was still as I remembered it. A couple of years later the house and grounds went on the market at over £700,000.

An odd aspect of this visit, that illustrates a clairvoyant ability I have that manifests itself but occasionally and of which I hope I can find more examples as this book progresses, was the way I thought to take with us in the car a copy of my second book, called *Guide To Arts Marketing*. Somewhere in my mind was the thought that it might make a useful gift during the course of a trip that would include Pauntley Court among several other places. David Ayshford Sanford turned out to be a governor of the Royal Shakespeare Company and was involved in a small theatre company as well as a festival in Newent. He accepted the gift of the book gratefully without, apparently, wondering how I had thought to bring it with me.

~

My parents were hard pressed to learn a new trade in the space of a few days – imagine it, moving from normal domesticity into running the equivalent of a hotel with absolutely no training – but they were young and, anyway, they had no choice but to succeed. Some staff arrived to help them. In those days the production of an illegitimate child was quite likely to have a young woman committed to a mental institution (yes, this is true!) and our Jane Irvine, who arrived complete with baby, was one such unfortunate. She had been released on licence, as it were, and could have been taken back into the 'Home' had she not proved to be satisfactory as a general do-anything-and-everything helper for my parents. She formed a bond of affection for them that lasted for many years, her letters telling us of what was happening in her life and how her baby daughter was growing.

There was a cook, George Lowden, an ex-miner from Newcastle, who had deep blue marks running under the skin of his arms and skull where coal falls had cut him open and dust had tattoed itself into his body. He was not a great cook but he was a genial soul and was always kind to me, volunteering to take me to school and collect me on the one form of transport that was available, a bicycle. I sat on the hard pillion seat and clung on for dear life as we whistled down the hill and freewheeled halfway up the other side. Once his poor eyesight failed to detect three sacks of potatoes that had been dropped by a tractor and as we whizzed down the hill on the way home he shouted to me if I could make out what they were. 'Sheep, they must be sheep,' he yelled, 'They'll move out of . . .' then *wallop*. A sprained wrist for George, a bent bike and an unscathed me.

~

I was enrolled in a tiny school in nearby Pool Hill. It had two rooms and two teachers, one of whom was the Headmistress. Children were divided up according to size. Big ones in this room and small ones in that. In those days children left school as young as 14 and not every one attended secondary school. This school would have taken some children through until the time when they left to work on the land.

I liked it there after the brutal teacher who had caned me on the hand for talking. Nobody mentioned caning but once when a big boy got cheeky the Headmistress went for him and gave him a good mauling with her bare hands.

~

It was exciting when the students arrived, both for me and for my parents, especially my Father who found the whole idea of being amongst people who were both intelligent and well educated very stimulating. Although he kidded them on a little (I once heard him tell a student that he had studied economics on the basis of his having read Karl Marx's *Das Kapital)* he had read widely and he did have knowledge and ideas in common with many of them. He was a musician and could start up a singsong at the drop of a hat. He could produce his ukelele banjo or his one-string fiddle and he could knock out a tune on the foot-pedalled organ in that little church that stood on the piece of high ground at the entrance to the drive down to the house. I still have a copy of the National Union of Students Community Song Book that formed the basis of most singing sessions – but I'll do these from memory just to show I can.

Cocaine Bill and Morphine Sue
Were walking down Fifth Avenue
Singing 'Honey have a sniff, have a sniff on me,
Honey have a sniff on me'.

Frankie and Johnny were lovers
Lordie how they could love.
Swore to be true to each other
Just as true as the stars above.
He was her man.
Wouldn't do her wrong.

Be kind to our web footed friends
For a duck may be somebody's mother.

They live in the woods and the fens
Where the weather's always wet.
You may well think that this is the end . . .
Well, it is.

Romans came across the Channel
Dressed in tin and bits of flannel.
Half a pint of woad per man'll
Dress us more than these.
Romans keep your armour,
Saxons your pyjamas.
Hairy coats were meant for goats,
Retriever dogs, gorillas, yaks and llamas.
Tramp up Snowdon
With your woad on.
Never mind if we be rained or blowed on.
Never need a button sewed on.
Go it, Ancient Bs!

~

Mushrooms grew in the field behind the house, huge ones that people called horse mushrooms. I found one as big as a dinner plate and took it to school to show the teacher, fully intending to take it home for Mother to use for her wonderful mushroom soup. Teacher thought it was for her and threw it in the dustbin, admitting to this when I asked for its return at the end of the day. Country folk do not always appreciate the country.

~

Some of the students befriended me and took me on a hike to Great Malvern. On the way, as I gasped my little town boy gasp, a girl promised me a drink of mineral water just as soon as we arrived. This sounded remarkably good to a little boy who would, under such exhausting circumstances, normally have reached for a glass of pop and, on arrival at the town, found that this was indeed what sparkled within the glass.

~

My Father found a pile of booklets in a cupboard. They were called, 'Pauntley Court – A Home for Wayfarers', and were intended to be sent out to potential philanthropists. It seemed that before the war the house had been run by a charity as a home for tramps. Bearing in mind the isolation of the place and the total absence of public transport, the home fitted into a sort of Darwinian scheme of things in that only the fittest of tramps could have made it there, the rest dying on the way no doubt.

The booklet had a foreword written by John Masefield, whom my Father told me was a famous poet and he dug out a book and gave me *Sea Fever* to read.

My education was coming on, you see. Mineral water. Wayfarer as another word for tramp. John Masefield and *Sea Fever*. And, of course, I knew where Dick Whittington was born.

~

Places like Pauntley Court were run by the YMCA for the War Agricultural Committee and it was this body that managed the supply of agricultural workers and serviced them. The same source also laid on a weekly lorry, a sort of liberty boat, to take my parents and me into Gloucester to go shopping and see a bit of civilisation. Students travelled with us, but in the back – we went first class, in the cab.

The lorry's return time was late enough to make trips to the cinema possible and the Diggle family, now with a weekly salary, the exciting challenge of a new job, status and a nice big house to live in, enjoyed this luxury to the full. Amongst many films, I particularly remember Jeanne Crain and Dick Haymes in the musical *Spring Fever*, Danny Kaye in *The Kid from Brooklyn* and *Up in Arms*, and Rhonda Fleming and Bing Crosby in *A Yank in the Court of King Arthur*.

~

The war in Europe was over and its end had been celebrated when we were living at Number 8 Pembroke Road, but the war with Japan continued. The price of seeing all the lovely films in Gloucester was the inevitable exposure to newsreels, and on one occasion the news contained footage of our troops moving in on the Japanese in some place or other, using flamethrowers. For a few seconds there ran across the screen some poor creature covered entirely in flames.

That image returned to me night after night as I lay in my little room. It appeared in my conscious mind and it reappeared in my dreams along with the ghastly pictures of the German concentration camps.

Then the war was completely over. There was Victory over Japan – VJ Day. We were too remote from the rest of the world to enjoy any celebration comparable to that of VE Day but, no doubt, we shared the sense of relief and hope for the future that everyone else in the country felt.

Only those horrifying images and dreams remained. They have never left me. For a good twenty years after the end of the war I would not pick up a factual book dealing with the war if I could see that it had illustrations. I learned to look at the edge of the pages to see if the texture of the paper changed from the usual matt finish to the art paper used for photographs. Today, even today, I have never been able fully to express to anyone the intense horror I experience when faced with news reports of similar atrocities nor the passionate hatred I have towards those who perpetrate them.

~

One day, at about midday, a van arrived. The driver and his three passengers, one in the front and two at the back, comprised an ENSA party. ENSA stood for Entertainment National Service Association and we, being part of the war effort, qualified for inclusion in their touring programme. The main common room was cleared, the old upright piano rolled into place, and the little troupe did a run through while I watched from behind the door. There was a comedian who claimed kinship with Bud Flanagan; he introduced himself as 'Tom Call Me Harry'. There was an elderly lady with huge front teeth who materialised for the performance in a very lovely frock and a thick layer of makeup, who sang, *inter alia,* an Ivor Novello song *Oi Will Give You The Stawrlight*. And there was 'Pat on the Mat', a tap-dancer who brought with him in the van something that looked like a rolled up venetian blind that proved to be a wooden-slatted tap-dancing mat; and his name was . . . Pat.

It would be nice if I could say that the experience of watching these good folk in their preparations and in their performance gave me a taste for the business that I would one day enter for I don't believe it did – but I did enjoy it and my Father was in a thousand ecstasies as he helped them in every possible way and led the enthusiastic applause for them. Oh, how much he would have wanted to play a part in all this!

~

The time of the delightful students passed all too quickly. Off they went, back to University, and then there arrived the wild Irish. Off the back of the lorry the men piled with a miscellany of boxes, cardboard suitcases tied with string and some with their possessions simply wrapped in a roll made up from an old garment and tied with string. Some were young, some old; most had brown or even black teeth; all were shabby. They spoke with accents that marked them out as being from the South; pleasant accents, voices that were easy on the ear. It didn't take me long before I could do a passing fair stage Irish accent.

The first impact of the new and different culture came on the first Saturday night when, without money in their pockets yet, they chose to entertain themselves with a *ceilidh,* a wild evening of dancing to the tune of a couple of fiddles and much banging on table tops. They all wore hobnailed boots, the same boots they wore when they worked in the fields, and in these they danced with great vigour. One tune they played over and again was a jolly jig called *The Stack of Barley* and this has stayed clear in my mind to this day just like the tune the children marked time and marched to in the school I attended in Bristol.

My, but they were *foreign.* All could speak English but mainly they spoke Gaelic between themselves. They were foreign in their dress – many would tie a string under the knees of their trousers (I never discovered why) and most would wear flat caps indoors, even in bed sometimes; foreign in their habits – older men smoked pipes either fitted with perforated metal caps or held the bowls upside down; foreign in their all male dancing and in their robust singing which quickly showed their nationalism. They sang *The Wild Colonial Boy* every evening when they got together after work and after dinner. They sang *If You Ever Go Across The Sea To Ireland* and when they came to the line 'And when they come and try to teach us their ways' they always sang 'And when the *English* try to . . . '. At 11pm every evening the big old radio in their common room was tuned to Radio Éireann and the Irish National Anthem blared out throughout the house, right through the walls into the rooms where were our quarters, just as the fiddles, the dancing boots and the thumped table tops did.

My Father was very sympathetic to them. He had heard about what the infamous Black and Tans had done to the Irish in the early part of the century and he admired Eamonn De Valera (one of the songs sung by these men had the line 'Up De Valera, champion of the right'). His history was shaky for he never referred to the period of the Irish Free State and never once spoke of Michael Collins but his information was based, as most people's usually is, upon casually read newspapers that do not exist to provide accurate history lessons. Father always inclined towards underdogs and lost or unpopular causes.

Part of his job was to collect up the letters being sent home by these men to make sure that the lorry delivered them to the Post Office in Newent and I remember him remarking unhappily on the habit these chaps had of always sticking the stamp bearing the head of George VI on the envelope, in the bottom left-hand corner and upside down. Perhaps he felt that this was going too far. Poor stuttering George VI had made a decent job of being a figurehead during the war and he and Queen Elizabeth were very popular. Such disrespect was going too far.

He came closest to the men in the matter of their music which he adored. From one of them he obtained the name and address of a Dublin music publisher and sent away for a pile of Irish music which he played on the old upright that had been provided for the entertainment of the residents. So we had *Galway Bay, The Rose of Mooncoin, Nell Flaherty's Drake, The Spinning Wheel, Bring Me a Shawl from Galway* and many others, the sheet music for which came each with its own frontispiece illustration in the form of a pencilled sketch. I still have all that music. I still can't read the dots but I know most of the words . . .

My name it is Nell
And the truth for to tell
Is I come from Coot Hill
That I'll never deny.
I had a fine drake
And I'd die for his sake
That my grandmother gave me and she going to die.

~

The river that ran across the back of the estate was the Welland. It wasn't particularly wide or deep but its water was pure enough to sustain trout. Once my

Father and I walked down there in the company of an Irishman who knew the way of rivers and the creatures that live in them, and he spied a lovely large speckled trout treading water, as it were, just resting in the shadow of the bank. Following his instructions I knelt down and slowly put my hands in the water around the fish and began to caress the lower sides of its body. The trout seemed to like this and it seemed a shame to follow the next instruction which was to yank it out of the water with all haste, but I did. Now if this was an Enid Blyton story the next scene would have Mummy proudly serving grilled trout to the assembled company – but it isn't; the fish was pulled up into the air and then fell back into the water where, no doubt, it resolved never again to respond to the physical blandishments of human fingers.

The same Irishman told me about eels. He was perfectly serious as he explained that eels were not born in the usual way, they were created and they could be created by anyone who knew the trick. You took a long horsehair and went to a shallow part of the river where there were a few rocks and you pinned the horsehair onto a rock using another rock and allowed the horsehair to run out, following the stream of the water. You then left it for two or three weeks and when you returned you would find an eel waiting for you. I tried to extract more precise information from him; was the eel still held under the rock or was it just . . . sort of swimming around? He wouldn't say.

~

Even before VJ Day POWs (Prisoners Of War) began to make their appearance at the house, sent to contribute their labour to the general effort to keep Britain (and themselves) fed. They were not resident, having to report back to their prison camps at the end of each day. They were the harmless kind of POWs. Italians. No-one ever took the Italians seriously during the war. During newsreels they were generally referred to as 'The Ice-cream Sellers' when far stronger and more hateful epithets were reserved for 'The Hun' and 'The Japs'. In my 1944 collection of the cartoons of the great Giles of the Daily Express, Italians usually had twirly moustachios and tightly-waved hair, and Benito Mussolini was always portrayed as the lapdog of the Nazi gang, usually wearing a dogcollar and a lead held in the hand of Hitler.

The British treated the 'Eyeties' with considerable affection and they enjoyed almost total freedom. After all was said and done most people had bought their ice-cream and fish and chips from chaps like these before the War, and their leaders had initiated no atrocities of which we were aware (apart from the assault on Abyssinia which was fairly remote from Britain and barely remembered – and if they did, they blamed it on that fat bastard Mussolini).

I first met them when I encountered a couple as I returned from school. One had come across a baby owl which he was holding tenderly and trying to calm down. He gave it to me and for a few seconds I treasured the thought that I might make a pet of it before it summoned up its strength and courage and took to the skies.

They were adroit craftsmen and good entrepreneurs. They made espadrilles out of straw and a bit of canvas, weaving the soles out of the straw. They sold for half a crown. Another product was the silver ring: you gave the man two halfcrowns, both of which were, of course, 99% pure silver in the years up to 1946, and one was made into a ring and the other kept as the reward for making it.

~

As Spring of 1946 came and progressed the wood on the other side of the river became filled with bluebells, and then the wild daffodils appeared, covering the hill. It was utterly beautiful and my parents and I delighted in walks there; it was a time of great happiness for us, and we all cried when the lorry came to take us away to our next assignment and dear old Pauntley Court was locked up once more.

~

When Lit and I made my sentimental journey there it was Spring and she was able to see that my stories of how lovely the place was were true. The wild daffodils were everywhere. David Ayshford Sanford told us that the present owner of the land there had tried and tried to destroy the flowers by ploughing but they hung on and just would not be eradicated. Bless them!

Chapter 5

Oh How I Feared Miscellaneous

Gotherington Fields Farm (1946-1949)

I don't recall it in any detail but I cannot imagine for a moment that the lorry that took us from Pauntley would have taken us straight to Gotherington Fields Farm, the place that would be our home for the next three years. Burnham-on-Sea would surely have intervened. Let us assume that it did and that we three came to the new job and the new place refreshed after a few weeks under canvas and not a few sessions of singing *Eedy Eedy Wop Tap Tap* on our passage through the duners. (You will have to wait for the section of this book called *A Resort Runs Through It* for an explanation of this arcane and apparently nonsensical reference.)

Looking at it on the map Gotherington is not very far from Pauntley, sharing as it does the county of Gloucestershire, but in those days it seemed so very distant and the move seemed to bring enormous changes in my life – largely centred around my schooling but also in terms of the scope of my life. This new YMCA hostel was a large farmhouse set in the midst of a working farm with fields that stretched for miles and all of this was mine to enjoy. Pauntley had grandeur and plenty of space but the estate of Gotherington Fields Farm seemed to have no limits.

There is a village of Gotherington but the natural point to turn to was the much larger village, Bishops Cleeve; beyond that is Cheltenham, a fine and beautiful town. So, from virtual isolation in the community of Pauntley Court, which for all its wonders was almost a desert island for us, to a home that was in easy contact with a thriving village and a town. It was a good move for all of us, much as we missed Pauntley.

~

I had barely been able to take stock of the new place, indeed barely had been able to adjust to the potential of my new and splendidly large bedroom that overlooked the courtyard, when the business of school had to be addressed. Oh dear! The sinking feeling in the pit of my stomach that I always developed at the prospect of a new school, a new class, a new term and even a new week (I've known it happen in the face of a new *day)* became extreme. I tried to convince my Mother that my condition was life threatening but she would have none of it and soon I was nervously entering Bishops Cleeve Junior School.

It didn't take too long to settle down for it was a benevolent place. My only serious difficulty lay with a slim book entitled 'Miscellaneous Examples in Arithmetic' with the word 'Miscellaneous' printed so large that it became the title for practical purposes. Oh how I feared MISCELLANEOUS, that collection of arithmetical exercises that were often used by the teacher to start the day while she did more important things. It was often there on the desks when we entered the room for registration, ready to perplex and humiliate me. I never had a head for sums and still don't – which is odd considering the way my career developed.

Pool Hill School had been a pleasant place but it soon emerged that it had added little to my education and I seemed deficient in almost every area – this was a serious business for it was from this school that I would be propelled into secondary education with Cheltenham Grammar School as the only target at which to aim.

So I started as a bit of a dunce and had to claw my way out of this position with about three years in which to do it. Of course I didn't see it in terms of this time-scale; for me then, as it often is for me now, getting through the day was achievement enough.

~

A major improvement over Pauntley lay in transportation. In the latter part of our stay there I had learned to ride a bicycle and now used one to take me every morning to the end of the road where I could leave it at the back of a petrol station and pick up the school bus. The bike could and did take me to meet other children, to build on relationships started at school – to make friends. I had made no friends at Pauntley for all the children lived so far away.

~

Our filmgoing now took on an even greater frequency. My parents would go into Cheltenham in the afternoon to go shopping and after school I would take the bus into town where I would meet them and then go straight on to the cinema. Tuesdays and Thursdays were devoted to this entertainment which my Father treated as High Art. So seriously did we take it that when a filmgoers' magazine's annual competition to choose the most popular actors, actresses and films came around we took home the forms so that we could discuss our choices calmly and rationally, for after all the careers of these people lay in our hands. Who would I go for? Stewart Grainger? Patricia Roc? Margaret Lockwood? Glynis Johns? Or perhaps Leslie Howard? Or James Mason?

~

We still had no mains electricity. Unlike the sophisticated Pauntley Court all we had were oil lamps. At the back of the house there was a Lamp Room and each evening the handyman (this was a recognised job in those days – and may still be in the remoter parts of the country) would take lamps around to every occupied room. There were basic oil lamps with wicks and chimneys for the residents and in the kitchens and our quarters there were the superior Aladdin lamps with incandescent mantles that were the equivalent of about 300 watts in their output. I recovered one of these works of art from my Mother's house when she died and still have it. I found a new mantle for it in an ironmonger's shop called Grover's in Boothbay Harbour, Maine, USA and I am still hunting for a new wick. Why? I don't know why. Useful for when the apocalypse arrives I guess.

~

We still had Irishmen in the house. There were many of those who had been with us in Pauntley and who had been transferred along with my parents. Dear Danny Heaton, a none too bright young man who looked to my parents to be his own. And Mr Durkin (always *Mr)* whom my parents helped in some special way to the extent that his wife, Mary, whom we never met, sent us by post a goose every Christmas for the next ten years in gratitude. The goose, still in the feather, would arrive by post from the Republic of Ireland only partially clad in a single sheet of brown paper barely secured with string and addressed with a label tied to its neck – and it arrived still fresh and wholesome.

~

Now being part of a social community at my school that was entirely rural in its character I wasted no time in learning to share the all-abiding passion for bird-nesting of my fellows – passion is what it was and all-abiding is what it was too, for one had no time for girls (although when I was ten I started to appreciate the inexpressible loveliness of a classmate, Anne Collins, but only from afar which is how these things so often are). That early seed, sown the day those boys on Rodway Common gave me a hedge-sparrow's egg, had lain dormant for a few years and now sprouted vigorously with the encouragement of peer group enthusiasm.

Gotherington Fields Farm was a perfect place for a young boy with a passion for *jewels* to grow up. There were fields, ditches, hedges, ponds, spinneys and, next to the house, a wood of monumental mature deciduous trees – almost every possible habitat for birds. Beyond the limits of the estate the potential was no less great; more woods and, half a mile down the road, a small pond fed by a brook with clear water where there were sticklebacks and where once a friend of mine caught an eel – fish are jewels too, remember.

The abundance of birdlife was, by today's standards, almost unbelievable. In the banks of the drainage ditches there were the nests of yellowhammers; not just one here and one there but enough to stretch the capacity of the habitat to provide for all the small families that were reared there in the Spring. To the side of the house there was a long, thin, narrow spinney of small trees and bushes, many overgrown with ivy, which was a perfect place for chaffinches and on one glorious day, when my bird-nester's eye was in, I found no less than fifteen nests in the space of a couple of hours. Of course one abandons the collecting of eggs in such abundance. Only one egg of each species is needed and once that rests safe in the collection bird-nesting becomes a matter of observation and detection.

But there are always new challenges and for me they lay in those nests that were out of reach, out there at the farthest edge of the reeds in a pond or *up there* swaying at the top of a tree. The eggs of the moorhen and the coot, water birds, were not too difficult to secure once one had accepted that the price was going to be a pair of water-filled wellington boots and perhaps even soaking clothes, but what about the magpie? The crow?

Magpies, with the strange, partial roofs to their twiggy nests, provided the first challenge for the lesser treeclimbing bird-nester. These birds like to be well away from the ground but not too high; 15 or 20 feet from the ground in a hawthorn tree is about right; there is enough height to deter and plenty of thorns too. I captured my magpie egg after only a few attempts in which I discovered that I suffered from vertigo and that if I was to extend my hobby upward from the ground I was going to have to be quite brave. The wood pigeon and the dove choose nesting sites in places similar to that of the magpie so as I overcame my fear my collection grew.

One day I faced the challenge that I had known would present itself to me eventually. There in the uppermost boughs of a fine, mature oak tree was a large nest, made of twigs, that showed the building characteristics of the crow. The tree was taller than I had ever attempted before but the boughs were strong and, most importantly, those directly supporting the nest were fairly robust, which meant that I had a good chance of being able to reach it. Crows generally build their nests in very high trees and pick a point at the top where the supports are no more than twigs – not one of my circle of friends possessed a crow's egg. Most of us had attempted a capture but when one is at 30 or 40 feet and the boughs are swaying, and the next reach and pull takes one into the snapping zone, courage is tested to the point where common sense takes over.

I climbed the oak – hard work but at least there were no thorns – and made it to the nest. I reached up and felt the eggs in the nest; they were warm. I took one and looked at it. It was not a crow's egg. I remembered the illustration in the Observer's Book of Birds and Their Eggs; it was the egg of a sparrow hawk I held in my hand. No-one I knew had such an egg. Following accepted practice when treeclimbing, I put the egg – warm and powdery – in my mouth and made my descent safely with a sense of such joy and achievement that I thought my heart would burst.

I know, I know, I *know* that collecting birds' eggs is not only morally wrong but is illegal also. Today, with so many birds facing extinction society must outlaw the practice, but with those memories of excitement and delight still fresh I cannot help but wish that those who have destroyed the habitats, sprayed the insecticides and liberally dosed the good earth with the artificial fertilizers had been stopped before they had destroyed so much. It was not the egg collectors of my generation that ravaged the bird population of our country.

~

The existence of a bus service had opened up our lives and I began to use it, frequently by myself, usually on Saturdays, to go into Cheltenham to visit stamp dealers and a junk shop that had acquired a birds' egg collection whose proprietor was prepared to sell individual items. There I bought exotic specimens such as the eggs of the Cormorant and the Guillemot – and even the Alligator (plain white, slightly elongated).

Stamps were small and could be beautiful. Stamps were jewels. Stamps were available from small shops run by dealers and you could even send away for them. Buying stamps by mail order was run on a remarkable system of trust that I cannot believe exists today. The dealer would send you a slender album containing stamps of the kind in which you had expressed interest, or perhaps a mixture to see if you could be tempted. Each stamp had its price marked on the page and you detached those you wanted, added up the cost and sent back a postal order. And you did. It would never had occurred to any of us, boys who collected stamps, to just swipe the stamps.

The stamps of Spain were big and grand. There was a series showing pictures by Goya. My favourite was *The Naked Maja,* a splendidly naked lady at a time when there were no naked ladies to be had, not even for ready money.

~

This was a time when my parents grew in stature. They had faced the challenge of Pauntley Court and had won through, showing that hope and determination can triumph over lack of experience; now they were professionals. There was a steady flow of hostel residents; the Irish continued to dominate for a long time but after a couple of years they were replaced by DPs. My parents' income was, by the standards they had previously known, not at all bad. We had good accommodation in the farmhouse, separate from the residents. We could afford to buy clothes and to take the annual holiday in the Resort That Continued To Run Through It. We went to the cinema twice a week. At school I was regarded as being fairly well-off.

My Mother was by now a most accomplished cook. Although a chef was always employed there were so many times when someone had to stand in, days off, holidays, periods between the departure of one and the arrival of another, that my Mother had no choice but to gets to grips with the job of catering for large numbers. She knew how to estimate quantities, how to order and how to cook on a large scale. This skill would stand her in good stead in later years.

My Father had taught himself how to handle all the administrative duties of a hostel manager and showed all the signs of self-confidence. He could handle accounts and he could handle, with considerable diplomacy, a drunken Irishman with blood boiling from nationalistic passion who was set on doing some damage to the first English thing he could see.

Father also had time for me and he initiated nature walks for us during weekends, school holidays and on long summer evenings after school. We would go to the very limits of the Gotherington estate, past the orchards of perry pears and right over to where the construction of a railway line had been abandoned years before, its embankment now covered with brambles and forming an habitat for animals and birds. It was lovely to go out together like that; I hope he realised how much I enjoyed it.

~

My parents also showed encouraging signs of entrepreneurism. It all started with the loan of a broody hen – which is what you need if you want to start breeding hens. A dozen fertilised eggs were bought from the market and the broody hen borrowed. She sat on the eggs in the corner of a shed and pecked at anyone who approached. Chickens emerged. My parents bought some pullets – young hens at the point of laying – and then things started to grow apace. My Father paid a couple of German POWs to put a six foot wire mesh fence around a large grassed area at the rear of the house and then the ducks, turkeys and geese appeared. Soon they were running a substantial poultry farm. How and where they sold the eggs I do not know but there was money coming in over and above my parents' basic salary.

It was a time when I felt secure and part of a family that was firing on all cylinders. It was a *good* time.

~

From this background of security it was fairly easy to make progress at school and I did my best with the goal of entry to Cheltenham Grammar School before me. In those days there was rigid selection at 11 years of age; an examination called the 11-Plus was intended to sort the wheat from the tares, with the former going to a Grammar School and the latter to a fairly recently invented type of school called a Secondary Modern. Make no mistake about it, my children, if you drew the short straw you were *second rate*. It may strike you as being worthy of thought that the Lit, who has had a distinguished career teaching English and Drama at the highest level in some of the best schools in the country, failed her 11-Plus examination and had to claw her way up with that millstone attached to her ankle. This should also make you wonder about the fairness of selection at the age of 11.

In my final year at Junior school I entered the class of Mr Carver who was a delightful man and a very good teacher. He treated me as though I was clever and

I became clever. He offered me duties and I assumed them. He asked me to write poetry and I wrote it. He suggested that I entertain my class every Friday afternoon with a story and so for one whole term I stood at the front of the class and improvised a serial story for half an hour every week. 'What about starting a nature table?' said Mr Carver, and I, being something of an expert on matters natural, started one. I had entered what the educationalist would term the 'pseudo-adult' stage of my life when for a few brief glorious months I would be self-confident, responsible, alert, helpful, articulate and, in my case, a most attractive candidate for admission to Cheltenham Grammar School.

I passed my 11-Plus. I was interviewed by the grammar school headmaster and was accepted for a place. When the news of this arrived my Father produced a gift that he had bought in anticipation; an ex-RAF box kite, made of very light hollow aluminium tubes and orange fabric, that was supplied to pilots who had crashed into the sea. That mark of his confidence in me was well taken by his son.

I wonder what life would have been like had I gone to that school? We had been deep in talk of uniforms and satchels when the news arrived that Gotherington Fields Farm would soon cease to be a YMCA hostel and that my parents were required to move to East Anglia, to a place called Honington, near Grantham in Lincolnshire. We would be there in time for me to start the Autumn term at King's School in Grantham.

~

What a god-awful change that turned out to be for me!

Chapter 6

I Must Ameliorate My Q List Average

Honington, Leasingham, Billingborough (1949-1951)

East Anglia was completely alien territory for me. They spoke differently there and they outnumbered me. The shock of moving into the collection of single storey brick buildings that comprised the Honington hostel, situated on a piece of land on the side of the well-used road between Grantham and Lincoln about fifty yards from the railway line spanning Edinburgh and London, about a mile from the village of Honington, was extreme. Where would I play? Where would I walk? Where would I go bird-nesting? There was nothing in mitigation; the place struck me as being entirely hostile. It had mains electricity and that was about its only advantage.

I huddled in my tiny new bedroom and waited for the axe to fall, my first day at King's School, Grantham. No Cheltenham Grammar School; that was left behind with all the other joys of Gotherington Fields Farm. The scholarship had been transferred effortlessly. A couple of bus rides into town had resulted in a blazer with school badge, cap with school badge and *canvas* satchel hanging in my wardrobe. I was unhappy about the satchel which by rights should have been made of leather – almost all children who made it to a grammar school had this mark of achievement bestowed on them whether their parents could afford it or not; leather was *de rigeur*. After about six months of use my satchel showed by its tatty state that this choice had been a false economy. I knew nothing of my Father's financial position and it could well have been that he had had to finance the move out of his own pocket, or that his salary had been reduced or, perhaps, his small part of the poultry industry – now abandoned – had been contributing more to our welfare than I had appreciated. Whatever the reason, I didn't feel that my loins were adequately girded for this major step in my life and I faced my first day at the school apprehensively – and would have done whether equipped with leather satchel or not.

~

The school bus, which picked me up outside the hostel, was full of curious and aggressive children, all much older than me it seemed. I travelled in a state of high tension, clutching my canvas satchel to me, staring out of the window and ignoring all attempts to make me speak. I had spoken to the driver once when entering the bus and my west-country accent amused everyone hugely. It took me a term before I could wear the edges off my burr but even then my voice marked me out as a foreigner.

~

Grammar schools like King's couldn't help being the way they were. They were proud of being old, proud of having educated some of the country's leading figures, proud of the part they played in moulding the section of society upon which they could lay their hands. King's School, Grantham was proud that Sir Isaac Newton had been educated there; it was an historical fact that our greatest mathematician and astronomer spent the years of his early boyhood at the school (before popping over to Cambridge to take up his professorship at the age of 13 years!) and this was a demonstration of how important was the school and others like it. These grammar schools educated the children of the middle classes and so, together with the public schools, had pass through their doors the officer class of the nation. The walls of these schools are clad with memorial plaques listing the names of their war dead alongside those listing the academic achievements of their pupils at the universities.

It was also part of their tradition that children were accepted from the lower orders if they had what it took intellectually. This was one of their great glories. The schools recognised that such children would not come equipped with the social niceties and might not even understand and appreciate the great good that was being done for them, so the culture of such places was to set great store by good behaviour and manners and to instil a sense of obligation to Society in them. It was also part of a tradition shared with public schools that children should be treated roughly. Beating by headmaster, by teachers and by senior pupils, once they were prefects, was permitted and practised. The class hierachy of society was harshly echoed by the grammar schools and right at the bottom of that hierachy was *me*.

Such a change in my life, wrought in such a short time! From being a happy and successful pupil in the charge of the amusing, helpful and youthful Mr Carver I was thrust into the dark corridors of a Dotheboys Hall, run by grim adults and malicious youths, and made to feel that I had no worth at all. I know now that I wasn't the only boy to have had the wind knocked out of his sails at this age but that didn't help me at all then.

~

Loyalty to the School (with a capital letter). Loyalty to the House (ditto). A system that linked academic performance with 'House points' so that failure to perform in class led to downgrading of your House, was operated. Every so often there was a collection of individual subject marks, brought together for each pupil, that were known as 'Q Lists' (Q for quarterly) and my first Q List result showed that I had brought about disgrace to my House although it was never explained to me why. Oh shame!

The shame was on the school (damn the capital letter; I will not give it one) not on the little boy who, with the stuffing knocked out of him by the grimness of it all, sat in a darkened room facing a jury of his superiors, prefects who were met to consider the fate of this traitor. The name of the judge will stay in my memory for ever; the house captain, a youth with short cropped hair – a crew cut anywhere but in an English grammar school – and ill-natured face garnished with extraordinarily ugly teeth, called Joppa Plough. T'is the truth I swear! Joppa Plough. *Joppa Plough.* Was he invented by Thomas Hardy? He could have been.

My judge read out the charge sheet and then asked his co-thugs to vote on whether I should be given lines or *whether I should be beaten.* The vote went in favour of my bottom and against the sadistic tendencies of this foul fellow who voted for the beating that he would administer. The line I had to write out many, many times – how could I forget it? – was:

I must ameliorate my Q List average.

Well, at least I learned a new word. It has come in quite handy over the years.

~

I met Latin for the first time. It was taught according to the strict practice of the time, with a name for every possible variation and conjunction of words. Primary school education at the time prepared a child very well in basic grammar so I came to the place knowing the difference between a verb, a noun and an adjective, but such an analysis of language that was the basis of Latin teaching – the breaking down of everything into parts and then the naming of those parts and then the account of how those parts worked one with another – was entirely new to me but I found it not altogether difficult. The rote learning of verb conjugations and noun declensions was a bore but it was achievable and within a term I was beginning to see the language as a whole. And it was, after all, the kind of thing clever chaps did at grammar school, something that was denied those who went to the secondary modern school – and I have never regretted the time spent studying the language.

~

I did not study French in my first year; this was something I was fairly soon to regret.

~

School work blurs into a mixture of impressions, none of them particularly rewarding in recollection. I could handle most subjects reasonably well and in my first year showed some movement upwards in my class position. First term: 21st. Second term: 12th. Third term: 14th.

~

As one might imagine in a school where bullying was institutionalised bullying occurred at almost level. My particular tyrant was a boy in the third form called Richard Haggart and he simply hit me whenever he saw me. After about a term of this my state of fear was so acute that my parents were forced to break the code of *omerta* and complain to the headmaster, a grim, skull-faced horror called Huggins who, to our surprise, took action and I was thereafter left alone.

~

Swimming took place at an outdoor pool some way from the school and one afternoon my form colleagues were there at the same time as a fifth-year form. I was walking alongside the pool when I felt something touch my calf, something that felt as though a fly had brushed it. I looked down and saw a tuft of red wool apparently stuck to my leg. Mystified I touched it and it appeared to be quite firmly attached. Then, as I pulled the wool, an inch of bright thin steel emerged from my flesh and blood started to run. Some yards way two older boys hooted with laughter.

The craze of the moment amongst older boys was to carry lengths of brass curtain rod in their satchels and blow darts, missiles made from long pins with flights made from teased out knitting wool. These projectiles, which were remarkably effective, were used everywhere, anywhere where there was no vigilance from teaching staff. They were fired at the backs, arms and legs of boys and readily penetrated clothing material and the flesh beneath. It was a foul pursuit and dangerous to an appalling degree but it was never stopped officially, it followed the pattern of schoolboy crazes and simply petered out.

~

I joined the boy scouts. Apart from the guidance of parents and teachers it was the first time that there had been an organised influence on me to *be good* for its own sake and for my own sake. Religion had never made much of an impact on me – perhaps because it seemed always to be saying that one should *be good* for some heavenly being's sake. I understood fully well that one should *be good* to other human beings – and animals – for their sakes. I had read Charles Kingsley's *The Water Babies* and fully went along with Mrs Do-Unto-Others-As-You-Would-Be-Done-By. Religion underscored all of the be-goodery of my times, including the boy scouts, but the scout movement did convey to me the notion that what happened inside *me* was important too. (Even today religion seems to believe that it has a monopoly on *being good* and that atheists have no right to enter the territory.)

Scouting is not now a fashionable movement and it is damned with accusations of homosexuality and paedophilia but, speaking as I found it, it was good for me at the time and no-one ever put a hand on my knee, thank you very much.

~

The hostel was now almost entirely stocked with DPs. We had Ukrainians, Lithuanians, Latvians, Poles, Estonians, Hungarians and one Yugoslav. We also had one Irishman, called McPhellamy, who was not one of the breed with which I was familiar; this chap had fought in the Spanish Civil War and had a chequered career the details of which he only hinted at mysteriously; heaven only knows how he came to be in our hostel.

Most of the men had had horrifying war experiences and had seen things that they fortunately did not share with me. In many cases DPs found themselves in Britain because they had been forced to fight in one part or other of the German army so they had been taken prisoner by the Allies and then, because of the element of compulsion in their service, had been given a category that stigmatised them less and did not mark them out as being of any potential danger to us. Many, many years later it was revealed that as the war ended in Europe a large number of SS personnel had pretended to be poor Central Europeans who had been press-ganged into service by the fearful Hun and thus escaped to a relatively pleasant life in Britain. Thus it is highly likely that a few of the men in the Honington hostel had actually participated in some of the atrocities they darkly hinted at having witnessed. The fact of this infiltration was something that would have had a bearing upon the investigation of a terrible crime that occurred within a few years, close to where we were to live, had the police known about it.

Most, of course, were poor victims of the hateful tide of evil that swept through their countries, both from Russia and from Germany, and were lucky to have escaped with their lives. Those that had worn German uniforms would have met with instant death from the Russians had they been repatriated after the war and indeed there is much historical evidence that Stalin set out to kill all from the USSR – that is, Russia and all its satellite countries – who had had any experience of the West during the War. So 'our chaps' were to be treated sympathetically and this was something that my parents could handle very easily.

So much could have been learned from these men. Did anyone – did they – think to record what they had experienced? What of our cook, a Latvian called Mikki Dakstins, who was 19 years old when he worked for us and so must have been only 14 years old when the war ended? An extremely handsome boy with wide open face and fine, wavy blonde hair, always smiling, who had lost all his family and who had a strange, taut quality sometimes that made me nervous of him – it was suppressed violence I think.

There was an Estonian man who was there with his 14-year-old son – only a few years older than me – who had been only nine when the war ended and had only recently managed to find and join his father. Where had he spent the war and the postwar years? Who had looked after him? I cannot remember what the boy did during the day when the men went out to work. Did he work too? I do not remember. I became quite good friends with him but he said very little about his past. Was his father, that gentle man, an escaped Nazi?

The only Yugoslav was a jolly fellow who once took off his shirt to show me the scars of eleven bullet wounds in his arms, shoulders and chest.

My favourite was a genial, young Ukranian called Yuri, who worked in the kitchen helping Mikki. He had bland, dark features, with good clean white teeth and a ready smile. His good looks and affable disposition were to get him into trouble during his time with us. One day my Father was visited by a local woman accompanied by her distressed daughter. My Father took this opportunity to give me one of his oblique lessons in human sexual behaviour but after a year spent at King's I could put two and two together. I think that Yuri thereafter had to face a regular deduction from his wages for 'maintenance' as it was called.

A few miles down the road, near Lincoln, in a village called Wellingore, was another hostel, occupied almost entirely by Ukrainians, and many were friends of Yuri. One day he asked me if I would like to go with him to a Ukrainian music evening at Wellingore. Now my tastes in music were strictly based on what came out of the radio when Housewives' Choice and Family Favourites were on – and, of course, the older songs my Father used to sing me – and, when I accepted the invitation, I had no idea of what to expect.

~

The hostel at Wellingore had a very large dining hall and a stage had been built at one end; the rest of the building was packed with chairs and an audience mainly of men, with some few women, and no children apart from me. The atmosphere was full of smoke for in those days most men and many women smoked and smoking in public places, such as cinemas, was generally accepted.

Yuri and I took our seats and the show started. It was a celebration of Ukrainian musical culture and it was done with great style and verve. There were men and women in the show (I never knew where the women came from for the hostels I knew were exclusively male. There must have been a woman's hostel nearby). The costumes were brilliantly coloured; all red and white patterned ribbons flowing against a background of black clothing and white caps for the women. To the rapid music of accordians they danced like nothing I had ever seen before. They performed those impossible Cossack dances, crouch down and balance on one foot while the other kicks out and then change feet and kick out the other, all the while spinning around and yelling like mad. These were people who would never lose their background it seemed and it was, to me, wonderful that they should live amongst us.

After the show Yuri took me to meet his friends who lived, as he lived, in a barracks building with bed alongside bed. They gave me strange food which I ate with gusto. This was what a boy would call a great night out!

One of the tunes stayed fixed in my memory just as others have done. A few years ago I met a Ukrainian woman who had come over to England after the war and in conversation told her about the Wellingore show. To illustrate the impact it had had upon me I whistled the tune and as I did she started to cry.

~

As end of the war became more remote so the need to provide accommodation for agricultural workers who were not indigenous became less as they were given the freedom to take up citizenship and to work on their own accounts. My poor parents seemed to find themselves in the position of cartoon characters running along a bridge that was collapsing behind them. Pauntley Court had closed. Then Gotherington Fields Farm. And now, after only one year, the letter came; Honington was to close as well. I had spent just three terms at King's School and now we were to go and live at a place called Leasingham, close to Sleaford, where there was another hostel for my parents to run.

The third term of school ended and off we went to Marsh Farm, Berrow for our Summer holiday. Then back we came to move our by now battered belongings to the even uglier cluster of one storey brick buildings that made up the Leasingham hostel.

~

But what to do about school? There was a grammar school at Sleaford, called Carres Grammar School, that was the obvious choice but we, the family, collectively decided that it was better for me to stay on at King's School. Travel was possible, barely possible, using buses and so when the first term of my second year started I got up at a very early hour and took the bus to Sleaford where I had to wait for ages to pick up the bus to Grantham. I don't remember how long the journey took but it was too long for me and, as Autumn moved into the beginning of Winter, it became too cold for me as well. I stuck it out for a term, the Michaelmas term of 1950 when I was 12 and approaching my 13th birthday.

~

In that first term of my second year I started to take French and wasn't very good at it but my end of term position was 8th overall. The subjects showed a variation in term classifications from C– to B+ and (Heavens!) I earned 2 house points. I did not even think to wait for a meeting of the Joppa Plough darkened Star Chamber where the vote would be on whether I should be given a day's holiday or a box of Quality Street chocolates for ameliorating my Q List average.

~

Then the Chief Education Officer of Lincolnshire, who seemed to have remarkable powers of perception, wrote to my parents and announced that the

The boy who succeeded in ameliorating his Q list average.

journey was too long for a boy of my age and that a place had been reserved for me at Carres Grammar School in Sleaford.

It was indeed easier to get there but once I had spent a day or so in the place, I found myself wondering, did I want to get there? God, but it was dire!

~

Here, at this school, my equivalent of Joppa Plough was the French master, a man named Cutler whose nickname was 'Butch', who took considerable exception to the fact that I had only studied French for one term whereas all the other boys in the class had been working on the subject for four terms. He bullied me, yelled at me, insulted me, gave me punishments – did everything except teach me French. My life, my miserable little life, revolved around whether or not my next lesson with this man was going to be absolute torture and humiliation or simply very unpleasant.

~

Then, after one term, the collapsing bridge caught up with my parents and the word came that Leasingham was to close within a matter of a few weeks. We moved rapidly to another hostel in nearby Billingborough and then, within no more than six weeks its closure was announced also. My parents would receive half pay but, it was much regretted, there was no job to go to just now nor would there be one until the Autumn. It was then April 1951. What were we to do?

Father made the decision. We would put all our belongings into storage and we would go to Marsh Farm, Berrow, there to enjoy the Spring and Summer and we would face the future when the future was there to be faced.

And what of my education? Carre's had been a beastly experience so we would face my educational future when my educational future was there to be faced. In short, Father gave me the term off and we went off to sing *Eedy Eedy Wop Tap Tap* on the duners for a few months.

~

A few years ago I drove up to look again at the Honington buildings that had been my home for a year. They had been used as a pig farm for a long time but were now derelict. I drove on to look at the Leasingham hostel. It could not be found. Either it had just been bulldozed out of the way or my memory could not hold on to one significant fact about its whereabouts but it was effectively gone. Just as well. And Billingborough? To tell the truth the very existence of the place and our brief sojourn there only returned to my mind as I was writing this; I did not even think to drive the extra few miles to take another look at the place.

~

One good thing to come out of my one term at Carre's was a school trip to Norway that was to take place several months in the future, during the Summer holiday. My parents had agreed to let me join this party and the deposit had been paid when fate and my Father's love of a good long holiday intervened. So, after nearly three months of indolence in Somerset, and when my parents had been told of their new assignment, I took my first journey abroad.

The train took us to Newcastle and then we boarded the boat, the *SS Jupiter*, that would take us to Bergen. We travelled steerage in a sort of dormitory in the bowels of the vessel with males on one side of a canvas partition and females on the other. It was all very primitive but exciting. On arrival we were each met by our host family. The arrangement had been the traditional exchange between families but due to some domestic problem with my Norwegian family my exchange partner, Ivar Moene, could not reciprocate by coming to stay with us later on, in the Christmas holiday period.

The Moene family gave me my first experience of what life was like for people with lots of money. Father was a consultant surgeon and the family, parents and two children, lived in Hunstatsvingen, an expensive street in an expensive suburb of the city, in a house larger than I had ever entered before. Until this time my personal standards of wealth were based on life at Number 8 Pembroke Road at one end of the scale and the one week I had spent with Aunt Marjorie (my Father's sister) and Uncle Dick in Surbiton, Surrey, at the other. Uncle Dick was a successful professional man and, I was told, had had a bit of luck with the football pools. So their house was very, very grand to this little boy. The house of the Moene family was even grander and I was awestruck by the opulence.

Norway, just six years after the end of the war, was not yet fully recovered. Things like oranges were never seen and chocolates and sweets were rare and when found not at all good. There was plenty of fish, however, and there I tasted my first smoked salmon and also ate a tunny fish steak. The tunny could be seen being transported through the streets on the backs of lorries, a dozen huge fish at a time, tied down with ropes, their swallowlike tails hanging out at the back, bouncing up and down.

Ivar, a boy of sixteen, older and much more experienced than me, never revealed to me his feelings about having drawn the short straw when it came to exchange partners. He and his parents made every effort to show me the city and the country and I left after a fortnight feeling, as travel is meant to do, broadened.

I returned to my new home and although I was by now getting used to living in strange places I realised that we could never have entertained a boy like Ivar Moene there and later on I even wondered if the 'domestic problem' of the Moenes had not been manufactured between my parents and the school to save us all embarrassment.

The new home was a collection of wooden huts set in the middle of Polebrooke Aerodrome, near Oundle in Northamptonshire.

Chapter 7

One Minute He Was Up In The Air And Then He Crashed To Earth

Polebrooke Aerodrome (September 1951 – July 1953)

Let us take stock of this growing boy who had had the benefit of a good long holiday with his parents and a couple of weeks in Norway to get over the trauma of the schools in Grantham and Sleaford – and was now seriously out of step in his educational progress. He was coming on 14 years old. He was philosophical about the changes that swept his life from one course to another and, being so close to it, could not see the downward pull that was acting on the fortunes of his parents. He seemed to take life as it came. He had no expectation of wonderful things so was not disappointed when they did not appear. His relationship with his parents was close and warm and this always gave him strength when life was difficult.

He had enjoyed many aspects of his school life so far and, in the main, the classroom held no fears for him. He did not feel that he was brilliant in any area but he was competent in most. The unpleasant things were always to do with people, people who were bullies, or were simply unkind or unhelpful.

~

His interests? He still treasured his collection of birds' eggs but these days found no-one who shared his love. He collected stamps but this interest was waning. He listened to the radio a lot and loved comedy programmes and knew all the popular songs of the day. He read constantly: there was the substantial collection of paperbacks, mainly Penguin books, of his Father and for some time he had been collecting the excellent children's books published by Penguin under the imprint of Puffin. So, even if he had not read them, he knew books like *Virginibus Pueresque* by R. L. Stevenson, *Chrome Yellow* by Aldous Huxley, *Erewhon* by Samuel Butler, *Kai Lung's Golden Hours* by Ernest Bramah, and many others. His Puffin books had introduced him to writers like Eve Garnett *(The Family from*

One End Street), the poetry of R. L. Stevenson *(A Child's Garden of Verses)* and many, many others. He had read *Tomorrow Is A New Day,* in the Puffin series, by Jennie Lee, so he even knew something of the person who would one day be the first Minister of the Arts of Great Britain. He had his William books (collected painstakingly during his holidays at Burnham-on-Sea).

~

He was aware that there was a different kind of music but knew little of it beyond some of the melodies of classical music that had been used to make popular songs and the music heard in films about musicians. A popular artist of the day was the American pianist José Iturbi, who also acted in films, and through these he knew that people sometimes played grand pianos or simply stood with baton in hand in front of orchestras and what emerged was generally held to be superior to the songs that Doris Day or Frank Sinatra or Frankie Laine or The Mills Brothers sang. (One day he would promote a recital by José Iturbi in Nottingham's Albert Hall and would get on with the artist very well.) His father often played music that had a classical inclination on the old upright he had bought in the Gotherington days. However basic his knowledge and naive his taste he did love the music he knew from films, radio, and the wind-up gramophone that had been 'brought along' with the family from the Gotherington manifest, and the songs he had learned at his Father's knee.

~

And girls? Did girls feature in his life? Well, during his extended Summer holiday, taken before arriving at Polebrooke, he had been somewhat smitten by one Cynthia Harrold, whose family were camping in a nearby tent, and had taken her to the cinema in Highbridge, near Burnham-on-Sea, but she was not interested in a much beyond . . . seeing a movie.

~

The boy seemed to spend a lot of time simply trying to do his homework properly which he did, as he had always had to do, without the benefit of assistance from his parents or from friends.

~

He had become used to owning almost nothing and this is not quite the same as being poor. Indeed, by the standards of many at this time, the Diggle family was not then poor. But a life where one was required to move from one place to another so rapidly did not lend itself to the acquisition of property. The rented house, Number 8 Pembroke Road, had long been let go and the furniture sold. So, rather as it must be for service families, there were no beds, tables, chairs, linen, cutlery, or even pictures, that made a home; everything was provided as part of the job and was left behind when the job ended.

Did this lack of property influence the man the boy was to become? Did this create a burning desire to own things? Not at all. In fact, quite the opposite. What it may have done was to instil a very passionate defense of those things that were owned rather than create an appetite for more things. The man hates to lose things, to have them stolen or have them broken or treated badly by other people. He also hates to waste *anything* – and that extends to people.

~

And now here the boy was occupying a small bedroom in a wooden hut that had, just over six years earlier, been the living quarters of the Officer Commanding of United States Army Air Force 351 Bombardment Group (Heavy) at Polebrooke Aerodrome. There was another bedroom for his parents, a bathroom, a toilet, a kitchen and a large sitting room. The cluster of huts also provided the living quarters of 'the men', all DPs, the camp kitchen and a communal hall. All of this lay to one side of a vast flat area that included runways and several hangars that had been used by the bomber aircraft of the USAAF. The area in which the living accommodation lay was dotted with buildings of brick, of concrete and of wood, all left as they were on the day the American forces pulled out. Had he known what he knows now the boy would have realised that he was about to live in the middle of a museum and would have taken steps to preserve and record the historical documents that stood there in the form of buildings that carried painted on their walls, material that varied from records of bombing flights to German destinations to ten-feet-high glamour girls of the kind made famous by artists such as Vargas and Petty and who featured regularly on the nosecones of the aircraft. His exploration was to reveal noticeboards left intact, complete with Station Standing Orders and instructions to personnel of all kinds. The drawing pins were by now rusty but the documents remained. There were buildings full of radio equipment left lying idle, with cabinet fronts left swinging open and thousands of valves revealed. As he cycled around the desolate runways on his rickety bicycle, a composite creation made from several sources, he found live machine gun ammunition lying where it had presumably been jettisoned by aircraft making landings deemed to be rather more risky than usual.

Just over the path that ran alongside the hut occupied by the Diggle family there was another, unoccupied hut. Following the practice of its time the names of the wartime occupants had been painted on a piece of wood that was nailed outside. The first name was that of Capt. C. Gable and it was subsequently discovered by the family that Clark Gable, yes *the* Clark Gable, had lived in this room during his wartime service. 'We'd better take care of that', said Father, approaching the shingle with a claw hammer. (The result of Father's understanding of the importance of artefacts of historical value now hangs on the wall of my study alongside the wooden dancing man Father made for me during the war, Willy Flapdoodle.)

In 1995 a small memorial to the lives and deaths of those who flew their sorties from Polebrooke Aerodrome was erected at the edge of the area, at the end of what had been the main runway. It says that from here 351st Bombardment Group (Heavy) of the Eighth United States Army Air Force flew 311 Group bombing missions between 1943 and 1945. It adds that 175 B-17 Flying Fortesses and their crews were lost and that 303 enemy aircraft were destroyed in aerial combat.

So, here we have a boy, freshly transplanted into a remote place richly endowed with three years of wartime history, on the brink of adolescence, facing a new life at another new school and with a rickety bicycle to get him there, to Oundle, a small town some four miles away.

~

The first face of Laxton Grammar School, Oundle, which I saw was that of the person I always regarded as the Headmaster, Mr S. J. J. Leech, a small man with a lined face that broke into a hundred wrinkles when he smiled, which he did frequently. He interviewed me in the presence of my Father in August 1951, a week or so after our arrival at Polebrooke, and we took to each other immediately. After the remote austerities that headed the schools in Grantham and Sleaford, this kindly man, with his quaint voice and his reference to me as either 'M'boy' or, miracle upon miracles, 'Keith' (I hadn't been a Keith at school for such a long time), prompted in me a great emotional response. I simply adored him on sight.

Mr Leech, known to all as I later discovered, as 'Quack' (was it his voice or his very slight physical resemblance to a duck? I never found out), was not, in fact, the Headmaster. Laxton Grammar School was the original school founded in the mid-16th century from the bequest of Sir William Laxton for the sons of local people that was in the 19th century metamorphosed into something much larger, into an English Public School – Oundle School – with fee-paying, boarding pupils who were not the children of local people. Laxton remained curiously independent, retaining most of the characteristics of a separate school and was physically separate also; you may point to one building in Oundle and say 'That is Laxton School' and, at that moment, you are not pointing at Oundle School even though recent history has bound the two schools ever closer.

Local boys went to Laxton as day pupils, usually after having passed 'the scholarship' and paid next to nothing, apart from small charges for lunches and 'extras' such as music lessons. Boys from other places, from families that were generally far better off, went as boarders to Oundle School. Laxton existed as a sort of enclave for the brightest of the local lads and was in many ways, most of them beneficial to the local lads, integrated into the adminstration and the teaching of the far larger and wealthier school. Certain distinctions were maintained: teaching of junior forms took place entirely within Laxton by Laxton staff; the school played soccer when Oundle School played rugby; Laxton boys did not row. When Laxton boys reached the senior forms they joined Oundle

School forms and then, when relatively poor shoulder rubbed against relatively rich shoulder, the other principal distinction became distinctly apparent as friction generated heat.

'Quack' was thus categorised 'Master-in-Charge' to make sure no-one confused his status with that of Mr G. H. Stainforth, the Headmaster of Oundle School. To my mind then, as now, the towering Mr Stainforth never approached the knee of our diminutive 'Quack' when it came to running a school well and with simple kindness.

~

The matter of the missing term worried Quack a little and so he decided to put me into the second year when I should, in the usual course of events, have gone into the third year. I found the work extraordinarily easy and at the end of my first term I romped home first in term work and first in examinations. For my second term I was upgraded to my proper position and everything continued to sail on successfully. The foundation in Latin given to me at King's School, Grantham held firm and now I was in good and caring hands my French improved steadily.

~

This was a time of great happiness for me. I biked into school quite cheerfully and when the weather became disagreeable there was a school bus that I could pick up a few hundred yards away. I made friends at school and I liked the staff. There were at the time only 90 or so boys at the school and a real family atmosphere was present. I played games ineptly but over time I found that I could run a bit, and so in Winter I did cross-country running and in Summer I took to athletics; eventually I even won races.

~

The school was, of course, still a school of its time and beating of pupils still went on, both from staff and from prefects. I had not been long at the place when I ran foul of the Laxton Head Boy, John Case, who determined that a beating was what I needed and he would administer it with the rather robust cane that NCOs in the school's cadet force used to . . . bolster their image I suppose. The cane was held at one end in the hand while the other end was pressed tightly into the armpit, the cane and arm thus making a triangle. This is not the caning position, of course, this is the 'I am a remarkably powerful and smart young man playing at soldiers' mode. The caning position was as you might imagine it to be.

Fortunately for me the school rules required young master Case to consult Quack before he physically abused a fellow pupil and my hero talked him out of it. Next day Quack had a word with me and told me to watch my step.

I did not, however, escape the school unbeaten. Three and a half years later my then immature sense of humour caused an Oundle School master, a chemistry teacher called Palmer, to demand retribution for what he took to be a slight, or cheek, or a challenge to his dignity, and Quack was no longer there to save me. Quack retired at the end of my first year at Laxton and we were all left to the less than tender mercies of his number two, an ex-Laxton pupil called Stretton, who . . . lacked sentiment, shall we say. At the age of nearly 17 I was required to bend down and receive six vicious slashes to my bottom from this man. It is customary to make light of punishments such as these and even to claim that they strengthen character but I will say that I found the experience extraordinarily painful – to the extent that I cried openly, noisily and without regard for anyone who might have been listening – and completely degrading. At a time of my life when contentment, confidence and a sense of security was fast ebbing (that collapsing bridge soon caught up with my parents again, sad to say) this was indeed a 'cruel and unusual punishment'.

(The experience with the teacher Palmer taught me that one should not be unduly influenced by appearance. This man had the appearance of one of Dickens' more genial eccentrics; plump, with a round face and a pair of granny glasses, a straw hat wedged onto the back of his head when in the street, he reminded me of a film actor of the time, one James Hayter, who played parts such as Mr Pickwick and other jolly fellows. The appearance of Palmer made me believe that he had a sense of humour although I had never once in my school career enjoyed the benefit of a lesson with him; had I had that experience I would have known better. The incident where he, an Oundle School master, reported my simple attempt at humour with a demand for punishment to the Master-in-Charge of Laxton School, illustrated one of the less beneficial aspects of the relationship between the two schools; had the complainant been a member of the Laxton School staff the beating would never have happened.)

~

I joined the Oundle School Combined Cadet Force (it was that or the Boy Scouts on Wednesday afternoons) and found I enjoyed it. The school had excellent connections with the armed forces so when it came to the 'Field Day', a day given over each term to some form of quasi-military activity, there were any number of exciting things going on. We played games with rifles and blank cartridges under the guidance and verbal abuse of real soldiers and Meteor jet aircraft were called in to conduct strikes on 'the enemy'. A waste of time? When each and every one of us were soon to be liable to conscription for two years in one of the armed forces at a time when Britain was engaged in armed conflict in several parts of its crumbling empire I think not.

After about a year, when I had passed the necessary cadet examination, I transferred from the khaki uniform to the blue, from the army section to the air section, where my heart really lay. Thoughts of a future career were never very far away at this time and the Royal Air Force, in which my Father had served, was a serious prospect for me. Everything about the RAF thrilled me. My love of birds and birds' eggs had been replaced by a love of aircraft and aircraft recognition became a passion of mine. The wonderful *Eagle* comic, launched just a few years earlier, often carried beautiful illustrations of aeroplanes such as the Spitfire, the Hurricane, the Mosquito and so on, and they decorated my bedroom wall. *Eagle* also carried magnificently drawn cut-away views of jet engines and turbo-props and these were carefully cut out and pasted in my special RAF scrap book.

Field days, summer camps, and holiday courses now took me to nearby RAF stations and I flew, as a passenger, in Tiger Moths, Chipmunks and once the twin-engined Anson, all the way up the east coast of England and Scotland to Aberdeen, for some of the time lying prone in the bomb aimer's perspex dome in the belly of the aircraft, enjoying the wonderful view.

~

It was while in Aberdeen, on a cadet Summer camp, that I made my first public appearance before an audience. It was in a fairground where there was a booth offering the experience of seeing a young lady, who wore very little, encased in a coffin made of ice. The barker was issuing a challenge as we approached: would anyone dare to challenge the young lady's record of lying in the ice coffin for two hours non-stop? 'You there, young fellow! Yes you, Sir. You in the uniform of Her Majesty's Royal Air Force (the man was mistaken, of course). Dare you take up the challenge?' He was pointing at me. I went for it and a few minutes later I was in the barker's caravan changing into a bathing slip and soon I was lying in the ice. The 'coffin' consisted of an open box of four inch thick ice with a lid lying on top in such a way that my face was fully exposed; I did not actually lie upon ice, there was a concealed sheet of clear perspex beneath me that was a very effective insulator. It was cold, however. Very cold. I lay there while cheerful visitors tried to feed me chips through the opening above my face. Some tried to pour me a little beer by way of encouragement but were persuaded away by my genial promoter who, after some 40 minutes told me it was time for me to leave. There was a ten shilling note and a packet of twenty Players cigarettes waiting for me. 'There's a reason we use girls for this job, laddy', he said, 'Men aren't really up to it. I'm speaking testicly, you understand'.

~

The school's Air Section possessed a simple glider known as a Grasshopper, a single seat device with a long skid (rather than a wheel) beneath that seat, that was intended to familiarise would-be glider pilots with the basic techniques. The student pilot would sit strapped into the seat while someone held one of the wing tips to keep the craft level; a long elastic rope known as 'bungee' was attached by its middle to a hook beneath the craft's nose; the tail was restrained by a cable attached to a hook screwed firmly into the ground; two equal groups of cadets would then take up the ends of the bungee and start to walk away from the aircraft at an angle of some 45 degrees from the centreline of the arrangement. When the bungee was fully extended a situation similar to that of a wad of paper about to be propelled by an elastic band obtained. The student pilot would yell out something to the effect that he was ready for takeoff, he would pull at a knob that was known inexplicably as the 'tit' and would then be catapulted forward at some speed. The speed would create lift from the aerofoil section of the wings, the elastic rope, its energy consumed, would fall away and . . . hooray, and up she rises.

Normally a launch such as this would put the craft some six or seven feet into the air, it would plane for a few seconds and then glide, quite swiftly, to earth whereupon it would slide upon its skid until friction brought it to a halt. Such was not the experience of young Diggle as he attempted his maiden flight. As he watched the yellow ball on the bungee being pulled into its ring, the sign that the rope was fully extended, he yelled the necessary 'All Out!' and released the cable that was holding back the aircraft. His fellow cadets, all acting on a predetermined and evil plan, then ran as fast as they could while still holding the ends of the rope. The result was that all the impetus provided by the energy contained in the rope was added to the effect of some 16 healthy lads adding their musclepower to the launch and the highly nervous novice suddenly found himself flying at a height of more than 20 feet with every indication that the flight would continue until the aircraft left the launch site and plunged into a hedge or worse. Without any understanding of the sensitivity of the control stick within his trembling fingers he translated his desire to be on good solid earth into a robust forward movement of the stick. One minute he was up in the air and then he crashed to earth.

After the impact he clambered to his feet but could not stand because he was still strapped into his seat. The seat was, however, detached from the rest of the craft which was in turn detached from itself in every significant particular. It was a pile of matchwood that the lad left behind him as he discarded the seat and offered a word or two of protest to his horrified companions.

~

Towards the end of my period at the school, after attending gliding courses and obtaining the gliding certificates A and B (and nearly C had not bad weather intervened) during my holidays I was a qualified glider pilot. I had flown solo on many occasions and had achieved this before the age of 17 years. The aircraft used were a far cry from the humble 'Grasshopper' the destruction of which I had contributed to; these were large, heavy two-seater craft that were hauled up to a height of 1,000 to 1,200 feet by a winch before the cable was released. It was, I found, an interesting experience to be alone in an aircraft that was being pulled upwards at an angle of about 45 degrees at what seemed a very high speed. The wind shrieked through the wires of the machine until the moment when maximum height was obtained and the 'tit' was pulled. Then suddenly there was silence. Below there was the map of one's world, the vaguely geometric shapes of green and brown, and then the gentle hiss of air now passing much more slowly through the wires. The knowledge that only *you* can get you back *down there* safely is a powerful discipline. Those lonely moments high up in the sky gave me something that remains with me today, an inner core of trust in myself.

I was promoted to sergeant and when the school had received back the repaired Grasshopper, I became the gliding instructor for the Air Section. On my final Field Day I gave a demonstration flight for the visiting VIP, Air Marshal Sir William Atcherly, which was deemed to be a great success as I flew a long flight, brought the craft down smoothly without bumping and slid along the grass with wings quite level. Then, when all forward motion had ceased, I finished with one wing tip resting upon a short post that marked the corner of a rugby pitch that someone had forgotten to remove. I walked from the glider leaving it neatly balanced, with wings horizontal. A fluke, of course, but it did make for a nice theatrical finish.

~

One experience as a cadet brought me face to face with a reality that I suppose I would have had to face some time or other but it happened in a way that caused me maximum embarrassment. The field day trip was to the Royal Air Force College, Cranwell, the place that has trained officers since the beginning of the service, and I was one of a group being shown around the main building that housed the officers mess and the principal offices by a young Flying Officer. Around the walls were group photographs of all the officers who had graduated since the very beginning. My Father had told me many times that he had held the rank of Flight Lieutenant and had attended the Cranwell officers' training college. It was only natural for me to want to find a picture of my Father on the day of his passing out and so, in the company of the young officer, I moved from photograph to photograph. In vain we searched. The officer was very patient and when he realised what the situation was he said that perhaps my Father had missed the Passing Out ceremony due to ill health on that day. Yes, perhaps. I never told my Father what I had discovered and I loved him none the less for it; I think he always wanted to give me someone I could be proud of and this simple piece of personal elevation must have seemed harmless when I was very young and then difficult to correct when I was older.

It had been my Father's influence, the tales of adventure in the canvas and string aircraft of his day, the 'snaps' of him in flying gear (but never seen in officer's uniform), the souvenirs of his time in India and so on, that had given me the taste for the RAF and that was no bad influence. Of course it gave me the unrealised ambition to be an officer and to fly but this is of no great matter. Few childhood ambitions are, in the end, fulfilled.

But I was left with a great affection for the *Royal Air Force March Past,* that became one of my great tunes, along with the primary school playground music, *The Stack of Barley* as played by our Irish residents and that wild and wonderful Ukrainian folk dance music that I heard at Wellingore.

~

I made friends with young people who lived nearby. At Papley there lived a farming family named Green and there were two daughters, Joyce and her younger sister Audrey. One of my very good friends and contemporaries at Laxton, Edward Lane (who was to die of leukaemia in his early adulthood), was seeing a lot of Audrey and his brother Tom, a darkly handsome and very senior youth, was very close to Joyce. So there was no romantic interest there for me but both girls were very jolly and friendly. Tom Lane eventually married Joyce and they still live in Papley and farm; now that time has made Tom and I virtually the same age he has lost the seniority he once had at school and he and Joyce are now good friends of ours.

There was another farming family that lived beyond nearby Lutton and here it was the wife, Mrs Selby, who added to my social life by organising a play in Lutton village hall and making sure that as many young people as possible were included. My Father was able to make our large communal hall available to the Lutton village community for Saturday night dances and for dancing lessons given by Mrs Selby. It was all simple stuff and very unsophisticated but it gave me some contact with people other than my parents and school friends and I enjoyed it. Without it, and without Mrs Selby, how else would I have become the expert dancer of the square tango that I am today?

It was through the family of Mrs Selby that I met my first real girl friend; her name was Jennifer Savill, she was very tall, she lived in Peterborough and it was a devil of a job to get to see her using rural bus services. She was soon to be taken from me by a devilishly good looking boy from Laxton called Derek Hadman.

I then took up with a girl who lived in Stilton, Anne Griffith, who was short, dark, slender, very pretty and perhaps, only perhaps, just a little more than I could handle at that time in my life. She was soon to be taken from me by the handsome and rakish Bob Mash who lived in Lutton and had until then enjoyed 'best friend' status.

~

During my first Summer at Polebrooke a local farmer, the father of the Head Boy, John Case, who farmed fields within the airfield's boundaries, met my Father and me and asked me what I was doing during the long holiday. I had no plans. Soon I was sitting on the back of a straw baler, threading wires through guides to make bales of straw, for a shilling an hour. It was terrific! I was thrilled to discover that I had something worth selling. The work was hot and sticky and occupied most of my days but the real money in my pocket, much, much more than I had ever had before, made it all worthwhile.

~

Travelling to school I usually bicycled in the company of Bob Mash and there were two routes open to us: the road that wended its way from Polebrooke Aerodrome, through Polebrook village, along past Ashton and the River Nene, over the railway crossing, over the bridge and up the hill, past the brewery and into town, and the Ashton way which took us right through Ashton Woods, on a metalled road that was flanked by trees the entire way. On a pleasant day Bob and I much preferred to pedal our way through the beauty of the Wold, going past the charming thatched cottage on our right before sweeping round and into Ashton Village itself, then down the hill to join the main road and the remainder of the conventional road route.

25 March 1952 was a Saturday and Bob and I were biking to school in the morning taking the Ashton Way; the weather was clear and bright and we were enjoying the ride and each other's company (the Anne Griffith business still lay in the future). We noticed one or two policemen in the woods; they appeared to be looking for something, turning over leaves with sticks and studying the ground. Then more policemen. This in a part of the world that really knew only one policeman and he Sergeant Wilde based in Oundle. We cycled past the thatched cottage on our right where the concentration of policemen and police cars was very high. We carried on our way to school puzzled by this strange occurrence.

At school we quickly learned of the awful tragedy that had taken place in the cottage the night before and was to remain in the memory of Ashton village and nearby communities for decades. The occupants, Mr and Mrs Peach, had been bludgeoned to death.

The investigation of the murder was massive by standards of the time. Eventually it took in the fingerprinting of every male physically capable of committing the crime for miles around and this included not only my Father but me. It also included all the residents of the hostel, the DPs.

For a while it looked as though the CID had found their man amongst our residents for they took one into the 'Clark Gable' hut over the way from us and interviewed him in shifts, for hours and hours. In the end, having eventually established an alibi, he was released. No-one was ever brought to trial for the murders.

Many years later, in the seventies, I read an article in the Sunday Times revealing that large numbers of German war criminals had escaped Allied justice by masquerading as DPs. It was, it seemed, highly likely that amongst our generally genial bunch of foreign fellows there were some few to whom the bludgeoning to death of an elderly couple would not have been impossible to contemplate or even execute.

Had the CID known this I wonder if they might have studied our residents just a little more carefully?

~

With so much land around me, land where I could roam to my heart's content without fear of a farmer popping up from behind hedges and threatening the trespasser with anything from prosecution to a backside peppered with shotgun pellets, I became something of a countryman. I learned how to snare rabbits and this soon became a source of pocket money for me. I would set my snares after school and then go around picking up my catch in the morning before going to school. The local Oundle butcher, Mr Brudenell, would look in to collect the rabbits when he called to deliver meat to the hostel.

I also talked my Father into buying a secondhand shotgun for £5. It had its barrel sawn down to within a fraction of an inch of the legal minimum (around 21 inches), no doubt to facilitate it being secreted beneath a coat and one can only wonder why the owner had found it necessary to keep it hidden. I roamed the aerodrome and tried to shoot rabbits but with small success.

~

There was one very odd occurrence that followed on from the purchase of the shotgun. It was the first of a strange kind of precognitive experience that has become part of my life, not in any kind of regular way, but just here and there, now and then.

I was out with the gun one Sunday morning; I looked along the length of a very thick, dense hedge and there was a rabbit, sitting on its haunches about five feet away from the hedge and probably well out of range. I took as much aim as was possible with that old relative of the blunderbuss and fired. The rabbit remained just as it had been and then ran, apparently unharmed, into the depths of the impenetrable hedge. Damn! I walked back to our hut.

Later that day, in my bedroom, lying on my bed and reading I started to wonder what had happened to the rabbit and then I formed a very distinct picture of it, lying on its side, dead, in the middle of the hedge. It was a brief but clear picture and quite realistic. I put on some very old clothes, borrowed my Father's tin snips and set off for the hedge where I had seen the rabbit. For two hours I cut my way into the blackthorn, receiving many punctures from the thorns, and still unable to see into the dark depths of the vegetation. But I *knew* what I was going to see eventually – and then, there it was, exactly as I had pictured it. I cut away with more enthusiasm and recovered the corpse.

Since then I have learned not to be surprised by my ability, my *occasional* ability, my ability that seems not to operate when I want it to, to anticipate things. I will not attempt a list here but I will give an account of a couple of recent incidents that illustrate what I mean.

Just a few years ago I attended a conference of arts managers in Vienna and sitting in one session I took up a pencil and a note pad from the hotel where I was staying and started to doodle. I drew a street scene, with tall buildings on either side of the sheet of paper. I put in a banner draped between two buildings but left the banner with no wording. Then I drew – now you will think this very odd but it gets odder – a very, very large bald head of a man, apparently pushing up through the surface of the street. This head was quite out of proportion to the buildings; it was, in relation to a building, as big as, say, a lorry. Then the session became more interesting. I stopped doodling and put the little note pad into my briefcase.

When I got back to my office I forgot about the doodle until a day or so later I opened my newspaper and saw a photograph illustrating the opening of an arts festival at the Barbican Arts Centre, London. In the picture there were tall buildings on either side, there was a banner strung between them – and there in the foreground was a huge bald head, a sculpture, resting on the paved surface.

I had not thrown away the note pad. I recovered it and compared my doodle with the photograph. It was . . . pretty close.

On another occasion the Lit and I were about to drive to London via a country road that led us on to the A1 road; it was a very familiar route to us. As we left the house I went to the kitchen and collected a plastic shopping bag. Lit asked me why I wanted a plastic bag. 'For the pheasant', I said with about as much thought as had gone into my visit to the kitchen. As we drove through the countryside something caught my eye from the grass at the side of the road. I stopped the car, picked up my plastic bag and went over to the verge where I found a large cock pheasant, unmarked but dead, recently dead, still warm. Into the bag it went. I was slightly surprised by this incident although it did seem to me that it was somehow appropriate that the bird should have been waiting for me. Why else would I have needed a plastic bag? Heather was much more surprised.

The interesting thing was that when I plucked and drew the bird ready for the oven (I'm afraid that we country lads do things like this) it was evident that the bird had not been hit by a car as I had first thought but had been shot – and the shooting season had not yet started.

It does not do to wonder about things like this too much.

~

During this year my Mother invited me to go into Peterborough with her one Saturday. She took me to a Gents' Outfitters near the centre of town and bought me a pair of grey flannel trousers, a sports jacket and a pair of brown brogue shoes with little leather tags at the end of the laces. At home I had a bright yellow silk tie that my cousin Roy had passed on to me, he not having the courage to wear it. The ensemble made me feel well on the way to being grown up. So often in this narrative my Mother exists in the background but she was insightful and quick to act when the situation called for it. I wonder if she ever knew how much I valued having that acknowledgement of my no-longer-a-child status.

~

My life at Polebrooke and at Laxton School rolled on happily. My academic progress continued unabated as I moved towards the first big hurdle of a young person's life, the General Certificate in Education at Ordinary Level, or GCE, the then new examination that had recently replaced the old 'School Cert' which was only awarded if the entrant achieved passes in at least six subjects. The GCE, which provided a separate certificate for each subject and did not require a minimum number of passes, was kinder. For reasons that now escape me, but were probably to do with school timetabling, I ceased to do Latin but the French went on apace. English too; it had always been a subject to which I was drawn and as I grew older I found it increasingly interesting. The GCE syllabus that required the detailed study of Shakespeare's *Twelfth Night* and C. S. Forester's novel *The Gun* was, for me, stimulating and rewarding. In mathematics, physics and chemistry I was competent and, to go by results in the examinations, successful but I was uninspired; I was never to be found talking about these subjects to my friends whereas the games of 'who said this, to whom, and why?' in relation to *Twelfth Night* went on.

~

My time at Laxton spanned four years of my life but only the first two were spent at Polebrooke, for within this period the bridge finally disappeared altogether and my parents were left clawing thin air. After just over a year the YMCA closed the hostel and there were no more hostels to which we could move. My parents became unemployed.

My Father then took a course of action that both saved our bacon and marked the end of his life as an active manager and my Mother took the first step that led to her becoming the major force in the breadwinning business. The collection of huts and all the furniture and equipment within them were technically Air Ministry property and if they were left unattended they would inevitably be broken into, vandalised and their contents would be stolen. My Father sold himself to the Air Ministry as a watchman. There was to be little or no salary; we were to live rent free. It was a mistake because at the age of around 53 my Father gave in to the temptation to take it easy. That he had my school career in mind as well, the fact that it had already been seriously disrupted and I was now doing extremely well with a glowing future predicted by all, cannot be denied but I believe that it was a wrong decision. As you will see, it was but a stop-gap measure.

~

My Mother thus had to find a job and, bless her, she went to it with a will. Stuck out in the middle of nowhere with only a bike and an infrequent rural bus service, she was, to put it mildly, handicapped. She became cook to the Watts-Russell family that lived on the Benefield side, that is, the other side of Oundle in relation to where we lived, and she went there by bicycle for five or six days a week. I was a healthy boy in my teens and I occasionally found the return trip by bicycle arduous; when the weather was bad I had the option of taking the school bus *and* I had plenty of school holidays. My Mother's journey was 12 miles a day and she had no respite. She was then only about 40 years old and in excellent health but the trip combined with responsibility for cooking lunch and dinner for a large family that ate along traditional lines, that is, heavily, must have been exhausting.

~

Her connection there found holiday work for me and in my Easter holiday I went to work on the Watts-Russell farm under the guidance of farm manager, George Little, and learned how to 'strip' a cow prior to mechanical milking (a simple test to check for signs of TB that involves knowing how to milk by hand), how to attach a milking machine, how to scrape dried manure from a cow's backside with a curry comb (there's more to this than . . . meets the eye!), how to make a really good barbed wire fence and how to cut and lay a hawthorn hedge. George Little was a good boss and made me feel that my contribution to the farm was of value – he also said nice things about me to my Mother which went down well at home.

~

I cannot be sure of the detail but at some time during this second year at Polebrooke Mother added to her workload by becoming a night nurse for two or three nights a week at the small hospital Oundle then possessed. She was working very hard and keeping us at that time.

~

At the end of our second year, that is, at the beginning of Summer, it became clear that this way of life couldn't continue and the remnants of the hostel were finally cleared away. My Mother gave up the Watts-Russell job and my Father's sinecure with the Air Ministry was terminated. The Diggle family put what few belongings they possessed into boxes and suitcases and into store – and went off to Brean Sands, near Burnham-on-Sea, where the caravan that had replaced the 196 square foot ex-Army tent a couple of years earlier now rested.

Father took a job as night watchman at Pontin's Holiday Camp, Mother took a job at Pontin's Holiday Camp, running the camp shop, and I took a job at Pontin's Holiday Camp, operating a dish washer. Thank God for Fred Pontin! Mine was simply a school holiday job; nothing to be ashamed of in that. To my parents it was bread and butter, plain and simple; without those jobs we should have gone under.

The camp employed two sports organisers who also arranged the nightly entertainments that consisted mainly of getting the happy campers to participate in a sort of smoking concert, with songs and sketches. It was corny old stuff but the two chaps, one youngish and one oldish, carried it all off with great panache and I loved to watch them at work making entertainment out of such rough raw material. My chores in the kitchen were over within an hour of the end of dinner and I was then free to do whatever I chose. I chose to help in the entertainments and soon became a sort of unofficial assistant. I got the taste for it and the experience of leading a hundred drunken holiday-makers in such classics as

I put my finger in the woodpecker's hole
And the woodpecker said 'God Bless My Soul,

Take it out
Take it out
Take it out my friend. REE-MOVE IT'

must have made *some* contribution to my future career. The sketches too, repeated each week as one crowd was replaced by another, and memorised by me, were to come in handy quite soon when I came to develop my promotional skills in Oundle with the start of the new academic year.

∼

The Summer came to an end. I had learned that I had achieved GCE 'O' level passes in French, English Literature, English Language, Chemistry, Physics and Mathematics. My parents got a job running a hostel for construction workers at Alconbury, near Huntingdon, which was far too far away from Oundle for me to travel daily and so arrangements were made for me to go into lodgings with a Mrs Oughton, at 29, Rock Road, Oundle.

I now faced my final two years at school. I would be living away from my parents during term time. I had made a cracking success of my school life so far. I had overcome the problem of attending three different schools in four years, had settled in to Laxton and had achieved six passes – good passes too, no near misses – at 'O' level. Why should I not go on being successful?

CHAPTER 8

NOT HEAVY ENOUGH TO WIN A PRIZE

Living in Oundle (1953-1955)

Mrs Oughton was a plump and kindly widow with a bit of a goitre and a daughter called Yvonne who worked at the chemists. They lived in a small house in Rock Road, Oundle. It had three bedrooms; two at the back, arranged so that you had to go through one bedroom to get into the other; mother and daughter occupied these. The new lodger was put into the front bedroom which, in the way of bedrooms in small houses of that time, had linoleum on the floor, a bed with small mat beside it, a wardrobe, a chest of drawers and a very small table where he could write; like the rest of the house it was unheated. It had a fireplace but the fireplace never saw a fire, no matter how severe the Winter. As with Number 8 Pembroke Road, only serious illness merited a fire being lit. Like Number 8 Pembroke Road the WC was outside the main structure of the house and flushed in the conventional way (unlike my Gran Staddon's). Unlike Number 8 Pembroke Road, the house had no bathroom, the bath being a metal affair that was kept in a shed next to the WC and was brought into the kitchen once a week (perhaps more often – I wasn't really counting). It had a back room adjoining the kitchen, in which we all ate, and sat and . . . did very little else. There was a front room opening directly out onto the street, with nice furniture and an upright piano, into which one never went. As with every house or hut I had ever occupied and as with almost everywhere else, there was no television with which to while away one's idle hours.

I washed myself in a large china basin in my room. I obtained cold water in a large china jug as required. In the morning Mrs Oughton would put a kettle of water on the gas for me and I would collect it for my morning wash. As with almost the entire British working class population truly effective personal hygiene was something of a new concept and only just beginning to catch on.

Mrs Oughton and Yvonne were nice people. They obviously needed the money that my presence brought with it and the terms of our contract were fulfilled quite adequately. I had my room and I was provided with breakfast and 'high tea' during term time. As I recollect, the arrangement was intended to span Monday to Friday, an extra payment being made if I stayed over the weekend, when lunch would also be provided. During weekdays I lunched at school and, by special arrangement with Laxton School's Master-in-Charge, Mr Stretton, I had free access to a bathroom in one of the school's upper floors. My laundry was handled professionally by a laundry service in town that required me to drop my bag into the shop on a Monday and collect it again on a Friday.

Yvonne was young and pretty and it was very, very fortunate for me (and perhaps even for her) that I was not remotely attracted to her. I was of an age when I was far from indifferent to pretty young women. Yvonne went her way and I went mine; it was only unfortunate when some time after joining the household her way caused mine to be discovered with disastrous consequences. Not that mine was so very outrageous. More of this later.

~

Entering the Sixth form puts one at the junction of the roads of destiny. My 'O' level passes were evenly poised between arts and science subjects. Which way to go? I am not at all sure that I had much say in the matter. The future of Britain lay in science and industry; that's what they all said. Mr Stretton leaned heavily towards the sciences and so did the whole of Oundle School apparently. If I ever had a thought on the subject – and I probably did although I don't believe that I ever felt that I could influence fate in this respect – the idea of . . . say . . . *engineering,* say, appealed to me. My Father had been an engineer, hadn't he? I had not by then ruled out the RAF either – and Father had been quite successful in the RAF, hadn't he? – and there were available RAF scholarships to study engineering at University. That must surely be the path to follow.

My parents expressed no views either way. No-one sat down and discussed with me which way my heart inclined, no-one asked me 'What do you *enjoy* most at school?' and so the decision to study Mathematics, Physics and Chemistry to GCE 'A' level was made and I stepped on to a conveyor belt that was to carry me along for the next 12 years. I wish I could say that I was conveyed kicking and screaming in protest but I cannot. I did not know myself at all. I had nothing to measure myself against. I had no sense of what was possible for me. I just wanted to succeed at *something.*

~

But I had brought with me to Oundle a minor ambition that tickled away and some slight experience that would help me achieve it. My time at Pontin's Holiday Camp had given me a taste of it and I took the first chance I could see to put my ideas into practice. It was not very ambitious but, for a boy of my age and of my background, I did not do badly.

Some friends invited me to join a group of young people who thought to form a youth club and we did, we set up the Oundle Church Youth Fellowship. How the church got into this I cannot remember and, once formed, we had nothing to do with either church or vicar. The important thing was that we had our youth club, we had a place where we could meet and . . . well, what could we do now? Let us put on a show, I suggested in the good, old-fashioned manner of a Mickey Rooney. Where? The Drill Hall! Let's do the show right there in the Drill Hall!

I have never been any good with committees for they come up with ideas like not doing a full scale show (which is what I wanted to do) but having a dance and then having a show and then having another dance – and calling it a Social – but I went along with it, the OCYF committee, and with the Social, and started to put together a show. During the time I was living in digs in Oundle I did two shows. They leaned heavily upon what I had learned at Pontin's and they were bracketed by what I thought were wholly unnecessary distractions but they were *my* shows.

~

I had been fairly friendly with a boy who was slightly older than me and considerably more clever. He was a scientist and he was also a good musician, playing the piano rather well. Now I was in my first year of the Sixth form I saw more of him and we became good friends. He too was in digs, staying with his Aunt Janet in St. Osyth's Lane, and I got in the habit of spending my evenings with him, doing my homework in his bedsitter while he did his. Richard Ellis, known to all at the time for reasons no-one can explain, as 'Dearie', became my lifelong friend. In the early stages of our friendship it was Richard's piano playing ability that I needed – plus his driving license and access to his aunt's car – and I exploited him mercilessly. He never complained.

The Drill Hall stage had no curtains. Mrs Selby (she who had turned me into an expert dancer of the square tango) had some curtains. Richard would borrow his aunt's car and the curtains would be collected and returned in due course. I needed an accompanist for my shows; Richard played what needed to be played.

I do not remember much about the shows. I wrote new words to fit tunes I already knew and I even attempted a bit of choreography in a number called *The Spider and the Fly* that I danced with Mrs Selby's step-daughter Daphne. I added a few sketches to the old Pontin routines. People did seem to like them. I did not attempt to lead the audiences in the song about putting one's finger in the woodpecker's hole.

I publicised the events as well. I visited the printer and had posters and tickets printed. In those days posters were printed from movable type made from large wooden letters and the smaller material was set from metal letters that had to be selected from a divided tray and laboriously made up into words. Illustrations of any kind were quite outside my budget as the technology of the time that was involved in taking, say, a photograph and reproducing it as a printed image was very costly. One relied upon words to convey the message.

Unwittingly following marketing principles that were then unknown to me I ensured that club members sold tickets to friends well in advance and that we did not rely upon sales 'on the night'. I trekked around all the town shops with my posters and learned that if one did not put up the poster oneself, or stand by with roll of sticky tape at the ready while the shopkeeper did it, the poster would go in the bin after one's departure. Our events sold out.

∼

Looking back on that time it is still a source of some wonder to me that what I was doing, primitive and insignificant as it was, took place quite independently and outside the knowledge of my school. No-one involved in my education and my guidance knew anything of what I was doing. In those days it was not the business of Oundle School masters to be aware of what Laxton School boys were doing and the Laxton School masters had no interest in what a boy who now took all his lessons in Oundle School was doing. Only the Master-in-Charge, Mr Stretton, ever came to know anything and he revealed this when he called me into his study to admonish me for smoking in public; I had, he said, been seen as I walked between the Drill Hall and one of the small brick huts where I stored some costumes, one Sunday afternoon. I had been rehearsing my show, I told him. He showed no interest and warned me that if I was caught out again the punishment would be severe. Nowadays, I should imagine, a boy would get a Duke of Edinburgh's Award or an National Vocational Qualification in Theatre Marketing.

∼

At around the time of my first show I developed another girlfriend. She was small and dark haired and physically she was a sort of prototype Lit. She lived in Oundle and the relationship was altogether more rewarding than my earlier ones. She was fairly quickly stolen away from me by the tall and devilishly handsome Derek Bunning, whom I have now forgiven for his unkindness and who now basks in the warmth of my friendship. Derek Hadman, who stole Jennifer from me, remains unforgiven for she was my first girlfriend and he, good-looking dog that he was, had the pick of all the available girls.

∼

My unsuitability for the course of studies that had been chosen for me soon began to show and Chemistry was the first to fall. I sat in a classroom mystified by something called Organic Chemistry and realised that I would never, ever, grasp it. A dramatically bad end of term result led to my being permitted to drop the subject. I was left with Mathematics and Physics and they, as my school reports show, began their own steady decline.

The timetable of my first year in the Sixth form included English, thank heavens. My teacher was a wonderfully urbane and witty man called Ralph Barber

The emphasis is on the concert

who affected foppish ways and possessed a far back accent and a drawling delivery that made him seem to have stepped straight from an upper class Edwardian drawing room. We aimed to gain a pass in what was known as Additional English Literature – a stepping stone between GCE 'O' Level and 'A' Level – and this involved the study of five texts amongst which were Lytton Strachey's *Eminent Victorians* and *Antony and Cleopatra* by Shakespeare. Ralph Barber's lessons were a delight and soon became the only bright light in my working week. I studied hard, loving every minute, and passed that examination with great ease.

The gap made in my week by the absence of Chemistry was filled with more lessons with Ralph Barber; French lessons. The group of pupils that I joined were a mixed bag of misfits who had been kicked out of or had dropped out of 'A' level courses; we were a sort of *salon des refusés*. Ralph Barber took us through a highly entertaining programme of French literature which he insisted should be read in the original language. Some found this hard to bear; I lapped it all up. We read a story of Russian emigrés in Paris called *Tatiana,* Pagnol's *Monsieur Topaz* and (seminal influence this) Merrimé's story that became a great opera, *Carmen,* and many more.

In my second year, when evidence of certain failure in my 'A' level subjects was becoming all too obvious in my end of term reports, non-examination English and French continued to make me feel that not all my time was being wasted. At the start of that *annus horribilis,* when I achieved the distinction of being placed in the bottom Mathematics set (I was later to be placed *bottom* of that set – quite a strange place for someone who was to become a teacher of Mathematics in a Grammar School), Ralph Barber launched his year of English with a long list of works of literature with which 'cheps' should be familiar and suggested, without any evidence of optimism, that the mixed bunch seated before him should take steps to read them in their spare time. With almost limitless spare time on my hands (I devoted very little to my main subjects) I set to and read the lot – which included Tolstoy's *War And Peace* and, of my own volition, *Anna Karenina.* The dear man was impressed, not to say touched.

Ralph Barber also set high personal standards of dress and behaviour and had his own way of suggesting improvements in his pupils. Once, following a common schoolboy habit of the time, I took out a comb and ran it through my (no doubt Brylcreamed) hair. He looked up and said in tones of limitless sorrow, 'Oh, Diggle', stretching out my name in his languorous way so that it seemed to take several seconds to complete. I never combed my hair in public again.

Ralph Barber still lives in Oundle and, as I write, is a familiar figure in the main street when he pops out to go shopping and appears at many artistic events in the town. I have attempted to let him know how great was his contribution both to my happiness at that time and to my education.

~

I think that my parents were having a hard time while I was at school and being a self-obsessed failure. My Father was the sole breadwinner at this time; he was running a hostel for construction workers and his employer was Tarmac Limited. My Mother had no official duties although she wielded considerable influence in the kitchen. Tarmac was not the kind and understanding employer that the YMCA had been. It was a tough company and it was tough with its employees. It treated my Father as being a very minor figure indeed and that was a shame because his dignity was important to him.

The accomodation provided was a Nissen hut; a rectangular floor space with neither walls nor ceiling but a curved surface with a semi-circular cross section that rose from one edge of the floor and finished its journey on the other side. Had we had any pictures it would have been the very devil to have hanged them. In the centre there was a diesel oil burning stove that, once ignited, roared and glowed and looked as though it was going to take off through that elegant corrugated iron covering. My parents improvised room dividers by hanging blankets from string tied to the metal bolts that protruded from the 'walls'.

Do I make this seem ghastly? It was ghastly. We spent a Christmas there trying to make the best of it but it was . . . ghastly. Travel by public transport, from Oundle to Alconbury, took ages and it became easier and easier just not to go home at weekends.

~

I have one memento of that time. One Saturday I had gone into Huntingdon to buy myself a hairbrush. I chose one that cost 10/6 (52.5p), which was not the cheapest hairbrush that I could have bought. My Father, who had said he would cover the cost, exploded with anger when I told him how much it had been. As though determined to prove that it was a good buy, and not mere extravagance, I have kept that hairbrush through thick hair and thin hair and still use it. Its distribution of bristles now patterns that of my own hair. The cost of the brush is currently working out at about 1.3p a year and, if I stay healthy, I hope to bring that figure down to under 1p. Do you forgive me now, Father?

~

Richard's home was in Godmanchester, just next to Huntingdon, and on the occasions when he could borrow Aunt Janet's car, he would drive past the site of the hostel and drop me off and then collect me on his way back. There was never any possibility of my inviting him in for a cup of tea for there was really nowhere in the hut that lent itself to hospitality. Sometimes Richard would not drop me off but would take me to his home for the weekend, a lovely half-timbered house on the bank of the River Ouse, where his parents would provide a welcoming reception, a comfortable bed and good food while Richard would take me on his round of friends, a small group of amiable eccentrics who seemed devoted either to playing in brass bands or fishing for eels. This made a great contribution to the quality of my life at the time.

~

At some time during my final year at school my parents packed in the Alconbury job and went to work in a small hostel for students in Wanstead, London. It was not very well paid but at least they did not have to live in a Nissen hut.

~

My school career dragged itself wearily to a close. Apart from the stress of beginning to realise that my parents were themselves on the start of a decline, and that my choice of academic subjects had been a horrible mistake, I was an adolescent (and that's bad enough); I was *lonely*. I remember very clearly Sunday afternoons in my last term when Richard was away at home and I would walk down to a public bench in South Road and smoke a cigarette, not giving a damn who might see me, and wonder what was going on in my poor benighted life.

~

During the week every evening was spent with Richard in his bedroom at Number 10 St. Osyth's Lane. I would go back to 29, Rock Road after school, eat, and then go back to see my friend. We would do our homework and then chat. Whenever funds ran to it we would prepare a meal that was invariably a shared tin of Irish stewed steak heated up in a saucepan on a Valor paraffin stove followed by tinned peaches and tinned cream. We kept a flagon of cider up the chimney. I would smoke a cigarette and Richard would light his pipe. On Monday nights we would listen to the radio programme 'Journey Into Space' and later in the week 'The Goon Show'. We kept each other company and our very different personalities complemented each other very well. We were good friends.

Richard helped me enormously with my school work through those two years; being a scientist he could help me with all of my 'A' level work and being a calm sort of person he could persuade me away from rash courses of action. He tolerated my occasional absences from his company due to feminine distractions and never succumbed to them himself while at school (in that connection, when he left school he found the girl he wanted to marry, Jenny, married her and they lived happily ever after). His one academic weakness – he was a sort of habitual English 'O' level failer – enabled me to repay him for his many kindnesses, in part at least, by coaching him for his English Language examination.

~

When I got the chance of feminine company I grasped it, and it took the form of a couple of girlfriends over those last six or eight months with whom, from time to time, I would stay out past Mrs Oughton's deadline of 10pm. On one occasion, in my final term, I had stayed out even later than usual and when I entered the house I locked the door behind me. What I did not know was that Mrs Oughton's daughter, Yvonne, who was also expected to respect a deadline, was still out of the house and was to return very, very much later. When she finally arrived back she was forced to wake her mother in order to gain entrance and mother was most angry. Somehow this became my fault and Mrs Oughton visited Mr Stretton in order to register her protest at my conduct. A letter was sent to my Father saying that my conduct was unacceptable and I would not be allowed to return to school when the new academic year started. So there was to be no second chance at those 'A' levels which was, it must be said, a blessing for it would have been a terrible, terrible waste of time.

∼

And there had been the beating, which I have already described. I had gone back afterwards to my bedroom and sat there alone for a couple of hours. Then I had gone to see Richard and he offered what consolation he could – almost certainly it would have been tinned Irish stew and mashed potatoes followed by tinned peaches and cream, accompanied by a glass of cider from the chimney.

To this day I cannot understand how someone could be so cruel as to do what was done then to a young person who was so vulnerable and alone.

All in all I had really done with being at school.

∼

Other than private satisfactions derived from doing essays particularly well, enjoying the lessons of certain teachers, the excitements of the cadets and rare occasions of entertainment such as the time the staff of the two schools staged 'Masterpieces', a stage review that featured the talents of C. A. B. Marshall (then known as 'Cabbie' and later, to a wider world, as television personality Arthur Marshall), there is almost nothing of my last two years that I may remember as being a success. I was not regarded as being worthy of elevation to the status of prefect and I won no school prizes. In those days the prizes handed out at the annual speech day were books; beautiful, leather-bound books with gold-embossed covers and I did so much want one of those books! I would sit watching the presentations, boy after boy marching up and returning with one of these gleaming treasures (sometimes more than one – it was too much to bear) and I would *envy*. It was not the glory I envied; it was simply the books. But I was just not heavy enough to win a prize.

∼

It was only at running that I did, in the end, excel. There was an annual cross-country race with The King's School, Peterborough and in my second year at Laxton I was chosen for the team; it was a gruelling course, I was not then a good runner, and I failed to finish. The following year the event was held on the Peterborough course and I struggled into fifth place. In my final year, the race took place in Oundle and I told myself I must win this. There were perhaps five really good long distance runners in the school by this time and we ran as a team, helping each other on. Within a mile of the finish, after clambering over muddy stiles and pulling through muddy fields we were all fairly well done for but were in the fore apart from one King's boy who kept ahead of us. I distinctly remember Jeremy Clarke, an excellent runner, stopping, exhausted, to hold up a barbed wire strand to allow me to pass through and take up a position second to the King's boy; Jeremy motioned me to go on. The course ended in South Road and the boy and I slogged over a deeply-ploughed field. The plimpsoll on my left foot pulled off in the mud and dangled from my ankle; I tore it off and discarded it. On through the mud and onto the hard surface of Herne Road I pounded and overtook the boy there. I maintained my position and, with blood pouring dramatically from my unshoed foot, I finished with him just a couple of feet behind me.

~

University was obviously not going to be an option for me and, although in those days it was possible for a young person whose parents were poor (and mine had slipped into that category since the early Polebrook days) to attend one had to be good academically and that I patently was not. Engineering still had an appeal for me although I cannot now say why, and I began to look in that direction. I also had to take into account that I had no home apart from the hostel in Wanstead where my parents worked and lived, where a room for me had to be negotiated, or my parents' retreat, a small caravan in Somerset. Wherever they were the available space would be shared with the Great Dane dog, Thor, that they had acquired somewhere along the way from the Watts-Russell family. So it wasn't that I made a decision to leave home – home rather left me.

~

Parental influence, whether conscious or not, can have strange consequences. My Father had been an engineering apprentice, having signed a five-year indenture paper at the age of 16. Here I was, aged 17 years and six months, considering the possibility of signing up for an engineering apprenticeship. Engineering apprenticeships were being advertised in the newspapers and could be secured before the awful reality of examination results came upon me. What tipped the balance against any deeply seated reservations I might have had was the fact that some apprenticeships were residential and I needed a roof over my head.

I applied for a five-year apprenticeship with the De Havilland aeroplane company. It was very famous at the time and had developed the jet airliner, the Comet, that was set to rule the skies for Britain commercially. The Comet later started to fall out of the skies with horrifying frequency and I was glad that the company had put me off by telling me that my parents would have to pay a small (but nonetheless too large) sum of money to secure the apprenticeship. At least I was never to have air disasters on my conscience.

The Atomic Energy Research Establishment at Harwell fell for my pitch and I signed up for the customary five years. It was to be an engineering apprenticeship with two days a week spent studying for 'A' levels necessary to put me into University to study engineering under the Atomic Energy Commission's sponsorship. It was a marvellous opportunity and I was to make a flop of it.

~

Note the beginning of the slippery slope. Study sciences at school – when you have absolutely no aptitude for the subjects – find yourself on the way to being an engineer – and facing five years of it.

Chapter 9

There He Stands, This Fine British Youth, Facing An Exciting Future!

Atomic Energy Research Establishment, Harwell
(September 1955 – August 1956)

It was September 1955 and I was three months short of my 18th birthday. I was free from the constraints of school and far away from that lonely bedroom of Mrs Oughton's. I stood at the doorway of Portway House, the hostel for apprentice engineers at Harwell, and I saw myself as an engineer of the future. What was that slogan from the 1951 Festival of Britain? 'Britain Can Make It'. Well, *I* would make it. I would be part of that new world!

I see it all now in terms of those optimistic British Movietone News items with that strange male voice telling us how this *British-made* machine could make more plastic eggcups than any other machine in the world and ending by saying that its performance was 'egg-straordinary!' And all the while the busy British music coming in and out, filling the spaces between the phrases of the jingoistic strange male voice that seemed to have found a new job for itself now that the war was over and could no longer tell us that 'Tommy was going to give those Huns one heck of a pasting!'. There I stood, in black and white, in profile, with the sun beaming down onto my noble features and in the background the outlines of tall modern factory buildings. The music played stirringly and the voice captioned the picture: 'There he stands, this fine British youth, facing an exciting future! Well, it's our future too and we all owe him one heck of a lot! Good luck with it, lad!'.

Reality was living in Portway House with 40 or more young men, all of whom were in various stages of apprenticeship at Harwell; I shared a room with one of them. I had a bed, wardrobe and chest of drawers. There were bathrooms and there was a laundry room. The hostel's kitchen provided breakfast and dinner seven days a week. I received a wage and a deduction was made for my accommodation and food. I suppose I must have been left with a couple of pounds spending money at the end of each week. It was, to me at least, a very heaven after what I had experienced over the previous two years.

~

The first year of the apprenticeship, when one was not on day-release studying at Newbury Technical College, was spent in the training workshop where one was taught how to use the basic engineering equipment: bandsaw, lathe, capstan drill, shaper and planer – but first the file, the common-or-garden file and the common-or-garden hacksaw. Our instructor, a genial fellow called Bob Wakeley, presented his new intake, a group of some 15 young men, with slabs of mild steel measuring about nine inches by five inches and half an inch thick. With our hacksaws and our files we would each make a pair of 'C' clamps. Later on we would need to know how to drill the holes that would carry the threaded part of the clamp and we would be shown how to 'tap', or create a thread, within those holes. Meanwhile, here's the blueprint. Get sawing and get filing.

We had a schedule of metalwork projects to accomplish during our first year; these 'test pieces' involved the expert use of all the basic machine tools and were so designed that if one had not achieved expertise the items – toolmaker's vice, scribing-block, tap wrench and so on – would not work properly and would look dreadful. It was a very traditional way of training engineers, the idea being that the young man, once qualified, would set out to face the world equipped with a full set of tools that he had made himself.

It was all very like 'workshops' at school but there was a lot more of it; our training area was located to one side of a real working engineering floor that was packed with machinery and men doing real jobs, so we constantly moved in the atmosphere of a factory. There was even a tea-lady with a trolley who plodded up and down the aisles and, in the manner of tea-ladies everywhere, kept back the best cakes for her favourite customers. Of our group approximately half were 'craft' apprentices who would continue to study the practical aspects of engineering for the whole five-year period. The rest, of which I was one, were 'student' apprentices and when we had finished our first year of practical training we would go on to study things like technical drawing while increasing the amount of time spent in theoretical study; from the third year onwards we were expected to go to University under the auspices of AERE Harwell. It was, for all but me, a fine scheme.

Although I was to spend only one year there I have always valued that experience of working in the factory atmosphere and learning the practical skills of an engineer. I still have most of the tools I made and sometimes find myself looking at them, admiring them and wondering how I ever managed to get them right in the end – the necessary skills certainly did not come easily to me.

~

It was wonderful to be living among lively young men. My social life blossomed. I had friends. I could afford to go out for a drink now and then. If I felt the need for company I could go down into the common room and talk to someone. I missed Richard Ellis but, as it is when you move into a new and exciting world, it was easy to lump him in with everything I had left behind me and concentrate upon the immediate future.

Of course the principal diversion was talk of girls. Portway House was an all-male establishment so girls were *out there* and had to be located, lured and captured. Most motives were based on good old-fashioned lust but there were some who sought out a local girl, with kind and understanding parents, with whom they could form the kind of relationship that would get them invited home regularly, so that whatever physical benefits there were would be supplemented by food; it was called 'getting your feet under the table'.

My immediate group of friends, the two Geoffs, Sinclair and Arnison, Roger Pelham and I believed that there existed places where girls were more likely to be found – rather in the way that there are spots in a river where one is more likely to catch fish or fields where one is more likely to find mushrooms – and Roger, who was a year or so my senior, held that it was a place called Nettlebed where dances were held every Saturday night. So for weeks we all set out, Saturday night after Saturday night, dressed in our killer clothes, in a borrowed car and spent the evening leaning against the wall of the hall, drinking and looking knowingly at the girls who were dancing. I don't think we ever invited a girl to dance. I don't recall ever speaking to one. It was, as these young male activities so usually are, pitifully funny.

~

I heard my first jazz at Harwell. Robin Turner, who went on to become a reporter for the *Daily Express,* lent me an 'album' (even that was a new thing for me – an *album),* a long-playing 33rpm record called 'Stan Getz at The Shrine' that began with words from the person introducing the live performance of which this was a recording, 'Ladies and Gentlemen, I'd like to introduce to you the leading exponent of the c-o-o-o-o-l school . . . Stan Getz!' and the cheering started until the sound, a new sound for me, of his tenor saxophone came in.

American West Coast jazz was beginning to be heard in Britain and I found it thrilling stuff. I bought an 'EP' (for 'extended play', a small disc that was played at 45 rpm) of the Gerry Mulligan Quartet – that I still have – and listened entranced to the sounds of Mulligan's baritone saxophone playing contrapuntally against and with the trombone of Bob Brookmeyer. Wonderful tunes; *Walkin' Shoes, Nights at the Turntable, Bernie's Tune* and so on.

Strangely, the music of the Dave Brubeck Quartet which is so linked with that period was not then heard. In Britain Getz and Mulligan definitely came first and Brubeck was to follow the year after when BBC presenter and pianist Steve Race introduced the music in his regular jazz programme and went on presenting it as a sort of one-man crusade.

Five or six years later I took photographs of Getz at Ronnie Scott's Jazz Club and many, many years later, after I had given a lecture in Capetown, South

Africa, a young man introduced himself to me as Darius Brubeck, son of the man who had been my hero when I was still in my teens. But these events are part of a later life.

~

I took up amateur dramatics and played a part in *A Lady Mislaid* with the Harwell Players.

~

One night another apprentice and I accepted the challenge of hitch-hiking to London and getting back to Harwell in time for work the next day. After a straightforward journey (hitch-hiking was commonplace and almost completely safe in those days) we found ourselves in Covent Garden market at about 1am looking for a lorry going in our direction. Finding no luck and feeling exhausted we sat down for a cup of tea in an all-night cafe at the end of Floral Street, just over the way from the Royal Opera House. I recognised the place when, some 23 years later, my future partner in business, Tony Gamble, and I looked over the premises above. I was to spend many years working on the first floor of that building and taking quick lunches in that cafe.

~

There was a central cafeteria at Harwell, where employees of all kinds, including humble apprentices, could go for an inexpensive self-service lunch – and there I met Yvonne Newman. We found ourselves sharing a table, started to talk, and within a few days were meeting to share our lunch break every day. She lived in nearby Didcot, had kind and understanding parents, and soon there I was with my feet under the table. It was never a very serious relationship – I was far too shallow a young man for that – but Yvonne and I kept each other company and that was fine for us both.

~

After recovering from the Alconbury experience and having spent many months working at 'Juniper', the student hostel in London, my parents managed to get a job running another hostel for construction workers in Bicester, which put them within hitch-hiking distance of Harwell. For a few months the job went well and during that time my Father very generously assembled £40 to enable me to buy an Austin 7 van (1938 generation) which made it much easier to keep in touch with them (although I drove without having passed my test). Then Father fell ill, the illness dragged on and in the end they had to leave the job. This was not a comfortable time for them.

I find it strange that my memory, which is generally good, should choose not to retain certain incidents, certain times, that were particularly painful although others, which seem now to have been just as hard to bear, are recalled with complete clarity. I remember the Laxton School beating as though it were this morning but what happened after Bicester is far from clear.

I do have one distinct scene from that blurred period in my mind and that is of a sort of snack bar or cafe that was close to an American Air Force base somewhere to the north of Oxford. It was not the Bicester construction camp and I think it must have been the place where my parents fled for work when the Bicester job was lost. I think they must have grabbed whatever was the nearest source of income.

I had arrived there in the Austin 7 van. The eating place was largely occupied by American service personnel. My Mother was behind the counter preparing and serving food. The most popular meal appeared to be steak and chips. My Father was clearing the tables. He wore a short white coat and his job was to collect up all the used crockery and cutlery and bring them back to the counter so they could be washed. At that time he wore a moustache. 'Hey Groucho', called out a serviceman in friendly tones, 'Howayerdoin?'.

It was not long before my parents had contacted the owner of 'Juniper' and, praise the Lord, discovered that he had not been able to replace them satisfactorily and that he would welcome their return.

~

The feeling was growing in me that although life was much more fun than it had been for years I did not want to become an engineer and, even had I wanted to, I had not the aptitude. The lectures at Newbury were incomprehensible and hence boring. Life in the training workshop had lost whatever lustre it had once had. For the first time in my life I prepared to make a decision on how my life was to go – and that was . . . to go.

I resigned the apprenticeship. Few had done this before. There were interviews. Even Bob Wakeley was asked to spend some time trying to talk me out of it (which he did with patent lack of sincerity – he could tell a non-engineer if anyone could).

One day I put my few belongings into the back of the Morris Ten Six, the car that I had ill-advisedly swapped for the Austin 7 van, and drove off into . . . wherever there was to drive off into.

My parents had meanwhile moved back to 'Juniper'.

Chapter 10

She Wrote Her Name And Her Telephone Number On The Back Of A Small Brown Envelope And Gave It To Me

Finding a Vocation (Summer 1956 – Summer 1957)

Very fortunately for us all, my parents had found in 'Juniper' a rock to which they could cling, to stop them being swept away entirely by the torrent of life (the collapsing bridge had long since fallen into the ravine and taken them with it). 'Juniper' was a hostel for students at Number 14 Grove Park, Wanstead, London E11, a large, detached, brick Edwardian house. They were appointed to run the place.

In fact it was run by the owner, Mr Arthur Cuff, a bachelor who managed his family's scrap metal business, who lived in one large room on the ground floor. He was an honest, god-fearing sort of chap who thought it better to use his home in this way – housing students and sharing their company – than to live alone. At dinner time all the students, there were perhaps a dozen of them, assembled around the table with Arthur Cuff who said Grace and then took his place at the head. After dinner, at 9.30pm, Mr Cuff would go up to a small room at the top of the house that he had converted into a small chapel, he would sound a gong very softly, and he would then conduct a short service of Compline, either by himself or with any students who felt inclined to join him. His was a non-intrusive form of active Christianity and my parents and I came to like and respect him.

But my parents were not running the place. They were now what was and still is known as a 'domestic couple'. My Mother cooked and my Father served at table, at the communal dinner over which Mr Cuff presided. They took joint responsibility for cleaning the bedrooms and the rest of the house. They occupied one large room at the top of the house and they shared it with the damned Watts-Russell Great Dane that was still getting in the way. The one large room was better than a Nissen hut I can tell you!

But there was no room for me and whenever I visited a negotiation had to take place with Mr Cuff to obtain one. He was very generous and if I turned up during academic vacations then there was always a room free of charge but during term time it was not always possible to find me a place. On one occasion, I had to pay rent in order to get a place to rest my head.

'Juniper' brought me into contact with the sort of people I would have met had I gone to University; this was an experience I valued greatly. In the eleven months or so following my departure from Harwell I was to get to know many people of my own age there and there I was to meet the first love of my life. Well now!

My parents were, for all the limitations of their accommodation, in a place where their competence and old-fashioned standards were valued – and no-one would call my Father 'Groucho'.

~

And where did *I* go when I drove that Morris Ten Six, that misconceived and mal-manufactured product of a bad Friday afternoon in 1934, after I left Harwell? I went off adventuring.

I drove down to West Malling to go hop-picking and there managed to nudge the leg of a Special Constable one night when I was driving out of the Hop Festival; unfortunately I was driving the car and he was standing in front of me, facing the other way with his arms in the classic policeman's Stop position. This later resulted in a conviction for 'Driving without due care and attention' and another for 'Driving without a licence'.

Despairing of the car's apparent inability to go more than a few miles without something going wrong, I left the car in Grove Park, Wanstead, and hitch-hiked up to Wisbech to join a National Union of Students fruit-picking camp where I picked apples and pears for a few weeks. I came back to London.

It was now Autumn of 1956 and the threat of impending National Service lay over me. The problem I encountered was that every potential employer knew that young men were liable to be 'called up' and so there was no point at all in taking them on if they were going to be whipped away at a week's notice. Even a humble pub job, that I had travelled some way by bus for, was denied me. Then I heard that jobs were to be had at Foyles Bookshop.

Getting a job at Foyles was easy and it turned out that losing it was just as easy. I worked in the Books Reception department, the entrance to which lay in Manette Street, off Charing Cross Road; my job was to open mailed packages and ensure that they went to the departments that had ordered them. It was then not possible to live with my parents at 'Juniper' so I obtained a room in a Toc H Hostel in Notting Hill Gate. I do not remember how much I was paid but after I had paid for the hostel, tube fares and the most modest of lunches, I had hardly anything left at all.

The first warning shot of National Service came when I was invited to attend the Officer Selection Centre of the RAF at Uxbridge. Young men of reasonably good education were offered the chance to submit themselves for consideration as trainee officers leading to a National Service Commission and the three-day selection process was generally thought to be worthwhile attending. Life as a National Service officer was held to be superior to that of a non-commissioned ranker although expenses were far higher and income not so very much greater. I accepted the invitation and asked my manager at Foyles if I could have the three days off work. He told me that I had better 'go up to the office' and ask.

Within a few minutes I found myself facing the legendary Christina Foyle. I explained what I wanted and why I wanted it. Her reply was very gentle and matter-of-fact; of course I could have the three days off, I could have as many days off as I wanted. I was fired. It was as simple as that.

I met a few of my fellow workers in the pub at the end of the day and we shared a farewell drink. Alex, the man who worked next to me, made a little speech, the burden of which was that they all thought it was a crying shame and they wanted to give me a small gift as a souvenir of my time with Foyles. Earlier that week I had opened a package from the USA that contained three copies of the complete short stories of Guy de Maupassant, beautifully produced books that I had handled with awe and admiration. Alex took up his briefcase and from it removed one of these books. 'To you', he said, 'From Foyles' he added pointedly.

I still have the book. It does not weigh upon my conscience. If you want it back, Miss Foyle, you may have it. But you'll have to say Sorry first.

~

The gentlemen of the RAF selection board at Uxbridge decided that I was not officer material and, of course, they were right. I was not heavy enough. I must await the call of Her Majesty to serve her in a more humble capacity, which summons would come in the fullness of time.

~

A period of blind panic followed and I went to the Employment Exchange (Job Centre in today's parlance) ready to accept anything, any old dead-end, mind-rotting, physically debilitating activity that paid money and that is precisely what they found for me; I ended up working in the warehouse of the toy factory of A. C. Wells & Co of Walthamstow. In the dark mornings of late Autumn I rose and caught my bus in time to punch the clocking-in machine at 8am and in the dark evenings I caught my bus back home, black from top to toe with dust – to 'Juniper' where, thank heavens, there was a bed for me.

I made up orders and packed them for despatch – the exact opposite of what I had to do for the lovely Christina Foyle. I worked with a delightful bunch of rough and ready local lads who accepted me as part of their crowd instantly. We were united by our common hatred for the foreman, Mr Weeitch. Now, could Charles Dickens ever have conceived a more apt name for such a wretched, mean-minded fellow? The quintessence of our various activities intended to thwart the fellow's insatiable desire to catch us at rest and punish us with loss of money was the Great Hollow Cube scam. Here we built a vast cube of boxes that was hollow inside. Whichever way one looked at it, it appeared solid but inside there was sufficient space for four or five of us to settle down for a smoke and chat. In the vast dark areas of the warehouse there were plenty of places where we each might legitimately have been but usually a few of us were within the cube, having pulled out the one loose box to gain entrance and neatly pulled it back again to cover our tracks.

The job was lousy, the people (apart from Weeitch) were wonderful. When I hear the expression 'the salt of the earth' I think of the half dozen or so fellows that kept my spirits up as Autumn blackness gave way to Winter blackness.

~

Christmas 1956 was on its way and in November there was a party at 'Juniper' to which all the students invited their friends. I drank too much and overcame my natural shyness sufficiently to approach one of the guests, a very beautiful auburn haired girl called Margaret Ann Devereux Mack; she came from Westgate-on-Sea, near Margate, her father was an ex-Army officer, a Colonel, and her mother was a nurse. She seemed quite pleased to talk to me and, yes, she thought it would be nice if we met again, after Christmas when she returned to Queen Mary College where she was taking an English degree. She wrote her name and her telephone number on the back of a small brown envelope and gave it to me. I still have the envelope.

Time to move on from humping boxes of toys I thought.

~

Ann, as she was always known, reappeared after Christmas and we became very close. She was intelligent, elegant and delightfully feminine. She was older than me by a year and more mature by several more years. She set higher conversational standards than I had been used to and simply expected more of me. Of course I was interested in theatre, wasn't I? Poetry? Music? Architecture? Naturally. She told me that she thought I was very good at explaining things that were complicated. She said that I should think about becoming a teacher. She was, without ever being patronising, simply a good influence on me. At first I was dazzled by her but the relationship became one of equals and we got on very well together. Did I fall for her? Do you really want to know? Yes, of course I did. Head over heels. Hook, line and sinker. All the usual hyperbole applied. None of it was wasted.

Unfortunately, when I made the inevitable visit to her family home one weekend, driving the monster Morris Ten Six (which did not break down on this one occasion), her mother saw through me instantly, a boy with no background and no foreground, and definitely not the one for her daughter. Ann did not let this bother her, she knew her own mind and the relationship continued subject only to her own reservations.

~

I returned to the Employment Exchange and asked them if they couldn't come up with something a bit more suited to my talents than shifting boxes. 'Why not try Supply Teaching?' they said, 'The primary school down the road needs a teacher to fill in until the end of term'.

Teaching? Me? Ann had suggested teaching. 'Yes', I said. 'Yes. Yes. Yes. Yes, please.'

The school was a bare ten minutes walk from 'Juniper'. The Headmistress was charming and after a brief chat introduced me to a classroom of some 30 children aged seven and eight. Apart from brief interludes with other teachers these children would spend all their time with me for a whole term. I had to take them for every subject except PE and music. A daunting challenge for an ex-humper of boxes.

I rushed back to Walthamstow and explained that I wanted to become an ex-humper of boxes with immediate effect. The Personnel Manager seemed slightly shocked that I should want to leave. I told her that I really thought I was not cut out for the toy industry and it would be better for both parties if the arrangement was severed. I was released.

I said my farewells to the charge-hand, known as 'Happy Smilin' Ted', to young Geoff who had once been dragged into the local police station for a beating, to Harry the lorry driver who had painted his sitting room with aluminium paint and thought it rather stylish and to Little George, the elderly cleaner who, as he swept the floors, would sing repeatedly a snatch of a TV commercial of the time, 'Bridge That Gap With Cadbury's Snack' – only he could not pronounce 'Cadbury' and made it 'Cagney's Snack'. I waved happily to Mr Weeitch as he sat scowling in his little glass box.

~

I loved teaching from the first minute of the first day. The kids were bright and lively and seemed to enjoy my lessons. The Headmistress issued regular pats on the head and told me I was a natural-born teacher. I felt I was. I knew I was. 'I told you so', said Ann. This was the real me and I enjoyed the sensation of discovering it. The term whistled by and suddenly it was the Easter holiday and I had to say goodbye to my class.

I was now on the books of the Essex Education Committee and I was offered another term's work; this time at a primary school in Dagenham. My class numbered 52 this time and at noon every day I had to move all the children out into a hallway so that their classroom could be converted into a dining hall; the result was that my class became so attenuated that I could barely be heard at the back and I could probably not be seen either. Formal teaching was almost out of the question but I improvised and galloped up and down the narrow space beside the children and kept the whole show going somehow. It was much harder than Wanstead but I still enjoyed it. This was definitely what I wanted to do.

~

I decided to take up teaching. I applied to enter a Teachers' Training College at Culham, near Oxford. I was interviewed but my application was not successful. I had not much to offer, after all, had I?

~

When I was fruit-picking in Wisbech I had met a Yugoslavian 'student' (he never studied and was not attached to any educational establishment) called Mico, with whom I got on quite well. At the time I landed my first teaching job he materialised in London and suggested that we rented a flat together. With the continual problems of staying in 'Juniper' I agreed and we found a place in Wanstead, close to my parents and the school. Mico worked all kinds of strange hours in a hospital and so I had the place very much to myself. Mico had a record player and bought records. I heard Ella Fitzgerald for the first time thanks to Mico. Ann gave me a little dish from the designer Susie Cooper as a flat-warming present.

~

One evening I made the trip to what was then the Davis Theatre at Croydon (now the Fairfield Halls) to experience (a far better word than 'see' or 'hear' in this case) the Lionel Hampton Orchestra and I began to appreciate something of the excitement and fun a Big Band can generate. Hampton, drummer, pianist, vibraharpist, arranger and bandleader, was part of Big Band history. He was American, he was black, he played swing and jazz, he was, ergo, a star. And he *was* a star.

I cannot remember since my teens when there has not been some kind of teenage movement or fashion to attract young people who cannot face the world without the crutch of hundreds of others who dress similarly. Mods and Rockers. Hippies. Punks. And so on. Then it was the Teddy Boy manifestation. Lads with long black suit jackets with lapels of velvet trimmed with black ribbon, very narrow trousers ('drainpipes'), black shoes with monstrously thick crepe rubber soles ('brothel-creepers') and hair. Such hair! Plumes of hair, anointed with strange emulsions and brushed up at the front and then allowed to fall forward and down over the brow, hair hanging low over the velvet collar of the jacket, hair growing down the sides of the faces ('sideburns'). The fashion caricatured the Edwardian style of male dress, hence the term Teddy Boy, but the behaviour of these fellows bore no resemblance to those early contemporaries of my Father when young; these were louts and sometimes dangerous louts at that. There was a female equivalent, the Teddy Girl, but she was a pretty sad sight and more worthy of sympathy than fear.

So a trip out to Croydon and the Lionel Hampton Orchestra promised excitement in more ways than one. The first film of Bill Haley and the Comets and the film *The Girl Can't Help It* had made Rock 'n' Roll infamous overnight as cinema seats were torn out and the auditoria turned into scenes of terpsichorean abandon by the Teddy Boys and their molls. Hampton did not play Rock 'n' Roll but that hardly entered into it; the perception was that it was going to be a rocking evening and so the Teddies turned up.

Whatever kind of music it was, it was something we had never heard before. In came Hampton leading the band through the audience, up on to the stage, and producing such volume! Such a beat! Such great tunes! In Britain we were listening to whatever came out of the radio: the Ken Mackintosh Orchestra playing *The Creep,* Dennis Lotis, Lita Roza, Dickie Valentine, and, by way of a change, Lonnie Donegan with his quaint interpretations of American Blues in a form of music known as 'Skiffle'. This was grown-up stuff all right. We loved it. We *all* loved it. The Teddy Boys flattened the folding seats and started to dance with their unlovely partners. The rest of us just applauded and jumped with joy. It certainly can calm the savage breast can it not?

~

When was National Service going to strike? The end of the Summer term was approaching and I received a letter putting me on notice that they were going to call me up fairly soon. The teaching job at Dagenham was over and I had to hustle for a living once more. I found a garage in Woodford Green, owned by an ex-racing driver called Dick Jacobs and went to work for him until 'the call'.

I learned much from the five or six weeks I spent working at that garage. I learned how well an organisation can work and how profitable it can be if it is led from the top by a person with energy and flair who knows how to keep his staff on their toes. I was one of two forecourt teams that worked turn and turn about, seven days a week, with a staff rotation that permitted each individual to work only six days. Our job was to serve petrol (no self-service stations in those days), and to sell oil, tyres and accessories.

Dick Jacobs was a whirlwind of energy laced with genuine charm; he was a likeable man and we all thought the world of him. He believed that we were all salesmen and gave us every inducement to change the traditionally passive rôle of the forecourt 'attendant' into a more active one. If we saw a bald tyre on a car we were expected to point it out to the owner and sell him a replacement there and then; if the owner agreed then two or three of us would move in on the vehicle and effect the change in a matter of minutes. If there was any case for replacing the entire set of four then we were expected to go for it. If oil showed dirty on a dipstick (and when did dipstick ever indicate otherwise?) we proposed a complete oil-change then and there, within minutes, while the owner waited.

Jacobs paid us commission on everything we sold that was not fuel. We each had our own keys on the cash register and the 1% and 2% and, sometimes, 10% grew daily. He would walk in to where we sat awaiting the next customer and say something like, 'I'm paying 15% commission on all tyre sales until the end of the month' or, as he did on one occasion, 'The salesman who achieves the highest commission figure next month is coming with me to my tailor and I am going to have made for him a suit that he will treasure for the rest of his life!'. Oh how we did zip into action!

It was manual work but it was not the same as the miserable Walthamstow toy company where the only pleasure came from the good humour of the workforce. In Dick Jacobs' garage the energy and good humour flowed from the top and infected us all. The only negative aspect I can recall was the owner's idiosyncratic way of showing appreciation by taking the successful employee 'out for a little spin' in his high-powered sports car; it was said that one was never quite the same again after 15 minutes in a car with Dick Jacobs.

So, during those Summer weeks, filled with the confidence derived from my teaching successes, happy in the company of Ann Mack, I learned that there is nothing wrong with good, old-fashioned manual work, but if one owns the source of the good, old fashioned manual work, one gets to own a high-powered sports car.

~

The letter told me to report to a London main-line station on 5 August 1957 where I would be taken to RAF Station Cardington, where I would spend one week after which I would be posted to another place where I would spend eight weeks doing basic training ('square bashing').

I assembled for myself a few treats. A box of 100 'Passing Cloud' cigarettes. A box of 100 'Pashah' turkish cigarettes by Abdullah. A box of 25 Balkan Sobranie 'Black Russian' cigarettes.

I took Ann down the River Thames to Greenwich and we sat on the grass as the sun went down watching a *Son et Lumière* performance at the Royal Naval College. This was my last night of freedom.

The popular songs that were pouring out of every radio were *Bye Bye Love* and *Dream* by the Everley Brothers and *Last Train to San Fernando* by Johnny Duncan.

Chapter 11

We Young Men Accepted This Form Of Sexual Discrimination Without Question

The Royal Air Force (August 1957 – September 1958)

I was always prone to a sinking feeling in the pit of my stomach on the first day of school terms, job interviews and first dates but waiting on the platform for the train to Cardington was beyond this; 'gut-wrenching' approaches the sense of apprehension that gripped me as my first day in the RAF dawned. There were a crowd of us, all about the same age, dressed variedly, most puffing away like mad on cigarettes (I kept my quality fags deep inside my suitcase and a packet of Senior Service in my jacket pocket) and all trying to look nonchalant whilst experiencing terror. Just as the young child is scared by the stories heard of horrifying initiation ceremonies practised at school so we quaked at the thought of what was going to be done in order to 'make men of us'. What we faced was, of course, a rite of passage, a coming of age, a puberty ritual. We were but boys and men had to be made of us. Some of us, some of those nervous boys waiting on the platform, would go on to face genuine dangers in places like Cyprus and Aden, where armed conflict was then a daily occurrence, and the older brothers of some had already experienced the horrors of fighting Mau-Mau terrorists in Kenya – but all we could think of just then was what would confront us tomorrow.

We were encouraged to enter the train that appeared by a nicely-mannered sergeant who appeared eager not to frighten us. The train moved off and we travelled non-stop to Cardington.

When was the horror going to start? Well, it didn't. Not at Cardington. You see there was a motive. National Servicemen did not offer the RAF such very good value for money. They had to be trained – some of them on courses that lasted for a year – and they were only enlisted for two years. Better by far to tempt them into becoming regular airmen, signed up for three, five or even more, years.

The carrot was more money and the promise (or rather, the hint) that at the end of the period they would have a trade and would thus have a *career*. The stick was that National Servicemen received very, very little money. So, for one week and one week only the RAF was very, very kind to its new recruits. The nicely-mannered sergeant at the station was the first part of what we would now term the 'charm offensive'.

The medical examinations offered the brave and self-confident one last chance to avoid the two years of servitude. If you failed the medical you were out of the service the very next day. The examining doctors were up to most dodges but the chap in front of me, as we queued naked waiting for inspection, simply fainted and that did the trick for him. He threw the back of his hand over his face (to save it when he fell), uttered a long and terrible 'Oooooh!' and smashed face down onto the floor. He came into the barrack room to say goodbye to us. 'Did you? Did you fake it?' we asked. 'I've been rehearsing that fall for weeks', he said, 'I've got a wife and baby to look after'.

We were kitted out with boots, shoes and uniform clothing that more or less fitted. It was advised that all our 'civvy' clothing be packaged ('There's the string and brown paper, lads') and addressed to our homes where it would be sent at the RAF's expense. We were given haircuts by a barber who was not too barbarous. The Teddy Boy who had sat near to me on the train seemed a little reluctant to lose his long greasy locks but emerged, shorn, and looking positively civilised. Those of us who had shied away from this symbol of teenage violence (they favoured the cut-throat razor as a weapon did some of these lads) were moved to make conversation with him now that we all looked the same.

We were given lectures on the noble history of the RAF. ('Don't call it the RAF. Don't ever call it that. It is the *Royal* Air Force and you must be proud that you are numbered amongst its ranks.') The advantages of signing up were explained at least once a day. A few blind fools were tempted and returned to our barracks sheepishly after signing years of their lives away. 'How long, then?' 'Ten.' 'Bloody hell, *ten* years! Bloody *hell!*'

We were politely advised of our square-bashing camps. Mine was to be in Bridgnorth, Shropshire. The advantages of signing on were pointed out to us as though for the first time. We were requested to board a train that was, mysteriously, able to travel from the RAF station at Cardington directly, without stopping once, to Bridgnorth. Was there a special RAF railway line? How *did* they do this?

~

At this point I find myself thinking of how we young men accepted this form of sexual discrimination without question – the fact that only males had to undergo this two-year loss of freedom. Our society accepted that the sexes were different and that there were advantages and disadvantages in being male as there were in being female. Men were obliged to give two years of their lives to 'a servin' of 'er Majesty The Queen' and that was that.

All males were eligible for call-up from the age of 18 years. The day of enlistment was deferred if the person was enrolled for further or higher education until the course was finished and then the axe would fall. This meant that a young man could leave school having gained admission to University, spend three or four years – or possibly more – there and then have to break the flow and occupy himself in one of the armed forces doing something relatively trivial for two years while receiving next to no money. Meanwhile his female contemporaries were making inroads into their careers and earning many, many times more than he. It was indeed, sexual discrimination and I await the first claim made to an Industrial Tribunal for loss of earnings, mental stress, degradation and the sheer buggering about that the National Serviceman received; when this happens successfully, as it surely will, the floodgates will be opened and I will be there, at the head of the queue.

~

The tone of voice that ordered us into the backs of lorries at Bridgnorth was markedly rougher. The voice that ordered us to jump from the backs of the slowly moving lorries on our arrival at the camp, was even rougher – it was an hysterical, eldritch scream, a wail of anger and frustration vented, it seemed, at the very sight of us. The voice propelled us into our hut where we extracted a towel from, and then dropped, our kitbags (towels were inevitably packed at the bottom) and out again *at the DOUBLE* to the showers where we were given sufficient time to undress and get wet but no time to dry ourselves so clothes went back onto wet bodies and then out again and back to the hut *at the DOUBLE.*

I won't bore you with more of this nonsense. It was all a silly act intended to impress upon us that these chaps with their hats with 'slashed' peaks (that is, doctored so that the shiny peak pointed down to the ground rather than at the horizon as our peaks did – an attempt to emulate the appearance of either the Gestapo or one of the Guards regiments, I cannot remember which) were *real tough bastards and you'd better watch it, Airman.* (Airmen was what we were called although few would ever fly, few would ever touch an aircraft and few would ever see an aircraft close enough to touch.)

The voices that propelled us came from Drill Instructors, a pitiable breed of lobotomised rotweillers who followed the classic routine of taking a crowd of raw recruits, treating them like dirt, and then slowly moulding them into fine, razor-sharp fighting machines (who could also do clever things like slow marching, presenting arms and funeral drill, which is all it was really about) so that at the end of the eight-week period they would fall on the feet of their masters, crying with gratitude and love, and buy them lots of beer.

~

Our home was a long wooden hut with metal beds set along the sides at right angles to them. Bedding rested at the foot of each striped mattress, folded and piled into a 'bedpack'. Each airman had a locker and a wardrobe. The floor of the hut was of linoleum and, naturally in this unreal world where hair was shorn, boots were polished to give them a surreal, almost fairylike quality, trouser creases were knifelike and bodies stood either at 'Attention' or 'At Ease' (Oh, how uneasy one could be when standing 'At Ease', awaiting the next scream of 'Flight! Ah – Ten – Shwah!'), such a floor had to be 'Like a bloody mirror, did you hear that Airman? Like a bloody mirror'.

We would enter our little home, first removing the hob-nailed boots that would, at first footfall, break the 'bloody mirror', and delicately place our stockinged feet onto square felt pads; we would then glide to our 'bedspaces'.

~

Arnold Wesker was called up into the RAF at about the same time as me and in the sixties he wrote a play about National Servicemen in the RAF, called *Chips With Everything*. I saw the West End production and found that it captured perfectly the atmosphere of the time and place – the bullshit, the stupidity, the occasional flashes of sadism but, above all, the true sense of cameraderie that soon existed between young men of disparate backgrounds who were forced to put up with all this nonsense.

It was the camaraderie that made the overall experience of being a National Serviceman satisfying in some strange way. The camaraderie developed because of the enemy that lay outside the walls of the hut (and occasionally made unwelcomed forays into it). We were as one in our dislike, contempt and, occasionally, hatred of *everyone else* – apart from the ladies that served in the NAAFI and the snack bar run by the Salvation Army (not sexually attractive, even to the most desperate of airmen, but the hot cheese pasties and pints of milk they provided – strangely, it seems now, just as popular with 'the lads' as pints of beer – compensated).

I suppose the most graphic example of how we regarded the life imposed on us by the RAF and how we reacted to it was demonstrated by several hundred airman waiting outside the mess hall at my next posting. They had been kept waiting outside locked doors because of some administrative cock-up and they were hungry. They stood in a broad queue and sang to the tune of *The Dam-Busters' March* the words, over and over again, joyously, 'I hate the Roy-oy-al Air Force. I hate the Roy-oy-al Air Force. Hate. Hate. Hate. Hate. Hate. Hate. Hate. Hate. Hate. Hay-ate. Hate.'. (You may observe the literary reference implicit in this. Orwell's 1984? Exactly. These were cultured chaps.)

~

The discipline imposed on us had a quality that could be described as amorally objective; it existed for its own sake and had no moral authority or purpose behind it. Thus, if one transgressed, it was then a simple matter of whether or not one was caught. If one was caught one was punished according to a simple formula that equated the breaking of a rule with a prescribed punishment. There was much screaming and shouting and pounding of boots in double time and toy-soldier-like saluting but there was no malice in it and, better still, there was no suggestion that your soul would burn in hell for what you had done. I found this unwritten contract between 'us' and 'them' curiously satisfying (just before my call-up I had read T. E. Lawrence's *The Mint,* the account of his voluntary period in the RAF under the pseudonym of Ross, and I could by now understand why he found the life gave him a strange kind of peace).

~

I may have failed my 'A' levels but I could do drill. Oundle School Combined Cadet Force had made me very good at drill as well as crashing gliders. I was thus able to avoid the bad breath of our drill corporal whose habit it was to stand a few inches away from recruits and scream abuse when they failed to slap a rifle butt at precisely the right moment. I was soon 'upflighted', moved to a flight (the RAF equivalent of a platoon) that was a couple of weeks ahead of my intake, so that my square-bashing was reduced in duration to six weeks.

~

At the end of our time at Bridgnorth there was, naturally, a great feeling of relief now that this rite of passage was over. There was also a sense of satisfaction, almost well-being. We had coped with all the silliness of drill and bullshit – but that had been no great problem. We had been exercised, physically exercised, more than most of us had ever experienced before and we had been fed a diet that for all its grease and carbohydrates seemed to be good for us. We had made friends across a wider social range than any of us would have imagined possible. We were, in terms of our ability to push our own feelings and wishes to the rear, disciplined. We were strong and oddly happy as we prepared to leave. Some of us, most of us probably, might even have been able to fight. Well, no, perhaps not on reflection.

~

As I boarded my train for my posting to RAF Station Locking, near Weston-Super-Mare, I was a few months short of my 20th birthday. I was an AC2, an Aircraftsman Second Class. My weekly pay was the equivalent of £1.30 (compare this with the cost of a Coca Cola from a slot machine in the mess hall – 2.5p or sixpence – that would cost 50p today: a net wage of £26 per week appears to be the equivalent). I was going to take a one year course on Radar at Locking (because I had been an engineering apprentice and because I had studied Maths and Physics at school – see how the conveyor belt moved me onwards!). And I wanted to see Ann Mack very much.

~

Why had I not fought against this posting, this Radar training? I could have expressed a preference for an overseas posting. I could have argued for a change of career direction and they probably would have listened to me. The reasons are embarrassingly simple. I did not want to go abroad because I wanted to see Ann Mack very much – as frequently as possible. I wanted to go to Locking because my parents had left 'Juniper' in London and taken a job as a 'domestic couple' in Cleeve, a village on the road from Weston-Super-Mare to Bristol. Such limited vision had this young man!

~

Oh but it was dull, that Radar training. An instructor would put diagrams and notes on a blackboard and we would copy them into a notebook. Every so often there would be a test, which I would fail. I do not understand Radar now and I did not understand it then. I was moved onto an easier and slightly shorter course from which I would emerge as a Leading Aircraftsman or LAC rather than Junior Technician, the glittering prize at the conclusion of the one-year course. Not heavy enough, you see.

~

I returned to amateur dramatics with the station society, playing a part in *My Three Angels* by Sam and Bella Spewak. Most of my hut mates attended the first performance and when I returned to my hut I found that they had laid out their programmes on my mattress in the shape of a cross. It was surely not so bad as that.

~

RAF Station Locking was visited by a jazz group, a 'modern' jazz group, called the Jazz Couriers, and with those earlier experiences of Stan Getz, the Gerry Mulligan Quartet and Dave Brubeck in mind, I attended. And there I saw and heard Ronnie Scott and Tubby Hayes for the first time. They knew what was going on in the USA and were impacting on British ears with their own music, influenced by the States no doubt, but their own music. Just as Dave Brubeck affected the 'intellectual look' with his (wholly redundant, according to his son Darius) thick framed glasses so these musicians, Scott and Hayes and the three others whose names escape me now, were 'smart and sharp'. Their hair was short and neat, they wore suits, collars and ties. Their music was original, exciting, often very beautiful and you never heard it on the radio. Being someone who appreciated modern jazz put one in a class of one's own and that, naturally, had its own appeal over and above that of the music itself.

As you will see, Mr Scott and Mr Hayes were, within a few years, to play a part in my eventual escape from the science and maths and bloody Radar conveyor belt.

~

I could visit my parents as often as I wished now. Cleeve was an easy hitch-hike away and, now that the rigid control of square-bashing was over, I was a free man in the evenings, at weekends and on the occasional sports afternoon (which, of course, I avoided). Hitch-hiking in uniform was the universally accepted mode of travel with motorists knowing the circumstances of the young, uniformed men they saw on the road-sides and most being prepared to stop. It was amusing to step outside the camp gate on, say, late afternoon on a Friday, and see dozens of airmen almost queueing up, waiting for cars and lorries to stop for them. I could be home in under half an hour under such benevolent circumstances. In these times of violence it is worth noting that during the several years of my life when I depended wholly upon this method of travel I never met anyone who threatened me, or appeared to be threatened by me nor did I experience any form of sexual overture.

~

Getting to see Ann was difficult and costly but I was not deterred. The distance and time available generally ruled out hitch-hiking so I often resorted to a coach that left Locking after work on Fridays and returned very late on Sundays. It was uncomfortable and longwinded (there was no M4 then, only the old overcrowded A4). Ann, now in her second year at Queen Mary College, was a paying guest in a vicarage in Leytonstone, and when I eventually got to London there was the problem of where to lay my sleepy head. Solutions that are common today were not available to young men then. I sometimes took a room in a small hotel or stayed at the amazingly primitive (plastic under the sheets and a blue light burning all night) Union Jack Club.

~

I have a copy of *Palgrave's Golden Treasury* inscribed 'On our first anniversary – November 1957. Ann' that she must have given me on one of those visits I made from Locking to London. That first meeting at the 'Juniper' party indeed turned out to be highly significant in my life. A whole year! But there was always a sense of uncertainty about my relationship with Ann. It started with my absolute rejection by her mother and then, naturally, there were other suitors. There was one, from her home town, John Gardiner, a captain in the Army, who pursued her enthusiastically. Bless her, she stayed loyal and once when I, desperately frustrated by my inability to *do* anything being stuck in the RAF and unable to get to see her due to lack of leave and lack of money, demanded that she made a choice, she sent me a telegram saying simply, 'You win'. But I think I always knew that in the end I would not win and, given that I was to meet The Lit within a few years it is just as well that I didn't, isn't it?

~

Eventually, after months and months, I came through the Radar course (I cannot bring myself to say that I 'passed' the course) and I was then promoted to the giddy height of Leading Aircraftsman. LAC Diggle K W, 5012991, with a weekly wage of £2/4/0 (£2.20), was promptly posted to RAF Station Wartling, near Herstmonceax in Sussex where he arrived some time in Spring 1958. There he helped tend a set of Coastal Early Warning Radar transmitters that were there to tell us all when Russia had launched rockets at us or that her planes were on the way to do us mischief. Thanks Be To God that she was never so bold.

My little piece of Sussex was half an acre of land, no more, in the middle of nowhere in particular that was much favoured by grazing sheep and enclosed by barbed wire with a padlocked gate. My special responsibility was a Type 7 Radar transmitter and the first thing you saw on approaching the gate was a large wooden sign on which some earlier airman had carefully carved the words 'LAZY '7' RANCH'. In the centre there was a large rectangular antenna (known as an 'array') that rotated six times every minute, its lower section some four feet or less from the ground. Beneath the array, concealed in the ground there was a concrete bunker that contained a transmitter and a room where a Junior Technician and I would . . . wait for something to go wrong. The bunker was entered through a horizontal steel flap that was located within the area swept by the array six times a minute. One ducked and ran and scrambled down a vertical set of steel rungs praying that the array would not strike. The sheep had no problem with the array, of course; they would wander about at will and play their favourite game of dropping their excrement down the hole and onto the metal rungs.

We did very little because there was little to do. We made coffee and toast. When there was a good radio programme, such as *Hancock's Half Hour,* we called up the chaps sitting on a hill miles away who looked at screens to see if any rockets or planes were on their way and asked if we might stop transmitting for a bit as the Radar interfered with the radio. Of course they agreed because they wanted to watch the television set they had installed behind a secret panel and the Radar interfered with that as well.

We worked in eight-hour shifts which meant there could be a lot of free day time if one was prepared to 'work' (I use the word loosely) at nights. I even managed to see Ann in London from time to time and she came down to see me on one lovely day when we had a picnic on the bracken-covered cliffs of nearby Fairlight Glen.

~

I had been in the RAF for about 11 months now and I was starting to get restless. I did not want to spend another year doing damn-all in a hole in the ground in Sussex. So, for what was perhaps the first time in my life I started to think *creatively* about how I might part company with Her Majesty and become qualified as a teacher.

I applied to take a Teacher Training Course at a Teachers' Training College at Saltley, Birmingham. I also had my Father write to the Commanding Officer at

RAF Wartling and ask if I might be granted an early release so that I might start a course in September – pointing out that call up had intervened in my earlier process of finding a suitable place. This was not strictly true but it could have been true in that had I not been called up I should surely have gone on trying to find a place. This is creative thinking.

Fortunately Saltley College responded promptly, called me for interview and offered me a place. My Father wrote again to my Commanding Officer and told him the position. Here was his son, able to start a course in just a few weeks time; how could they hold him? They let me go. After a total of 13 months they just let me go – and I went.

~

While I was moving from Locking to Wartling my parents had stopped being a domestic couple in Cleeve and had started being a domestic couple in a lovely place called Somerton Erleigh, near Glastonbury and Wells. This movement from one place to another is – or was – the lot of many domestic couples. For my parents it started slowly at first with several years spent at Somerton Erleigh and then the pace was to quicken. Meanwhile I simply saw a lovely estate of apparently limitless boundaries, with a room for me if I could get there to use it, in the most glorious part of England.

I stood on the platform of Bexhill railway station, dressed in my 'civvies' with almost everything I owned in the world in a white kitbag with a blue band on which was stencilled 'DIGGLE 5012991'. The RAF had provided me with a travel warrant so my journey was free. Better still, I was free. I was going to stay with my parents. Ann was due to arrive there within a day or so. I was going to be able to spend day after day with the girl I loved.

Gosh, but things were looking up!

Chapter 12

'Oi 'Ave To 'Ave 'Im For Moi Own!'

Saltley College, Birmingham (September 1958 – July 1960)

It is September 1958. Time to take stock once more of this young man about to face a new future and who will be 21 in under four months. He is walking up the grimy road that leads to the Victorian-built institution, all blackened stone, with heavy oak double gates, known as Saltley College of Education, in Birmingham. Weighed down with a couple of battered suitcases he has left the bus that dropped him off in the Alum Rock Road and has struggled up the road past poorly-dressed children in the street and even, here and there, mothers breastfeeding their babies while sitting on front door steps. Ahead of him is the back of a car factory, Morris Commercial, and at the top, on the left, is the entrance to the place that he believes, accurately enough as it turns out, will show him how to do the job he wants to do for . . . for ever? He does not think so far ahead. He has no real idea of *future*. For all of what has been his adult life (and when did that start?) it has been enough to get by. Just as it has been for his parents in recent years, surviving is enough.

Physically he is undistinguished. Just a fraction under six feet in height. A high forehead that already suggests the baldness that will develop within ten years or so ('Too much testosterone' he will later aver, hoping that this is indeed the case). Glasses; just a shade better, that is more expensive, than those provided free by the National Health Service. Clean shaven; even now a razor is needed only infrequently (what was that about testosterone?). Inevitably he will be wearing a sports jacket, unpressed trousers and barely polished shoes. He smiles very readily with that rather sensual mouth of his. He's not a bad-looking fellow at all come to think of it but no heart-throb, he's not likely to drive women wild at first sight; never has and never will. He is just one of the hundreds of ordinary young men who has trudged up that uninspiring street with hope in his heart or wherever it is that one keeps the stuff.

He has a sense of who he is or, at least, who he might be. He has a sense of the spirit too, in that he believes there may very well be a god and that this god has some influence on what happens to him. At one period in his RAF life, when despondent (probably because of Ann), he took to praying in his bed just before he went to sleep. He did not do it in an obvious way as some others did – he could see them, often as many as two or three out of 30 or so, kneeling by their bedsides, in their bedspaces, in the darkness – it was just a silent one-way conversation in the dark. He knew enough about the courtesy of praying to start with the whole world and then to narrow down the field quite quickly so that there were just his parents and then Ann and then himself to concentrate on; it seemed the only proper way to proceed. It, the praying, seemed to work in a funny kind of way, as though it helped him to be honest with himself by being honest to this god and the being honest did the trick.

This private faith will lead him to be confirmed within the next twelve months for this is a Church of England College of Education and the Principal is a Canon of that church and, even if these were not the case, he would be driven to do this by his desire to fit into the world. He feels very much an outsider just now as he stands before the large oak gates and he wants to be part of the college and part of the world.

Enough of this introspection. Open those gates, young man, and get started!

~

But first, the bad news. The conveyor belt of life extends beyond school and Harwell and the RAF Radar training course and the maintenance of Radar equipment: from RAF Locking to RAF Wartling and through those oaken gates of Saltley College with this young man being propelled forward, incapable of resistance, to be dropped unceremoniously at the doors of the Mathematics and Physics departments.

~

I still cannot be sure how it happened. I was interviewed by two members of staff, both members of the Drama department. David Turner (who was to go on to achieve worldwide recognition as a playwright with his play *Semi Detached* and others), the deputy head of the department saw me first. 'Tell me a story', he said, 'Any story. Make one up.' I told him a story my Father had told me about how he, a teenage boy in 1915, had been lying ill in bed in the family home in Southampton and had heard the feet of men marching past the house on their way to embark for France. All day and night the feet could be heard marching by. Men marching three abreast for the whole time he lay there. His mother had told him later that of this particular regiment or these regiments, he didn't know who they were, none had returned. When I finished I saw that tears were running down David Turner's cheeks. That concluded the interview.

He passed me on to Philip Dunn, the departmental head. He had a wonderful Brummie accent and a radiant personality. He asked me to tell him about my experiences as a supply teacher; he had before him the testimonials supplied by my two head teachers. When I had finished he pulled out the letter from the Dagenham head teacher who had said, *inter alia*, that I had had one or two problems with handling children. Before I could say anything Philip said, 'And how many children had you in the class?'. I told him, 52. 'Well, there's no wonder is there?' he said and then we went on to talk about other things.

I don't believe that my being interviewed by the Drama department had any special significance; Philip and David just happened to be available and were probably better suited at sorting out the kind of men that could benefit from the College. I certainly had not expressed any interest in Drama as a subject to study. After the two had conferred Philip called me in to say that the College would offer me a place but he very much regretted that the drama course was full and I should have to take Mathematics and Physics as my main subjects.

Well, I had climbed onto the conveyor belt out of my own free will, I'd stayed on it voluntarily and even then, at this critical moment when I could have changed the course of my life by refusing the courses offered, I stayed on. No-one to blame but me. Bloody fool!

~

The money situation was not good. The Somerset County Council Education Committee would pay my fees and hall charges, I would receive money to cover the cost of one return rail fare home and £14 each term. This was less than I had been receiving in the RAF. Something would have to be done about this.

~

Once through the gates, the College could be seen to be an oasis amidst the blackness of industrial Birmingham. It was built on the traditional hollow square model with a Green in the centre. Lecture halls were on the ground floor and in an extension of the square going off to one side. Students' rooms were on the second and third floors. There was a chapel beyond the limits of the main building and within the high wall that kept the rest of the world at bay. There was a refectory and a main hall where the entire student body could congregate and which served as a theatre. Beyond this old building there was a huge open grassed area, large enough for cricket pitches and athletics ground. Beyond that there was a fully equipped gymnasium and another block of student accommodation, much newer, known as ... you guessed, New Block. The Principal's House and other tutors' houses were dotted about the perimeter of the open area.

It was a perfectly designed instrument for accommodating students and tutorial staff. I could find no fault with it.

I was allocated a room on the third floor, overlooking the quadrangle. It was plain but it suited me well. I liked it.

~

The timetable was similar to that of a school. There were subjects to which much time was devoted, main subjects (Physics and Maths in my case) and there were subjects such as English, Religious Education and Physical Education that everyone had to take. This was a College of Education of the old style and they were seen as being extensions of school, I am sure. The essential difference was that there was another subject: Education, and that made all the difference because this was what was to make teachers of us.

Physics was taken by a inadequate fellow who gained popularity by not requiring his students to do any work; his system was to accept students who were roughly up to GCE 'A' level and then to set them examinations that were roughly of GCE 'A' level standard. *Ergo* no work was necessary but he would chat happily about vaguely scientificky things.

Maths was taught by a small, quiet man who saw it as his sacred duty to push his students to their intellectual limits on every occasion and then to set work to occupy the space between the occasions. He was rather awesome and as my first year progressed I slipped into my habitual position at the bottom of the group.

But there was so much more to this place than studying the academic subjects I had studied at school. It existed to create teachers and somehow it generated an atmosphere in which everyone wanted above all else to be a *good teacher* and tried their damnedest to become one. There were men here who wanted to be good primary school teachers, men who wanted to be good secondary teachers and men who just wanted to be good teachers. Education was studied as an academic subject and, through long periods spent in local schools under tutorial supervision, put into practice. And the place produced good teachers amongst whom I am proud to include myself. Of course, being a teacher is pointless if one does not have something to teach and it slowly dawned on me that I had better do something about this as well.

~

In an attempt to add balance to my life at college I joined the Literary Society and, as my first contribution, gave a talk on the work of John Steinbeck. When the committee was discussing its future programme of events I realised that I had read most, if not all, of Steinbeck's books and I volunteered to prepare and present the talk. My Father had loaned me *Grapes of Wrath* several years before and I had sought out secondhand copies of his other works ever since.

I joined the Debating Society. My first appearance was as proposer of the Motion that 'This House believes that one should live fast, die young and make a good-looking corpse'. (We in Britain were becoming aware of the writings of Jack Kerouac and the notion of the 'Beat Generation'.) In the following year my membership of this society was to have very far reaching consequences for me.

I joined a strange group that set out to arrange visits to breweries in the West Midlands during which the members would drink as much beer and eat as much food as their hosts, usually generous, would provide.

The dramatic activities of the college were plentiful and of a high quality, driven as they were by the excellent Dunn and Turner combination, but dominated, as one would expect, by students on the Drama course. I picked up tiny parts here and there. The highest point of my career was being chosen to be compère of the college Review, *Merry Go Round,* that featured wonderful *pastiches* of Edwardian Music Hall songs written by Philip Dunn with music by the college head of music, Barrie Grayson. Philip Dunn had difficulties with my voice when he rehearsed me. It was not the accent, it was the dipthongs. As a professional theatre man Philip couldn't abide dipthongs but, sadly, they were not to be expunged. Dipthongs are as much a part of my voice as is the Gloucestershire accent.

~

It was wonderful to have my parents happily settled at last. Somerton Erleigh had turned out to be a lovely old country estate occupied by a family that had come over with William the Conqueror and owned not only this beautiful house and hundreds of acres but another estate in Ireland as well. My parents occupied a wing of the mansion and, at last, had some space; two living rooms, a kitchen, a bathroom and two or three bedrooms with the option of using more, as bedrooms sprouted off the corridor leading into the 'big house' (as was always called) and they were there to be used if necessary. They also had an understanding and congenial employer.

We, my parents and I, were positively encouraged to enjoy the estate to the full. There were no restrictions on our movements and I could explore places like the old ice-house where winter ice had been placed to keep until and through the summer, the passageway under the main road that was completely lined with ammonite fossils up to one foot in diameter and the distant wood where there was a heronry. A wonderful place for bird-nesting – but, sadly, the passion had gone by then.

There was a narrow country road running along the edge of the estate and walking along it in the balmy atmosphere of a Summer evening I saw *glow-worms.* Oh! Small, beautiful *jewels.* I had almost forgotten that there were such things as small, beautiful jewels in the world.

Ann had visited Somerton Erleigh in the Summer of that year, in the brief period between my leaving the RAF and setting off for Birmingham. We had spent a few days together there and I think she loved it as much as I did. We walked everywhere there was to walk and just enjoyed being there, together. The difficulties of the RAF period were over and there, *over there,* was the light at the end of the tunnel, or a bright future, or a new beginning – something like that, anyway. I might even have had marriage in mind. I do not think she had, but I cannot be sure.

~

The money matter, the lack of money matter, soon became pressing. My needs were small but they could not be satisfied by an income of £14 a term. So poor was my wardrobe that I volunteered to be the collection point for clothing contributions for a charity so that I could find myself a pair of trousers, jacket and overcoat.

I went to work as a barman in a nearby Working Men's Club for four nights a week and Sunday lunchtime. I had done some hard physical work in my life but holding a tray bearing a dozen pint glasses in one hand whilst pulling beer into them with the other (imagine the weight when the glasses are full!) for hour after hour, tested me. The customers were understanding and would wait patiently while I made up their orders and then laboriously added up all the amounts in my head and then they would invariably add, 'And one for yourself, lad'. Their orders for beer, mainly a dark and mysterious brew called Mild that seemed anything but, were vast – the round of a dozen pints was commonplace and to this might well be added the barley wines, the ports and lemon, the gins and lime, the rums and blackcurrant, for 'the ladies' – and always that tip, that one for myself, that meant half a pint of Mild to be drawn and drunk and no taking the money and pocketing it. 'Twas hard to stay sober and I didn't. I rolled back to college bursting with beer . . . and the late night supper.

The man in charge, the bar steward ('Careful how you say that, son') was Harry, known as 'H' to all, and, unlike that damned Chemistry master at school, did have a personality that matched his appearance. He was rotund, tightly packed, with ruddy cheeks and hair that was parted right down the middle. He looked jolly. He was jolly. His wife, Dot, was just as jolly and just as tightly packed. Together they jollied the bar staff through the long evening with hoots of laughter and, when it came to me, sexual harassment. 'Ooh, he is *luvly*', Dot would shriek as she approached me, 'Oi 'ave to 'ave 'im for moi own!'. And she would lunge at me, bosoms like extravagantly stuffed pillows, hands trying to work their way beneath the metal tray that I held before me in protection.

When it was all over, when the spillage and the ullage (a fine distinction here, roughly the equivalent of flotsam and jetsam, which you will know about because of the song I referred to several chapters earlier) were poured back into the barrel of Mild – everything went in, the dregs of the barley wines, the ports and lemon, the rums and blackcurrant, *everything* – H sent out for Fish and Chips. Then the whole bar staff would sit down together, with their (one would think, wholly unnecessary) glasses of Mild before them, and there would be a convivial half hour of conversation and joking. And *then* I would go rolling home.

I made money. I got fatter. It was worth it. I met a wonderful crowd of 'salt of the earth' people. I learned that to serve does not humble you. It was definitely worth it.

~

Ann and I had now passed our second 'anniversary', two years of keeping a relationship together in spite of all the separations and strains. She was now in her third and final year at Queen Mary College, London and was sharing a flat in Balham with two friends, Eileen Carss and Margaret Shaw. This was a most sophisticated and adult group. They organised their life together with quiet efficiency so that there were never rows about money or who was supposed to do what or any of the other irritations that bedevil groups of young people. The three-bedroomed flat was always clean and tidy. There was a weekly menu that they took turns in cooking, working from a pool of money to which all three contributed. The atmosphere was always calm and friendly and, as the academic year progressed and the time of Finals approached, there was no evidence of pre-examination hysteria. The girls just worked at it in the same down-to-earth way that they handled the business of living together. I loved my visits there.

~

Margaret Shaw and I shared the same date and year of birth, 19 December 1937, and we all agreed that a joint 21st birthday celebration would be highly desirable. Term had just ended and a party was arranged. The trio had plenty of friends to invite. I had a couple of ex-RAF people who were still in contact with me, and we were gate-crashed by a large number of Cambridge students who claimed acquaintanceship with someone or other and arrived in a very boozy and jolly state. The whole evening – the whole night – was very boozy and jolly but, in keeping with the way these young women organised their lives, it stayed within those generous limits. No-one became aggressive. No-one got sick. There was a modest amount of sinning. No-one had to call the police. It was a nice 21st birthday and I still remember it with pleasure . . . and a touch of *angst?* Oh, yes. Just a touch.

~

The end of my first year at Saltley saw me distinctly undistinguished in the academic stakes, something of a rising star as a teacher following an outstandingly successful teaching practice in a local primary school, better off financially and so able to see Ann more often. I felt good as I set off back to Somerton Erleigh to spend the Summer vacation with my parents.

The letter from the Principal of the College that arrived a couple of days later bore a remarkable resemblance to that sent by the Oundle School Headmaster, Stainforth, towards the end of my school life. The message was essentially to 'shape up or ship out'. There was indeed little point in becoming a teacher if I had nothing to teach. But why did it have to be *bloody Maths?*

It was too late to change.

Clearly the job at the Working Men's Club had to go if I was to start studying seriously. But how then would I live? I kissed goodbye to an idle Summer spent looking for glow-worms and went out looking for work that would finance my next term or so at College.

~

The George and Pilgrims inn at Glastonbury provided the answer. It had recently acquired a new manager, an ex-football player, Dick Stoneley and his very much younger (and lovelier) wife. Dick was full of energy and wanting to do everything *now*. I was taken on as a barman for the 'back bar', the place where the local rank-and-file went for their refreshment and where tourists, looking for atmosphere, found their way.

I worked throughout that Summer vacation for every week bar one and that was devoted to Ann who came to spend what was to be her final time with me at Somerton Erleigh. I worked at the George and Pilgrims for ten weeks, seven days a week, eleven hours a day. I stocked the bars in the morning. I ran the back bar and the saloon bar at the front. I worked in the dining room as a waiter, as the wine waiter and, for a couple of weeks when he was taken seriously drunk, as the head waiter. Not all at once, naturally, but I was Dick Stoneley's *largo al factotum*, ever willing, ever available. Each night as I settled down in my room in the hotel I spurred myself on by adding up the money earned that would enable me to devote myself to studies when I returned to college.

I derived the same buzz from this frantic activity that I had had when working at Dick Jacobs' garage. Once you got down to it, there was genuine satisfaction to be had from it.

~

One day John Steinbeck and his wife came into the back bar. They walked in one lunchtime when the bar was empty. She sat down on a bench and he came up to me and ordered two pale ales. He looked just like his photograph on the back of the Penguin edition of *The Grapes of Wrath* and even wore a checked lumberjack's shirt as he does in that picture. I knew it was him within a few seconds of hearing his deep, quiet voice with the American accent. I said nothing to show I had recognised him; it was not a conscious act, I was just so full of awe that I did not know what to say or even if I should be saying anything. So they sat there and I, the Maths student who had given a talk on the work of John Steinbeck just a few months before, stood there leaning on my bar, staring, smiling inanely, trying to think of a way to start a conversation so that I could tell him how much I admired him. Mr Steinbeck ordered another couple of pale ales which they drank and then they left.

I did not realise then that famous people have to be *somewhere* and one should not be too surprised if they happen to be close to you. I also did not know that recognising and acknowledging that you recognise someone is more often than not appreciated by the person recognised. I now know that Mr Steinbeck would have happily chatted to a barman who had read all his books.

~

And then back to college where I had been allocated a room in the New Block. The rooms were arranged in groups of four, each group with a small cooking area and bathroom. This automatically put four men into close proximity with each other and it was thus important that they rubbed along together easily.

I had made some contact in the previous year with my 'group mates' and at the end of term we had agreed to live together; they seemed a decent bunch if distinctly older than me and it turned out that these men were to make a major contribution to the restoration of my academic fortunes.

Mike Evans was 26 and had been a Flight Lieutenant in the RAF. Ken Greenwood was 30 and had spent his adult life as a French polisher before throwing it all up to follow his heart's desire to become a teacher; he was married and had a young son. Alan George Leach was 40 and had served for 20 years in the Royal Navy, latterly as a Chief Petty Officer, and was on a pension; he too was married. I, 21 years old, made up the quartet.

These men were serious about their chosen careers. Yes, they would go out for the occasional drink. Yes, they would talk for hours. Yes, on Saturday evenings they might consider a trip to the cinema. All such activities took place only after *the work was done.* Those were the rules and although they were never overtly imposed on me I followed them. It was the ideal atmosphere for me who had returned to Saltley determined to crack the Maths challenge. I knuckled down to it and, reminding myself constantly that there were plenty of dumbwits out there who seemed to be able to get their heads around these concepts, I studied hard.

~

My studies were assisted by the arrival of a new tutor who was a better teacher than the excellent mathematician who had the year before failed to make progress with me. A good teacher myself, I still find that I can only learn from good teachers. This man had the knack and with patience and good humour he slowly brought me to the point of 'critical mass' in Mathematics, the state where one knows enough to be able to learn more at a much faster rate. It is the same with learning a language; one reaches a point, perhaps laboriously, when basic communication is possible and then everything one learns fuels the move into fluency. I became rather good at Mathematics and began to feel that a career of teaching the subject would not be so bad at all.

~

I do not believe that it was this rather sudden application to my studies that led to the break with Ann although it took place within this crucial term of developing self-confidence for me. It was just the old, old story of girl meets another boy.

Ann had completed her degree course and as I moved into my second year at Saltley she started a one-year Post Graduate Certificate in Education course at University College, London. She, Eileen and Margaret kept on the Balham flat. Then she met *someone else.* There had always been the threat of *someone else* but now I found myself having to face the reality. She had met him at a party and ... she was so absolutely honest and open about it ... why couldn't she have done what most women would have done? ... why couldn't she have just gone out with the man, given herself time to see how she felt about him after a few weeks? But Ann was Ann and after nearly three years with me she was compelled to tell me about her wish to see this man. I think the idea was that he and I were to be run in parallel, for a while at least.

I sat with her in a Chinese restaurant off Shaftesbury Avenue while she tried to explain how she felt. I watched the tears pour from her eyes as she sensed the pain I felt as the end of our relationship became more and more apparent. In those days I could hold back tears. I don't do so now.

I wrote one of those dreadfully wounding letters, full of anger and resentment. I could not bear to think of her with someone else. No matter how innocent that relationship might or might not be I just could not take it; this one had to be ended.

And that was that. Get back to the text books.

How did I feel then? Awful. How do I feel now? It is strange but for so many years I have not thought about her at all, and then when I came to write about this time of my life I started to look through photographs and I came across two studio portraits of her. There was one inscribed 'March 1957. To Keith – with my love – for lack of suitable quotation! Ann', followed by three crosses, those symbols of affection or passion in which I would have invested much hope. The second, dated March 1959, 'With my love – Ann', was in a card frame with a folded cover and this was secured inside a stiff board cover so that the photograph and frame had to be pulled from it before the picture could be seen. At some time in my life I had obviously decided that this was private and did not want anyone to happen upon it by accident; this was secret stuff. Inside the frame there was a folded piece of tissue paper containing a curl of her auburn hair and the small brown envelope on which she had written her name and telephone number at the party in 'Juniper' in November 1956. Forty years ago! Oh! Oh! Oh! *Oh!*

Looking at the 1959 picture of this young woman, in mortar board and gown at her graduation ceremony, and holding in my hands these tangible proofs that she had existed for me, was like a punch to the heart. No, I do not love her now. I have not secretly longed for her throughout the wonderful years of my marriage to Heather. I have scarcely thought of her. But I loved her *then* and this has never left me.

~

Christmas vacation 1959 was spent working hard at the George and Pilgrims in Glastonbury. I was able to hitch-hike home to spend my afternoons with my parents. They were now very comfortably settled and had started to buy furniture. They bought a television set. This was a step on the road to recovery indeed. The work was as drear as domestic work always is but my Father seemed to accept his rôle as 'houseman' (as I think he was called) and Mother was always happy as long as people enjoyed her cooking and gave her plenty of praise. It was a beautiful place in which to live and the dog, that damned Great Dane, had almost enough space in which to stretch his legs.

I was able to put aside a goodly sum of money and returned to Birmingham a relatively well-off young man, albeit a lonely one.

~

The College Debating Society, of which I was now Chairman, received an invitation to take part in a debate with the City of Birmingham Training College in Harborne. CBTC, as it was generally known, was an all women's college, on the other side of the city. The Motion: 'This House believes that a man should always tell a woman the truth'. We were to propose. I travelled over with the team and there met the young woman who had organised the event. She was very young, quite tiny, and wore a beautiful green dress and a necklace of large beads that she occasionally put up her hand to hold in a slightly nervous fashion. Her name was Heather Ellis.

In my speech I remember giving as an example the way I had sometimes gone along with the assumptions of me made by 'someone I used to go out with' and by not correcting them had thus not always been entirely truthful. I think I cited examples of poetry, music and architecture as where I had not truly shared Ann's enthusiasms. I don't remember whether I argued that it had been right or wrong, wise or unwise not to have told the complete truth to 'this woman' – but I think I made it fairly clear to the assembly that whatever the relevance to the debate, I was currently available.

A couple of evenings later I was called to the public telephone in the college. It was Heather Ellis. After an exchange of pleasantries she said something along the lines of 'I was very interested by what you said about your former girlfriend. It sounded sad'. 'It was', I replied. 'Then you must tell me more about it', she said. *Ah!*

I took Heather to the cinema. We saw *Anatomy of a Murder* with Lee Remick and Ben Gazzara. Coming out of the cinema, waiting to cross the road, without thinking I took her hand in mine. It was a very beautiful hand, small, soft and very fine. I had never been taken by a hand before but then as I held it I thought to myself that this was indeed a very lovely hand. Then I took her to a Chinese restaurant.

She was 19 and in her first year of the two-year Certificate in Education course at CBTC. Although she had, *unlike me,* all the necessary qualifications to gain a place at any university, she had decided that she wanted to be a teacher and so to CBTC she came where she, *unlike me,* was taking Drama and English as her main subjects and being more than merely quite successful at it.

After our first meeting Heather formed the conclusion that she had found the wealthy man everyone told her she should secure. Heavens – the cinema *and* a meal! She has still not fully forgiven me for my quite unintentional deception.

Heather (not then the Lit, of course) has always had the knack of charming my friends and the minute she was introduced to Mike, Ken and Alan, they became her champions and she their mascot. I got on with her pretty well too. We saw a lot of each other during that Spring term and I found she was becoming an indispensable part of my life. She was such a pretty, colourful little jewel of a girl.

When I took her home (you see, I actually had a home then) my parents took an instant liking to her. My Mother named her 'Littlin' within a day or so of her arrival and she soon became Littlin to us all and, later on, when you came on the scene boys, Lit. I do not remember when the definite article was added but *The Lit* she became and remained.

~

Just as I had recycled my experience at Pontin's Holiday Camp to produce the shows in Oundle the time now came for me to make use of what I had learned at the George and Pilgrims. The college May Ball was approaching and it was tentatively mooted that a bar, a bar that sold *alcoholic* drinks might be good to have. This was a Church of England Training College, remember. Somehow the Principal unbent and I, the one with all the experience of setting up bars from scratch, was the one to do it.

It was just like running a show. A thousand things to think of. Telephone calls to make to strangers. Arcane trade practices to unravel and understand. It all went well and the Students Union made a fortune.

Heather, who came dressed fit to kill, spent far too much time on 'the night' waiting for me to grab a few minutes for her from the constant round of checking that everything was going smoothly, changing a barrel here, serving a gin and tonic there. I apologise for this fairly regularly to this day but she has not fully forgiven me for this either.

I organised a bar for the college on several occasions and soon the Principal decided that a bar was a Good Thing. The year after I left the college opened its own bar, running seven days a week.

~

When the end of the Summer term came along my course at Saltley was over. The examinations had gone well for me, thanks in no small part to the influence of my three colleagues who insisted on group revision every evening, a process which had them talking through the topics while I listened, followed by my giving a summary of what they had said. Only when we had completed a full two-hour session was it permitted to go out for a pint. This discipline prepared me for the Education papers and my own studies in Mathematics had me well tuned up for a good examination performance. Flushed with my conquest of Mathematics I decided to take a one-year Diploma Course in the subject at St. Luke's College, Exeter.

Heather still had a year more to spend at CBTC. How would our relationship stand the pressures of separation? Mike, Ken and Alan were emphatic. Their verdict, that Heather was the girl for me and that I should commit myself to her was delivered as a committee decision. 'Take heed, lad', said

Ken 'You'll not find a better one anywhere, she's a grand little lass'. Ken came from Huddersfield so he probably went on to call her a 'right little bobby-dazzler' as well.

'Right', I thought to myself, 'You'd better be best man if it comes to the crunch'.

~

In September 1960 I took myself to St. Luke's in Exeter where I was lodged in a room of a house in College Road. I started the course. It was a perfectly acceptable course but I found it, as I found the college, as I found my lodgings and as I found Exeter, boring.

Heather and I found it difficult to meet. The journey by car from Exeter to Birmingham was long and even when I managed to beg a lift or persuade my own limp-along car to make it there was no accommodation for me. We found it easier to meet at Somerton Erleigh with Heather taking the train to Taunton and me picking her up and bringing her home. We both have good memories of those times, talking and walking down the leafy lanes of that most beautiful of places. For Heather, a city girl who at that time had never seen an apple on a tree, much less picked one, it was all new and romantic. To me it was all familiar and romantic.

Towards the end of the first term I asked Heather to marry me and she accepted. It was all very simple and straightforward. We met, we fell in love and we decided to get married.

I spent most of my Christmas 1960 vacation staying in London as a guest of Heather's parents and working for the Post Office as a casual employee taken on to cope with the Christmas rush. I was following my custom of using holidays to finance my college term expenditure – but this time I had to gather enough together to buy an engagement ring as well. We chose a ring, a beautiful ring of white gold, with a huge, high moonstone and three tiny diamonds on the shoulders of the mount, from Green's Antique Galleries in Kensington Church Street; I paid a deposit early in December and then, on Christmas Eve, having earned enough money, we went along to collect it. The cost was £18/10/0 (£18.50 in today's money).

Many years later the ring was to be stolen by a burglar. It was unique, irreplaceable. For our 25th wedding anniversary I had a copy made but it was but a shadow, a puny thing lacking all the *oomph* of the original. I fear that one day, when travelling on a train or sitting in a restaurant, I will see it on the hand of someone . . . and then what shall I do?

We took the train to Langport that same day and eventually arrived at Somerton Erleigh. I had asked Heather to take off the ring which she had been proudly wearing during the journey and to put it in its box so we could surprise my parents with the evidence of our engagement. My Father waited for us to tell them that we were now engaged and examined the ring that Heather showed him, now back in its box. 'That's not where it should be', he said, 'This is where it belongs', and he took it and put it firmly onto Heather's finger. Then he reached for the bottle of pink champagne he had kept on ice ready for the 'surprise' that we had sprung upon them. I remembered how he had already bought my present for passing the scholarship examination at Bishop's Cleeve before my success was known.

∼

Heather and I succeeded in getting through that difficult year of separation. She took her examinations and achieved her customary high pass levels. I took my Diploma and passed that too although by then I was starting to have serious doubts about whether I wanted to teach this subject. Oh, but it was boring!

We had thought each to complete a year of teaching in London before getting married. Heather would live with her parents and I would get a small place somewhere. We would have time to put aside some money and then set out together. We did not reckon with Heather's wise old Grandmother. Nanna, a Scot, spoke to Heather about our plans; 'Don't wait a year, child', she said, 'Do it now'. And she offered us an interest-free, long-term loan of £40 by way of encouragement. So we agreed to act in haste and hoped that we would not repent at leisure.

∼

In March of this year of 1961, the Somerton Erleigh idyll came to an end. My parent's employers decided to go to occupy their property in Ireland and leave their son to run the estate in England. He had no need of a domestic couple and so it was time for them to go. There then began the start of what was to be the long, slow slide downwards of my parents' fortunes.

They could not wait for a better 'situation' to come along. There was no home to which they could retreat, in which they could scan the Situations Vacant columns of *The Lady* magazine at their leisure. There was no money to provide support either. Just as domestics have always had to do, they grabbed the first opportunity and fled to it. They went to work for a farming family in Piddlehinton near Dorchester.

In order to be close to them I took a job running the bar of the King's Head Hotel in Dorchester for the Easter vacation of that year and as soon as I arrived to take up the job I hitch-hiked over to see them. From the relative splendour of their Somerset Erleigh accommodation they were reduced to a one-half share of a small labourer's cottage, with one living room and one and a half bedrooms. The half bedroom, that I occupied for one and only one night, was a room divided by a single sheet of plasterboard; on the other side there slept the farm labourer and his wife who occupied the other half of this chicken shed of a building.

My Mother was instantly put to work to satisfy the social demands that had been building up on her employer for several months prior to my parents' arrival.

This became a familiar phenomenon over the years that were to follow; for half the year the employer would accept social invitations and then, when it was time to reciprocate, a domestic couple would be taken on, worked furiously and then 'let go'. Within a few weeks my Mother developed some kind of problem with her leg; she found she could not stand in the kitchen, working non-stop cooking meals for the family, cooking for dinner parties, making cakes and preserves and so on, for ten hours or so each day, six days a week. Her employer took her to the local doctor who, on examination, said that my Mother would have to stay in bed for at least a fortnight.

Then, before they returned to the estate, an odd thing happened. The employer went in to see the doctor and stayed in his consulting room for a few minutes. In the car going back, the woman dismissed my parents. One week's money and out.

This was Thomas Hardy country, mark you.

I do not know what they did then or how they survived but I presume that the advertising columns of *The Lady* came good in quick time for another job for within a very short time I learned that they were moving to Rowberrow, close to Churchill, near Weston-Super-Mare, to where there was another 'big house' and, most conveniently, a lovely little church. Rowberrow, although it was to provide Heather and me with the most romantic of memories, was but a small upward blip on the graph of my parents' progress, the trend of which was quite definitely downwards.

Chapter 13

Heather Would Have To Do The Bedrooms On The Morning Of Her Wedding So That Mr Maxwell Could Make A Proper Job Of Polishing The Car

Getting Married (September 1960 – September 1961)

The Summer terms of our respective colleges over, we set out to earn enough money for our wedding and the first month of our new life together – for salaries are paid one month in arrears. That we should have salaries was, by this time, a certainty, for in those times, dearly beloved, it was held that teachers were important, that teaching was important, that the education of children was important – and there was small point in training teachers if you did not put them to work immediately. This is not to say that jobs fell from the trees like ripe fruit but it is to say that if you wanted to work and were prepared to travel, or to live in what was perhaps an unfashionable spot, then you would probably find a job. Heather had been appointed to a post in Brent, Middlesex and I to one in Tulse Hill, London. We should start to earn money from these jobs in September but it was now the end of June. July and August were the months in which we should have to assemble all the money we should need to carry us through to the first of October when the first pay cheques would appear.

~

With my parents living so close to Weston-Super-Mare we opted for that town as the place where we would assemble our nuptual fortune. I quickly found a residential job running the public bar of the Royal Hotel and when I was settled in I suggested to the manager that another vacancy that existed be filled by Heather. In theory the 'spit and sawdust' bar would be run by the two of us. It seemed like a good arrangement.

Heather did her very best; she seemed overshadowed by the bar – she could barely reach the optic measures for the spirits and pulling the arms of the beer pumps took all her strength but she would have overcome these problems had it not been for the Local Hard Man. He, the LHM, was a regular drinker in the bar, a man with a prison record for assault, brawling and generally beastly conduct – and he took a fancy to Heather. She had only been working in the bar for two or three days when, as we were closing down, the LHM decided to give her a goodnight kiss. He reached over the bar, pulled her halfway over it and planted a horrid kiss somewhere on her reluctant face. She struggled free and he laughed triumphantly. I shouted my protest. He suggested that he and I should leave the bar together in order to sort the matter out in the manner of LHMs the world over. I declined. He clearly thought that we were not worth further trouble and left. Heather resigned the job that night.

~

We found a job for Heather in the Hampton Hotel, a small seafront place that was a step up from Bed and Breakfast accommodation. It was a residential job. She was the chamber-maid. On her first free morning we met and she wailed, 'No-one told me why they call me the chamber-maid!'. In those days bathroom and toilet facilties *en suite* were almost unknown in smaller hotels and residents were provided with chamber pots, usually placed in small bedside cupboards, that were colloquially known as 'chambers'. One of Heather's jobs was to empty these foul things.

~

So together we started to prepare for our wedding and the first month of our life together. When we started I had in my post office savings account £11, my half share of the proceeds from the sale of the battered old Singer Nine I had bought jointly with another student at Exeter. Heather had nothing at all.

~

We decided that we should get married in the church at Rowberrow. It was a beautiful church and it was so very tiny that the few people we planned to invite (and we thought we could afford to invite) would not look lost within. We chose Friday 1 September (1961, in case you have lost track) for 'the day'. A Friday because Canon Leslie Alford, who would marry us, advised that Mrs Lucas, who ran Penscot guest house in nearby Shipham, where we would obviously hold the reception (but, of course!), would much prefer to have it on a Friday, rather than a Saturday when she was busier.

During our two months we had to make trips back to have chats with Canon Alford in his home, (the now incongruously titled) Gay's Cottage; the sessions that he deemed to be an essential part of the whole business were delightful conversations in the cool, calm of a sitting room smelling of beeswax and looking out onto a perfect English country garden. Canon Alford's home might well have been designed by Clarice Cliff. But we only had about three hours off each afternoon and for transport had to rely on the kindness of the Royal Hotel's Assistant Manager, Peter Clayton, who ran us out there and back in his Renault Dauphin and waited patiently while we took tea and conversation with the Canon.

In those two months we spent almost nothing. We had accommodation and food as part of our jobs, so we needed to spend nothing more. We worked, we accumulated money; that was how we spent July and August of 1961.

~

The wedding was scheduled. Among our guests there would my parents and Heather's parents, Charles and Cathie Ellis. My best man would be Ken Greenwood (how could he refuse?). Heather would be given away by her Father and her solitary bridesmaid would be her best friend from CBTC, the marvellous Maggie Morgan. My maternal grandmother, the old lady from Chipping Sodbury, would attend in the company of her latest consort, an elderly gentleman called Billy, who had one tooth. Trevor Bell, the student with whom I shared the room in the house in College Road, Exeter, would come and bring his camera (he was thus the official photographer). My cousin, on my Mother's side, Maurice, would come too (and he, fortunately, brought his camera as well – fortunately, because all our 'official' wedding photographs were later to be lost). Heather's best friend from her childhood in Scotland, Sheila McClean and Wendy Boot, another close friend from CBTC, and her friend Pat would be there. My cousin on my Father's side, son of Aunt Monica ('Mona'), Kenneth Poolman, already then an established writer, would join us as well (the experience would provide him with the basis of a 'Morning Story' on BBC radio within a month or so, a story that featured a great dane and a family wedding).

Plenty of people for such a small church.

~

But what about a wedding ring? White gold. Had to be ordered. Had to be sent to Birmingham assay office for hallmarking. Delayed in the post. Lost in the post? Perhaps. No, delayed in the post. Arrived just in time. Phew!

~

And the wedding car? No money for a wedding car. Heather's employers, Mr and Mrs Maxwell, had a wonderfully vulgar American style car, a pink Vauxhall Cresta. Yes *pink*. Almost a pink Cadillac. Mr Maxwell would drive Heather and her bridesmaid to the church (but Heather would have to do the bedrooms on the morning of her wedding so that Mr Maxwell could make a proper job of polishing the car).

~

Honeymoon? You've got to have a honeymoon – and after two months of slaving over a bar and chamber pots a holiday would be good, never mind a honeymoon. Cornwall would be lovely. Keith had discovered Boscastle when he went on a camping trip with Trevor Bell in the Summer term. Boscastle then. The Wellington Hotel which he remembered as being quite nice. I wrote and booked us in for two whole nights . . . er, days.

~

But how to get there? In the centre of the Hampton Hotel there was a room that was never available to residents. Within it there lived a desiccated old misery of a woman who owned the hotel. The lovely Maxwells did not own the Hampton, they merely rented it for the season and hoped to Heavens that a profit would be made sufficient to last them through the Winter. This stick insect of an old lady lived in her room; food was brought in to her, she used a chemical toilet and on entering the room *you could tell.* She was a creepy old lady.

The old hag owned a car, a Hillman Californian, that lived locked in a garage at the back of the hotel. The car had only been driven a few hundred miles and now, after years of stasis, its brakes were fixed solid to the wheels, the cylinders were fixed solid to the cylinder block, the tyres were fixed solid to the concrete floor of the garage – just as the old buzzard was fixed solid to her chair that was fixed solid in the middle of the room in the middle of the hotel. This was a car that Miss Haversham might have been proud of.

Keith struck a bargain with the old lady. He would unstick that which was fixed, he would coax sparks from an inert ignition coil, he would introduce oil into the minute gaps between big ends and crankshaft – he would bring the car to life – if he could then use it for his honeymoon, to take him and his bride to Cornwall. Yes. That would be *almost* acceptable. Payment of £20 would make it completely acceptable. The old lady had not got where she was by being kind to young people starting out on married life.

~

Oh God! It's always money, isn't it? . . . Isn't the bride going to need a wedding dress?

Keith's cousin on his mother's side, Margaret, had just got married in Bristol. Perhaps her dress would do? Discreet enquiries were put in train. Cousin Margaret would co-operate, bless her heart. Heather took the bus to Bristol and, oh yes, there is a God, it fitted not just well, but perfectly.

Now I could get back to worrying about the cost of the wedding reception.

~

The wedding took place on a sunny day. The ceremony went well enough. We had chosen some lovely hymns, all of which would be well known to our small gathering. Sadly the organist had other ideas and used a completely different set of tunes. We muddled through. Heather looked lovely and that was all that mattered.

The wedding reception went very well too. In order to save money I had bought the drinks from my hotel's supplier in Weston-Super-Mare and they arrived on time; the cost was £7/6/6 for 13 bottles, including three of the nearest thing to champagne we could run to, Veuve du Vouvray, a snip at £1/11/6. The bill from Penscot guest house, that I still have along with the drinks bill, shows that our party consisted of 25 people and we paid 11/6 a head for our wedding lunch, a total of £14/7/6. Altogether we spent £21/14/0 on the reception.

I cannot work out how we became 25 people for the most I can put a name to is 20; there was Canon Alford and his wife, the kindly Maxwells, Peter Clayton from the hotel ... never mind, it doesn't matter now. It was an altogether jolly affair and everyone had a grand time.

And then Heather, now changed into her 'going away outfit' (is this term still used today? I rather think it might be) and we entered the unstuck, revitalised Hillman Californian, and set off for Cornwall. It was very hot and the confetti that had found its way under my collar became damp and the colour started to run through my shirt. Apart from that everthing else was lovely.

~

We moved out of the Wellington Hotel, Boscastle, the expensive part of our honeymoon, after two days and went in search of something cheaper. We discovered Rock, just over the River Camel from Padstow, and booked into a charming little guest house called 'Gleneglos' where the proprietors, twigging in an instant that we were honeymooners, treated us lovingly. The bills reveal that the Wellington cost us £7/17/6 and four days of 'bed, breakfast and evening meal' in 'Gleneglos' came to £10/8/0. Total outlay: £18/5/6.

After just six days it was time to return to face the world. My arrangement with the Dessicated Female permitted three more days use of the car. So back to Rowberrow where we collected all those worldly goods with which I had endowed Heather, plus the wedding presents, and then Off To London And A New Life Together!

(Cue jolly travel music.)

~

Should you, boys, ever have imagined that your Father was always the sagacious person that you know and no doubt love, now is the time for me to disabuse you of this notion. At this time in his life your Father was ... let us agree on *naive*.

We left Rowberrow on the Friday morning for London. Where were we to stay? Well, it was all very simple. I had obtained the telephone number of an agency in Clapham that handled rented property; I had spoken to the manager a couple of weeks before our wedding and asked if he had anything that would suit us. 'Can't say just now' he said, 'Come in when you are ready and we'll soon sort you out'. So, we turned up at the agency at about 3pm on that Friday afternoon, our borrowed *(rented)* car containing all our possessions, ready to be 'sorted out'. The agency was closed. Closed for ever, it appeared.

After three or four hours of scanning newsagents' windows looking at cards and getting rather worried we found a couple of grim rooms in the home of a grim Irish family as an interim measure. We paid a week's rent, £4, in advance. When we had unloaded the barest minimum of articles necessary to our needs – unloading everything and 'settling in' would have implied a commitment to the place – the brave face that Heather had been wearing all afternoon finally gave way to tears.

The next day was spent scurrying around the agencies that were open and after one very nasty experience that involved viewing a flat that was jam-packed with furniture – hardly enough room to squeeze between the many sideboards, tables and chairs – that was being offered by a woman who was very mad, we found the first-floor flat in Number 62, Ansell Road, Tooting, owned by Malcolm and Janet Over who were not at all mad, who were indeed very decent, pleasant people, and who were prepared to let us occupy the top of their house (sitting room, kitchen, bedroom and shared bathroom) for £5/5/0 – five guineas in old money – a week.

At some time during that Saturday Heather had found time to shop and after a Sunday lunch in our grim Irish kitchen, of roast lamb, our first real home-cooked (Home? Pah!) meal as a married couple, we minced the remainder of the meat (one of our wedding presents was one of the old-fashioned mincers with a long handle that are temporarily attached to a table by means of a screw) and Heather made a shepherd's pie. We carried that pie to Ansell Road early on the Monday morning and when the car was unloaded I set off to return the car to the Witch of Weston. I returned to London by train and later, sitting together in our bright little, over-patterned little, unsophisticated little living room, we ate our shepherd's pie, looked in each other's eyes and prepared to face the world.

We had paid four weeks rent in advance, £21. We had paid for our wedding, our wedding reception and our brief honeymoon. Nanna's £40 was long gone. We were due to start our new jobs within a few days and would have to pay fares and feed ourselves at lunchtimes. We would have to feed ourselves at breakfast and dinner times as well. Our first salary payments would not be made until the first of October. This first month together was going to be a close-run thing. I was 23 years old and soon to be 24. Littlin was 20 with eight months to go before she was 21.

Come on now, everyone, say 'Aah!'.

Chapter 14

They Were Such Sweet And Simple Young People

First Year of Marriage (September 1961 – August 1962)

We started our grown-up lives in September 1961. Married and with jobs we immediately assumed the ambitions of almost everyone else in the same situation. We wanted our own house. We wanted more space. We wanted decent furniture (we found that the bed Malcolm and Janet Over had bought for the flat had come from a secondhand shop in Tooting High Street and had been stored out-of-doors – the mattress was *damp*). When Winter came we wanted central heating.

(Thank Heavens we didn't want children!)

But our combined monthly income was only about £85, and after we had paid the rent, paid for our travel to work and bought food, there wasn't much left to go towards the achievement of those simple ambitions. Our lot was no different from that of most young couples then nor from that of most young couples today. The cards are stacked against you when you are young. Oh, but what an advantage the children of wealthy parents have! How much more *fun* they can have. Not having to work during their holidays, how much more time they have for that fun. During our college holidays neither Heather nor I had been able to take a holiday, she working in shoe shops for Lilley & Skinner, the company that employed her father, and I in hotels.

Now that does sound miserable, doesn't it? This is just the *tristesse* of nostalgia, pay no attention. At the time we were just thrilled with it all and not remotely miserable. At weekends we would go down to the market and plan our meals and how we were going to cook them. We had a copy of the Good Housekeeping Cookery Book and that provided us with a steady stream of challenges in our tiny kitchen – there were not then colour magazines of Sunday newspapers to tell us that in social terms we were what we ate. We would go into a pub and have a drink, just the one, and talk about our dreams. We would go to the cinema at the end of the road, just the one visit every so often, and be very happy with that. A bottle of wine once in a while – sweet, of course; all we knew of wine was from poetry and song and there all wine is sweet *(She had – Ooh Ooh – kisses sweeter than wine)*. We had no television, but then few had. We had the secondhand radio that we had bought with the £3 the staff of the Royal Hotel, Weston-Super-Mare, had collected for us. Oh, but they were such sweet and simple young people those two at 62, Ansell Road, Tooting!

~

Heather drew the short straw in terms of her job and in getting to work. She had been appointed to the English Department of Brent Secondary Modern School. The nearest tube station to the school was Hendon and she left each morning at 6.30am from Tooting Bec underground station. On arrival at Hendon she had a 40-minute walk. The school was not a particularly pleasant one; the journey to and from it was costly and stressful.

My school was the Dick Sheppard Comprehensive School for Girls in Tulse Hill, a nicer place and an easier journey. I was a member of the Mathematics Department and my boss was a chain-smoking old biddy with skin like leather called Doris Bass; she was pioneering the introduction of calculating machines to the classroom, heavy little brutes with levers and handles that I could never master. Imagine it, the electronic calculator had not yet been invented!

~

We celebrated Heather's 21st birthday on 15 April 1962. So young to be a married woman of eight months standing! We bought a magnificent car to mark the occasion, a light blue 1948 Triumph Roadster, a car that sat three across the bench seat, had another two fold-down dickie seats with their own fold-up windscreen in the boot, and a canvas top. Hire purchase made possible the outlay of £140. Heather could not then drive, of course. We would teach her. But Heather's feet could not reach the pedals. Heather would never drive that car. This is another matter for which she has never truly forgiven me.

~

We two were not long into 1962 when we decided that this way of life was not for us and started to scan the jobs columns of the *Times Educational Supplement*. A move out of London, to where we could afford to live in a slightly better style, was what we had in mind.

A job in Corby Grammar School caught my eye. Corby was a town some twelve miles from Oundle; I did not know it well but, of course, I knew the area. Then a vacancy in the English department of Oundle Secondary Modern School appeared in the TES columns. That could turn out to be a happy combination. The Corby job advertisement mentioned that teachers would be given priority in housing allocation by the Corby New Town Corporation. This looked even more promising.

I went for my interview in Corby and when I was there I felt that I was regarded as potentially being an important part of the growth of a new enterprise. The town itself was old but as a designated 'New Town' it was funded for growth and the approach was based in part upon the introduction of young professional people who would give the place some life. Subsidised housing was the most immediately visible evidence of this and I, on my appointment to the school, was offered a recently-built, two-bedroomed maisonette for £9 a month. Remember that the Tooting flat was costing us 5 guineas a week. All other things being equal the move was immediately worth a quite substantial pay rise.

With this achievement in mind Heather went for her interview at Oundle Secondary Modern School bearing a feeling of some responsibility. Fortunately for her the Diggle name did not stir any unfortunate memories amongst the board of governors, some of whom were Old Laxtonians (indeed, who knows, it might even have counted in her favour) and she landed the job, teaching English and Drama under head of department, Leo Dunham, an Old Laxtonian of considerable fame in the town, a bachelor whose lanky frame could be seen almost any day bicycling somewhere or other through country lanes and the town's streets. Leo really preferred to teach gardening to the lads so he welcomed an enthusiastic young teacher to lead the way in teaching the two subjects (to both boys and girls) that were his titular responsibilty.

So the Diggle family found itself a new place to live, two new jobs and, to make not too much of it, a bit of a future.

~

At the end of June 1962 we gave up the Ansell Road flat and moved into the home of Heather's parents in Willesden Green, who kindly offered us a roof while we prepared for the move and enabled us to save the money that would otherwise have gone on rent. As the end of my final term approached I took another job working in a nearby garage (making use of the Dick Jacob's Woodford Green garage experience, you see). I would serve petrol until closing time and then work cleaning however many cars that had been booked in for an overnight valeting service. When this was done I became a night watchman – but I was allowed to sleep. I found myself the comfortable back seat of a Bentley that was always kept there overnight and settled down. At around 10pm Heather would come in to see how I was, bringing a sandwich and a flask of coffee, and then it was sleep until early morning.

~

We did sums and planned how we were to fill this two-bedroomed maisonette. A visit to Bentalls in Kingston-on-Thames filled us with awe. Could we really buy *our own* bed and bedroom suite? Dining table, chairs and sideboard? Chair and sofa? Oh, thank heavens for Hire Purchase! We placed our order and stated the required delivery day. This being married stuff was taking on a whole new adult dimension now.

~

Less than a year ago all our worldly goods had fitted into the boot and back seat of a Hillman Californian; now we had very little more – but too much for a Triumph Roadster – and too little, far too little for a removal van (even supposing we could have afforded one). Through a friend of a friend we negotiated the hire of a 'gown van', a vehicle that was tall enough to carry garments on racks but which proved to be inherently unstable when loaded with anything heavier. It had a two cylinder engine and was . . . well, knackered. On the great day of our removal we loaded up the van and started to move northwards up the M1. The maximum achievable speed was 10mph. If the vehicle went faster it developed an awe-inspring speed wobble and threatened loss of control.

At some time during the loading or unloading of this van from the nether world we dropped and lost the little box of photographic transparencies that recorded our wedding.

Heather waited in our little maisonette, all empty but for our boxes, while I drove the van back to London (rental was only for the day), collected the Triumph Roadster and returned to Corby. On my return I found a travel rug laid out on the floor and two cushions (our only cushions) lay waiting for us to take our places for our evening meal, which was a simple salad. No, the furniture had not arrived although it had been promised for midday. The electric cooker had not arrived either. We put on our brave faces to show each other that of course it would be all right, of course it would. It did not feel as bad as it had when we had been trying to find a flat on our first day in London. The cooker arrived soon afterwards and the Bentalls van arrived at 7pm when our bravery was beginning to wear thin. There we were, at the beginning of a new phase of our lives.

CHAPTER 15

NO MORE MATHS! NO MORE MATHS!!

Corby (September 1962 – December 1966)

Teachers automatically use September as the reference point for their personal histories because that is the month when the academic year begins and so when new jobs usually begin; lives move from September through to July and it is in July and August when job and house moves take place or when, given good times, ambitious holidays are taken. So life in Corby began in September 1962, one year having passed since the lovely day in Rowberrow.

Over the next four years the life of Keith and Heather Diggle was to change very significantly for the better. It was a period of personal growth and growing up. Heather was to establish herself as a very well-qualified teacher of drama and to become ready to take on professional responsibilities that others, older and more experienced, might have shied away from. Keith was to grow away from teaching mathematics and into a career for which he had absolutely no qualifications but which was to provide him with a never-ending stream of professional challenges and satisfactions.

So the two of them joined their new schools, Heather in Oundle and Keith in Corby, and worked away as hard as they possibly could. There were no upsets, no set-backs. They furnished their maisonette. They were given an old black and white television by Heather's parents. They eventually swapped the Triumph Roadster for a Fiat 500 station wagon (yes, there was such an animal) and then an Austin Mini-Cooper and then an MG Midget, bought *new* (by the quality of their machines shall ye know their progress in life). There was never much money but that was ever so in the lives of young teachers and was a problem this pair addressed by taking on more work. Their focus may appear to have been material, and so it was to a considerable extent – and why should it not have been, this pair had not so far been treated very generously under the circumstances ('under the circs' as my Mother would have put it) of their birth and upbringing – but there was also a side to them that the outside world would not have seen, namely personal growth as an end in itself, a desire to make the most of what talents nature had provided, not for reasons of material gain but because it seemed the only way to approach and to make the most of a life.

~

This was also a time when their belief in a god, which had been waning, finally disappeared. There was no dramatic incident to prompt this. They simply realised that their life and their philosophy must be based upon what they believed rather than what others told them. They learned that if they kept their mouths shut they could live happily among believers in a god for in practical terms the way they lived their life and treated others was no different.

~

Corby, not now a pleasant place and never particularly pleasing in architectural terms, was then an exciting place for the young professionals who had been attracted there by the promise of subsidised housing. It seemed as though whatever contribution one wanted to make could be made and would be welcomed. So the clubs, societies and evening classes thrived, run by those young professionals and attended by them. The heart of the place was of steel, for this was the home of the steel giant, Stewarts and Lloyd, and its famous chimney, the Corby Candle as it was known, that burned off waste gases from the steel-making process could be seen from miles around. Being the home of a large company there were employees of all ages and backgrounds living in and around the town, from senior managers through to the horny-handed manipulators of the Bessemer process. All shopped in the same shops, sent their children to the same schools, went to the same pubs, joined the same clubs and societies and attended the same evening classes. It was, in sympathy with its principal industry, a melting pot of people – and Heather and I felt very much at home there.

~

There was an interesting core of jazz musicians working and living in the place. I discovered that some 15 or 20 of them met every Sunday morning in a pub where they formed a Big Band, a rehearsal band that played for its own pleasure with no serious thought of giving performances. Individual members looked for work to supplement their incomes from their day jobs but there was little call either for the kind of modern jazz they played when they came together as trios and quartets or for the swing they favoured when they all met up together. I invited a few of them to come to my school to give my older pupils the chance to listen to music that was different from the music that was being pushed out from the record industry and the radio – not that I was in any way critical of that more easily available stuff, indeed I liked most of it a lot – but jazz was . . . more interesting I thought. Before I knew it I had started an informal kind of jazz club for the school.

I soon realised that any music that does not easily find a large audience needs financial help while it finds that audience, and so I looked for an event that would make money and would also make a memorable impression of what we were soon calling the Corby Grammar School Jazz Club on the local population. I picked the Monty Sunshine Jazz Band and on signing my first contract committed myself (it had to be me, there was no other) to paying a fee of £100 for the Saturday evening performance. My monthly salary, after deductions, was then around £50 a month. I made all the other arrangements, booking the school hall, bribing the caretaker to be tolerant, buying in the coca-cola, printing the tickets and handling the publicity. We had a great success my group of sixth-formers and I.

I invited that local Big Band to give a concert in the school hall, so it was no longer just a rehearsal band, and it was wonderfully successful. The musicians appreciated what I was doing and offered to help in all kinds of ways. I was soon able to offer a programme of regular Friday night events in another part of the school, somewhere smaller with more of a club atmosphere. We put candles on the tables and somehow we got away from the schoolroom feeling – and it was fueled with no more than coca-cola and the occasional trip outside for a cigarette. Of drugs there was then not even a suspicion.

Meanwhile the larger school hall demanded a different kind of programme. I had by now paid several visits to Ronnie Scott's Jazz Club in London and knew who was who in the British jazz scene. Ronnie Scott and Tubby Hayes were the front rank in those days, the same two who had formed the core of the Jazz Couriers, the band I had heard at RAF Locking several years before. Full of quite irrational fear I telephoned Scott's business partner, Pete King, and tentatively suggested that Mr Hayes might like to appear at the school. King, who always behaved as though he were in a strong seller's market (that is, he was brusque and unhelpful) even when he was not, said that the only possible time for a performance would be on a Sunday afternoon. A jazz concert on a Sunday afternoon? I did not like the idea but, so thrilled was I to secure the great Hayes, I agreed to it.

We drew the curtains tightly. Stage lighting created atmosphere. Better still, a full house created atmosphere. We had a great concert. We lost a little money but we had a great concert. Corby Grammar School Jazz Club was beginning to establish a reputation in the town.

I took my club members to concerts in the De Montfort Hall, Leicester (Count Basie, Sarah Vaughan, Jimmy Rushing and Ray Charles) and to recordings of BBC's Jazz Club programme held in the Paris Studio, Regent Street, London.

But we needed money to subsidise the ambitious programme I planned for the Sunday afternoon concerts. I came across a noisy, raunchy, wild-sounding band called the Apex Rhythm and Blues All Stars, that came from Northampton. Each member was a solid, respectable citizen (the lead guitarist and singer 'Fearless Frankie Short' worked for the gas board) but when together the whole was substantially more than the sum of the parts. I loved them and invited them to perform. This time there were no rows of chairs. Along the sides and the back

A typical Corby Grammar School Jazz Club poster

of the hall we placed tables with candles and plenty of space was left for dancing. This great little band let rip and my 'kids' let rip too. Great music and lots of fun produced money to make possible the next jazz concert in the school hall. The Apex Rhythm and Blues All Stars were my equivalent of an Arts Council funding body.

Ronnie Scott was the next to visit. Then a visit from the American jazz singer, Mark Murphy, whom I had heard at Scott's club and who accepted my invitation to come and sing in aid of the then recently formed Amnesty International (I believe that this was the first fund-raising concert for that worthy charity ever staged). Imagine, after some two years we were in a position to raise money for others! Then Dick Morrissey and Bill Le Sage.

At no time did I realise that I was doing anything unusual. The headmaster and staff of the school regarded me as being a harmless enthusiast (I was once referred to by the Head as 'Mr Diggle, who teaches jazz with some mathematics') and I saw myself as just another among all the people in Corby who were doing things to make the place more interesting. It was only when the then jazz columnist of the *Sunday Times* Derek Jewell wrote an article about me in the paper, 'Maths Masterminding Jazz', that I saw what I was doing was unique. Jazz musicians of national stature were then not generally travelling outside London and certainly not performing in schools. What neither Jewell nor I realised was that as well as promoting music in an unusual place, I had stumbled upon the system of self-subsidy, making possible loss-making events through the promotion of profit-making ones, that had underpinned the arts and entertainment from the very beginning. I was simply applying an old technique to an area of music promotion that carried with it a risk much higher than most people would accept. This approach provided me with a stepping-stone into a whole new world of music and eventually a new career.

~

Heather, meanwhile, was being her usual highly-successful self within her Oundle school and had added to her normal workload by running evening classes. I joined a pottery class in Corby and realised that perhaps there were within me 'things' that needed to come out. I detected a hint of a creative side to my personality, not that it would be expressed through fired clay in any valuable way, but the poetry that I had attempted at college and the desire I clearly had to make 'things' happen – my little shows in Oundle when a boy, the college bar, the jazz promotions, the interest in amateur dramatics – all pointed towards a need to do something different from . . . teaching mathematics. I wrote two plays for television during this time, *Queen Bee* and *in just spring,* and started my collection of rejection letters. Together, busy as could be, Heather and I were beginning to enjoy a full and creative life in this new town.

~

The graph of my parents' fortunes had taken another dip. Before we had moved to Corby the Rowberrow job had ended (all social obligations now being satisfied) and off they went to be a domestic couple at a residential adult educational centre near Torquay. It was not a success and after a few months they went to assist another family make reciprocal their social life. By now they knew the signs and they moved their bits and pieces into the cottage in the grounds of another big – well, biggish – house on the road from Yeovil to Dorchester, Princes Place, with resignation. My Father was now about 62 years old and he was *tired* of all this. My Mother, still several years short of 50, reacted to it with pugnacious optimism; she would not let it get her down and she threw herself into her cooking as though she were feeding her own family. Her strength was formidable.

One image of this time stays with me. My Father's brother Harold, who lived in Southampton, had died and I drove down to take Father to his house so that he could make the arrangements for the funeral. Father had been ill a few days before and had had to visit the doctor in Dorchester. I asked him how he had travelled, for there was hardly a bus service worthy of the name. He had hitch-hiked. My Father had hitch-hiked. What kind of employers were these who would let a man, any man, no matter how important to him was his sense of dignity, a man of that age, stand on the roadside outside their home and beg for a lift to go to the doctor when there were a couple of cars in the drive? In my memory, in my collection of sad memories, this ranks with the Groucho episode at the American air force base and I weep inside.

Then they were ready to be 'let go'. Mother knew the signs by now and had been studying the columns of *The Lady* for some time. The downward movement of their life's graph hesitated for a while and changed course for they found a job that was almost the exact equivalent of the Somerton Erleigh position. It was a *real* big house, called Midelney Place, on the edge of Curry Rivel, and their employers, the Maude-Roxby family, were solid, decent folk who knew about *noblesse oblige*. My parents occupied the lodge house and within a few months had established themselves as though they had been there all their lives. The damned Great Dane, Thor, was still around, dominating their lives but they adored him and keeping him had become a kind of symbol to them; lose Thor and you lose your grip on life – a bit like the Barbary apes on Gibraltar.

It was lovely visiting them and seeing them so happy. We, full of life and the thrill of being in Corby, were happy and energetic and saw much more of them now there was a place where . . . there was a bed, apart from anything else. They were good times.

~

I was in conversation with my headmaster, John Kempe, over coffee one break time, and the subject of teachers' salaries came up. Almost as an aside I mentioned that there I was, now three years or so into my career and I possessed but one suit and that the suit in which I was married. I was, I pointed out, wearing that same suit that day. The dear man must have taken this to heart for a week or so later he called me into his office and told me that he was awarding me a 'special responsibility allowance' (for which special responsibility he did not say – perhaps it was the jazz) that was the equivalent of a whole month's salary extra every year.

~

Another one of the young Corby professionals was an ex-actor who had taken a job with the steel company in an administrative capacity and now wanted to get his hand back in by directing a play for the town. There was already an amateur dramatic society but it was established, had its own way of doing things, and would not have wanted to handle the then controversial play *A Taste of Honey* by Shelagh Delaney that was his choice. There were open auditions and Heather was cast as Helen, the mother of the girl Jo, and I was given the part of Peter, Helen's repulsive boyfriend. The play calls for a black actor to play Boy, the sailor who makes Jo pregnant, but in those days one saw few black faces in Corby. One day, while we were still pondering the black actor problem, one of us saw a man, a man of afro-caribbean descent, walking through the technical college. He was wearing RAF uniform, had the rank of Chief Technician and was taking a course at the college. He was considerably older than the part called for and no-one knew if he could act – but the man was *black* for Heaven's sake! He was approached nervously. It seemed awfully rude to offer someone a part on the strength of skin colour but we did and Jim Stewart was not at all offended. He was no great shakes as an actor but he worked hard at the part and his natural charm, his rich voice and accent, made him a great success.

Rehearsals for the play developed a quality, an atmosphere, unlike any play I have ever been involved in. A young local newspaper reporter, Roy Coates, came to see what was happening and was so staggered by the intensity of the work that he attended every subsequent rehearsal and all performances. It was electric stuff and entirely appropriate for the Corby of those days that wanted and expected unusual things to happen. Roy Coates had a photograph taken of Heather in her rôle of Helen, standing in the dramatic light cast by a streetlamp, looking every inch a tart; the caption said 'This is Helen. She likes her drink and she likes her men. See her in *A Taste of Honey* at Corby Technical College this week'. The picture went down very well with Heather's pupils at Oundle Secondary Modern School.

Controversy took over temporarily when a local councillor, on the board of the Technical College where the production was to take place, read the script. He became disturbed when he realised that one character, Geoffrey, the boy who gives Jo a home, is homosexual. He became inflamed when he counted the number of swear words. He produced a list showing the frequency of all the swear words in the play. Delicate negotiations took place. The rôle of Geoffrey could not be negotiated away, however, and Corby had the thrill of seeing its first openly gay character on stage – as well as seeing a black man kiss a white girl on stage for the first time.

Pioneers, were we!

~

While my jazz activities were gaining me some small reputation in the school and the locality, there was beginning in Corby another musical venture that illustrates yet again how it was possible to start new things in this place at that time. It was a chamber orchestra, called Midland Sinfonia, that the Corby Grammar School's head of music, Neville Dilkes, had started. Neville was a talented musician with serious conducting aspirations but his academic background, although sound, did not meet what was deemed to be one of the absolutely vital requirements of the musical establishment of the time – it did not include either of the magic words Oxford or Cambridge. So Neville started his own band, not with local amateurs but with high-quality professionals drawn from wherever they could be found. Many came from London and were the same musicians that could be found playing in the English Chamber Orchestra and the London Mozart Players. They all had to be paid and their travelling expenses had to be covered; it was an expensive business.

When I came to know about the Midland Sinfonia it had given a few concerts (Heaven only knows where the money came from; it certainly did not come from the sale of tickets). Its potential had been recognised by a donation from the Calouste Gulbenkian Foundation, and the Musicians' Union had just made a grant, spread over three years, to enable the orchestra to establish an administrative base. Until then all aspects of the orchestra's life were handled by Neville and his friends. Neville got to know about me when he looked into the school hall one Sunday afternoon and saw me putting out chairs for a concert that would attract some 300 people. (It is odd, is it not, that some two years of jazz concert promotion in a school could go almost unknown – and completely unattended – by its music department?) Neville's concerts attracted perhaps 50 or 60 people. Neville determined to have a meaningful conversation with me.

Neville's idea was that I should become the manager of his orchestra, part time, while still working at school; the funds from the Musicians' Union grant would stretch to an annual honorarium of £250. Now this was Big Bucks to young Keith Diggle. The only snag was that young Keith Diggle knew nothing about the kind of music played by the Midland Sinfonia and he suspected that if he heard it he would like it not at all.

At the moment of this opportunity Heather and I had been awaiting the outcome of an application to take part in a UK/USA teacher exchange scheme that would have put us both in the USA for a year. It was a very exciting project and we wanted to participate very much. The news came through that we had both been accepted for the scheme in the same week that the offer from the orchestra was made. We must have realised that the orchestra job, for all my lack of knowledge of classical music, offered a better chance of eventually escaping from the teaching of mathematics than one year in the USA spent ... teaching mathematics. Heather's sacrifice was the greater but, as it turned out, our decision based on what was likely to be better for me turned out to be better for Heather as well.

So I accepted the job and started to run an orchestra from our spare bedroom.

~

I did not like the music. I had been used to music that generally set out to achieve its aim within a few minutes and it was the duration of this music that I found most difficult. In this respect I, although I was then in my mid-twenties, was in a situation similar to the child at school who has heard nothing but popular music with a typical duration of 2 minutes 20 seconds. Jazz had, naturally, led me into an appreciation of music that had greater ambition and depth but it, being substantially based on treatments of popular songs, tended to express itself relatively briefly.

I had no background of listening to classical music, no experience; I could not set it in any kind of personal context. I did not know what it was *about* and did not even know that this way of looking at it was entirely irrelevant. So, not only was the length of the stuff too much for me, I did not know how to let my ears and emotions do the work. Fortunately for me my ears were in perfect working order and so were my emotions; it was simply a matter of putting them in touch with one another. All those years of listening to my Father's popular songs were not at all wasted.

I started by going to the small number of concerts that had been arranged in the Midlands; places like Derby and Rugby. The first thing I realised was that the programme an orchestra plays is determined by its size and size is determined by money. Of course an orchestra like the Midland Sinfonia did not have aspirations to become a symphony orchestra employing 80 or more musicians, it was a chamber orchestra – but a chamber orchestra can be anything from 11 strings alone up to a band of 40 or more, including woodwind, brass, timpani and appropriately large string resources. We tended to field a small string orchestra of 12, as often as not directed by Neville Dilkes from the harpsichord.

This orchestra size, although limited in its repertoire, nevertheless has plenty of great music available to it and it was this small-scale music that gradually won me over. Soon I was beginning to remember short sections of a few pieces of music and to recall them when I read the titles. The orchestra played pieces such as the *Serenade* by Dag Wiren, the Tchaikovsky *Serenade For Strings*, Benjamin Britten's *Simple Symphony* and the *Holberg Suite* by Holst. Later, when Ronald Thomas the Australian violinist, who was an accomplished soloist, became the Leader, we included Vivaldi's *Four Seasons* and then, as more musicians became known to us, Bach's *Brandenburg Concertos*. There was no shortage of good music to be played and our programmes began to delight me as much as the folk who paid out good money to hear us.

Being able to recall music has always been important to me (remember the music that was played outside the school when I lived at Number 8 Pembroke Road, Bristol? And the Irish jig, *The Stack of Barley?* And the Ukrainian folk music?). Recall plus the ability to play the music inside my head and so to hear it with a kind of inner ear is at the heart of my enjoyment of music. Classical music is far harder for me to take in than the simple tunes of my childhood but I can carry substantial chunks around with me and they pop into my consciousness without warning to give me a quick burst of music at the most unlikely times.

As the repertoire of the Midland Sinfonia became familiar to me I came to like it more and more and today I owe the considerable pleasure I get from a far wider range of music to those times spent in halls in Midlands in the mid-Sixties.

~

My job was first and foremost to obtain more concerts for the orchestra and Neville Dilkes. This could be done in two ways. One was to persuade concert societies to include the orchestra in their season of concerts and choral societies to use the orchestra in their productions of the great choral works. The second way was to raise enough money from the local government – or from any other source that presented itself – to promote concerts ourselves and then meet the inevitable deficit from those funds. With no reputation and costs that were hardly any lower than those of better-known orchestras the first way proved to be largely unfruitful, so the second had to be explored vigorously. As an organisation we were constructed so as to make self-promotion possible: we were the Midland Sinfonia Orchestra and the Midland Sinfonia Concert Society.

The system of arts subsidy hardly existed at this time. The beginnings of a network of what were to be known as 'regional arts associations' were visible in the North of England, in the West Midlands and in the South West, but for our part of the world there was nothing. To the East there had just begun the Lincolnshire Association; this was in the hands of a delightful alcoholic gentleman who apparently saw the job as a glorious sinecure that would (and did, as long as it lasted) sustain his habit. One of the main functions of the regional arts associations was to receive money from the Arts Council of Great Britain and from local government and then to use it to support the work of people like us. A regional arts association would have been very useful to me in those days. Or maybe what I really wanted was the equivalent of an Apex Rhythm and Blues All Stars in every town.

I became a self-taught administrator, orchestral manager, concert promoter and fund-raiser, all operating out of the spare bedroom of Number 75 Farmstead Road, Corby. Somehow I managed to carry on a teaching career that was, remarkable as it now seems, highly successful. I had become a good Mathematics teacher and could hold up my head in the department when it came to results at examination time. It seemed as though all those years of failing to comprehend made me understand how hard it was for those young people to come to terms with what was for them an alien subject and helped me find ways of casting light on it.

~

What was happening to the Corby Grammar School Jazz Club while all this was going on? It faded. As the demands of the orchestra grew my time became more limited and I could no longer plan the interesting, self-financing programmes that had given my school club members and me such satisfaction. For a while I fought to continue and did, in the end, manage to keep the club active up to the end of our time in Corby but before this I succumbed to the temptation to enter the big time in jazz promotion and lost my shirt.

An agent offered me the opportunity of booking the American jazz tenor saxophonist, Ben Webster. Webster's place in the jazz hall of fame will never be questioned. His was a great talent and, in his time, he was respected – treasured – by his contemporaries. His breathy tone was unique and even today, when I do not seek out jazz for my pleasure and when the sounds of many who were once familiar to me have faded, I can spot Webster's sound from a couple of notes. So, the chance to present Ben Webster!

Impresarios often start by promoting those things that they themselves like and are familiar with, and because of this their judgement on what is worth promoting and what people may be persuaded to sample and enjoy is often good. If they become too specialist, however; if their personal taste becomes too refined, then they run the risk of losing contact with their public – and failing. This is what happened to me; the failure that was to come was brought about by my belief that my taste was shared by a large number of people and that my judgement was always right – after all I had enjoyed a remarkable string of successes with the school jazz club, had I not?

Webster's fee was high enough to rule out any hall in Corby. I needed capacity. I also needed to sell that capacity – but assumed that this would be no problem for I was a successful jazz promoter, wasn't I? I knew about selling tickets. I did not know about selling tickets in Leicester however and it was in that city's De Montfort Hall (capacity 2200) that I chose to locate the Ben Webster concert.

The Webster package included the Bruce Turner Jump Band as backing and to make more of a concert of it I invited Mark Murphy, the American singer, to sing in the first half. It was an attractive programme but sadly, not attractive enough.

What I remember most about that evening was sitting backstage talking to Webster while the Bruce Turner Jump Band played and Mark Murphy sang in the first half. Webster's grandmother had died a couple of days before and he was in a state of deep melancholy. The night before, when he was performing on another stage, he had drunk too much and had been told to get off and go home. But in spite of his sadness and his feeling of shame he talked; he needed to talk and he told me about his life, the people he loved and admired and his music. This man had been part of jazz history, he had seen them all, heard them all and played with them all and, a fact that hovered about in my mind as we spoke, he had been a lover of Billie Holiday.

I really don't remember his performance. I was by then trying to come to terms with the fact that there were only 400 people sitting out there when I needed for there to be at least 2000! Financial disaster! I lost much of what we had been saving towards the deposit on a house.

~

After three years of teaching at the school in Oundle Heather had the notion of taking a one-year course at Central School of Speech and Drama in London to obtain a drama qualification that would cut some ice with future employers. She applied, was accepted and then successfully applied to her County Council employers for permission to spend the year away from the school on full pay. So for the period September 1965 to July 1966 Heather spent the academic term time in London, coming back home at weekends; when she had finished the course she was ready to face a challenging professional appointment – and that is what she got. I beavered away at my Midland Sinfonia work.

~

The Midland Sinfonia job became a success for me. All those evenings and weekends spent typing out letters and making telephone calls slowly started to make an impression and the orchestra's schedule began to grow. I soon realised that if I was to make any real progress I should have to kiss goodbye to teaching. How was this to be achieved?

Nottingham had the appearance of being a go-ahead city. It was currently basking in the glory of its new Playhouse whose artistic director was the charismatic actor and director of impeccable background, John Neville. I approached the Town Clerk, Phillip Vine, and suggested that the Midland Sinfonia based itself in the city and became the city's own orchestra. At the heart of my scheme was a series of concerts in the Albert Hall, then Nottingham's only hall suitable for concerts. Financial support for this concert series, if sufficiently generous, would make possible the establishment of an office in the city and would finance a full-time job for me. Well, not completely. More money would be needed – but that was what I was there for, surely?

A few months later and I was nervously awaiting the outcome of the City Council's deliberations. I was nervous because I had already resigned my teaching job. Three month's notice were required to resign and the way the timing of the proposed move to Nottingham and the start of our first season fell did not permit me to be sure of my future before casting myself adrift from the relative safety of teaching. Then the news came through; the Council had bought the idea and our season would start in September. Phew! Only then did I truly appreciate the extent of the risk I had taken.

~

In the city people were friendly and made encouraging noises about the new project. I invited John Neville to join the board of the Midland Sinfonia Concert Society and he accepted. We started to look forward to this next step in the orchestra's life.

We rented a two-roomed office on the top floor of 72, St. James's Street, Nottingham that had been occupied by a small company that made greetings cards. The walls were splattered with paint. We got down to some serious decorating. As well as Neville Dilkes and I there were two others, David Cound, who was an accountant who gave of his time most generously and Bernard Lucas, an old friend of Neville's, who was the managing director of a Derby paint company. We all pitched in – and the paint was free.

We were ready to go.

~

But first a holiday. The relative stability of our lives in Corby, two incomes, cheap housing and school holidays had allowed us to take holidays just as soon as we had recovered from the initial costs of setting up home there. Our Summer break in 1963 had been spent with our Fiat 500 Giardinera, surely the smallest station wagon ever built, driving to Yugoslavia. We took a shabby little green tent, borrowed from my school, a hotch-potch of cooking equipment, very little money and set out bravely through France and Italy and then down into what was then a peaceful, although poor, country. On the way back, when driving up a motorway to Milan, the car's engine seized. We were towed into a little garage just off the motorway. Where were we to stay? The Signora, wife of the proprietor, waved us towards the one small piece of grass in a nearby field that was not covered with the rotting hulks of long dead cars; that was where we would stay. We had no *lire* on us, having expected to be beyond the country's boundaries by nightfall; the Signora indicated that a bus ride into Milan would be necessary. No money? The Signora produced a purse and gave us money that we could pay back later. She was a gorgeous little plump hen of a woman who communicated her intentions perfectly with every part of her personality.

The week we spent in the little community around the garage was as interesting and as memorable as any part of the holiday we had just had. The garage petrol attendants and mechanics (men to whom I could relate after my happy days spent at Dick Jacobs' garage) took to us and adored Heather. They delighted in taking time out to stand us coffee in the little bar next to the forecourt, these charming young men who showed Heather complete respect and flawless courtesy. One, having sought my permission, had Heather sit side-saddle on a Gilera motorbike and then whisked her off at high speed for a few circuits of the nearby Monza motor-racing track – from which she returned quite speechless to the amusement of all. There was Antonio, the raffish taxi driver with the looks of a David Niven, all crinkled black hair and pencil thin moustache, who operated out of his melon stall (the selling of the water melon, by the slice, was his main source of income) and had a smattering of English. And there was the Signor himself, a vast handsome man with wavy grey hair, always clad when we saw him in a pair of overalls that buttoned up on one shoulder, of the kind that the chauffeur of a twenties film star might have worn, whose arm swept down to enfold the Signora and to hold her close in to him whenever they were near to one another. As we were entertained by these jolly people we were always aware that our future lay in the hands of the Signor because it was he who was working on our Fiat 500 engine, now stripped out and disassembled, and he who would determine the size of the bill.

When the time came for us to go the Signor presented us with a bill that was about one fifth of what I had expected. The entire garage team and community took us to their favourite restaurant (we went in style, being driven in the breakdown truck, complete with flashing orange light) for a farewell dinner. Antonio gave us a whole water melon and the brother of a petrol pump attendant, who worked on the motorway toll station, gave us a ticket that would take us out of Italy free of charge.

Other holidays were less exciting as we tried to make the best of our own country. We took the shabby little green tent down to Cornwall and it rained and it rained. Whenever we went to Cornwall, it rained. I always had in my mind the memories of my childhood holidays in Somerset (about which you will read in the section headed *A Resort Runs Through It*) but those golden times were gone and only the blissful honeymoon remained with them in memory as times when we had enjoyed free time in our own country.

So when Heather's course at Central School of Speech and Drama was over and before I was due to start work in Nottingham we took our new car, our green MG Midget, over to France. We had been to France only once before and that was when we had taken the Fiat and the shabby little green tent to Yugoslavia. France had felt an alien place, not unpleasantly so but slightly uncomfortable and made worse by our inability to speak the language. We had been very poor so most of the delights of the country were experienced through a plate glass window, as it were. This time I planned to use hotels and to give Heather a wonderful holiday as a reward for all her hard work at Central School of Speech and Drama as well as to mark the beginning of a new phase of our life.

We drove to Dinard and spent a couple of days *demi-pension* in the Hôtel de la Paix and then we drove on to explore more of Brittany. On that first day of touring we discovered St. Cast and our further exploration of Brittany and, indeed, the rest of France, more or less ended there and then. We had found what we wanted. The story of Keith and Heather Diggle and their love affair with St. Cast is told in *A Resort Runs Through It.*

Then back to face the real world.

~

Where were we to live? What about Heather's job? We still lived in Corby and Heather was still expected to return to Oundle when her course in London was over. I was now running the orchestra full time and driving to Nottingham when circumstances dictated. In September I would need to be occupying that newly decorated office.

Ben Webster had not wiped us out totally; we just had to look around for mortgage deals where 5% cash deposit was needed rather than 10%. We found a small housing development in the village of Cotgrave outside Nottingham and our 5% secured a piece of land and the promise that there would be a house on it, designated Number 4 Rectory Road, by Christmas. The year was 1966.

~

Now, what about Heather? She was still at the Central School of Speech and Drama when we spotted an advertisement in the *Times Educational Supplement* for a very interesting job (I make it seem far too casual – we were scrutinising every page of Situations Vacant like bible proof-readers for months); it was for an Assistant Drama Adviser in the County of Nottinghamshire. How very appropriate! Heather applied.

They didn't want her. Was she too young? She was only 25; could be. Was she too inexperienced? Probably – but she had lots of energy and was very bright. How would we know why they didn't want her if we didn't ask? So we asked. I telephoned the County Council education department and asked them. Such a cheek! They were so surprised to be asked that they told me; Heather had no experience of teaching Infants and the job called for someone experienced in the broadest possible range of ages. 'That's easily put right', I said. 'Give her a job teaching Infants for a term and if you get good reports then give her the job.' We did the deal over the telephone and they confirmed it in writing a couple of days later. She would be attached to an Infant school for one term and then, subject to favourable reports, she would become Assistant Drama Adviser responsible for the teaching of drama in no less than 70 schools in the Arnold and Carlton area. She would need a car – and plenty of energy.

~

While all these exciting things were going on Corby was building itself a leisure centre with a concert hall and theatre; it was finished during this last year of ours in the town. The first concert in the concert hall was given by Midland Sinfonia with soloist Semprini (Schumann Piano Concerto) and conductor Neville Dilkes. The first event in the theatre was promoted by Corby Grammar School

Jazz Club and featured a group led by Bobby Wellins performing his recently recorded *Under Milk Wood Suite* and then going on to accompany our friend Mark Murphy. I felt that these two events were a fitting crown to our time in the town; we had contributed just as we had benefited.

∼

We spent an uncomfortable three months working in Nottingham, first commuting daily by car (in the new MG Midget, so it wasn't too bad a journey) and then, for just a few weeks, as paying guests with a friendly family in the city. We watched the slow progress of our Cotgrave house and harried the builders whenever we could. It was finished by early December and there we were, in our own house each with a new job to tackle and a feeling of crackling excitement in the air, another phase of our life completed. We invited both sets of parents to join us for Christmas and then we were all together, the six of us, for the first time since our wedding.

∼

By then Heather's appointment to the County Council education department's drama advisory staff had been confirmed so she faced 1967 with excitement and apprehension, a combination of feelings that I still see in her at the beginning of every new term no matter what the school and what the job.

Although I had spent the best part of three months working in the St. James's Street office and the first season of Midland Sinfonia was well under way, I too felt a similar *frisson* as I thought about what lay ahead. I had cut myself off from the one job I was qualified to do but, at last, at long last . . .

I was off the bloody conveyor belt! No more Maths! NO MORE MATHS!!

My Father, with one-stringed fiddle, as a member of the Syncopated Six (1920s)

My parents on their Wedding Day, 22nd February, 1936

My Father in 1960

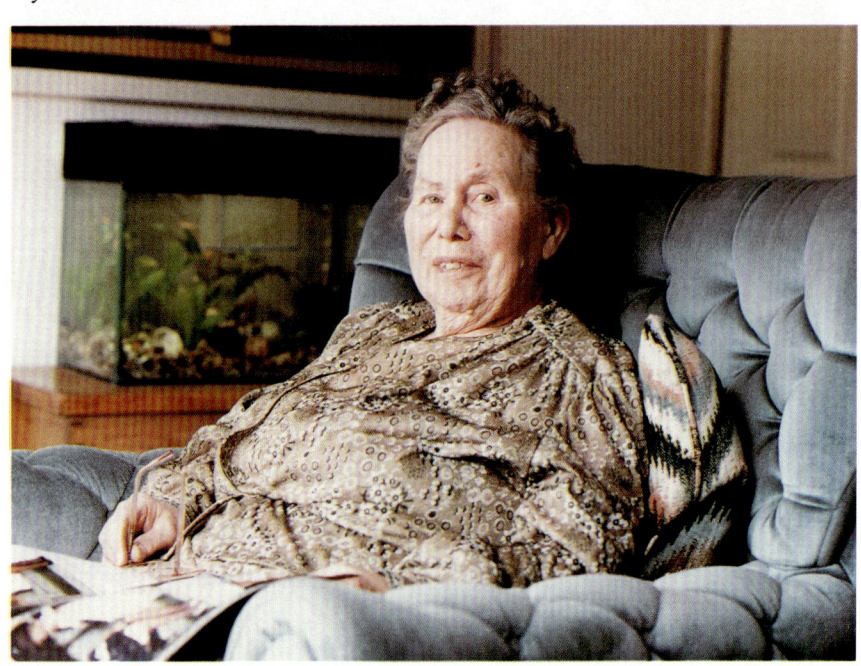

My Mother in 1992

Our Wedding, 1st September 1961 (left to right: my Father, my Mother, Kenneth Greenwood, myself and Heather, Charles and Cathie Ellis)

Off on our honeymoon in the Hillman Californian, property of the 'desiccated old misery'.

MYSELF WHEN YOUNG...

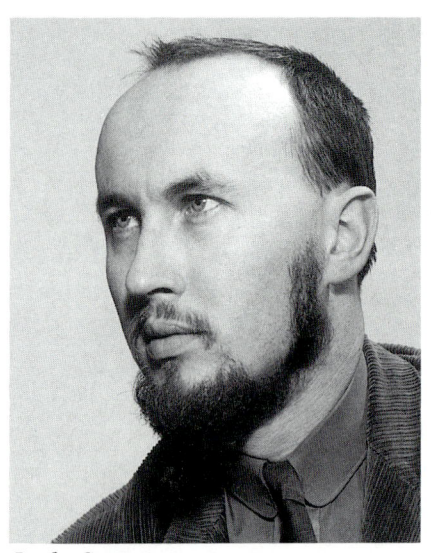

In the Sixties

In the Seventies

In the Eighties

In the Nineties

...AND OLDER

Looking apprehensive on the Second Great Sea Adventure. Mid English Channel. April 1974

In Numero due, Christmas 1976

The road to Canonica

Numero due

Interior – after whitewashing    *View from interior*

Carey Clarke painting The Canonica

The day they arrested the students (our R16 is in the centre)

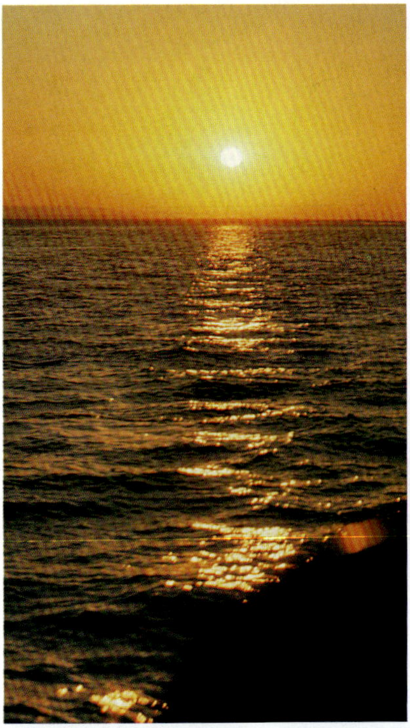

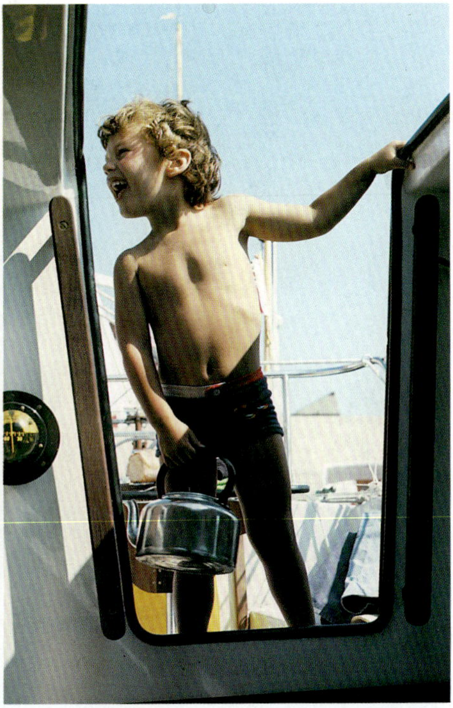

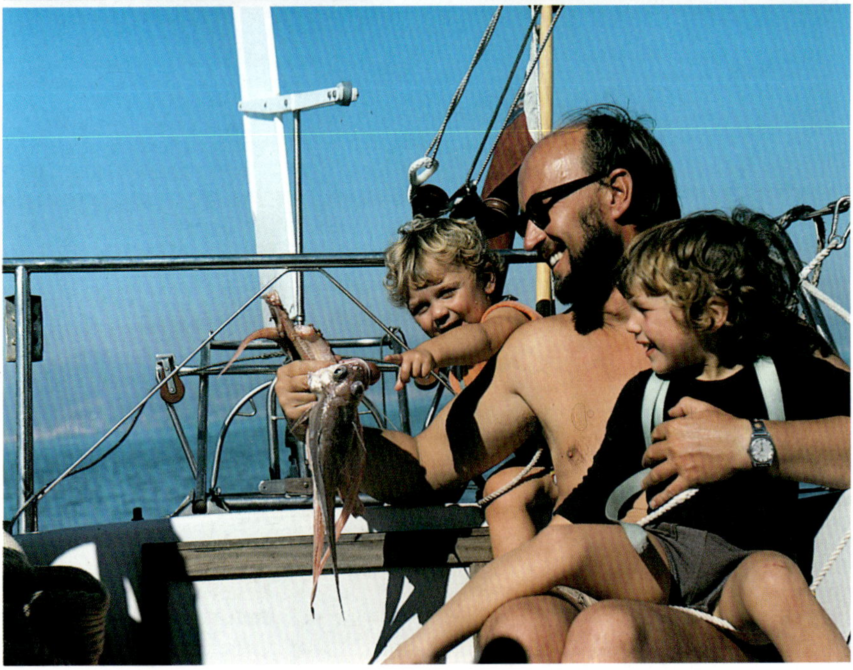

SCENES FROM THE THIRD AND FOURTH GREAT SEA ADVENTURES

HEATHER

In the Sixties

In the Seventies

In the Eighties

Julian with his Grandfather ('Poppa') in the early Eighties

Cathie Ellis ('Momma') in 1997

Myself on extreme right, next to conductor Richard Hickox; Simon Rattle 4th from left.

A Classical Music magazine editorial meeting c.1980. Left to right: Andrew Peggie, Leonard Pearcey, Robert Maycock (Editor), John McMurray, Tony Gamble, Myself, John Pick.

The founders of Subscribe Now! (UK) Ltd. Left to right: Hugh Barton, myself, Tony Gamble

History from our door plates

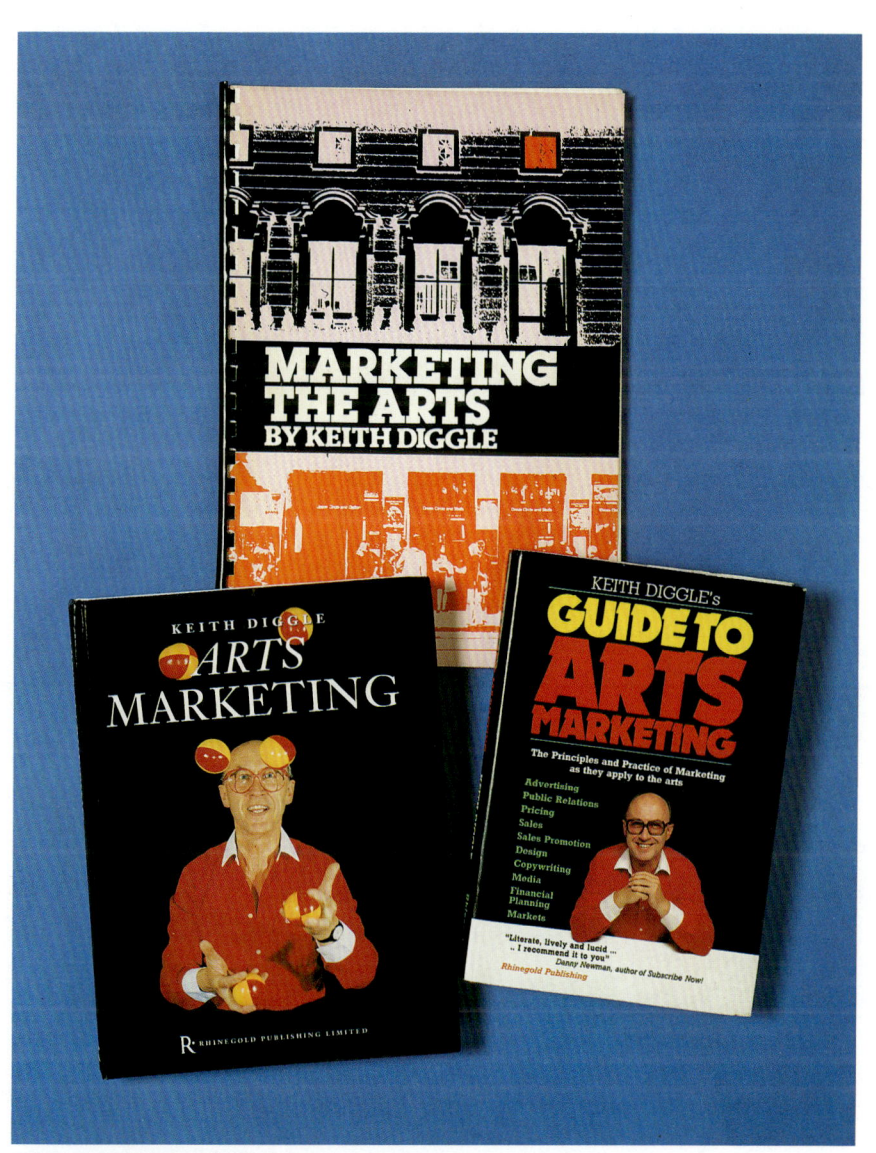

The Arts Marketing books

And so to A RESORT RUNS THROUGH IT. Mother, Father and Thor on the duners Berrow, 1960

A RESORT RUNS THROUGH IT

Keith Diggle

Chronology is a tyrant. Have you noticed that when most people tell a story 'right from the beginning' your eyes begin to glaze over and when they get to the nub of the story you have most likely forgotten why they ever started? I'm going to have to break away from it – the chronology of my autobiography – for a while.

You can divide a life up into chunks as I have done in the main book but when you do you risk missing the continuity of influences that are strands of a life, lines that run throughout from beginning to end. I'm going to tell you about one strand that started when I was six months old and will, I hope, continue . . . forever, if heredity plays its part.

A Resort Runs Through It (to plagiarise the title of a rather pleasant film directed by and starring Robert Redford) – a resort called Burnham-on-Sea/St. Cast that runs through this life, the life of my parents and your lives. Given fair winds and robust deckchairs it may well run through the lives of your children too. I hope it does.

Burnham-on-Sea is a small seaside resort in Somerset to the south of Weston-Super-Mare. The class distinction perceived by our Victorian forebears is apparent; Weston merited the Latin, crummy old Burnham didn't – and the 'Super' has an upper-case 'S' whereas the 'on' of Burnham is always in lower case. Even the word 'Sea' is a kindness to the place for Burnham is on, if it is on anything, the Bristol Channel that leads up to Bristol, which is its principal port. The water is a swirl of silt – dark, thick brown and tastes, heaven forbid that one should taste it, of salt – so that qualifies it to be sea.

From Burnham, going north towards Weston and stopping at a massive rocky protruberence called Brean Down, which is one of the last outcrops of the Mendip Hills (they finally peter out in the Bristol Channel as the islands Flat Holm and Steep Holm), there are miles and miles of sand dunes, wonderful piles of soft sand held together by grass but with exposed flanks that look quite solid until you, a child of, say, four or five, run up the grass and jump from the high edge, arms held high, whooping with joy, flying for a moment and then falling feet first into the sand that collapses beneath you and cascades down with you, breaking your fall and tumbling with you to the soft base of the hill. These sand hills, dunes, were called by my parents, in the language they had invented for themselves, the 'duners' (pronounced 'dooners'), and they loved them as much as I did when I was taking my first breathtaking leaps.

I don't know precisely when Mother and Father discovered Burnham-on-Sea and the village, a few miles away, located just behind the duners, called Berrow, which became the base for their camping holidays for much of their life together, but it was definitely before I was born. Many years later, when I had left home, they moved a few miles along the coast road to Brean Sands, just to the South of Brean Down. My Father had always gone camping for his holidays. I think that is what he did when he left the Royal Air Force; he returned to England from India – perhaps with a little money, who knows? – and he went off a camping.

In the cardboard case I inherited there are 'snaps' (that is what people took then, not photographs) of him in fields with a crowd of young people wearing strange clothes that look very much like the stuff turned out by Armani for the gilded youth of today. There are tents in the background. He stands there with his thin body, his wispy hair and those double dimples in the cheeks of his smiling face. I think, I cannot be sure, but I think that one of the laughing girls was the one – not my Mother – who first took his heart. The name Freda comes to mind, I don't know why. I'll never know now.

The place of those pictures was Lulworth Cove in Dorset and he loved it with all his heart. The scenery there is lovely with rolling hills, dramatic cliffs and blue, blue sea. That was where I believe he went when the doctor told him he would 'never walk or work again'. I think he must have had at least one glorious Summer season living under canvas (living with Freda? I certainly hope so) and then what?

I know that some time after his camping days he went to live in Bath. He was unemployed and he lived in a boathouse on the River Avon. My cousin, Kenneth Poolman, the son of my Aunt Monica, my Father's sister, who is more than ten years older than me, was living in Bath at that time; his father, a merchant seaman, was away for weeks on end and so my bachelor Father became a surrogate parent for the boy. Ken, whom I visited in the course of writing this book, told me how Father had built himself a small sailing boat out of scrap materials and how in the boat there was a special compartment for the fish he caught. The fish were his staple diet and he supplemented this protein with vegetables stolen from gardens that lined the river. Father was definitely in the middle of his 'all property is theft' phase. Ken would visit Father and listen to tales of earlier adventures and hear him romance about the books he would write and what he would do when he was a writer. Ken, who went on to become a successful author, kindly attributes his motivation to the pictures painted in the air by my Father in those distant days.

Father met my Mother in Bath. She was working in a 'big house' as a nanny and when she visited Father in his boathouse she would take for him food stolen from the kitchen; she used to go sailing with him in the tiny sailing dinghy and to swim with him in the River Avon. The snaps tell the story. The cardboard case also held a couple of newspaper cuttings showing pictures of that boat with Father and ukelele banjo, looking very dashing.

Eventually he was persuaded – or volunteered – to give up his gypsy life, to get a job (which he did in 1935) and to get married. After their marriage they moved to a rented house in Bristol and they took their holidays 'under canvas'. That was the only affordable form of holiday for young people then as it is for many today. He did not choose to return to Lulworth Cove.

Somehow they came across the village of Berrow and the nearby town of Burnham-on-Sea which could be reached by train from Bristol. No car, remember. Nobody had a car. So, emotional considerations aside, Lulworth Cove was ruled out by virtue of its distance from Bristol.

So, a train and then a bus from Burnham-on-Sea to a bus stop about one mile beyond Berrow, a bus stop next to Marsh Farm, the place where the Diggle family pitched its tent (or its caravan) from 1936 until the early sixties. I didn't come into the picture until 1938; I was born, you will recall, in the December of 1937 and I was first taken to Berrow in the summer of 1938 when I was six months old.

The owner of Marsh Farm was Farmer Coombes – yes, that was his official title, he was referred to as Farmer. Not Mr – *Farmer*. He could have stepped out of a Donald McGill postcard. Indeed, as we walked around the little shops of Burnham and studied the comic postcards in their windows or in display racks on the pavements outside them – a favourite pastime of holidaymakers on rainy days in seaside resorts all over Britain in those days – I saw Farmer Coombes in a variety of guises. A rotund bishop. A fat fishmonger. A tubby army sergeant. The large girthed man in the striped one piece swimming costume scanning the horizon with hand to brow and saying 'I haven't seen my little Willy for years'.

Farmer Coombes was not merely fat, he appeared to be inflated; he was so full of internal pressure that every part of him was convex. His cheeks were as red and firmly rounded as the most artificial of apples. His buttocks did not only fill the seat of his vast breeches, they packed it so tightly that when he walked there was no sway, no movement. His calves were similarly constrained by polished leather gaiters. Apart from Sundays, when he appeared more formally clad, he was never to be seen wearing a collar to his shirt but there were studs at front and back should he have suddenly have found himself in a situation calling for collar and tie. An unbuttoned waistcoat completed his dress.

Farmer Coombes smoked a clay pipe and his teeth were gappy and brown. He suffered from gout and he was nothing like as good tempered as his appearance suggested. He terrified me and he seriously intimidated my parents for whom he made the rental of a tiny part of his orchard for a few weeks each year seem a major act of philanthropy on his part. My parents may have been paying him good money but there was never any doubt as to who was doing whom the favour in the transaction. He was, in truth, a fat old bully, who bullied his shabby wife, his daughter Cissie and his labourer, a gentle fellow called Toby who walked with a bad limp and whose clothes seemed to be entirely covered with encrusted cow manure.

When the bus stopped at Marsh Farm after the long journey and we alighted accompanied by all the impedimenta of basic camping, the odds were that Farmer Coombes would be standing by the milk churns, next to the bus stop, and he would be as welcome a sight as that of Brent Knoll, that strange conical hill, clearly visible from the train that showed us that the holiday had really begun. He did not have to utter a greeting; his grunt was enough. We were here!

Our little ridge tent in faded green canvas was allowed to occupy a pitch in the field, the orchard, nearest to the bus stop. The apples on the trees were a now long-dead variety known as Morgan Sweet and they were used to make cider. Farmer Coombes would have an old wooden wagon, the kind pulled by a horse, dragged into the field and the children of the families staying there in tents and caravans would be exhorted to fill it up with fallen apples. No promise of reward from Farmer Coombes. No offer of a glass or two of the cloudy cider to co-operative parents. Helping the Farmer was part of the tythe the fellow took of our holidays and no-one thought to question it. And why should we have questioned it? It was fun enough and what else would we have been doing with our time?

We would have been running to the beach over the duners. This trot of jubilation was repeated many times during a holiday but the first one, when the tent had been pitched and the bags unpacked and a cup of tea made on the Primus stove, was an essential part of our ritual. As the clouds of my memory clear and reveal me to be old enough to walk and sing and run I am there, between my Mother and Father, all hand in hand and facing the first view of the duners. We had walked sedately from the orchard, through a field where tents might be pitched when the orchard was full and where one caravan, occupied almost all the year round by Mrs Campbell and her daughter Susan, whose husband had deserted her, rested, and into a dark and mysterious tunnel of overhanging trees where there were wild flowers and butterflies and a lovely smell of wild thyme and then into the sunlight (of course it never rained, never, never) and there they were, the duners!

At this point the walk would become a trot, hands still held, legs synchronised – left legs together, right legs together, a little faster now, keep them together, a little faster now – teamwork that was suggestive of Liberty Horses in the Circus. Indeed, the Lit and I, when by ourselves on a beach somewhere, might still break into such an arm-linked trot, which we call 'Liberty Bodices'. I will not attempt an explanation of this strangeness. You either understand or you do not.

Then we three would start to sing the song that was only ever sung on such occasions. To appreciate this song you have to recollect the melody of the Minuet and Trio from Boccherini's *Quintet in A major*. Now the words of the song may help you recall this very famous tune; they go:

Eedy, eedy wop tap tap
Eedy, eedy wop tap tap
Eeeedy wop tap tap tap
Eeeedy wop tap tap tap
Eeeedy wop tap tap tap ta-aa-tap

It's good isn't it?

The duners were indeed a wonderland. Not only the great cliffs and pits of white sand that I would throw myself into, but the flowers that grew there, gorse and broom, sea holly, mallows, scarlet pimpernels and many more whose names I never knew – all jewels. In the sky there were skylarks doing what skylarks always do, in the words of that animal impressionist of the period (and decades more), Percy Edwards (whom I saw only once in the flesh at the Windmill Theatre, then, as now, specialising in naked female bodies but with a good line in speciality acts – and who died just a few days after I wrote these words), 'throwing us a handful of silver by way of a song'. The larks nested in the duners and one of my later ambitions was to locate just one nest, to take my one, just one, beautiful memento, but I did not succeed.

Hidden within the duners there were indications of the war that by the time the eye of my memory opens was consuming most of the world. There were concrete pillboxes and deep communication trenches with walls of corrugated iron, hidden within the sand hills. They were never occupied but were there against the time when the miles of beach might attract an enemy invasion and machine guns could rake their landing craft. Meanwhile the constructions provided people with very public toilets and the less discriminating with places for lovemaking.

After the opening run and *Eedy Eedy Wop Tap Tap* song we started our walk over the duners, slowly and contemplatively, in appreciation of their wonders, but when the beach came into sight the pace quickened – mine did anyway – and became a rush down onto the dry sand that was rarely, if ever, covered by sea. In fact most of the sand was rarely, if ever, covered by sea. It was that kind of beach and was famous for its absence of sea. The part where the sea did regularly make its twice daily call was not sand, it was a thick, squidgy mud that was supposed to possess therapeutic properties to the extent that in nearby Weston-Super-Mare there were municipal health baths in which people paid money to lie in containers of this mud. Disgruntled holidaymakers had been known to call our town Burnham-on-Mud.

The first sight that met the eye of the little boy running down from the duners was of the tank traps; the whole of that immense stretch of beach, from Burnham to Brean Down was also protected from an enemy that might choose to make a landing there by ferro-concrete posts that were in places erected vertically, stuck deep into the sand so that they could resist all onslaughts from sea and wind, and were also piled into crisscross arrangements so that four, six or eight posts lay in an interwoven square arrangement. Effective? Well, Jerry (as the mighty German forces were known) made no attempt at a landing on *our* beach, thank you very much. Of course, it being on the west coast of England, that is, the side that faces away from the rest of Europe, might have supported the enemy in its decision to stay away.

There was not much more on our beach. The skeleton of a long dead boat was about it, apart from the concrete posts. The sea did occasionally approach beyond the mud and then we swam but this involved a longish walk out to meet the tide and the fear that we would be 'cut off'. It was one of Father's peculiarities that although he knew that tides arrived roughly every twelve hours and that the time of arrival was roughly one hour later every day, he had never grasped the concept of the range of a tide, that is, the cyclical variation of the height of the high water and the depth of the low water. He knew that there were 'spring' tides but he had never heard of their opposite, the 'neap' tides, so he assumed that spring tides that brought the sea much closer to the land only did this in the Spring. Thus, if one took one's holiday in the Summer or Autumn the tide would never even think of approaching the land. But the tide was a treacherous beast and could at any time decide to sweep the sea in *behind* the unsuspecting bather and approach the land in this way leaving us on an island of sand that would get smaller and smaller until it was covered – and then we would all drown and be swept out to sea.

Apart from the usual ball games (and kite flying, using kites made from bamboo sticks and newspapers) the best diversion was to walk along the most recent high water mark of beached seaweed and search for flotsam and jetsam. It was one of those small pieces of knowledge that distinguished between a man of education and the other kind – knowing the difference between the two types of waterborne rubbish. It is, even today, deemed to be something that a semi-finalist in University Challenge might be expected to know, for example. So I knew what was what from a very early age. In addition there was a popular male singing duo heard regularly on the wireless, called 'Flotsam and Jetsam'. Sang the two:

Flotsam and Jetsam
Flotsam and Jetsam

and then one, in a high voice, sang

I sing the high notes

and then the other, in a low voice, sang

And I goes and gets 'em

Very droll, it was.

Amongst the detritus brought in by the sea there were occasionally to be found small pieces of evidence that a war was being fought: bits of aluminium from aircraft and even once a large piece of silver painted canvas that had come from a boat. My Father and I once came across part of the life saving kit from a life-raft in which there was a waterproof pack of lemonade crystals which we took back to our tent and after a few minutes hesitation broke open and used to make lemonade.

And then back across the duners, through the dark tunnel, across the field and into the orchard, back to our little tent and back to the odd little social hierachy that existed there. The community of orchard holidaymakers was marked at its lower end by the Diggle family and at its upper end by the Haynes family, people who owned two – yes, two – greengrocery shops in Bridgwater and who kept a rather smart caravan close to the gated entrance to the field. The Haynes family, Mr, Mrs and overwhelmingly beautiful daughter, Wilma, spent their weekends at Marsh Farm and travelled by car. The Haynes family were top of the pile; they knew their place and we knew ours. We felt rather pleased when they greeted us and bade us farewell. In between there was the unmarried hairdresser from Bath, Miss Bakewell, who travelled to and from Marsh Farm by Morris 8 and who holidayed in one of those graciously curvilinear 'streamlined' caravans that were a delightful by-product of pre-war design. Others came and went but they were not regulars like the Haynes, the Bakewell and the Diggles and so had no place at all in the society.

It was in this orchard, when I was three or four, that I saw my first black faces. At the lower end of the orchard, close to the bend in the road, there was a wide ditch filled with water and one day my father found me talking across the bright green expanse of weed to two black American soldiers who were trying to persuade me to pick them apples and to throw them over to them. I was fascinated by these broad, black, shining, smiling faces and voices that sounded friendly and kind. Father came to my assistance and we loaded up those two doughboys so that their pockets were bulging.

It will be hard for you, my sons, and your children, to imagine what it was like to live in a world where all skins were white. Black people were only to seen on film and only then – with the notable exception of the singer Paul Robeson – in the rôles of servants or fools. It does not surprise me that people of my generation and older hold attitudes towards people of different racial backgrounds that shock you. In those days all races were seen in terms of racial stereotypes. You have only to read books of the period to see how all Chinese were cunning, all French were slightly soiled, all Japanese were wily, all Blacks (or Negroes, or Niggers) were lazy and untrustworthy; unless, of course, the author befriended one and then they became the exception, loyal, decent, godfearing and so on.

I was lucky. My Father had prejudices but they went the other way. He exhorted me to admire people of African descent. Paul Robeson was the perfect example, for not only was he a great singer but his politics matched my Father's. There was a black folk singer called Josh White, a sort of precursor to Harry Belafonte, who could be heard on the radio. We jointly adored the Ink Spots and the Mills Brothers. Later on Winifred Atwell, the honky-tonk pianist, was added to the Hall of Pro-Black Prejudice.

So, you can imagine my Father's delight when these two real black men appeared on the far side of the ditch that day. They looked as though they might break into song and dance any minute. None of us then knew of the extent to which racial segregation and oppression was practised in the USA and in the American armed forces. We saw these men simply as black Americans, people who came from the Land of the Free, nice men out for a walk in the country – who were closely related to some very famous black people.

The walk to the village of Berrow was not far, perhaps a mile, and it was there that we shopped. We passed the farm of Mr Case, who did not do camping but seemed to me to be a much nicer person than Farmer Coombes with his weatherbrown face and ready smile. The road took us away from coastal scenery for a while and then, on the right, the duners reappeared and amidst an area of houses and trees there was a sign for 'Thorne's Steam Bakery' which lay hidden behind tall broom and blackthorn. To approach this bakery, to smell the bread from a far distance, to hold a new loaf that was almost too hot to handle, wrapped in tissue paper, and to be allowed to pull off pieces of crust to eat as I approached the main part of the village was a very heaven. No French child today, tearing off the end of his baguette on the way home, could derive more pleasure than I did in those days.

Berrow was famous for the names of its shopkeepers; on the left as one entered the village proper there was the shop of the baker, Mr Bunn. On the right was the village shop and post office, owned by Mr Chick, where Mr Ham worked. Through the village, just past the garage owned by Miss Welland (what a shame her name wasn't Jaguar or even plain old fashioned Morris), on the left, there was the butcher, Mr Horsey, and next to him was the ironmonger, Mr Steele.

Beyond, a bus ride away was Burnham-on-Sea, where we went for pleasures that Berrow could not provide. When I was very young it was donkey rides, playing on the beach with other children and a splash about in the pool that the Council had made by building a large circular wall about two feet high within the reach of one of those spring tides on which my Father was so expert. The tide would withdraw and leave a substantial amount of itself contained within the wall. Later our visits were built around attendance at the cinema; we were passionate about the cinema. We would buy fish and chips and take them to eat in a discreetly located seafront shelter and then join the queue for whatever James Mason, Stewart Grainger, Margaret Lockwood, Glynis Johns and Patricia Roc of the home stable or the glittering delights of Hollywood had to offer. Oh, the wondrous Gene Kelly! To how many young people then did he introduce the dance? Recently I saw on television a compilation film showing scene after scene from the great American musical films; Fred Astaire, Ginger Rogers, Gene Kelly, Vera Ellen, Cyd Charisse, Anne Miller – and realised how much I truly loved the work of these people. They called their work 'hoofing'; I think of it as great art. If you think I am exaggerating then see *An American In Paris* with Gene Kelly and Vera Ellen and look at the 'Slaughter On Tenth Avenue' sequence – and listen to the music. *They don't make films like those any more.*

When not going to the cinema with my parents or playing on the beach I would pursue my other passion which was collecting the William books, by Richmal Crompton. In Burnham there were six or seven small shops that carried a stock of books and William books, hardback with colourful, illustrated covers, almost always featured but never was there to be found the complete set of . . . twenty-five I believe there were. So I would take my five shillings (25p today) and hunt and sometimes I was lucky and take back to Berrow a treasure to occupy me in the evenings, reading by the light of the oil lamp in the tent.

The event that remains most vividly in my memory is the Berrow Flower Show, an annual event held in Farmer Coombes' field, next to the orchard, that I must have attended four or five times, perhaps more. It always seemed to coincide with our holiday and it was a definite high point. A vast marquee was erected and around it were all the stalls that you would expect to find at a country fête. Inside the marquee there were the entries for the vegetable, fruit and flower competitions with the cards indicating their level of award from the judges. There were races, three-legged, sack, egg and spoon and get to the winning line as quick as you can, for grown-ups and children and there were small cash prizes. Everywhere was bustle, excitement, the smell of crushed grass and small boys, myself amongst them, and small girls running around, 'having goes' on the stalls and even, yes even at that age, indulging in very minor and innocent forms of flirtation.

The little faded green ridge tent was eventually replaced with a government surplus ex-Army tent, 14 feet square with very serious looking sectional poles and a proper ridge pole (although the tables I learned in school only went up to the 12 times I worked out, with my unmathematical brain, that the floor area of this tent was 196 square feet – a fact that enabled me to enhance my reputation amongst my fellows, '*our* tent covers 196 square feet, so there!'). We acquired three camp beds and a big wooden folding table, also government surplus; we graduated to having two Primus stoves and folding chairs. After my father got the wonderful new job in 1945 we went up in the world and these things became possible. Our status in the orchard social hierachy didn't alter, however, because as we went up in the world so did the Haynes and the Bakewell. We moved our regular site from the orchard to the field so our lack of social position was not so apparent and, indeed, amongst the tent dwellers in the field – people taking their holidays in little faded green ridge tents – there were some who looked up to us.

There was now far too much stuff for us to carry (there still was no motor car and never was there to be one – neither of my parents could drive) so my Father had a word (I'll bet it was a nervous word) with Farmer Coombes who, with uncharacteristic generousity, agreed to allow us to store it all in the loft of one of his barns. We feared rat damage over the Winter but every year, when we climbed the dangerously rotted ladder to bring it all down again, it emerged uneaten – dusty and cobwebby but all in one piece and nothing ratlike leapt out at us. Whatever our emotional commitment to the place, we were now well and truly physically committed.

Father bought a portable radio too. It was a very heavy portable. A Pye, covered in green, mottled rexene, it required a very large battery and a small one (High Tension and Low Tension) and it picked up the Home Service and the Light Programme which was just wonderful. We could lie on our beds and listen to Housewives' Choice in the mornings. Housewives' Choice regularly played all the

Berrow Flower Show
Keith Diggle

The flapping, fluttering white marquee,
Hired for the day from King's of Bristol,
Holds a chattering, flattering crowd
All freshly washed and starched and ironed
And the smell of sweat and stampled grass.
Linen-clothed tables bear their burdens
Of carrots and turnips, potatoes, tomatoes
And every flower and fruit that grows.
The centre of attention is the marrow;
Plump, complacent, smug it lies
Secure and safe in a wicker basket
That is painted gold and lined with silk.
A red-faced man – the happy father,
Smart and hot in his best blue worsted,
Smiles and nods at his friendly rivals
Who peer and point and wish they had a dungheap of their own.
Bean-bags fly and tin-cans fall
And the Wheel of Fortune goes spinning around.
A dusky lady, late of Weston pier,
Swings her earrings and plays Patience.
Careering cannonballs bump towards the boxwood skittles
And the wriggling piglet squeals hysterically.
Beneath a yellow, yawning awning the vicar grasps his halo,
Throws and wins a china shepherdess.
Beaming and benevolent, the Bishop gaiters past the stalls,
Stops to buy a pin-cushion and to pass the time of day,
Nibbles at a Morgan Sweet and still retains his dignity.
Congratulates the Vicar who mumbles modestly
And speaks hopefully of a new steeple.
And a little boy watches a patch
Of slightly flattened, shining, steaming grass
And absent-mindedly adjusts his trousers.

really good songs and because of it I came to know not only the kid's stuff like *The Teddy Bear's Picnic* but real music, music that had quality written right through it.

Hogey Carmichael, that genius of a songwriter and performer who also acted in films, was a particular favourite of mine. The song *Buttermilk Skies,* which was often played on the programme, was sung by him in one film: as he sang it he played with a little homemade toy consisting of a piece of wood with a propeller at one end; he rubbed another stick up and down the stick and as he did the propeller rotated. Fascinating! How did he do it? I made things that resembled what I had seen but they wouldn't work. I was left with a very nice song but no toy. In 1996 I sat with you, Marcus, in a tiny diner close to the Rockies National Park in Colorado and at a table nearby there was a father and small child playing with one of these things. You'll never know, my son, how much I wanted to go over and ask to examine it. I still don't know how those things work!

As you will see as this story progresses, the lives of my parents moved into a period of relative success when we left Number 8 Pembroke Road, Kingswood, Bristol but within seven or eight years it had started its irreversible decline, slowly at first and then almost headlong until my Father reached the age when he could legitimately call himself retired (at that time he been so, in practice for several years) and draw his state pension and expect little more from life.

Throughout the whole of this time this holiday place was central to his life and that of my Mother. The 196 square feet tent eventually gave way to a caravan, which we named 'Valhalla', that was based all the year round in the same field as the tent had occupied. My parents acquired a Great Dane dog from the Watts-Russell family in Oundle called Thor (you see? Valhalla? Thor?) which made their various trips to Berrow by public transport quite complicated. Dear Thor had the distressing habit of sitting on train seats with his hind legs resting on the floor just as a human would do, supported by his front legs on the seat, thus exposing his lower belly. He would then allow his imagination to wander and his huge, red, conical penis would emerge from its hiding place and all would try to pretend it wasn't there. There is humorous potential in such a scene but, at the time, sitting in a railway carriage otherwise full of people, I confess I did not appreciate it. God but he was an ugly brute!

When I brought the Lit back to one of my parents' many homes during the start of the period of 'the great decline', the evil creature decided that he did not like this newcomer. He waited his time and on the second or third day of her visit, when she was alone with him, he attacked. He leaped at her, towered over her, and bit her, very hard, in the upper arm. The Lit swears that if my Father had not come to her rescue the dog would have finished her.

Why did they keep him? After this attack on my Lit why did they still keep him? My Father once explained; when he took Thor out for a walk people used to open conversations about him and he liked that. The bloody dog was a conversation piece!

Farmer Coombes died and the field was sold for housing development. Valhalla was moved a few miles along the coast to Brean Sands to Warren Farm which lay behind sandhills that could never, by any stretch of the imagination, be called duners. The land was flat and over the years became infested with caravans; the beach became infested with motor cars. The whole place became simply . . . *infested.*

But my parents stayed true to the place. Valhalla gave way to a slightly better model which they named Valstar (why I never knew – it is the name of a French brand of beer but that couldn't have been the source). When my Father was properly retired and a little house eventually obtained in Nottingham he and my Mother used to move down to Brean Sands in March and they would stay there until as late in the year as the weather would permit; until, say, October or even November. He bought a portable typewriter and took up his writing again. He grew huge flowers in old Walls ice-cream tins – marguerites and sunflowers which attracted butterflies and bees. The size of the flowers was very typical of my Father's taste as was his way of assessing the quality of the portable Pye radio; he would turn the volume up to full blast and say 'Just listen to that tone'. My Mother provided support services as usual. They walked on the beach and my Father took a daily dip in the chocolatey water. They had television so they did not go to the cinema. I think they were very happy there.

And then, on 4 July 1972, my Mother went out to the nearby shop leaving my Father typing. When she returned he was dead. His heart had stopped. He had had one warning heart attack a couple of years before and had tried to take it easy but he'd been taking it easy for years. There is a limit to how far you can take things easy. It was the diet I think. High fat diets did not come any higher. They used to eat cheese sandwiches and drink cocoa made with full cream milk every night just before they went to bed. Theirs was a generation that saw good in animal fat in all its forms.

I think I can truly say that there has hardly been a day since he died when I haven't thought of him and wished that I had known him better – and he me. He was a dear, dear man and I loved him so.

And that was the end of that. No more Berrow, no more Burnham-on-Sea, no more Brean Sands.

Long before this I had met the Lit and we married in 1961. She had come with me to Berrow and to Brean Sands and had even walked across the duners and had sung the song (it was one of the ways I knew that she was going to be *all right)* but we had our eyes on more distant horizons.

In 1964 Lit had been given a year's secondment from the school where she had been teaching (Oundle Secondary Modern School) to take a course at the Central School of Speech and Drama in London. When her academic year was over in the Summer of 1965 we drove our MG Midget over to France for a holiday; Lit was quite drained after the rigours of the course and badly needed a break. We took the ferry crossing to Cherbourg and drove down the Cotentin peninsula to Dinard and booked into the Hôtel de la Paix for three nights. It was, I believe, the first hotel we had stayed in since our honeymoon and definitely the first where we had lashed out and opted for *demi-pension*. We adored the place and we, entirely inexperienced little folk that we were, were thrilled with what we saw as the sheer luxury of the hotel. These days, when we leave the Portsmouth to St. Malo ferry early in the morning, we often go to that same rather modest hotel for our first breakfast in France; we sit out in the sun and take our breakfast and feast on the memory of the place. We always recall the visit of a troupe of open-air entertainers who, on our first evening there, had erected a tightrope right across the square, high above the street, the pavements, the traffic and the people, and with apparent disregard for their own safety performed right in front of us, right above us. It was all so different, so *foreign*.

When our three days in Dinard were over, with map in hand, we explored this northern part of Brittany and, before darkness fell, we came across a small coastal resort called St. Cast. It had a very large beach and promenade – a bit like Burnham-on-Sea really. It was about the same size as Burnham-on-Sea as well. It felt very comfortable, almost familiar. The main difference lay in the beach, the *Grand Plage*, which had lots of those pretty little striped tents that you see in pre-war postcards of France and it had children's beach clubs, something quite new to us. We saw groups of children under the supervision of adults, playing games, doing physical jerks, and clearly enjoying it; these were the clubs. We learned later that the children's beach club was a commercial undertaking, usually owned by a person trained as a children's physical education teacher, that ran throughout the Summer season. There were then just a couple of clubs but later on, when you boys got to know St. Cast, there was a wider choice.

The traditional St. Cast beach holiday would have the family first select its tent and pay its rental in advance for the full period – in those blissful days this might well mean the entire month of August – and it might well also contract to rent its deckchairs at the same time from the same provider. The children would then be enrolled in their chosen club for the duration, a choice usually governed simply by the choice they had made the previous year; tradition and loyalty pay a major part in the selection of a beach club for there is great competition between them, both between the proprietors and between their charges and once one has been part of the team it is almost impossible to change sides.

The *Grand Plage,* for all its activity, was a very quiet place and this made it different from any town beach I had ever known in Britain. With families occupying all the tents, young children crawling around, older ones participating in the club activities and all the usual activities of a busy beach it was perfectly possible to hold a conversation in the midst of it all without having to raise one's voice.

We booked into the Hôtel de France (room only – three days of lavish eating in Dinard had seriously impacted on the savings). The room had no plumbing at all. There was a china bowl on a cupboard and along the corridor there was a WC and a bathroom. Early in the morning there was a knock on the door and a young woman stood bearing a large china jug full of hot water; this was the plumbing. When we left a couple of days later the bill turned out to be exactly half what I had expected it to be; my French has always been weak when it comes to numbers and I had misunderstood what the proprietor had told me when we booked in. It was a good mistake to have made because it compensated somewhat for the dinner we had taken at the Hôtel Ker Louis the night before.

For years afterwards the Hôtel Ker Louis was our idea of what a good hotel and restaurant should be. On the evening of our first whole day in St. Cast when we first saw its lighted windows, the illuminated menu outside, and the packed dining room of the hotel we metaphorically pressed our noses to the glass and by the second evening we had talked ourselves into believing that we could afford to dine there – which proved to be the case once we settled up with the Hôtel de France. In truth it was not all that expensive and it was a delight to be there.

I still cannot determine what there was about St. Cast that made an impression upon us apart from the strange Burnham-on-Sea quality and the *Grand Plage*. It was . . . comfortable. It was as foreign as could be but we felt at home there. We had stayed there for only a couple of days but the memory lasted.

It was in the Springtime of 1970, when I was working in Liverpool, that I took a trip to Rennes with two colleagues from work. It was a visit to the Maison de la Culture in Rennes, sponsored by the French government, and Peter Bevan, Lynne Burton and I went there in my car via the usual ferry route to Cherbourg. After three busy and very pleasant days we set off on the return journey with a night to spare before having to catch the boat. St. Cast came to mind as a possible place to stay over and off we went there, arriving in the early evening. Very little was happening. The sound of boules being played in the little court just behind the Place des Mielles was all that could be heard. I booked us into the Hôtel Ker Louis and we chose our evening meal from exactly the same menu that Lit and I had used five years before. Even out of season the place had a definite attraction for me.

I returned from France loaded with all the good things that contributed to our love of the country – food mainly but also, for me, a pack of cigarettes, not the commonplace Gauloise but the yellow 'maize' paper covered Boyard in their sturdy blue and white packets of thick card that I liked to smoke from time to time – things that we call, in the language, 'we-gots' (as in, 'look what we got'). I discussed the location of our Summer holiday that year with the Lit. Could . . . St. Cast possibly fit the bill?

I telephoned the Hôtel Ker Louis and booked us in for a fortnight, *demi-pension*. How much would that be? Fine. Fine. That was affordable.

Seen from the inside, our room in the Hôtel Ker Louis bore a strong resemblance to that stayed in by Monsieur Hulot on his Holiday. It was very nice but it fell short of five stars, or indeed any stars. The room had a nice wooden floor with a scattering of sand here and there (always a good sign in a small holiday hotel), a bed, a wardrobe, a cupboard, a mat and a handbasin. The WC was at the end of the corridor and there was a bathroom, access to which was obtainable on payment of a small supplement (bit of a shock that). It was *all right*, let me assure you. The food was splendid and we passed a blissful week towards the end of which an odd thought crossed my mind. I had been wrong over the cost of staying in the Hôtel de France and I had received a pleasant surprise. Could I have misunderstood what I had been told over the telephone when I had called this hotel? Without giving too much away I told the Lit that it would perhaps be a good idea to check on how the bill was going. Perhaps we could go for the lobster *en supplement* next week?

I had misunderstood. Pension rates are given per person. Room rates are given per room. The hotel bill for the first week was precisely double what I had allowed for.

And that is how the Lit and I had a week of improvised camping using our picnic equipment and the folded down seats of our car, the first of several Renault 16s, known throughout France as the 'Ehr Sez'.

In the early Spring of 1975, when there existed a two-year-old Marcus and a very recently arrived Julian (who was almost the same age as I was when I first met Marsh Farm, Berrow), Lit and I abandoned our children with their maternal grandparents for a couple of weeks and went off to Normandy where we had arranged to hire a touring caravan that was based in Domfront. We hitched it to the back of our car (which had a very floppy rear suspension and hated pulling this box making its feelings known by regularly bashing the exhaust pipe on the road surface) and set off for the Loire Valley. After a day of pipe bashing we abandoned the Loire valley trip and made for Rennes. We dumped the caravan in a camping site outside town and took a night in a hotel in the city. Returning to the caravan the next day we thought it might be interesting to tow the little box – very slowly and carefully – to . . . the coast somewhere . . . to St. Cast perhaps?

A few hours later the caravan was resting beneath an apple tree in full flower at the farm campsite at Pen Guen, just outside St. Cast.

St. Cast was, naturally, on its best behaviour for us. After calling to us and bringing us there it was not going to spoil things now, was it? We enjoyed the weather, the scenery, the whole atmosphere of the place and we realised that this was really the place for the whole family and not just for us. I won't say that we felt guilty about being there alone but I'll admit that we pictured the two of you being there with us.

We went to the Hôtel Ker Louis for dinner, got into conversation with the proprietor, Madame Rouxel, and enquired about the possibility of renting accommodation later in the year. She recommended that we pay a call on Madame Matisse who lived in the higher part of the town, known as St. Cast Bourg. This we did and met the eighty-year-old lady whose large house was divided into flats. Yes, a fortnight in June would be perfectly possible, in the second-floor flat. The price? 60,000 francs. Even with my limited grasp of French numbers I thought this sounded like a very large sum. The old lady was, of course, giving the price in old francs; the currency had been revalued downwards by a factor of 100 to 1 many years before. Our bill would be 600 francs and that was affordable. Madame Matisse told us that now we could tell our friends that we were going to spend our holiday in Singapore – you say it the French way and you get a very close approximation to how you pronounce St. Cast Bourg. It's not a great joke but it came free from Madame Matisse.

We returned home, via Domfront, where we left the little box on wheels, and two months later we were there, the four of us plus the daughter of friends, Beth, a very lovely person, who came to help us spend a little time, from time to time, not looking after two baby boys.

Not everything went perfectly well. There were three flats in the building and Julian, who did not sleep well at night, had a yell that could penetrate all walls and ceilings and he chose to exercise it from about midnight through to the wee small hours. The outcome was that the only way we could co-exist with our French neighbours was for me to take young Julian out to the car at about 1am, when he usually awoke and started his amazing yell, unfold the seats to make a sort of double bed, put him beside me all nicely wrapped up, put in my Boots wax ear plugs, and settle down for the night with Julian belting it out as hard as he could and me in restless slumber.

The nearest beach was that named *Plage de la Fresnaye,* one of St. Cast's seven beaches. Not the *Grand Plage* but one favoured by slightly lower orders. Not the lowest of orders for they occupy the *Plage de la Mar* that is close to one of the less favoured camp sites. *Plage de la Fresnaye* stands to the *Grand Plage* as a Regimental Sergeant Major stands to a Captain or perhaps (on days when there is a good *basse mer* and the sand eels – or *lançons* – are there to be caught) as a Lieutenant to a Major.

Well, my dears, we had a wonderful time. We played on the *Plage de la Fresnaye.* We drove into the centre of town and played on the *Grand Plage,* we peddled pedalloes, and we looked at the children's beach clubs, of which there were now six, and wondered whether this might be the place where we should all go for our Summer holidays and if we did, which club would suit Marcus and Julian. Every evening the boys would go to bed nice and early and the three of us would eat and drink robustly. Then the ladies would retire and I would slump in a chair until Julian started his first yell; then off I went for my period of exile.

From that time on St. Cast became our Burnham-on-Sea. At first we did not visit every year but by the time Marcus was seven years old and Julian five, we were regulars. We got into the habit of renting apartments in the centre of town so that it was not long before the boys could be trusted to make their way to the beach without supervision to join the activities of the *Club des Benjamins* – the chosen one – in the mornings and afternoons.

The song of the *Club des Benjamins*

C'est moi, Benjamin, le roi des gamins.
Choisi au cours d'une fête.
La reine c'est la p'tite Babette
Oui mais le Roi,
Le Roi, c'est bien moi.
Laissez passer Benjamin, le Roi des gamins.
Mais le lendemain j'allais à l'école
J'etais dans la lune la tête un peu folle
Dans mon vieux confortable j'avais emporté
D'objet merveilleux de *la royauté
C'est moi Benjamin, le Roi des gamins.
Laissez passer Benjamin, le Roi des gamins!

(Words as recalled by Martin Gasqueton, member of the *Club des Benjamins* thoughout his St. Castine life.)

Oh how wonderful was the *Club des Benjamins* during its heyday when it was run by the energetic and handsome Monsieur Hamon who owned it with his wife, Annie, who administered the business of taking the money and keeping safe lost property from a small caravan on the beach. Annie spent all the summer days secure within the caravan because she was allergic to sand. Imagine that! And outside, with one or two assistants, inevitably young PE students, Monsieur Hamon would organise, create new games, amuse, exhort, chastise and generally make himself very busy indeed with a morning programme of exercises and an afternoon one of competitive sports all spread across four age ranges. He was a short, powerfully built man, with beard, tanned skin and, cliché though it may be, twinkling eyes – and he laughed a lot. He was ideally cast in his rôle and he was adored by all.

Although Julian 'came on' later he was always in the shadow of brother Marcus during the great years of the *Benjamins* for Marcus became the winner of almost every first prize, almost every day, at the competitive events. The Hamons had so organised things that each of the five working days of the week was sponsored by one commercial company or another and sponsorship meant donating or financing the prizes for the competitive events. The Hamon policy was that there should be prizes for the winners and prizes for the losers. At the end of the sporting day, at 5pm, there would arise from the sector of the beach occupied by the *Benjamins* a great shout: *AS-SEM-BLE-MENT!* Children would assemble by the stone steps leading up to the promenade. Parents would assemble. So would passersby, to see what all the noise was about.

Monsieur Hamon would stand on the steps and bid the crowd to silence. He would then announce the name of the person who had come third in, say, the senior

---

* Jean-Pierre Montier holds that 'ma' is the correct word here.

long jump and that child would step forward to receive his prize, a book, a school bag, a tee shirt or something equally attractive (the prizes were always worth having) and Monsieur Hamon would call for three cheers *Pip Pip!* and the crowd would roar back *Hoo Rah!* Then the second prize, then the first, all treated with the same organised but nonetheless spontaneous celebration. This would be repeated countless times until every winner had been prized and cheered. Then Annie and one of the assistants would stand at the top of the steps and all the children would move from the beach and each would collect a small prize, a comic book, a sample of toilet soap – once, I recall, a small packet of washing up powder.

This ceremony was repeated every day, Monday to Friday, throughout the Summer season months of July and August. It must have taken some organising and some stamina to have carried this routine out year after year and, as they did during the most popular weeks of the Summer, organise a Saturday morning exercise and games session for the parents at no charge at all.

You boys grew up usually spending one full month each Summer there, moving through the age groups of the *Club des Benjamins,* becoming increasingly familiar with the French language and self confident amongst French people. We made good friends with French families who came originally because they wanted a good place in which to holiday with their children and then fell in love with it. We came to know the town and all its hidden corners. When the boys grew up and moved away from home we took many holidays in many different places but we tried never to let a year go by without spending at least a week in the place. St. Cast has definitely become to the Lit and me what Burnham-on-Sea was to my parents and we even hope that one day we may spend the larger part of the year in our favourite place, just as they did.

We would study the free tide-table obtainable at *La Maison Blanche,* the sports goods shop, and time our visit to the *Bec Rond,* the island just off the port, straight after the lowest of *basses mers.* Then there were exposed rocks that had not been exposed for about a month and they had again been colonised by crabs and even – one prayed – by lobsters. We wore 'jellies', clear plastic sandals that strapped on and did not slip as we clambered over rocks carrying our crab hooks (purchased from *La Maison Blanche).* I also wore thick gardening gloves against the ravages of barnacles that tore at the skin as I strained to turn over large rocks. We hunted two kinds of crab. There was the *dormeur* or *tourteau,* that the British would recognise as the ordinary edible brown crab that is to be found in fish shops in Britain. They lay under rocks and you reached them either by raising the rock that hid them or by jostling them out from their cover with a crab hook. The second variety exists in Britain but is almost never taken and eaten; it is the *étrille,* a small but fearsome beast that fights back with vicious pinches when it is approached. It has a blueish shell, tinged with red, with sharp spikes on its legs and its pincers. It is packed with sweet meat and is a far better bet than the *dormeur.*

In the hunt for supper we inevitably came across the little green crabs that the French called *demoiselles;* they were not recommended eating. (Who recommends these things? I cannot say. They do not recommend the spider crab in Britain but it is eaten throughout France. Perhaps the absence of the *demoiselle* from any *poissonerie* I have even seen in France, where almost anything that moves finds a human mouth in some part of the land, is evidence enough.) We would approach one of the women who always appeared on the rocks at this time of low water, armed with a bucket and an implement, sometimes no more than an old kitchen knife, and offer our catch of *demoiselles* to go with theirs of mysterious small creatures for which they had some culinary purpose. Their response was always to accept with a grateful smile and the view that even the humble little green crab was 'bon pour la soupe'.

Once, when hunting by myself, I overturned a rock and beneath it there was a pool of water made murky by the disturbance. Within the clouds of mud and sand I momentarily saw a long thin blue-red antenna sweep through the water and knew that *I had one!* A few seconds later, with blood dripping from a well pinched finger, I bore a lobster – not a vast lobster but big enough – back to the tent where the Lit was sunbathing. The boys came running back from the Club and for a day or so I was a star, not only within my family but amongst all the French families with tents near ours who wished that they had fathers who caught lobsters.

I repeated the experience a couple of years later when out on the rocks with Marcus and once more in nearby St. Jacut with Julian, but these lobsters were much smaller and I haven't had a sniff of one for the past five years.

Maybe next year.

It is possible to eat the clams found in St. Cast without contracting some awful disease that will destroy your liver. The slogan that goes on a car sticker that one may buy at *La Maison Blanche* says 'St. Cast La Pure' and, to date, that seems to be true. The talent for catching the clams, *palourdes,* is not given to all. I have it (well, I am the Father) and Julian has it. The two of us can outcatch the French any time.

We own clam forks, bought from . . . yes, you guessed . . . that have two prongs about five inches long, and wooden handles. These implements only come into play when you have located your clam. Some use them to find the clam but the expert does not do this. The trick is to know how a clam behaves when it feels threatened. If a clam feels the sand in its immediate vicinity disturbed it will squirt out a tiny jet of water, sometimes large enough to project beyond the sand and sometimes only sufficient to disturb the wet sand that surrounds it. So one sets out to disturb clams by poking into the sand with a stick or – the most sophisticated of techniques – the big toe. Old French ladies who have been hunting clams all their lives use the big toe. When a clam is approached the telltale sign of disturbance is noted and the clam is hoicked out by means of the two pronged fork.

Clam hunting in St. Cast is practised at low water – it need not be the low water of a real *basse mer* – between the *Grand Plage* and the port, where many small boats are moored. The clams are brought back to the beach tent for the admiration of one's family and neighbours.

Clams are the true *fruit de mer;* they are eaten raw, like oysters, and taste much better. They are sweet and scrumptious. There is a knack to opening the shell – one uses nothing sharper than a blunt kitchen knife or blood will flow. They make a simple and delicious meal.

How sad it is that the Lit, who is allergic to bivalves, cannot share my catch.

In the sand of the *Grand Plage,* when the tide is out, it is possible to catch the *couteau* or razorshell, a bivalve long and thin that lives in a hole some 15 or 20 inches beneath the surface. The *couteau* is edible but, to take a line from Ogden Nash, myself I find this claim incredible. By the time one has cleaned it and cut away the inedible portions one is left with a piece so small that it does not seem worth taking the life of even such a humble creature. Catching the little beast is something else, however, involving as it does a choice of two quite remarkable techniques both of which should be part of the armoury of the regular St. Cast holidaymaker. Whichever is chosen, the *couteau* should always be returned to its native habitat (throw it in the sea and it will quickly dig another hole for itself) or, if you cannot bear to waste it, find a French woman with a bucket and an old kitchen knife and give it to her, saying that it will be 'bon pour la soupe'.

The hunt for the *couteau* involves either a packet of salt or a piece of wire about two feet in length with the final one eighth of an inch bent at right angles to it. The salt technique involves 'putting salt on its tail'. Find a *couteau* hole – there are plenty, don't worry – it usually has a funnelled entry and the hole itself is about half an inch in diameter. Pour salt into the hole (about a dessert spoon full) and wait. When the salt reaches the creature it responds by getting the blazes out of this place just as fast as it can. It comes up the hole very fast and before you know it there is its top half protruding for you to grab; just be quick about it.

The wire based technology is even simpler. Pop the wire, bent end first, into the hole. Push it down until you reach the end, twist the wire round through ninety degrees and then pull out. If there was a *couteau* in the hole the wire will have hooked beneath one of its shells, the bivalve will have closed around the wire so that when you remove the wire the shellfish will appear, neatly kebabbed.

Having demonstrated your skill and knowledge to an admiring crowd simply slide the unharmed *couteau* from the wire and make your choice as to the method of disposal.

While on the subject of bivalves, let us not forget the humble cockle which grows in some abundance in the *Baie de la Fresnaye.* It is another of those creatures to be hunted when the tide is out and one's mood does not incline one to the pleasures of the *Bec Rond* or the pursuit of the clam or the razorshell. It is a gregarious little beast so that, in general, when one has found one cockle one has found many – but finding that first one has made many a tyro give up in despair after an hour or so on his knees, on wet sand, with a strong wind blowing across the flats, scrabbling with increasingly sore fingers, searching for that first unmistakeable small, solid mass with deeply striated shell that is the precursor of *hundreds* of his kin.

There is a tool for the job, naturally. A five pronged rake with a handle of, perhaps, 18 inches in length*. I have one but its original bright blue paint is in almost pristine state because . . . I also have the Lit and when it comes to the cockle hunt the Lit has no equal. Although she may not eat them she finds the exercise of her almost superhuman powers of detection irresistible and once persuaded from her deckchair and book and appropriately clad she knows no equal in *la chasse*.

The British method of cooking cockles is not, I believe, commonly used in France. We simply boil 'em and souse 'em in vinegar, eating them cold. The French make a little more of them, as you might imagine, but in whatever form they can never be regarded as part of *haute cuisine*. They are common food for common people but are no less good for that.

An interesting and little known fact that I will share with you here is that the eating of a large number of cockles will turn one's urine the most amazing shade of incandescent orange. It's a phenomenon I merely note in passing.

It is the sand eel or *lançon,* a thinnish fish of between four and seven inches, that offers the best opportunity for sport and excitement and the greatest likelihood of catching something delicious for the pot. The habit of the *lançon* is, when it senses that the sea is ebbing, to move close to the sandy sea bed and just before the sea goes, to bury itself in the sand – wherein it waits until the sea returns. But the fish only does this when the departure of the sea causes it some surprise; that is, when it has become used to having sea in which to swim, and then all-of-a-suddenly, the sea goes – which it does periodically when the cyclical sweep of tides causes a *grande marée* that is followed some 12 hours later by a *basse mer.* Just as it is with lobsters and crabs on the *Bec Rond,* the *lançons* are only to be caught when the water is at its absolute lowest.

It is not the case that very low water only occurs at three in the morning but it is true that only the low waters that occur at this unearthly hour that carry with them the atmosphere of excitement sufficient to make us, our French friends and the Diggle family, set out for an activity that is such hard work. The *lançons* are there to be caught at low water in daylight – but it isn't so much fun.

Lançons are only to be found on the lower reaches of the *Plage de la Fresnaye.* One meets one's friends in the small car park there and one is equipped with a good big torch and someone to carry it (Lit does this very well). One has an *houette,* a ploughshare on a long pole, obtainable from . . . yes, that's right, and someone to pull it through the sand (this has traditionally been me but I am willing to relinquish the honour just as soon as I can). Then you need a couple – one will do but a couple is better – of keen-eyed boys (girls will do but I haven't any and I think that girls might not enjoy getting their knees abraded by wet sand) to catch the fish. And you need a bucket – for the fish – which the torchbearer carries.

It is dark but you know where the water's edge is because you can see the torch lights of all the French people who got there before you. You find a spot and

---

* The rake is generally available from a well known sporting goods shop in St. Cast.

start to operate next to your friends, another family almost certainly, so that the competitive spirit may develop.

The *houette* is pressed hard into the sand that the sea has only just left behind and it is pulled through it so that a deep furrow is created. The torch follows every move of the instrument and so do the other two members of the crew, one on either side of the trench. Suddenly a *lançon* leaps. The crew has but a fraction of a second to catch it and pop it in the bucket. Miss it, misgrope for it in the wet sand and it is gone for ever. A sand eel can swim through wet sand as though it were water. Catch it and you all yell out in triumph. Your nearby friends redouble their efforts.

And so you go on. You search for more fruitful areas for like clams the distribution is not uniform; in one place you may start a dozen or more, in another none at all.

The puller of the *houette* gets well and truly tired after about an hour and hopes that by then one has sufficient fish for a good meal for three (the Lit rarely eats more than half a dozen) or, at the very least, more than the Gasquetons have caught – for these are your friends, the great enthusiasts for seafood hunting in all its forms and very competitive people. Now the Diggles are not competitive but when in the company of the Gasquetons they become so.

And what does one do with these poor dead fish? Well, much later in the day, after a nap, when one has recovered, they are rolled in seasoned flour and deep fried. It's as simple as that. They are truly worth the effort. They are also obtainable from one of St. Cast's several *poissoneries* at a price comparable with that of the humble mackerel but that is not what it is all about.

Now, who are these friends? They are part, as we are part, of *la famille St. Castine,* a group of people, all French apart from us, who have brought their childen to St. Cast almost every year from the time they were able to walk and talk. Those children were, I believe, all members of the *Club des Benjamins* at some time or other.

You have met the *lançon*-hunting Gasquetons. Father is Martial, mother is Colette and son is Martin. They live in Rheims and after years of renting the same primitive but very pretty little house in St. Cast, *Ker Nic,* they have built themselves a house and clearly intend to stay there forever with, no doubt, an eye on the next generation when Martin gets going on that front. Colette is a brilliant cook and speaks her own version of English that is heaps more effective than my version of French. Martial is a financial investment adviser; he plays Bridge and loves to eat and drink. When Martial comes to St. Cast he brings with him Perrier bottles filled with 40 year old (and occasionally even older) cognac; there is a family connection with the trade and he appears to have barrels of the stuff at home. A visit to the Gasquetons at around 11am is likely to result in an invitation to take a small glass of the wonderful drink, as Martial says, 'pour remonter la coeur'.

When we first met Jean-Pierre Montier, who lives in nearby Rennes and has been spending the two principal Summer months of the year in St. Cast all his life because his mother has a lovely house there, he was married to Henriette. They were a devoted couple and we became very fond of them. Then we learned that Henriette was dying of cancer. When we went to St. Cast in that fateful year she stayed indoors but invited all the ladies of our family to visit her so that they could say goodbye. We remember Henriette at our one and only 'grand party', the occasion when we managed to bring all the family together and to entertain them in such a way that they revised their views on English cooking. This is the memory of Henriette, laughing in the company of the people who loved her, that we shall never lose.

Jean-Pierre, now retired, was until very recently professor of violin at the Rennes Conservatoire of Music. His mother, known to us all as 'Mami' (pronounced *mah-mi*), was a professional violinist and, now in her mid-eighties still plays for pleasure. One of Jean-Pierre's daughters, Catherine, has recently left the Paris Conservatoire, and is a professional violinist. On one occasion in Rennes, in his last year at the Conservatoire, Jean-Pierre played a Vivaldi concerto grosso for three violins and chamber orchestra with his mother and his daughter.

After many years without Henriette, Jean-Pierre started keeping company with an old friend of hers, Monique, who is a very senior member of the Rennes educational inspectorate, specialising in English. Monique has quietly slipped into his life and now they are virtually man and wife. Those of us who love him are very happy about this.

Having both a combination of a house in St. Cast and the luxury of academic holidays all his life, Jean-Pierre has the advantage of us all. He arrives earlier in the year and leaves later. He does not have to put up with the inconsistencies of rented accommodation as we do, although when Henriette was alive and when his children, two daughters and a son, were with them he had to, the family presumably being too large for Mami's house. He owns a nice little sailing boat, about 21 feet long, that may winter in Mami's garage and spend the Summer at a mooring in the harbour. Trips from St. Cast out across *La Baie de la Fresnaye*, where occasionally dolphins may be seen, with Jean-Pierre are a delightful part of St. Cast holidays.

Jean-Pierre is very close to us. He was one of the first of the family with whom we became friends because, I suppose, along with his cousin, Jean-Louis and his wife, Sybil, he speaks excellent English.

Jean-Louis and Sybil Delage live in Paris, their two sons, Josse and Simon, are almost the same age as you, Marcus and Julian, and the family also spent its holidays in St. Cast. Like us, they always rented accommodation and like us, when circumstances called for it, were always able to transcend its inadequacies.

Jean-Louis' sister Jacqueline seems to visit St. Cast once a year but never predictably. She will suddenly appear, sometimes in the company of a personable man, to whom we will all be introduced, sometimes not. She has a son, David, and a daughter, Sophie, from a now long dead marriage, both of whom we meet occasionally but the lives of our children never crossed with the lives of hers and now both are well and truly grown up.

And then there is Colette Alric and her consort, Bertrand Canard. Colette teaches art and Bertrand, once one of her students, is an artist. Both live in Paris but in recent years Colette has been able to buy a lovely stone house in the *rue de la Semaphore* in St. Cast and now the two spend many weeks of the year there. They are very hospitable people and one of the first events of any holiday in St. Cast is a visit to Colette and Bertrand for dinner – drinks in the garden and then something delicious roasted on the open log fire. Bertrand is particularly close to Jean-Pierre and our trips out in the boat are usually accompanied by him.

The St. Cast family, during its heyday, traditionally met and socialised on the *Grand Plage*. A place would be chosen. Who chose it and how it was chosen remain a mystery to me. There would be a place and during the course of the morning everyone would drift down to that place and form a seated circle on the sand. The children would go off to the club. Groups would form for the purposes of discussion. Books would be read. Sun cream would be rubbed in. The women would all get up and drift off to look around St. Cast's limited supply of dress shops – the favourite was run by the elegantly tall and slim, sun-tanned and raffish-looking Guy, whom they all adored. Good looking and want to make a fortune? Open a dress shop, fellows. If the sea was in Jean-Louis and Martial would go out on their *planches aux voiles* for an hour. If it was out I might go off and find some *palourdes* or take a stroll across to the port.

At noon the children would return, desperate for food, and the beach would empty. Strangely the habit of making a picnic on the beach was not adopted by these folk and we all went back to our houses and apartments for lunch. Afternoons would follow a similar pattern. Children might well rush up seeking money with which to buy an ice-cream, a *crêpe* or a *pomme chausson* from the little stall run by St. Cast's classiest . . . what do I call the establishment that calls itself *A la belle meunière?* It is a *salon du thé*, a sort of tea-shop that serves pastries, tea and coffee at its elegant, if slightly faded, tables but it also serves all the usual alcoholic drinks and the most fanciful of ice-cream confections. The granite columns that present it to the main street seem always to have been there and they appear in the countless postcard views of the town over the years that are for sale in the several antique fairs that take place during the season. The columns frame a shop front that houses only a small part of its seating area, for the main business of the place occurs outside, on the pavement, where people gather during the day to take the sun with their drink or ice-cream or in the evening to watch the sun go down. Lit loves to leave the beach with me at around 5.30pm and drift over to the *belle meunière* and for us to take our aperitif there. At this time in the late afternoon we are each served, in addition to our drink, a small plate of freshly cooked – hot, straight from the oven – *feuillités,* savoury puff pastry snacks that almost compensate for the extraordinary cost of taking even the most humble of drinks there. The place is expensive by any standards but only there can one sit and watch the world go by and feel that you are truly on holiday.

With the absence of children the beach family is smaller and, what is sadder, the Delages seem to have abandoned the place in favour of trips to North America, the Far East and other excitements. To Jean-Louis and Sybil, who will inevitably read this book, I say 'All is not lost. Come home and be welcomed. The Diggles also take holidays in strange and exotic places – but we try always to spend a few days every year, at the very least, in St. Cast. Come and join us!'

The family corporate memory records a small number of excellent social events in its life. The first for us was a dinner party given by Sybil and Jean-Louis in a very sparsely furnished rented house. The theme of the table was mauve and purple, the colours of summer fruit, with clusters of blackberries decorating the room. The food was superb for Sybil is a very good cook. There Lit and I began to know something of the life in St. Cast.

Then there was another house party. Held on a balmy evening in an old, almost tumbledown cottage that was even more sparsely furnished than the earlier one and located in a square piece of land that appeared to have been cut out of a field of maize, the party took place out of doors against a background of these huge plants and was memorable for not only the large number of new friends we made but for the meal which had been improvised at short notice and had as its centrepiece sufficient *étrilles* (caught by a party led by Jean-Pierre who had taken his boat on the long trip to the islands known as the *Les Hèbihens* to catch them) to provide at least one for everyone present.

It was the great night of the *éclade* that made us feel we were becoming part of the family for until then we had always felt we were guests of our friends. An *éclade* is, I am told, an event most commonly held much further south, but it is particularly appropriate for a place like St. Cast where mussels are cultivated in profusion. In my earlier list of creatures to catch and eat in St. Cast I omitted the mussel because although they grow on most of the rocks they are usually very gritty and rarely turn out to be worth the effort of gathering and cooking them. In the *La Baie de la Fresnaye* they are reared on long poles stuck in the sand, *buchots*, and are free from sand. In St. Cast one buys mussels. When in Rome . . .

The *éclade* is a sort of mussel bake or roast. You take a large piece of waterlogged wood – we had an old, old door – that will not easily burn and has no paint on it. You prepare your mussels – a massive amount of mussels – and during the afternoon you carefully arrange them in a circle made up from a tightly packed spiral, all arranged the same way with the edge uppermost. I'm sure that the precise arrangement of the mussels does not make a tuppenny damn's worth of difference to how they eventually taste but this is France and tradition is important. We learned later that this business took three men of the party all afternoon to complete.

The large piece of waterlogged wood, bearing its burden of carefully arranged mussels, was carried carefully in the old van of one of our party to the remote little bay a few miles from St. Cast where all had agreed to meet. As we arrived several plastic sacks full of pine needles were produced – all gathered from nearby woods during the day. It was now nearly nightfall and we gathered on the small beach with the wine that had also arrived in the old van. What was to happen next?

The arrangement of mussels was placed on the sand and then covered with the light, dry pine needles. And then a match was put to it. Whoooosh!

After no more than a few minutes the roaring inferno subsided into a faint glow. The grey ashes of the pine needles were blown away and there was revealed a very large number of delicious roasted mussels – and we all (with the exception of the Lit who had to make do with some bread, cheese and a peach) piled in.

Eating mussels cooked in this way soon turns you into something resembling an end-of-the-pier minstrel for it is impossible to do justice to them without your hands and face becoming quite black. Imagine then the St. Cast family, well blackened, well into their umpteenth bottle of wine, now munching into the bread, cheese and peaches. It was a happy gathering.

Most of us also remember the evening for the decision of Jacqueline, Jean-Louis's sister (usually referred to by him as 'my naughty little sister'), to go for a swim in the sea which was some distance off across a rocky beach. She and her daughter, Sophie, stripped down to economically styled pants and they went off for what must have been an uncomfortable walk and a very brief swim in the cold, cold sea. It is a strange thing but although most of the ladies of the family sunbathed topless on the beach in full view of everyone the reappearance of Jacqueline, dripping wet, virtually naked, with goose pimples, made an impact and has stayed in all our memories and is still recalled in conversation. Colette Gasqueton has a photograph to commemorate the event and it reminds me that Jacqueline did look *very* good that night.

And that is how one conducts an *éclade*. Martial and Colette Gasqueton celebrated the completion of their new house in St. Cast in 1994 with another and the Lit and I collected the pine needles for it. It was another wonderful St. Cast evening with many of the family present – including Jean-Pierre's mother Mami, looking great as always – which we ended each with a balloon glass of Martial's 100 year old cognac, 'pour remonter les souvenirs'.

We made our contribution to the 'events' of the St. Cast family in 1985 when we were staying in a house right at the end of the *Impasse de la Poste,* just off the *rue de la Colonne.* The Lit and I decided to say thanks for all the good companionship and entertainment we had had over the years and lay on a really good party.

The house had a very large sitting room so we set out to create a table that would almost fill it. We put together every table we could lay our hands on and we assembled a massive affair that was almost exactly square with the various surfaces almost even. The whole was covered with white bed sheets. We went into a supermarket in St. Malo and bought the place out. Lit created a monster paella with langoustines, huge prawns and chorizo sausage poking out of saffron coloured rice. We had three complete brie cheeses, the ones that are about one foot across, and we had trays of peaches. We had wine to float the navy, including three bottles of a great *premier grand cru* sauternes, *Chateau Rayne Vigneau*. The room was soon filled with our friends and any of their assorted relatives who happened to be around at the time.

Outside the children had their own barbecue and a firework display – *feux d'artifice* are readily available in the Codec supermarket in the middle of town, no need to wait until Guy Fawkes Day.

It was on this evening that we first met Bertrand who accompanied Colette Alric; he was darkly handsome, looked slightly battered by life, and was reserved. Lit says that he scared her at first but he warmed up when the wine had started to flow.

As I have already told you, this was the evening that provides us with the frame for the picture of Jean-Pierre's Henriette. There she is, with huge smiles illuminating her bronzed face and us, a glass of wine in one hand and a cigarette in the other, radiating pleasure as she involves herself in animated conversation with those nearest to her.

The St. Cast story still has a few chapters to run (I hope!). As I write this I know that in just one month's time Lit and I will be setting off to Portsmouth for the overnight ferry to St. Malo. These days we take a de-luxe cabin which has television and video and a refrigerator full of soft drinks, a bowl of fruit and a man to wake us up in the morning with breakfast. It is hugely expensive and no doubt we'll succumb to the tunnel one day but just now it seems well worth it to travel in style, to enjoy a good dinner on the boat, and then to take breakfast in Dinard before driving the few miles to St. Cast, arriving in time to catch M De La Motte Rouge of the *Agence de la Plage* who has arranged this year's rental. Will it be all right? Just how 'oblique' will be the 'oblique vue de la mer' claimed by the descriptive leaflet for the apartment? Will it continue to be true, that statement I have drilled into all the St. Cast family, so that it is part of our lore, that in terms of weather, atmosphere, activities, events, food and drink, the number of *palourdes,* the new films being shown at the Cinema Eden, the pretty girls sunbathing topless on the beach, and the quality of the beds in one's rented accommodation, 'St. Cast never lets you down'?

I will leave St. Cast, the place that together with Burnham-on-Sea, is the resort that runs through it, our life, with one more story that adds to the reasons why I love the place. It does not take place in St. Cast but if we had not been staying in St. Cast we certainly would not have experienced the *Fête des Moules* at Tregon, which lies on the coast between St. Cast and Dinard.

The posters were up all over the area, advertising this village fair. There were lots of similar posters for *Fêtes* celebrating all kinds of things, corn, agriculture, agricultural implements, fishing, leisure, horses and so on; the one at Tregon was going to make a fuss of the mussel. It was scheduled for a Saturday in August. It was 1994.

Lit and I turned up at about 11am and expecting the usual car parking problem we left the car in the upper part of the village and walked down the hill to where we could see marquees and general fête type activity. There was a car park down there; an uncultivated field backing on to another bearing a fine crop of mature maize (which, on such festive days, traditionally doubles as a public convenience) and no admission charge. There was plenty of space – just park where you like.

The field where the main activities were to be held was just at the edge of Tregon's somewhat inadequate beach and was already well attended. The principal activity was clearly to be eating and drinking for the marquees were devoted to this. There was also a stage set somewhat incongruously in front of a huge road vehicle, a trailer of some sort that was entirely enclosed, identified as being the property of a milk company; this had an opening leading out onto the stage that was closed with a gaudy curtain made up of sequins. Our attention was drawn to the marquees.

This little village, with a population of only a few hundred, had set out to attract thousands and then to feed them with freshly cooked food. As you might find it in an English village putting on a fête, the organisation was based on old fashioned class lines and sexual demarcation. The organisation was under the tight control of middle class ladies in their fifties and sixties, all carefully made up, who wore neat white blouses and managed their labour force, which was predominantly male of all classes. We sat down at one of the several wine bars – a square of tables for serving, a canvas roof and tables and chairs for the patrons. It was possible to buy a single glass of wine but there seemed little point; a bottle was about £3. Service was provided by a horny handed son of the soil supervised most amicably by one of the ruling lady class.

The large marquees contained the equipment necessary to boil sufficient mussels and to fry sufficient chips for . . . however many people were going to turn up. Now consider this. Have you ever seen in Britain, anywhere, at any time in your lives, anyone attempting a feat of this magnitude? Think of what is involved. By mid afternoon my estimate was that there were at least 3,000 people there. Well, they had everything in place and were ready to go. The queues started to form and we joined one. Yes, we had to wait a while – behind a *France profonde* family the mother of which delayed our serving somewhat by trying to negotiate a price reduction as she was buying for six people – and when I had recovered from the shock of having the lady's casserole (she had brought one, planning to take out her spoils, I think) dropped on my sandelled foot, I had my plate filled with steaming *moules marinaires* and masses of those exquisite chips that only the French can turn out. Lit took the ham baguette option. We returned to our table, bought another bottle of wine and lunched.

But a French lunch does not consist of one course, surely? Of course not. There was another marquee and when we drifted over to it we found it full of tables and chairs. Service was in the hands of the female teenagerie of the village

– smart, attractive young girls delivering said service with a smile at high speed, all under the supervision of the same members of the village equivalent of the Women's Institute (Rather Well Off Division). Service of what? The far end of the marquee opened out and led into the back of a large refrigerated lorry that appeared to be packed to the roof with the highest quality, professionally made, patisserie. These folk were not relying on a few homemade cakes brought in by the locals. A row of machines was producing freshly made coffee. Coffee and *patisserie* completed the meal. All delivered in an atmosphere of calm bustle to a marquee packed with people. Very pleasing.

An announcement called us out into the sun where we found the crowd assembling around the stage. There was to be some dancing! Breton dancing. On to the stage trouped the local equivalent of Morris dancers, who stumped their way through some pretty turgid old folk dancing, interspersed with explanatory announcements from an equally turgid folk dance expert. Oh Lord! Then they were replaced by a children's accordian band. Oh Double Lord! My enthusiasm was flagging and it was beginning to look as if a third bottle of wine was going to be needed when there was a distinct change in the mood on and around the stage. The kids' squeeze-box band cleared off and a man took the stage bearing a hand microphone. 'Ladies and Gentlemen', he announced in voice that rose to a great crescendo, 'I present to you, LADYSWING!'.

At that a battery of loudspeakers produced a blast of music and the gaudy, sequined curtain in the side of the trailer opened. One after another, at high speed, came the most astonishing sight one could ever imagine seeing in such a truly rural setting. Beautiful, beautiful, *beautiful* girls! They wore the full showgirl costumes; huge plumed head-dresses, fishnet tights, bosomy costumes cut high on the thigh, glittering shoes. The music delivered volume and rhythm and out of the box danced these amazing creatures. They danced and they danced. The audience swelled to its maximum, quickly regaining all it had lost to accordians and Breton dancing.

There were half a dozen of them but it seemed as if there were more for no sooner had they delivered the first number than five of them disappeared back through the curtain leaving the sixth to take the microphone and sing, which she did *beautifully*. Then back came the five in a completely different costume, including short blonde wigs this time, all bearing microphones and then they all sang – *beautifully*. For half an hour or more these girls rang all the changes imaginable in their dress, their dance routines, their songs, their individual performances, whether singing or dancing. I counted about 15 costume changes. That trailer, the property of a milk company, must have been choc-a-bloc with racks full of costumes.

Lit and I stood about ten feet from the edge of the stage and studied this phenomenon closely (in truth, I studied it a little more closely than Lit). The girls, clearly a team from one of the Paris nightspots such as the Crazy Horse, stood close examination. Their skins were flawless under their stage make-up, which was, in itself, exquisitely applied. Their bodies, most of which were exposed, were slender and strong. They exuded youth and energy. To the pre-recorded music coming out of the loudspeakers they could dance and sing to the highest standards and yet, in spite of their professionalism, they did not once appear to look down on their rustic (present company excepted of course) audience.

Once or twice one of the girls went to the front of the stage and invited members of the audience to sing, offering them the radio microphone, and the invitation was instantly taken up without hesitation. Amazingly the people, chosen at random, appeared to know the words of songs that I had never heard before in spite of all my experience of France. Would this be so in Britain, I wonder? It seems to me that whenever Britons gather together and some form of singing is called for they cannot get much further than *My Way* for individual efforts and *Yellow Submarine* for singing *en masse* and even then there is a lot of fudging on the words.

Then it was over. The girls disappeared behind the curtain leaving every single one of us dazzled and delighted. We drank another bottle to them

Then it was not over. After a short break the music struck up again and out they came to do another show, with different costumes, routines, and undiminished vigour. Before the finale, which was delivered with amazing *brio* and included those terrifying splits that are approached from several feet in the air, there was one item that reduced us all to silence.

The group had started to sing a song the words of which were hard to pick out at first. They were singing a song called *Deshabille Moi*. Gradually the stage emptied and one girl was left alone on stage to finish the song. As she approached its end her clothes drifted away and she was left, not naked, but poignantly half naked and in that bizarre setting, standing in the sun before the astonished gaze of many, many people, she was applauded with our silence. And then, with consummate judgement of the moment, back came Ladyswing to pick up the music for their finale and the roar of appreciation for her and for them was unbearably joyful.

I will leave you with this image and you will know why my heart is in France.

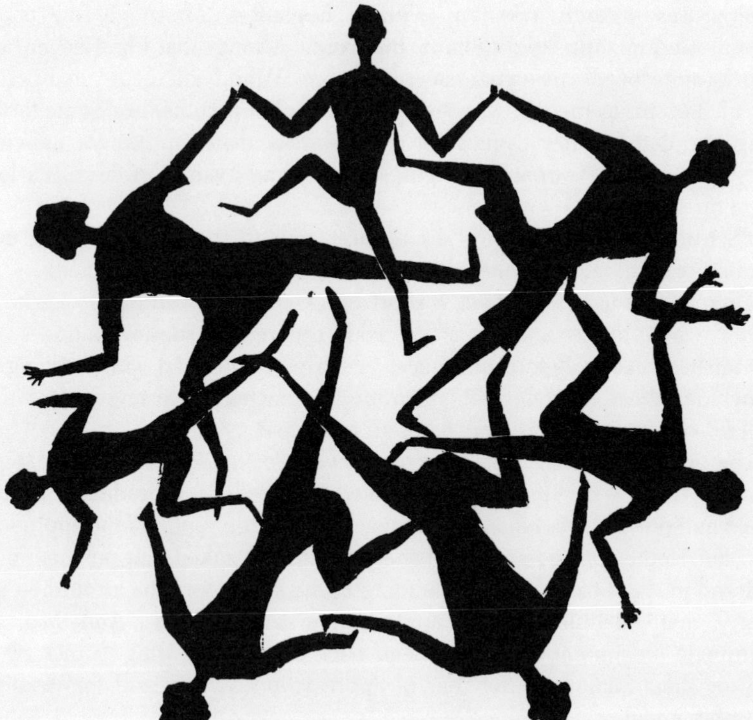

Chapter 16

'Give Him The Money, Godfrey, For Heaven's Sake Give Him The Money!'

The Midland Sinfonia, Nottingham (1967 – 1968)

So 1967 started with Keith and Heather in the first house they could, with only a moderate amount of self-deception and a polite nod in the direction of the building society, call their own. Keith's work with Midland Sinfonia produced a cheque at the end of each month and so did Heather's work with Nottinghamshire County Council; together the two cheques produced about as much as they required to live. They had two cars, the MG Midget that Heather now used for her peripatetic drama advisory work and a Triumph Herald for Keith that he used for daily travel to Nottingham, for his various journeys around the country to find work for the orchestra and to attend rehearsals and performances. They dressed better. They ate better. They had a little fun, sometimes. They were a happy pair.

At the beginning it looked as though it would last for ever but it couldn't and it didn't; that inner sense of dissatisfaction that had driven Keith through and away from his teaching work was to drive him through and away from the job he had worked so hard and risked so much to create within two years, and this, in turn, would take Heather away from the job she valued so much.

~

One day we bought a boat. It was a secondhand 'Mirror' dinghy that had been made by the owner of the Cotgrave garage and his son; they had outgrown it and had bought themselves a new 'Osprey', a terrifying craft with trapezes. I saw the 'Mirror' on the garage forecourt with a £50 price tag. A brief discussion with Heather and it, together with its trailer, was bought. It was, I believe, the first non-essential purchase of any substance we had ever made. There now, married for just over five years and we were wasting money on luxuries.

I couldn't sail. Sailing was one of those activities I had always wanted to do but there was never the opportunity of getting anywhere near a boat. My Father had owned a boat, one that he had made himself, during his bachelor days in Bath but he had abandoned sailing before he married and I came into the world. I had tried once or twice to teach myself but with near-disastrous results. Now I had a boat, but I couldn't sail it.

Our house was set within a small cluster of new houses, many of which had yet to be completed when we took over Number 4 Rectory Road. One house, in a court just over the way from us, had just been occupied by a young couple with a very small daughter, a child just old enough to toddle around pushing a toy pram. On the afternoon of the day when the 'Mirror' dinghy had been placed in my garage, when I was standing looking at it, admiring it and wondering how I was ever going to sail it, the male half of the young couple appeared. He smiled and nodded towards the boat, 'Nice boat,' he said, 'can you sail it?'. I admitted my deficiency. 'I can,' he said, 'would you like me to teach you?'.

That afternoon Heather and I, our new neighbours Roger and Heather Wilby and their daughter, Sarah, set off for a quiet spot on the River Trent, with the 'Mirror' dinghy in tow; there Roger taught me how to sail.

The Wilbys soon became good friends and still are.

~

This was the period when my parents' life went into serious decline. Curry Rivel went the way of Somerton Erleigh. It was not that my parents had outlived their usefulness in terms of helping to meet short-term social obligations – the dinner parties all crammed together into one short period of time syndrome – it was just a matter of changed family circumstances. Either way the result was the same; time to move on.

There was a damp thatched cottage near Wimborne in Dorset. We visited it once and found my parents very reluctant to talk about the job or the people they worked for. Then another move to Boxford, near Newbury, to an even damper thatched cottage and a *nouveau riche* employer of unspeakable awfulness.

At this point it seemed that we had to step in and do something to resist the gravity that was pulling these good people ever downwards. I found a small terraced house in Arnold, Nottingham and, on behalf of my parents, applied for a local government loan to buy it. I do not remember how much it was – a few hundreds of pounds I think. I applied for a council grant to improve it – to add a toilet and bathroom. At some point I discussed all this with my Father and obtained his, albeit reluctant, approval. At this stage in our lives and our relationship he seemed to view me with mistrust, as though the small, almost insignificant improvement in my fortune was the outcome of some fundamental dishonesty, some kind of smart-aleckry and he was at risk of being exploited by me. He was by then 66 and drawing his old-age pension and my Mother was the official breadwinner of the household.

I showed him all the figures: how much the house would cost, the size of the loan, the cost of the improvements (which I would put in hand and supervise), the amount of council loan and the amount of cash that would be needed. He would have to find £150 and we would come up with the rest, a similar sum. We would also pay him sufficient each month to cover the repayment of the council loan, which we would also guarantee. He trusted me sufficiently to agree. Am I being unkind to him? It must have been hard, very hard, now to feel beholden – and this is how he must have felt – to his son and daughter-in-law who were, to him, barely out of school. But his unwillingness did look like lack of trust at the time and, in view of the size of the commitment we were making, seemed ungrateful.

At last, *at last* the desperate, erratic movements, the expensive launch into the unknown of new employers and accommodation, the downward sweep like the ball of a pinball machine, knocking into this obstacle and being propelled into that obstacle, being swept upwards for a while and then dragged back down, was over. My parents ordered their last removal van and it deposited them and their furniture outside 172, St. Albans Road, Arnold. The removal men, ever scornful of those with little, bashed their belongings and left pieces of objects on the pavement. But it was over, at last it was over.

The caravan remained on its site at Brean, Somerset and as soon as the removal was complete and the first bright days of spring appeared they were off, the house locked up in March or April and left so until November while Mother and Father enjoyed a little retirement, a little time – a few years as it turned out – without having to bother about anyone but themselves. I am sure that Father hated the Arnold house; it was small and mean and it represented the material failure of his life, but it was nonetheless of value to him. While he and Mother spent their seven or eight months by the sea, living on the state pension, the house was there, all expenses paid, waiting for them and making clear to all that they were not the sort of people who had to live in a caravan; they were simply taking their annual holiday and would return to their Nottingham house at the end of the season.

This was the time when Father resurrected his writing ambitions. He dug out the piles of handwritten material he had produced during his bachelor days, bought a tiny, tinny portable typewriter from Boots, and set out to rewrite and type his first novel *The Life Chain* and then to start another that he called *The Youngest Hilton*. He also wrote a children's book *Trouble in Dogrose Dell* and another book, his last before his death, *Diadem for a Dog*. This last book was, like his first two, an ill-concealed autobiography but very much more transparently so; it covered the period from 1951 onwards and was about a domestic couple who moved from job to job accompanied by a Great Dane called Thor. This is a very revealing piece of work and reading it (which I did in the course of writing this book) made me sad. I learned, for example, that when they were working at 'Juniper', the students' hostel in Wanstead, and I was working as a supply teacher, their combined income was less than mine. In the book he comments ironically how Keith, his son, was complaining at the time about being paid 'shirt buttons'. Oh, Father! Oh, Father.

The writing occupied him happily when he was in the caravan. Mother provided the life-support system, enjoying the business of shopping and cooking and keeping him company. They were both in quite good health and I believe that the five years or so that they had together, wintering in Arnold and summering in Brean, wholly free of responsibilities, were among the best of their life together.

1967 then, also saw the end of my parents wanderings. Their list of places of residence dating from the move to Polebrooke in 1951 when I started at Laxton School to the time when Heather and I were able to obtain the Arnold house for them runs:

Polebrooke, Northamptonshire
Alconbury, Huntingdonshire
Wanstead, London
Bicester, Oxfordshire
Wanstead, London
Congressbury, Somerset
Somerton Erleigh, Somerset
Piddlehinton, Dorset
Rowberrow, Somerset
Kilve, near Torquay, Somerset
Princes Place on Yeovil to Dorchester road, Dorset
Midelney Place, Curry Rivel, Somerset
Wimborne, Dorset
Boxford, Nr Newbury, Berkshire
Arnold, Nottingham

It averages out at almost one job, one house a year. They, my parents, were surely benefactors of the furniture removal industry.

~

It was a time when we were forced to realise that the migraine from which Heather suffered and generally rose above on wings of aspirin, paracetamol or sometimes stronger drugs, had the potential to do serious damage. One evening, when driving home in our second Triumph Herald (the MG Midget had been traded in against the purchase of the more sober vehicle) Heather blacked out for a second or two and put the car into a ditch. A few months later, when driving the Fiat 600 that replaced the Triumph, the same thing happened again and she and the car passed through a large wooden bus shelter on the main road into Nottingham from Newark. In neither case was she anything more than shocked. Heather still has migraine but she has fortunately not developed what did at that time look like becoming a habit.

~

The most important thing in my life then was the orchestra. I had built the small administrative and financial base so I had my factory; what then was my factory going to produce? The Nottingham concerts were going well and I had managed to build up a respectable number of performances in other places. The need for a London performance grew within the small management group consisting of Neville Dilkes, David Cound and myself; we felt that we needed this in order to make the orchestra more significant to the Nottingham people, to the freelance musicians upon whom we relied and to the music press whose favourable reviews would help in obtaining more engagements. So on 21 February 1968 the Midland Sinfonia appeared in the Queen Elizabeth Hall on the South Bank, London. The conductor was Neville Dilkes, the piano soloist was Louis Kentner and the programme consisted of:

Divertimento for Strings, Bartók
Piano Concerto No 23 (K488), Mozart
Dumbarton Oaks, Stravinsky
Symphony No 39 in E flat (K543), Mozart

Wasn't that a lovely programme? Oh, how I had come to love Mozart! He alone made the career move worthwhile. It was a good concert and pretty well attended. We six, Neville and his wife Pamela, David and his wife Margaret, Heather and I, booked in to stay overnight at a hotel, waited up after the concert until the first editions of the papers were on sale and then scanned the reviews for mentions of Midland Sinfonia. They were not too unkind to us. We did get a review or two – I cannot remember how many, nor in which papers they appeared but I do remember that what they said was not at all bad.

~

You must remember that in those days, the mid-Sixties, there was little or no system of financial support for the arts and what there was was sporadic and as likely to be based on whim or old school tie as anything else. There was an Arts Council of Great Britain and it was gathering strength very rapidly but it concentrated on the major arts organisations in London and the major cities, and devoted little time or money to piddling little outfits such as ours. The network of regional arts associations was beginning to grow but there was not one for the East Midlands where we were based; in those days if you wanted subsidy you carved it out of granite. I devised a scheme that anticipated the funding base of the regional arts association and used this to make the orchestra grow.

I listed all the local authorities in Nottinghamshire, Derbyshire and Leicestershire and located within each county a place that had a hall suitable for a concert and an immediate population from which to draw. I then associated a small number of local authorities with each venue, using as criteria for selection their size of population and their relative wealth. For each 'concert centre' I then chose one of three basic orchestra sizes according to population within my chosen catchment area and capacity of the hall, and calculated how much money would

The First Concert of the MIDLAND SINFONIA ORCHESTRA
Leader: Ronald Thomas
in LONDON

QUEEN ELIZABETH HALL (South Bank)
General Manager: John Denison C.B.E.

Wednesday 21st February, 1968, at 7.45 p.m.

Programme
Divertimento for Strings . . . . Bartok
Piano Concerto No. 23 in A (K488) . . . . Mozart
Dumbarton Oaks . . . . Stravinsky
Symphony No. 39 in E flat (K543) . . . . Mozart

Conductor NEVILLE DILKES, Soloist LOUIS KENTNER (Piano)

Tickets 21 - 15 - 10/- 5 - from the box office, Royal Festival Hall,
London S.E.1. Telephone 01-928-3191, and usual agents.

*Presented by the Midland Sinfonia Concert Society Ltd.,
72 St. James's Street, Nottingham. Telephone ONO2 43653.
Concert management by Christopher Hunt Ltd., 5 Draycott Place, S.W.3. Telephone 01-589-9277.*

The Midland Sinfonia's London debut

be needed to subsidise a concert. Then I divided each sum of money between the local authorities in each concert centre (according to their wealth, the amount raised by a penny rate) so that if all contributed the sum required the concert would take place. I thus had a plan of concerts across each of the three counties and three lists of grant applications for the local authorities in each county. My message to each of them would be very simple, 'Give us this relatively small amount of money and an orchestra of this particular size (capable of performing a programme such as *this*) will give a concert in this place that is either within your area or close to it. If we have not planned a concert in your locality this year, we will give you one next year or the year after'. When I had done my sums and drawn up my three County Plans the idea I had to present was easy to understand and was not over-ambitious. I sent copies of the County Plans to the then Director of Music of the Arts Council of Great Britain, John Cruft, with a request that the initiative be backed with ACGB money.

Well, it worked! Many of the local authorities (which were in those days not tired of being pestered with requests for money) agreed to the scheme. Most important of all the ACGB came back to me with the equivalent of a hearty pat on the back; John Cruft thought the idea fine and dandy and some money would flow; most of the planned concerts would take place.

~

We added a series of Summer concerts to the Nottingham season and this led to my first steps in the field of commercial sponsorship of the arts. The tobacco company, John Player and Sons, had already started to assist arts organisations such as the Nottingham Playhouse and obviously saw this as being a way of showing the local community that it cared. I put my proposals for the series of Summer concerts to Godfrey Seager, the company's Head of Public Relations. He liked the idea but had to seek approval from Managing Director, Tony Garrett. The dates for the concerts grew closer and I heard nothing. The company was irritatingly concentrating more on making money from manufacturing and selling cigarettes than on sponsorship. There are a hundred and one arrangements to be made when promoting concerts and there comes a time, many weeks before the performances, when the financial side has to be buttoned up safe and sound; this time was getting distressingly close. My telephone calls to Seager's office were beginning to cause embarrassment for he was clearly unable to persuade his boss to approve the project.

In the week of this crisis I had an appointment with a photographer to take some publicity photographs and during the session an idea occurred. I had the man take a picture of me at prayer, hands pressed together while I looked pleadingly into the camera. The next day I had a print delivered to the public relations office with a note asking Seager to have the photograph placed, without explanation, on the desk of Tony Garrett.

The story of what happened next became part of company lore for many years after. The photograph duly appeared before the great man. Seager, waiting outside, heard nothing for several minutes and then he heard a huge guffaw of laughter from behind the door which then opened. Garrett called out to Seager, 'Give him the money, Godfrey, for Heaven's sake give him the money!'.

Midland Sinfonia's first series of John Player and Sons Summer Serenade Concerts took place and were held to be a great success.

The relationship with the company was maintained so that in the Autumn of that year of 1968, John Player and Sons made it possible for our orchestra to give a series of delightful concerts in the Wigmore Hall, London.

~

During this time we gave serious thought to the name of the orchestra which was, we believed, restricting the growth of our work. The word 'Midland' said that we saw our scope as being mainly the Midlands, which had been true and was still largely the case, but it also suggested that our musicians came from the Midlands – when everyone knew that the top-flight freelance musicians mainly lived in London. We decided to become the English Sinfonia. At the same time the Newcastle-based Northern Sinfonia, which employed its own group of full-time musicians, made the same decision to change its name for almost certainly the same reasons and it too chose to become the English Sinfonia. A dispute arose.

It was at this time that I learned something of how the 'system' works. I was in the studios of the newly launched BBC Radio Nottingham when I was called to the telephone. I had been tracked down by a very senior member of the Arts Council's Music Department who needed to speak to me urgently. The burden of the man's message was that it had been decided that Northern Sinfonia should become the English Sinfonia. What right had the Arts Council to make such a decision? I asked. It wasn't a matter of a right, the man said, it was just that they . . . preferred it to be so. He became a little more specific. If we didn't go along with the Arts Council's preference then the orchestra would suffer financially and . . . now mark this, dear readers . . . my own career would not exactly benefit either. I told him that the decision to change had been made, the changes had been registered at Companies House, and that was that.

I'll never know to what extent the orchestra suffered nor if I ever suffered personally, for the way the system works makes it impossible to tell.

~

What was I doing in the studios of BBC Radio Nottingham? I was presenting my own record programe, which I did every week for more than a year. There was then something of that exciting atmosphere of Corby in the air (indeed, I believe that Britain then was generally a much more exciting place than it is today) and when I came up with the idea of doing a record programme entitled 'The Best Of Everything' it seemed only natural to put the idea to the station manager. I had in mind just one programme made up of eight records that were each in their own way absolutely the best of their kind. He invited me for a chat and I was asked to do eight such programmes under that title – so I had to come up with 64 records that were 'The Best Of Everything'. After eight programmes I was asked to continue so that by the end of a solid year of broadcasting I lost count of how many 'bests' I offered my listeners. What I loved about doing the programme was the way it called on my musical tastes in the broadest way and enabled me to share them. Thanks to Father for developing those tastes in me.

~

Everything seemed to come together in 1968. All the plans that we had worked on when the orchestra was being managed from the spare bedroom of 75, Farmstead Road, Corby now came to fruition. But the frustrations also matured.

The frustrations stemmed from the fact that although it is easy to throw one's energies into building something like an orchestra it is harder to devote those same energies to the welfare of another human being, particularly one who is reluctant to share the workload. A situation had developed where the income of our conductor and musical director, Neville Dilkes, depended almost entirely upon my success in finding work for and promoting the orchestra. He appeared to me to be sitting at home doing very little while I devoted most of my time to working at projects that would ultimately benefit him – and, after a while, I found this . . . frustrating.

It was better that we parted and towards the end of the Wigmore Hall series of concerts I resigned. Just as when I had resigned from my teaching job I had no job to go to. Oh, that is such a dangerous thing to do!

The newly formed Merseyside Arts Association advertised the post of Director in the *Sunday Times* a week later and I applied. I was shortlisted for interview and on a grim November day I travelled to Liverpool to meet those who were to be my new masters. Soon I was to wonder just what I had let myself in for.

Chapter 17

I Remember Darkness ... But There Was To Be Light As Well

Merseyside Arts Association (December 1968 – September 1973) and the First Great Sea Adventure

I have only the most miserable of memories of those first few months in Liverpool as director of Merseyside Arts Association. I remember darkness, rain and snow, loneliness and unfriendly people. My feelings towards the place improved with time but there was hardly a day in the five years I spent there when I did not want to be somewhere else; indeed I started to apply for jobs within three months of my arrival there.

There also lay ahead in our lives darkness far more profound than that of a gloomy city in Winter but there was to be light as well.

Looking at the other candidates for the job when I attended the interview by the selection sub-committee that dismal November day in 1968 I was struck by the overwhelming impression that no-one of any merit wanted the job. My appointment was a walk-over, not because I was an outstanding candidate but because the knowledgeable folk stayed well clear of the political hotbed that was Liverpool. When Ron Hodson, the Town Clerk's left-hand man (his right-hand man was one John Fennell who was a very much more senior and infinitely craftier fellow) came out to announce that I had been selected my feeling of elation at having pulled myself out of the ranks of the unemployed so soon was at war with the sinking feeling that was taking my spirits to my boots.

I had faced a small group of people, some councillors from local authorities in the Merseyside region, including Liverpool, and some local arts representatives, all of them under the chairmanship of an elderly Tory Liverpool alderman who, I later learned, was holding the chair to keep another alderman, a Labour man, whom he detested and who had designs on the job, off it. This was very much the Liverpool way of doing things. The chair of this new arts association was seen as another relatively easy way of getting some power and an almost certain route to getting an 'honour', letters after the name or even a knighthood. That was why the Tory alderman wanted to keep the other one out. The experience of the interview remains filed in my memory alongside the 'star chamber' interview when the head boy and prefects of King's School, Grantham, met to decide whether I should be given lines or a beating.

I was required to return a week later to meet the full executive committee, some 25 people. The timing of the meeting made it necessary for me to stay over in a hotel. When I telephoned Ron Hodson to confirm details he told me that he had booked me into a hotel for the night and that I should submit my claim for expenses immediately afterwards. I asked him how much the hotel would cost; it would be 12/6. I told him I assumed that the Merseyside Arts Association would cover this cost. Er . . . um. I would receive the official allowance paid to a Principal Officer Grade 3 for an overnight stay; it would be 11/6. Not a lot of money was involved but it symbolised the nature of the relationship that would exist between us.

~

MAA had been set up by Liverpool City Council which saw itself, quite accurately, as being the principal provider of the arts not only for the City but also for a much wider region controlled by local authorities that paid not a farthing towards those pleasures enjoyed in the City by their inhabitants. Now that money was starting to flow from national government into the Arts Council of Great Britain and from it into the regions, and now that the regional arts association idea was drawing support from the ACGB and local authorities, Liverpool saw a way of pulling in some national money and money from those other local authorities that had been hitherto sitting on their hands.

So MAA was set up by Liverpool and run by Liverpool during its first phase. The other local authorities, places like Bootle, Birkenhead, Ormskirk and so on, were invited to nominate representatives and so the executive committee was, in terms of geographical spread, representative of the region as a whole. When Liverpool looked to the arts organisations themselves they could see only those that were Liverpool-based, because there were very, very few outside Liverpool. When a meeting was held to select and elect arts representatives the people chosen were almost exclusively from the City. The local authority representatives held a constitutional majority on the committee so in geographical terms it was a regional body but the arts organisations were from Liverpool and the most powerful local authority present was Liverpool City Council. When I surveyed this group of people that made up the committee there was little doubt in my mind that this was a Liverpool piece of mutton dressed up as a regional lamb.

To make matters more difficult MAA, having been created as a Liverpool initiative, was from the outset in the hands of Liverpool local government officers which meant that all meetings were convened by Liverpool City Council officers, the Honorary Secretary of MAA was the Town Clerk of Liverpool, the Honorary Treasurer of MAA was the Treasurer of Liverpool. Meetings of MAA executive committee were held in Liverpool Town Hall. The Liverpool piece of mutton was firmly placed in a Liverpool oven.

My job was to develop the arts in this region and the only way I could do this was to carry this disparate group of people, councillors from all over the region, representatives of arts bodies from Liverpool and officers who were the paid servants of Liverpool City Council, with me.

Had I, poor soul, appreciated at the time the depths and currents of the political maelstrom into which my desire to find honest employment had thrown me, I do believe I should have willingly gone back to schoolmastering!

~

When I started this difficult job at the beginning of December 1968 I had nowhere to live in Liverpool. Heather was still doing her job in Nottinghamshire and our home was still in the village of Cotgrave, outside Nottingham. Heather gave in her notice of three months as required by her contract but that had to be worked out and meanwhile she had to live in Cotgrave. I took a rented room in a benighted part of Liverpool; a cold, unfriendly room in a cold, unfriendly house, and travelled to it early on Monday mornings and returned home from it on Friday evenings. I naively waited for the gestures of simple friendship towards the new director, the 'Do pop in for a drink after work one evening' or 'Would you like to come to dinner one evening, say on Wednesday, when you probably need company the most?'. Eventually there was one invitation to dinner but that turned out to have a hidden motive.

~

Ron Hodson had done a little of the preparatory work necessary to setting up the new Association. There was a written constitution and an executive committee – and he had hired a room for me in the Crane's Building, Hanover Street. That is all there was when I arrived – a room, a bare room with nothing but a telephone.

At least I had done it before, the starting out with the barest essentials, but the fact that I could do it did not seem to me to be sufficient justification for requiring me to do it. Looking back over my life it has struck me that since I left teaching I have never once occupied a warm chair, never taken a job that someone else had done before me so that the snags were ironed out, the policies established, the structures worked out and put in place. With the MAA job there wasn't even a cold chair. There was a catalogue of office furniture with pictures of several chairs – a telephone – and me.

~

The salary was poor also. On the day I arrived to meet the executive committee the Liverpool Post carried a story on my appointment, 'Earning

£3000 a year will take real art', its headline said. Apparently the size of my salary was already a controversial issue and there on the page were photographs of Liverpool arts people (including a couple of members of my committee, which worried me slightly) with their quoted views on MAA and its decision to pay me so much money. I had been appointed at £2,500 a year. I took the newspaper cutting and before filing it I crossed out 'Earning' and replaced it with 'Getting'.

~

Heather and I hunted high and low for a house in Liverpool, somewhere close to the centre so that it would be easy to get to all the evening events that I should have to attend. Of straightforward, non-professional social contacts there were none but my diary was full of invitations to exhibitions and performances. Why was I so popular? The newspaper article had also spoken of MAA's job as an arts funder and therefore many saw me as being the driver of the gravy train. Whatever the motives of those who invited me to spend an evening with them my first task was to familiarise myself with them and what they did, so I accepted the invitations and became very busy, very quickly.

We could not find a house that we liked and could afford in Liverpool. We learned of a house in Lower Heswall, on the Wirral, that large lump of land between the Rivers Mersey and Dee that is situated between Liverpool and North Wales. Lower Heswall was in Cheshire and was posh. In tones of warning I was told to bear in mind that only middle-class folk lived *there*. Of course a lot of middle-class people lived in Liverpool as well but they played the Liverpool game, even affected Liverpool accents, and so escaped censure. Liverpool loves to despise things. The accent and speech patterns of the place lend themselves to vituperation. The people of Liverpool are romantic and sloppy about their ugly city and its people and viciously contemptuous of those who live 'over the water' (or anywhere else for that matter). I quite liked the idea of being thought of as middle class; it would make a change.

So, for about £5000, we bought the house we could afford in Lower Heswall and damned the warnings of the Liverpool folk who somehow thought it wrong that the director of the region should live in the region. We bought it in a hurry, in the dark. We saw a large semi-detached Victorian house in an appalling state of disrepair occupied by a strange family that appeared never to clean anything, whether the house, the furnishings or the children, and a St. Bernard dog that was tied to the door of the refrigerator. It was cheap enough to be afforded by a couple with only one member earning a salary for, you will remember, Heather had resigned her job in order to be with me.

Most young couples dream of buying an old house to renovate. We, in our haste, ignored all sensible precautions and leapt in to commit ourselves to this house because we too had this dream. When we revisited it and saw it in daylight we were . . . thrilled. The house, 'Glenelg', was in a wide road, Park West, that led down to the . . . sea! We did not know this when we viewed the house. There was the Dee estuary just 100 yards down the road, seven miles of sea and then there was the Welsh coast. As the local estate agents had it, 'Uninterrupted views of the Welsh hills'. The road was lined with grand and beautiful houses and ours was the only one to let the place down. At the end of Park West there were boats bobbing at their moorings. What are the 'Three Ps' of property buying? Place. Place. Place. We had all three. We had a fourth as well: Potential. We could even add a fifth P for we were soon to live in a Palindrome, were we not?

We could (and did) do something about the state of the place later on. Perhaps later on we might even buy a bigger boat, who knows?

So, in the Spring of 1969, we moved to our thrilling new house, leaving behind our friends the Wilbys and taking with us their promise to visit us often. They did not break their promise and they became regular visitors. We still had the 'Mirror' dinghy and sailing was now rather more exciting than it had been on the River Trent in Nottingham and was to become even more exciting later on.

∼

After a short while I worked out my plan for developing the arts on Merseyside. It was simple enough, it reflected the situation that existed at the time in the region as a whole and it took account of the political realities. Within Liverpool there were plenty of arts bodies and grants from MAA would help them do more and do better; this was essentially all the Liverpool people on the committee wanted but I added another element. If nothing much was happening in the wider region then MAA would make it happen by promoting events itself. My theory was that an active promotional policy would galvanise local people into action. We would make contact with the groups that did exist and invite contact from the individuals who wanted to see more going on. Eventually, we would encourage the formation of local arts associations, run by amateurs, that would exist to promote small-scale professional events. MAA could then help by organising regionwide tours of appropriate performing groups and by providing money to support their promotion.

At the beginning by no means all local authorities had agreed to join MAA and to support it financially (a regional arts association was intended to be funded from national and local sources) and I believed that a policy of regional development that would promote events and provide grants only in the areas of local authorities that had joined MAA, would ultimately create a 100% local authority membership. Liverpool need not be excluded from the direct promotion of events; if there were gaps (as there certainly proved to be) then we might well attempt to fill them.

I hoped that this policy, sound as I believed it to be for the people in the region, would also be the best way of approaching the politics of the executive committee. There was always to be a constitutional majority in favour of local authorities but the voting bias of the committee as a whole was, at the beginning, very much in favour of Liverpool. By adopting a truly regional policy the support of the local authorities outside Liverpool would be strengthened and their number would grow in time. Even the Liverpool councillors and their officers could see the advantage of getting more support from the non-Liverpool local authorities and as none of them were particularly passionate about any of the art forms they did not seem to mind if MAA spent money on the arts outside the city; their initial hope was that eventually a strong MAA would reduce the cost of supporting the arts in the city but this disappeared with the passing of time. Opposition would come, as I knew it would, from the representatives of the Liverpool arts organisations, who did not really want a regional body at all, they really wanted a Liverpool Arts Association – and bugger the rest.

~

Looking around the room when I met my committee, as I did every month for five years, I saw little to love in the faces of these members of the Liverpool arts community. They were not artists. They were people who, for whatever reason (and they were in most cases perfectly good reasons) were involved in running amateur arts organisations. In London they might have been called 'the great and the good' but in Liverpool a more appropriate description would have been 'the average and the not bad'. They proved to be more of an impediment than a benefit to a director whose brief was to develop the professional arts across a region. It was a shame that the professional managers of the City's great symphony orchestra, two subsidised theatres and art gallery of national reputation had not been voted onto the committee but I suspect that the chairmen of *their* committees had indicated that they should not stand. In such a highly politicised place it would not do for paid officers, no matter how experienced and how great a contribution they might make, to speak for organisations that had perfectly serviceable, unqualified, inexperienced chairmen to speak on their behalf – and the MAA committee was, after all, one of the routes to that Honour that they all had in mind. If this seems cynical I will cite the Labour alderman whom the Tories had decided to keep out of the chairmanship when MAA was founded. Labour alderman Harry Livermore was at that time chairman of the Royal Liverpool Philharmonic Orchestra and of the Everyman Theatre; eventually, when the Tories lost control of the city, he became chairman of MAA as well. Three of a kind is a winner. Harry got his knighthood.

In the early days, when I was fresh and innocent, I was wooed by one of the non-local authority members, a man who was chairman of one of the local societies. He was the one who issued my only social invitation during my first lonely three months; I went to dinner at his splendid house and met his charming wife and was encouraged by his friendliness. When Heather joined me and we moved into the Lower Heswall house he offered us the use of a holiday house he had in North Wales and we spent a week there in the early Summer of 1969 with Roger and Heather Wilby and daughter Sarah. Soon after he invited me to lunch and told me quite directly that he fancied being the next chairman of MAA and

arts alive merseyside

THE FREE MONTHLY MAGAZINE OF
THE MERSEYSIDE ARTS ASSOCIATION
NUMBER 26 DECEMBER 1971

Outside Woolworths in Church Street/by the traffic lights, opposite the Tatler Sinema/ stands the little God man/He's only a little God man/standing there in his waterproof spiritual waistcoat/blessing people as they cross the road/He blesses me every day/and as he does/the changing lights/confirm his special relationship with God

An issue of my first magazine, *Arts Alive Merseyside*.
Sketch by Vincent Finn. Poem by me

suggested that I might set about arranging it. Soon after that embarrassing incident (for I could not and I would not help the man) the chairman of the day, a Tory, a nice man who knew nothing of the arts and cared less, saw me and commented that I seemed to be fairly close to this committee member. 'Be careful of him', he said, 'He was, you know, the only member of the committee to vote against your appointment'. Oh, we live and learn, do we not!

~

I put my policy in writing – a paper of only three or four pages – and set it before my committee. There was some discussion and it was accepted. It formed the framework of everything that I and the small staff that I was able to enlist did over the next few years. The programme of directly promoted events was labour intensive, requiring our personal supervision during both day and evening when there were performances and a considerable amount of travelling as touring programmes were required to visit as many parts of the region as possible. The numbers of events that we initiated and promoted ran: 1970/71 – 76; 1971/72 – 90; 1972/73 – 78. It would have been far, far easier to have stayed in the MAA office armed with a cheque book and to have made policy through grant making – and some other regional arts associations did just that. We also had a cheque book and maintained a grant-making policy in parallel with our direct promotions. We were thus a busy little team.

At the beginning there were hardly any local groups to help us but there were volunteers, people who showed an interest and made themselves known to us. One was an employee of the Inland Revenue, Peter Bevan, who was involved in one of the first local arts associations, that of Birkenhead. Peter made himself so useful that when I advertised for an assistant director and he applied for the job his appointment was a foregone conclusion. Peter was my assistant for some four years and when I left he took over as director. After I had gone Peter recruited yet another person from the same amateur-run local arts association to help him.

I started a magazine, called *Arts Alive Merseyside*, that was based on an earlier listings sheet called *Arts Alive* that the Bluecoat Society for the Arts had been publishing for a few years. It was monthly, had but eight pages, was printed in a variety of colours but almost never more than two at a time. It carried events listings and news about local arts activities. With a free circulation of around 16,000 it was also a very valuable communications tool for MAA and we used it to explain what we were doing and why we were doing it. It was a modest little thing but it stands comparison with contemporary publications with similar intentions.

Much committee business consisted of discussion on applications and my accompanying recommendations. As you might well imagine, this activity was the most divisive as local authority people attempted to fight their own geographical corner and Liverpool arts people fought to keep money in the city.

My ally throughout most of this time was the Labour alderman, Harry – later Sir Harry – Livermore, the man who had set out to obtain the clutch of arts chairmanships that would get him his Honour. He was a solicitor and had a strange reputation – for being surprisingly rich for a Labour man and for his creativity in court; the local saying went, 'If yer guilty, get Harry'. He was a rough, tough old philistine and I did not like him very much but he was of the old school and did not believe in barking when he owned a dog. The understanding I had with him was that I would make sure that all favourable publicity went to him and in return he would back me. Harry's aldermanic seat had been abolished by the Tories and when I first met him he held his place on the MAA committee by virtue of election; he was not a local authority member. He was thus able to associate himself with those elected arts community members while knowing precisely how the political machine of the city functioned. Harry had favours he could call in and strings that he could pull.

Harry's roughness and toughness helped establish MAA's regional status. Although MAA was described as a regional body by the Liverpool City Council people it was not recognised as such by the Arts Council. We were seen as being a 'sub-region' of the North West Arts Association that was based in Manchester and it was intended that our national money should be funded through NWAA. The rivalry between Liverpool and Manchester is legendary and only someone based in London could have ever believed that such an arrangement would work. Harry determined to knock this idea on the head within a few days of taking office as chairman.

Harry wrote to the Chairman of the Arts Council of Great Britain, Lord Goodman, and asked for a meeting. Harry and I then travelled to London with Harry going over and over his strategy for the meeting. I would say this and Harry would say that and they would probably say this, and so on. We went in to see Lord Goodman. Harry told him what we wanted. Lord Goodman agreed. And that was that. Could anyone else have achieved such a walk-over? I doubt it. First there was motivation: Harry detested the idea of having to go 'cap in hand' as he put it, to Manchester. Then there was reputation: Harry was known far and wide as a street fighter who generally won his cases. There was doggedness: Harry gave every impression of being capable of carrying this fight on for ever if need be. Lord Goodman, who had defeated many more eminent and powerful opponents, just couldn't see this particular fight as being worth the light – and probably the issue did not matter so very much to him anyway.

~

While the affairs of MAA were bubbling away and I was doing a fair job of implementing that policy of mine, we, Heather and I, were developing other personal ambitions, the most important of which was the desire to become parents. The need grew and as it grew it seemed harder to achieve. We had almost reached the state of desperation, the point where Heather's gynaecologist was talking about the possibility of adoption, when she became pregnant.

(I will take a break here from what I hope will have read so far as easy narrative and admit that at the time I am writing this I do not know how to describe what then happened, nor if I can begin to convey how I felt at the time. What I can say is that until this time I have kept the dates of the birth of our first son and of his death just a few weeks later so deeply hidden in my mind that I have never been able to recall them. Until I asked the Lit to tell me – these dates being branded into her consciousness – I could not even have stated the year in which our awful tragedy occurred. I have simply blanked out the memory of his short life until this time when he takes his place, his tiny little place, in our life story.)

Piers Winfield Diggle was born in Alder Hey Hospital on 29 August 1970. His was a long and difficult birth. Full of the bravado of the novice father I was present throughout and I emerged a more sober person. After a few days Heather and Piers came home and there we were, a proper family. I will not attempt to describe our son nor how we felt about him; your own imagination will tell you this.

Most babies have a tendency to regurgitate their food and so neither we nor our doctor saw anything to concern us in Piers' difficulty in keeping his food down, but after two or three weeks the problem seemed to be more severe and we sought advice. We were offered the usual solution of using a thickened feed and Heather persevered, patiently helping our son to eat and coping with the results of his body rejecting the food. The regurgitations became more severe and developed the character of projectile vomiting. The specialist to whom we were referred diagnosed the problem as *pyloric stenosis*, a condition of the pyloric sphincter muscle at the top of the stomach that will not allow food easily to pass through it, a condition that most children grow out of, but some do not and for these an operation is necessary.

I do not remember for how long we waited in the hospital for the consultant to find the time to examine our son and I do not remember why he took so long before he decided to operate. Piers was getting weaker by the hour and I could see the concern on the faces of the nurses as they too waited for the man, the consultant, to act. I do remember the feeling of complete helplessness in the face of this man's refusal . . . even to speak to me. He was such a *grand* man, such a superior being that even his decision not to make a decision had to be accepted.

Piers died on 20 October 1970, during the operation. The coroner decided that there would be a *post mortem* hearing and the coroner's officer, a retired police sergeant, told me that I must go to the hospital mortuary to identify my son's body. I was distressed and I was angry. I could not do this. He told me, quite brutally, that I had no choice.

As I hesitated before entering the room where Piers' body lay the attendant who escorted me, a kind man, held me by the elbow. He whispered to me that all I had to do was enter the room and then leave it, and added that no-one would know whether my eyes were open or closed. He held me as I took a step or two through the door and then gently pulled me back again.

At the hearing several weeks later I was greeted by the same coroner's officer who had by now read the *post mortem* report. He apologised for the way he had spoken to me before and said that now he could understand why I had been so angry; it was all contained in the report.

It was strange to see a battery of lawyers facing me as my son's death was discussed so calmly and clinically. The lawyers were there to represent the consultant, the anaesthetist, the male nurse who assisted them and the hospital. Why? Did they feel guilty about something?

I made no accusations. I was given the opportunity to ask questions but I declined. I did not want vengeance and I could not have understood the explanations of what went wrong beyond the fact that air had entered a vein, a vein that should have sealed itself after an incision, and that my son had been in a very weakened state prior to the operation and had not the strength to survive. Or something like that.

What I remember most about the time after our son's death was taking Heather for a walk after his funeral, a walk on heath land on the Wirral, where there was growing heather in profusion. The air was clean and the wind stung our faces as we walked, hand in hand, and thought of . . . I don't know what we thought of, we were just feeling very, very sad.

I remember the physical effect of grief on me at the time of his death, a cry that tore itself from me, that overwhelmed me, a cry that I could not control.

∼

My dear Father died on 4 July 1972. I came into the office one morning and one of my staff, Lynne Burton, took me by the arm and gently walked me into my own room. My Mother had telephoned to say that he had died that morning, in the caravan at Brean. He had been writing, typing away at that old portable typewriter of his, when his heart stopped. She had been out shopping, doing what she loved to do, preparing for the midday meal, ready to sit down with him, for a chat about nothing in particular, perhaps about the number of butterflies fluttering about the marguerites planted in the old Walls ice-cream tins around the caravan, 'Valstar', and when she got back he was lying on the floor. His heart had just stopped and he was gone from us. Those few years without having to be a sort of odd-job man in the houses of the wealthy, of doing nothing in particular, of not worrying very much about money, those years of not realising exotic dreams but just being with the Mums, walking in the duners, swimming in the dark brown sea, imagining what it might be like to be a successful writer, were over. I sat at my desk and the crying tore itself from me just as it had done when Piers had died.

∼

Marcus Charles Winfield Diggle was born on 15 December 1972. He was as beautiful as Piers only stronger and he thrived. He became the focus of our lives.

∼

Just as the desire to move away from teaching grew in me and eventually caused me to throw it in I was now developing a very serious desire to write. I did not necessarily want to be a writer (although that would come). I just wanted to write. I wanted to be in print. The little monthly newsletter I had started, *Arts Alive Merseyside,* gave me an occasional opportunity to produce something that was not simply news in brief, but this was not enough. I set my sights on *The Guardian.*

My first submission was on the topic of infertility (of which we had experience as for a couple of years it was thought that we would not have a family) and the death of Piers. The newspaper accepted it and, without telling me, carried it in the weekly digest newspaper it produces for overseas readers. I was deluged with letters from every part of the world and the newspaper carried a representative sample of them a few days later. I felt that I had made my breakthrough.

Subsequent pieces, written late at night, often while waiting for Marcus' first night-time feed, did not find favour. I sent my articles to *The Guardian's* Northern Features Editor, John Course, and I soon became familiar with his economical style of rejection. But I had managed to avoid the standard letter of rejection, the 'The Editor thanks you . . . but . . . ' letter. John Course would often give a reason and would sometimes even offer a word or two of encouragement.

Then I had an idea. The wife of Prime Minister Harold Wilson, Mary, was coming to give a reading of some of her poems with a well-known Liverpool poet and artist, the then rotund Adrian Henri. I called Adrian Henri, whom I knew very slightly, and suggested that I interview him for a piece that would 'hang' on the poetry recital. The piece started *'Worth his weight in stolen hubcaps', they say in Liverpool 8. 'One of our cultural heavyweights' they say in Bluecoat Chambers.* And the dear old Grauniad bought it. I spoke to John Course and he said that this was 'good stuff', not like the first piece which hadn't been at all well written but was 'real', which was why he took it. It was just as well he hadn't told me that at the time or I might never have gone on with my ambition.

So, I felt I might have some future at the writing game.

~

The sailing desire did not go away. The 'Mirror' dinghy was no good for those waters at the bottom of the road that rushed in and out at a furious pace twice a day. It was no place for a sailing dinghy. A small cruiser perhaps? Something that could live down there together with the other boats. A boat that would float when the sea came in and would settle down comfortably onto a pair of bilge keels when it went out. Not too big but big enough to be stable, big enough not to capsize – and big enough to . . . sleep in? *Sleep* in?

A man in West Kirby was selling his 'Caprice' sailing cruiser because he wanted some money to enable him to install central heating and he was happy to accept £600. I trundled the boat home behind the car with its unstepped mast

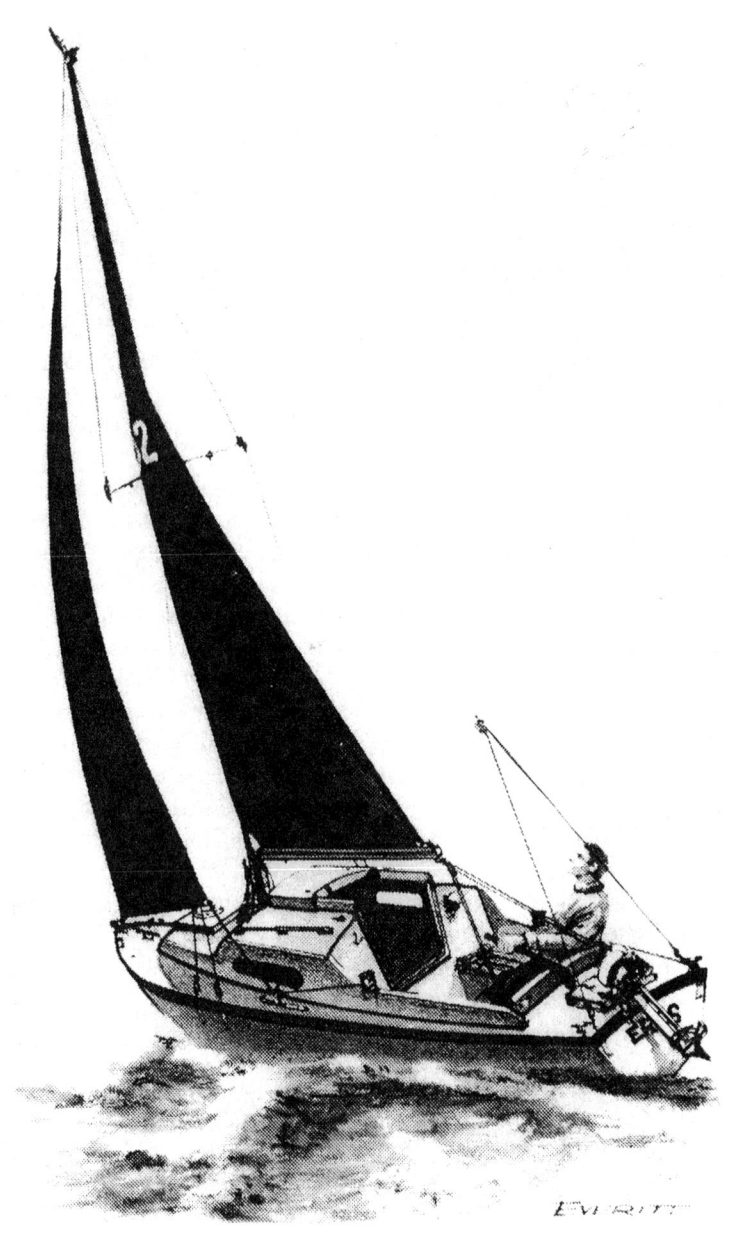

My boat *Eros,* as sketched for Practical Boat Owner
by Dick Everitt (used with permission)

flapping and bits of wire, rope, fenders and other miscellaneous items threatening to spill out of the cockpit. I uncoupled the trailer in the drive and as I examined the boat more carefully, both outside and inside, I realised what a bargain I had. It had two berths in the main cabin and a fo'c's'le that could accommodate children but was more suited to containing a rapidly struck foresail that was hauled down by someone standing protected within the boat whilst reaching up through the forehatch. There was a gimbelled two-ring gas burner. There was not much else – certainly no marine toilet but when would I need anything more than a bucket? (The time would come . . .) The boat, just under 20 feet in length and about 18 and a half feet on the waterline, had been maintained by one of those enthusiasts who is more happy sanding and varnishing than actually sailing and she looked very neat and seaworthy. Her name was *Eros*.

But how would I sail this boat whose size seemed to increase every time I looked at her? Roger Wilby expressed great delight when I called him to deliver the good news but he was not in a position to give me the personal tuition he had provided when I bought the 'Mirror' dinghy. There was a sailing man, Ken Stubbs, who lived at the bottom of Park West in a lovely house that faced directly on to the estuary and I approached him. Ken was a member of a boat-owning syndicate but its boat was moored at Anglesey, miles and miles away, so he was most enthusiastic about teaching me how to sail *Eros,* the boat that would be moored almost in front of his house.

I had anchors made by the local blacksmith, bought heavy chains, dug deep holes for the anchors in the hard muddy bottom of the channel and eventually, after much heaving and hauling, there was 'Eros' resting serenely on her twin keels awaiting the first rush of the tide which, when it arrived, swirled around the hull and then swept her downstream to the full extent of her moorings. Ken, who turned out to be every bit as good a teacher as Roger, kept an eye on her and advised when higher tides or bad weather were expected so that extra attention could be paid to the boat's security.

I found I could walk onto the boat quite safely a few minutes before the tide was due. I would make everything ready, take the sails from their bags and attach them to the various bits of wood, wire and rope (I avoided sailing terms and nomenclature whenever possible because I found them impossible to remember; 'sharp end' and 'blunt end' were good enough for me). The old Seagull outboard that had come with the boat was attached to the stern and primed for starting with the cord wound ready for the first pull. Then I would make a cup of coffee on the stove, light a cigar and sit there blissfully until Ken joined me at the last minute, clambering aboard with the water almost lapping around his wellington boots. When the channel had filled and with the bow pointing upstream we would start the engine (easier said than done with the good old British Seagull) and motor out to the broad spread of the estuary, where six miles or so away there was the Welsh coast, and then we would set the sails. On a high tide we could reach that coast and get back to the mooring before the sea left us high and dry again. With the sun shining and the wind filling the sails, with seagulls overhead and seals clearly visible in the water it was paradise.

~

I was, by now, ready for bigger professional challenges and I started to apply for jobs that would give me more to do and put me up a rung or two. I was making a fair success of Merseyside and I thought that this would inevitably propel me onwards and upwards. I needed a new challenge, needed something more, needed . . . to move away from Merseyside. The arts were booming with more and more jobs being created and I felt that I must inevitably find the better job sooner or later.

After countless job applications, immaculate presentations of my professional history and reasons why I would be the perfect choice for whatever job it was, after interviews by the dozen it seemed, I found myself facing the simple and obvious truth – I was wanted by no-one. I had been successful enough with the MAA job but I had not dressed my window, I had not spent time making sure that people outside my little region knew what I had achieved. The arts world consisted of lots of people like me, heading small organisations, sitting on the top of their own pyramids, some big, some small, and my pyramid was a very tiny one that was remote and was mainly under heavy cloud cover. It was depressing.

~

My head was by then filled with dreams of sailing. I read magazine articles and books about sailing and I thought constantly of my little boat *Eros* there at the bottom of the road waiting for me to . . . to . . . do something *significant.* To meet the needs these dreams created and to take my mind off my failure to take the next step on the stairway to fame and fortune, I planned an adventure.

It would not be a huge adventure but it would involve a sleeping bag, food, a compass, and a chart. It would be a trip to Rhyl, on the coast of North Wales, just around the corner of the Point of Air once the Dee estuary had been crossed.

So, one Saturday midday, when the flooding tide set *Eros* afloat and she swept downstream to the full extent of her mooring chain, I started the Seagull engine, cast off and punched against the tide, up the channel to the open water of the estuary. I waved farewell to Heather who stood on the tiny promenade at the bottom of Park West holding son Marcus. Then off with the engine, swing it up and clear of the water, up with the sails and Ho for Rhyl!

The journey was only seven or eight nautical miles but it was an adventure holding for me a similar sense of excitement merged with fear as my first solo glider flight. I arrived off the beach at Rhyl in the afternoon and sailed in towards the fairground until my keels touched sand. The tide was ebbing fast and soon I was high and dry. I walked across the sand and secured my two anchors fore and aft before returning to the snugness of my cabin. As the sun went down the lights of the beachfront fairground grew brighter and the music from roundabouts and all the other noises of entertainment filled the air but the sounds were not intrusive, merely atmospheric. To this background and as the tide started to flow in, I cooked and ate my dinner and settled down to read a book by candlelight before pulling my sleeping bag up around my shoulders and snuggling down for the night.

As I slept the tide came in and by breakfast time it had gone out again. It had been a tranquil night, the lifting and drifting of the boat lending a lulling effect and putting to flight any tiny, lurking fears that this gentle experience might be transformed into a desperate fight for survival had the weather turned nasty. As I made my breakfast, hot and sizzling and plentiful, two or three small boys, early risers, walked over to inspect us and put tentative questions to me. Their awe was very much as mine would have been had I come across a real, live sailor and a proper seagoing boat on the sands at Berrow or Brean.

When the tide flooded again and *Eros* had lifted clear I hauled in my anchors and motored out to sea. Engine off. Sails up. A nice breeze would get me home in no time. So, now, Ho for Heswall!

The fog that then quickly settled about me gave me my first real taste of . . . not fear exactly but apprehension, the realisation that there is always a dark side to sailing. I could not see the Wirral peninsula and I could not now see the Welsh coast. I took out my chart, on which I had already marked a course, and consulted the large compass I had borrowed from Ken Stubbs and wedged into a plastic bucket by way of a mounting. I knew my course to sail and I sailed it through the fog with the confidence that only the ignorant possess. There was, in fact, next to no chance of meeting or colliding with another vessel in these waters and the biggest danger, that of running aground on sand banks, was offset by a rising tide that would have floated me off had I run aground.

Then there was the end of the channel leading back to my mooring. Down with the sails. On with the engine. Back to Heswall's minute promenade and there was Heather with son Marcus waiting for me, having walked down the road once or twice already to see if there was sight of me. It was the end of the First Great Sea Adventure.

A couple of evenings later I wrote my first article which I knew would be accepted. I called it 'Single Handed To Rhyl' and I sent it to *Practical Boat Owner*. Within a few days there came back a letter of acceptance and an offer of £40 from the Editor, Denny Desoutter. I am still naively proud of that piece.

~

The Chairman of Granada Television in those days was a splendid man called Dennis Forman and one day he took it into his head to organise a party to go to the opera in Manchester where his company was based and where the Welsh National Opera company was then visiting. His charming PA, Gerry Hagan, called me and asked if Heather and I would like to join the party; naturally, I accepted. There was, in truth, not much of a social life in Liverpool and a trip to see Berg's *Lulu* in the company of such a genial and gifted host could not be missed.

Heather and I turned up at the Granada main offices and were whisked up to the penthouse suite where a pre-performance supper was laid out. There were about a dozen of us present. I do not remember who all the other guests were but I do remember that when it was time to go to the theatre I was asked to escort a lady in her fifties called Peggy. We entered the theatre in our pairs as requested by Gerry Hagan and I took my seat with Peggy. Heather was seated further along the row with her partner for the performance.

I do have trouble with opera. Some operas, such as *Carmen* and *La Traviata*, I enjoy without reservation. *Lulu* I found difficult but extremely interesting; it was one of those situations where I felt, I knew, that any failure to appreciate it was my fault and not that of the opera or the performance. *Lulu* merited my concentration.

Concentration was what the opera did not get because of the vivacious and irreverently inclined woman on my right, Peggy, who took against the whole idea of the opera from the first instant and started to whisper in my ear comments like 'She's no better than she should be', 'She'll get 'er come uppance, you mark my words, young sir' and 'What on earth is going on? Are you making any sense out of this'. She was very funny and soon we were suppressing giggles instead of concentrating upon *Lulu*.

We went back to the penthouse suite for drinks and a light snack afterwards and there the conversation, led by Dennis Forman, turned to the world of theatre and the focus of attention soon became Peggy who was being treated as something of an authority on the subject. Who was this woman? It was Peggy Ashcroft.

(In the week in which I write these words a biography of this lady, later made a Dame and now dead, has been published in which the author claims that she possessed a voracious sexual appetite. I am happy to confirm that during our entertaining evening together she made no gesture, nor offered one word, that could be interpreted as an advance – what a pity.)

~

We re-acquainted ourselves with Italy in the spring of 1973, when Marcus was a few months old. We had not been there for nearly ten years, the last time having been our grand tour to Yugoslavia when the Fiat 500 broke down outside Milan. This time we booked a villa just outside Lerici with a couple of about our age who had a baby daughter. Lerici is near La Spezia, on the Gulf of Livorno. It was April and, as we now know but did not know then, the weather in this part of Northern Italy is often very bad at this time of the year notwithstanding its Mediterranean location. We were very lucky with our Italian April weather and we basked in Spring sunshine as we ate glorious food prepared by the two spinster sisters who owned the villa. Marcus, now with rolls of puppy fat and an entirely bald head, and nicknamed 'Abel Magwitch', rolled happily on sand and sat contentedly in warm sea water. He was to us the most wonderful child and more wonderful for two people who had lost their first and adored son. Abel Magwitch was the most precious thing in the world – and the boy slept well! He didn't keep us awake at night!

To what extent the wonderful weather we experienced influenced later decisions about the course our life should take I cannot say but it certainly contributed substantially to a romantic view I had of the country – which to some extent I still hold. As you will see, it would not be too long before Italy became part of our lives and this particular part of Italy, Lerici, part of one of the great adventures of our lives.

~

I returned from the Italian holiday to face yet another batch of unsuccessful job applications. Convinced that I would never find a suitable job in arts management I turned to the recruitment advertising pages of *Campaign* magazine, where arts jobs were never to be seen, and saw that the Nottingham firm of John Player & Sons was advertising for a person to be second in command of its public relations department. A job in the *real* world, that's what I wanted. I applied. I got the job. I felt quite proud of myself.

Farewell to Sir Harry Livermore and his Executive Committee. Farewell to my staff (I would miss them). Farewell to 'Glenelg' that was by now looking much better than it did when we bought it. Farewell to the lovely Dee estuary – but not Farewell to *Eros* which would follow our Renault 16 to Nottingham pending plans for future trips.

Our souvenirs of Liverpool would be the pictures we bought. Works by artists now famous, Maurice Cockrill and Sam Walsh, and excellent but not famous, John Baum, Tony Clews and George Wallace Jardine. A first rate, hilarious, ink and wash sketch, *Hot Pants in Hackins Hey,* from the Pat Cooke touring exhibition that was one of my first Merseyside promotions. A Sam Walsh spray painting that my staff and Liverpool City Council friends gave me on the day of my departure. There had never been much money to spare in those Merseyside days but once in a while a picture had generated an irresistible tug on my cheque book and I had succumbed; we never regretted the purchase of a painting once the decision had been made and we left the region with marvellous mementoes.

Chapter 18

We Were At The Mercy Of A Tide That Was Steadily Carrying Us Backwards Into The Maelstrom. Oh, The Horror!

John Player & Sons, Nottingham (September 1973 – September 1974) and the Second Great Sea Adventure

We made a profit when we sold 'Glenelg'. The sixth P. It enabled us to buy a delightful house (c. 1910), 23, Villiers Road, Woodthorpe, which lay in the northern part of Nottingham. It was just a few minutes drive from the factory and headquarters of John Player & Sons (JP&S). We were not able to make the move neatly so that we left Heswall together and arrived in Nottingham together on the same day. Complications over the sale of one house and the purchase of the other meant that I had to start work with JP&S a couple of months before we had a home in the city. JP&S simply put me into a hotel during the week and I commuted on Friday evenings and Monday mornings. When it was time to make the move JP&S put the three of us into a hotel, a better hotel, for a few days while we settled in. It was a definite improvement on the start to the Merseyside job.

~

In my memory the whole of that period of moving into the 'real world' is characterised by money, by the vast amount of money that slopped around in the tobacco industry. My new job was second in command of the Public Relations department and plenty of money slopped around there. Not as much as in the Special Events department that handled the sponsorship of motor racing, cricket, power boat racing and anything else that would enhance the image of the different brands of cigarette, and most particularly the brand that came in a shiny black pack with gold insignia, John Player Special – but plenty of money by my humble standards. My salary was excellent, the company insisted on paying for the move and made a generous contribution to the cost of new carpets and curtains, there was a company doctor and a dentist to whom the fitting of gold crowns seemed to be as commonplace as recommendations to use dental floss, and almost any extravagant whim might be paid for out of 'expenses'. There was also, in the PR department, a cupboard stacked high with samples of the company's products, from the humblest fag to large cigars packed in white metal tubes, to which PR executives had free access. All other employees had a small weekly ration of tobacco products but we PR fellows could smoke ourselves to death if we chose to.

Death? The anti-smoking lobby was beginning to develop muscle in those days but I was still a smoker and working for a tobacco company did not bother me – although I certainly would not do so today and ethical considerations would play a part in that decision. I had moved to a small cigar (non-inhaling) mode several years earlier so the presence of unlimited free cigars did increase my throughput of potentially fatal smoke while I was with the company. The tobacco cupboard became for me part and parcel of the whole style of life enjoyed by senior executives of a company that did not have to be very, very clever in order to be very, very wealthy. Like the cigars the memory leaves a bad taste.

~

The problem for me was that there appeared to be no work to do. When I was interviewed I learned that the PR department had continued the local sponsorship of the arts that I had helped encourage them in with my English Sinfonia concerts and was ready to consider arts sponsorship on a wider scale. It was my understanding of the appointment that my special contribution would be to bring my experience to bear on these embryonic programmes of sponsorship and expand them. By the time I moved into my office, met my own personal secretary and been out to lunch with my boss, David Way, and a couple of colleagues a few times it dawned on me that the company's enthusiasm for my involvement in the sponsorship of the arts had ebbed very slightly.

It may have been that I simply misunderstood the way big companies worked and that my perception of an involvement with sponsorship was not the same as that of my new colleagues who, as far as I could see, never had any significant involvement with any of their projects. Involvement was the territory of *consultants* and I was not told about these fellows until I had moved us all into our lovely house in Woodthorpe and was past the point of no return. It may have been, therefore, that nothing had changed and that what the company saw as a personal involvement, a direct responsibility, was something far more remote than was familiar to me.

But the point remained that there appeared to be no work to do. The programme of local concerts had been proposed and was managed by a self-employed consultant, recently started up, an ex- W. D. & H. O. Wills tobacco man, Bill Kallaway. There was also a much larger PR consultancy outfit, F. J. Lyons Ltd, that was most securely plugged into our PR department.

A couple of charming chaps from F. J. Lyons Ltd would travel to Nottingham from London once a week for a meeting that was always held in the directors' conference room where lunch could be served conveniently. We would meet, we would chat about how the week had gone, we would consider a proposal or two, we would decide not to do several things and then we would eat a jolly good lunch, smoke a few jolly good cigars, bid farewell to our charming chaps from F. J. Lyons Ltd and then repair to our separate offices where we would tidy up our desks and then pop off home a little earlier than usual 'to put the final touches to that report I've been working on'.

~

A few months drifted by and took us into 1974. Something happened. Heather became pregnant. Julian Caedmon Diggle, who would be born on 14 November, was on his way.

~

With so little to occupy my mind my thoughts turned to *Eros*, still on a trailer parked on the driveway of our new house and very visibly deteriorating, with varnish and paint peeling.

There was in those times, on a narrow canal running by the River Trent, a small boatyard run by an elderly boatbuilder, Tom Trevellick. Imagine such a Cornish name in such a place. Tom took *Eros* into his small shed and undertook to carry out certain vital repairs giving me open access to his yard at weekends so that I could rub her down and paint her up and bring her back to respectability.

After one visit from our friends Roger and Heather Wilby my weekend work took on a new urgency for we, Roger and I, had hatched a plan. We had an adventure in mind.

We would sail *Eros* across the English Channel, from Shoreham to Cherbourg. We would then return from Cherbourg to the Helford River in Cornwall. Heather and I knew a pleasant little guest house at Pons-a-Verron, the owner of which had a mooring and he agreed to let us leave the boat there on our return so that we might collect it later in the year when we came to take our Whitsun holiday with him. We would complete the whole trip in a week.

Heather Catherine, my Heather, booked a week's holiday in Ibiza with her friend, Maggie Morgan, to coincide with our absence on the high seas.

~

Now this was a pretty crazy idea. *Eros* still had no compass (I bought a Japanese one for £9 and bolted it in the cockpit). *Eros* had no way of measuring speed or distance run (we'd hire an old-fashioned trailing log). *Eros* had no liferaft (we'd hire that too). *Eros* had no Radio Direction Finding equipment (we'd hire that as well). *Eros* had no signal flares (we'd buy a couple). Charts? Waterproofs? Safety harnesses? Radar reflector? Nothing that money couldn't buy. But all these acquisitions did not stop it being a pretty crazy idea because the journey we had planned was very long, about 90 nautical miles out and about 110 on the return leg, and *Eros* found it difficult to move at more than three knots. We were inexperienced to a high degree; Roger had sailed on open water, had been through some bad weather, but had never tackled anything like this. And me? Well I had sailed Single Handed To Rhyl.

Once we had committed ourselves, metaphorically shaken hands on the deal, and told our friends, there was no way out of it and, to tell the absolute truth, we did not even try to find a way out of it. This week in April 1974 was going to be the adventure of our lives.

And so it was.

~

We tipped and hauled the boat off the trailer onto the hard at Shoreham on the evening of Saturday 20 April and then put my car and the trailer into a public car park to await our return. As I used to do at Heswall we set an anchor, climbed onto the boat while she stood on her twin keels, and made ready while we awaited the tide. At 10.30pm we upped anchor and motored up the western arm of the harbour into the eastern arm. We anchored again and 'took the mud' as Roger's note in the log has it, at 2.30 in the morning of Sunday 21 April; then we took to our bunks. At 10.30am we set off on our adventure, motoring out to sea.

Soon there was sufficient wind to fill the sails and to enable us to follow the course that we planned on our brightly coloured Stanford chart (which had quite the wrong scale for a trip like this but I preferred the way Stanford's sea was coloured a nice bright blue, shallow coastal areas a sandy sort of brown and navigation lights were given nice bright colours – altogether more cheerful than those Admiralty charts all austere black and white with only the merest hint of magenta here and there). About five miles offshore the wind stopped and, of course, so did we. We waited patiently. There, in full view, was Shoreham harbour.

Nothing happened for a long time. This Sunday was definitely a day of rest. We ate and chatted and admired Shoreham Harbour. I felt vaguely seasick with the continual bobbing up and down, but nothing more serious. When evening fell I heated up a tinned curry and as I was passing a plateful to Roger the bobbing became more vigorous and I slopped the lot on the carpet that I had laid on the cabin sole. The carpet went over the side and we shared the remainder. A nice, big, fat JP&S cigar helped dispel the smell.

I went to my sleeping bag while Roger took the first watch. I awoke to the sound of water rushing past the hull. The wind had come up and at 2am on the Monday morning Roger had set the sails and we were now whistling our way through the blackness of night at . . . well, all of three knots. It *seemed* very fast. Soon the both of us were kitted up for wind and weather and enjoying an exhilarating night sail.

Navigation proved a problem. To know where you are at sea, even only approximately, you need a chart (ours was not entirely appropriate to our needs), a reasonably accurate compass (ours was only so-so or even, being Japanese, only ah-so), a timepiece of some kind (our watches were, I suppose, up to the task) and a device for telling you how far you have gone – a log. Most logs, even in those days, were electronic but my boat, having no electrical supply at all, had only the old-fashioned mechanical log that I had hired. It consisted of a lump of metal so contrived as to spin when 'streamed' in the water, the cord holding the piece of metal then spun as well and a meter to which the whole was attached recorded the number of revolutions per minute and from this one could tell the speed through the water and the number of nautical miles travelled. All very well but the thing only worked if the speed of water relative to the boat was at least 4 knots. You will remember that *Eros* could only manage about three knots and a bit.

RDF, Radio Direction Finding equipment, in the form appropriate to our needs and pockets was a hand-held compass attached to a radio receiver that would pick up signals from a fixed transmitter. One pointed the thing very roughly in the direction of an RDF transmitter and listened through a pair of headphones for the morse code signals it transmitted. The Cherbourg transmitter put out the signal CB (– • – •   – • • •) and when this was detected the device was swung slowly from side to side. When the compass was pointing directly at Cherbourg the signal disappeared and the compass reading at this 'null point' gave you the bearing of your position in relation to Cherbourg. Another transmitter was then chosen and you repeated the procedure. The two bearings were marked on the chart and where the lines crossed, there you were. Do it once more and you had a triangulated bearing. A piece of cake. The RDF we hired, along with the log and the inflatable life-raft, did not work we discovered.

But no matter how approximate is one's navigation, when crossing the English Channel from the English side one may be fairly certain that France will appear sooner or later. So we sailed on through the night and across the first shipping lane. Big boats in the Channel are expected to stay in shipping lanes; the one nearest England is for ships going up and that nearest France is for ships going down. When a boat is ahead of you at night you can see from their lights which way they are going, because they carry a red light on the port side and a green light on the starboard. Thus, if you see a green light alone you know the craft is passing in front of you from left to right; if you see two lights, a red on the left and a green on the right, it is moving in the same direction as you and, being bigger, it is inevitably going faster, so there is no danger. Crossing the first shipping lane you might expect to see only red lights ahead, with all the boats going from right to left but it does not quite work out like that. As you cross at your miserable three knots you look over to the starboard side and see two lights, a green on the left and a red on the right and you know that there is every possibility that you will be run down. It is exciting stuff.

We emerged into the daylight unscathed but with no sight of land. In spite of taking spells of rest down below we were a little tired by then. It is something that sailing does to you. We carried on, confident that very soon we would see the Cotentin peninsula where lies Cherbourg.

There was no sight of land. We had not allowed for the tidal streams that moved us with the tide as it flooded and ebbed but as Roger observed, 'They cancel each other out, don't they?'. In our slightly fatigued state we agreed that the absence of land was something of a mystery by now. We had been sailing on this course for nearly 20 hours. We sailed on.

We sailed on and on. Just grey sea and mist and evening drawing on. At 7.30pm, as we were were trying to work out how it was that France had managed to disappear, Roger's keen eyes spotted the green light of a buoy marking a wreck. There were plenty of wreck buoys off Gold, Utah and Omaha beaches, some of major sites of the D Day landings. We were right in the middle of the Baie de la Seine, miles to the east of the Cotentin peninsula which we had simply missed. Oh, dash!

At least the wreck buoy told us where we were. Now quite seriously fatigued and not a little depressed we put *Eros* on a course for Cherbourg. It was now dark and we were about to spend our third night at sea. We were getting fed up with all this water and my bottom was getting sore from sitting for so long (never go to sea without a cushion, me hearties).

The wind was on our side and we sailed swiftly and easily without having to waste energy and time in changing course or messing about with the sails. We were very tired and although we took turns at the helm the lion's share of responsibility increasingly passed to Roger whose stamina far exceeded mine. We sailed on, confident that soon we would be in Cherbourg for a shower, a shave and a big dinner.

At 4.30am (Tuesday 23 April) the wind stopped. This in itself offered no serious problem in that it would give us time to freshen up, eat something, tidy up and so on – but we had reckoned without the dreadful . . . *Barfleur Race* (cue: dramatic music containing powerful elements of impending doom).

The Barfleur Race is a tidal phenomenon that occurs off the Pointe de Barfleur when the tide turns. The result is an acqueous nightmare, with great swirling whirlpools, walls of water shooting up into the air and as much chaos below the surface as above. Tidal races are *horrible* things that sink boats.

Our night sailing had brought us up to the north of the peninsula and to within ten miles of Cherbourg but now there was no wind. Then there was a flutter and a very slight breeze that enabled us to continue for another couple of hours. We thought we were making progress but the tidal direction had changed and as we went west the water moved east, only more so.

It was 7.30am and I was at the helm (sitting on a padded lifejacket in lieu of a decent cushion) while Roger was down below organising some food. I had become aware of a strange, low sound behind me but in my fatigued and befuddled state probably put it down to the sound of the calor gas on which Roger was heating water for tea. Roger came up from the cabin and looked over my shoulder. He seemed concerned at what he saw.

I turned and saw what appeared to be a wall of water and it was *roaring* at us. We were at the mercy of a tide that was steadily carrying us backwards into the maelstrom. Oh, the horror!

We rushed to the Seagull outboard engine that was attached to the stern, propped up so that the propellor cleared the water. Down it went into its proper position, the carburettor was primed, the choke was set, the cord wrapped around the flywheel starter. Pull. Nothing. Wrap the cord again. Pull! Nothing. Wrap the cord again. PULL!! Nothing. Only this engine could get us out of the impending disaster and only then if it was powerful enough to fight the awesome power of this ripping tide which seemed to get stronger as we approached the race. And the *bloody* engine wasn't firing.

Grimly we prepared for serious trouble. The lifejackets were put on and tied tightly. The few flares we had were tucked inside close to our bodies. The hired liferaft was hauled from its locker and into the cockpit, its container unlaced, all ready to be thrown into the water when it would automatically inflate (we hoped and trusted – not too optimistically for it came from the same company that had hired us the log that only functioned at speeds over four nautical miles per hour and the RDF equipment that found nothing).

Then we felt a zephyr of wind, just a puff; enough to fill the sails and give us enough oomph to turn the boat in a northerly direction, to run parallel with the race. The wind force increased and we started to move. The course we were able to steer took us through the edge of the race (an experience I intend never to repeat) and into clear water.

For hours we sailed fitfully as we moved against the easterly flowing tide, making little progress. The atmosphere between the two of us became more and more bizarre as our fatigue worsened. Roger went into a kind of trance, never once taking his hand from the tiller, reacting automatically to the wind, doing his best to gain some progress from it, hardly speaking. I had started to hallucinate the night before; when I was at the helm I had looked into the cabin where Roger was lying and counted five people sitting there quietly, staring into space. There was an old black man with white hair and a school girl in gym slip; the others I cannot now recall.

The tide slackened at around 11.30am and we started to make some better progress. The sun came out; that always helps but we were exhausted and my hallucinations started to come back. In the bright sunlight, I saw more strange things. We passed a buoy that had within its upper cagelike structure a device that produced a strange whistling noise as it moved up and down in the water; I saw within the cage a little man, holding the bars of the cage and whistling for our attention. The sheet of the foresail was of white rope tied into a short loop by blue whipping cord and this was clipped into the sail by means of a brass snap-shackle.

As the foresail flapped idly in the intermittent light airs my brain turned this part of the sheet into a little dancing girl whose head and Barbie Doll-like hair were made up from the loop, whose neat waist was the blue whipping cord and whose legs were the two lengths of rope beneath it.

I had a strange and serious conversation with Roger, which he did not treat as being as foolish as it was, about how we could persuade a ferry boat in Cherbourg to haul the boat on board and take us home nice and safely.

But we continued and that afternoon we slowly made our way into the port of Cherbourg and the moorings. For this kind of manoevre one really needs an engine but ours was still not in the mood. Roger responded to the challenge in characteristic style and with a following breeze he gull-winged us right into the heart of the moorings, sheeted in, turned and there we were, ready to tie up, as neat as a whistle. Brilliant stuff, Roger! It was 3pm in the afternoon of Tuesday 23 April. We had done it. We had been on the water for 69 hours and had travelled (including the deviations in our route) 140 nautical miles.

We found a nearby hotel, showered and then slept all evening and all night. We spent the next day, Wednesday 24 April, in Cherbourg enjoying Rest and Recreation as sailors do (not as some sailors do, I must add) and to putting ourselves and *Eros* in a fit state for the return trip. We dried out our sleeping bags (the forehatch was found to let in water very badly) and attended to the outboard motor. On examination the Seagull's problem turned out to be that when I had changed the sparking plug (as a diversion from staring at Shoreham harbour on the first day of the trip) I had not attached the high tension lead properly; a matter of a couple of minutes to sort out (but not if you are being scared witless by the sound and sight of a lethally inclined tidal race).

We caught the tide at 11.30pm that evening so that we would be swept away from the Barfleur Race rather than into it. The wind was just right and we travelled as fast as *Eros* could go. Sailing back to the Helford River was long, cold and hard work but there were no serious snags. After a day at sea we sighted the light of Start Point at 9pm (Thursday evening) and that of Eddystone at midnight. We sailed through the night, the wind continuing good, if rather vigorous, the sea was kind and the effects of the tidal streams did seem to cancel each other out this time. By 8.30am we were fast approaching Falmouth with very big following seas so that *Eros* appeared to be surfing through the water. The wind was so strong that we had to take down the mainsail and we raced along propelled only by the foresail. At 11.30am we entered the Helford River, finding quiet waters there. We found our mooring. Roger had done most of the work on this passage and was, as my Father would have put it, flaked out. We sailed onto the mooring and once we were secure Roger stretched out on the cabin floor and went either asleep or unconscious – he was very, very tired.

We were almost immediately greeted by a Customs man who had spied us entering British waters and, suspecting smugglers, had followed us along the coast in his Mini. At Pons-A-Verron he had commandeered a dinghy and duly appeared at our stern asking to come aboard. I wondered if this might be the old hallucination problem again but as he looked real enough close to I allowed him to throw a leg over and climb aboard. We had an odd conversation sitting in the cabin on either side of a completely collapsed Roger, drinking tea. He signed our 'Certificate of Free Pratique' (a quaint nautical term meaning A Clean Bill of Health – which was ironic bearing in mind Roger's state) and at 1.15pm he left.

Roger soon recovered and that was the end of our adventure. We had sailed 285 nautical miles in all – 140 on the outward leg and 145 on the return – and we had spent five nights and almost six days at sea. Maybe Ibiza would have been a better choice but I doubt it. It was one of those tough experiences that one enjoys more in the recollection; writing about it now I am enjoying it hugely.

Then back to John Player & Sons for me.

~

By this time my Mother had moved back to Nottingham and was in a constant state of anguish now that she lived alone. After my Father had died the year before she had stayed on in the caravan for a while and then tried life alone in the Arnold house. She made one or two trips back to the caravan before Winter came but could not settle. She took a job as a cook in an old people's home in Weston-Super-Mare but without the reassuring presence of my Father, who could always calm her ruffled feathers after a disagreement or a slight, she soon ran foul of the boss and was asked to leave. Our move to Nottingham encouraged her to return to the area and once based there she found a live-in job as a cook in a crumbling pile of a big house near Newark, not too far away for days off to be spent in Arnold. She remained lonely and confused. She desperately wanted someone to look after.

Through a newspaper Lonely Hearts advertisement she found a man. I believe he had described himself as a widowed farmer and his name was Bob. He was in fact divorced and was a cow man; he looked after dairy herds. He drove them into the milking parlour, attached tubes to their udders and scraped their backsides while the milk was being extracted. He owned nothing but what he stood up in as far as I could see. I believe he saw my Mother as a wealthy widow for she owned a house and a caravan and these were riches indeed to him.

He came up to Nottingham and moved in with Mother, who had resigned the Newark job, and this is where we first met him. He was a profoundly stupid man with an West Country accent so thick that I do not believe I ever understood what he was saying. Heather and I were horrified but there was nothing we could do. Mother needed someone and she had grabbed the first man that came along. I do not think I could be blamed for finding her choice of a second partner a fearful insult to her first.

Soon he got a job looking after Lord Waldegrave's dairy herd in Compton Bassett in Somerset and a house came with it. The two of them left the Arnold house and then Bob started to milk my Mother of her limited resources. He had a penchant for new cars and would walk into a car showroom, trade in his current model and sign a legally binding hire purchase agreement without any thought as to how the agreement would be kept; this would be my Mother's responsibility. The Arnold house was sold, the money going in part to pay for a car and to buy a depreciating asset in the form of a large caravan on a fixed site in the west country. The caravan provided them with a few holidays before it was sold, at a substantial loss, to pay for another car.

On the plus side the man gave my Mother what she needed – company and someone to cook for. The cars enabled him to take her out for trips and that was new for her. They managed to take a few holidays abroad, something she would never have been able to do with my Father. So there were benefits for her from the relationship but years later, when she fell seriously ill with a mentally degenerative disease, Bob was wholly unable to help her.

~

Back at JP&S there was something, at last, to look forward to. The independent consultant, Bill Kallaway, had talked the company into sponsoring an international competition for young conductors which involved the Bournemouth Symphony Orchestra and would take place in Portsmouth. Once I accepted that my job consisted of no more than . . . being around and representing the company, I began to enjoy myself.

The John Player International Conductors Award attracted entries from all over the world and lasted for several days. Heather and Marcus, now a golden-haired toddler, accompanied me to Portsmouth and we lived luxuriously out of the pocket of Mr Player and his son. On the final day we sat in the audience next to the parents and younger sister of the 19-year-old Simon Rattle and shared their delight when he was announced the winner.

Then back to Nottingham and unrelieved boredom. I recollect that the highpoint of that time was the preparation of an audio-visual presentation for employees on the life and works of the tobacco beetle.

~

I started to enjoy JP&S much, much more the minute I resigned. I gave plenty of notice and then started to relax and make the most of it. My boss, David, knew that I was hating the corporate life and accepted my imminent departure with good humour and grace. He had some private reason for wanting me to stay on the payroll (probably to do with his own salary) until the end of September so we did a deal that would have me working three months notice until August, followed by an all-expenses paid visit to the Edinburgh Festival.

The new baby was due to be born in November. When I thought of this and of all the problems that would arise out of not having a regular income I found myself getting scared. I was coming up to my 37th birthday and I still had not found what it was I could do that would make me happy, that would make use of my talents, that would give me scope for expansion, that might conceivably make me better off, even – dare one hope for this? – wealthy.

How many times had I resigned a job with no guarantee of another? Teaching. English Sinfonia. This one made three. What was I to do? I was clearly never going to find another arts management job. I had no enthusiasm for the private sector now that I had tasted it. It would have to be the freelance life, doing a bit of this and a bit of that until some sort of pathway opened up in front of me.

So while I still had regular money coming in I started to write again and did a good piece for *The Guardian* reviewing the Summer Special edition of *The Stage and Television Today* (which made me a friend for life of the Editor, Peter Hepple, a charming man) and then another on arts sponsorship. I made contact with The City University, London, that had just taken over the Arts Council sponsored post-graduate diploma course in arts management, and was taken on to do a weekly session on the subject I had invented, Arts Marketing, from October of that year.

There would be lecturing and there would be writing. Would it be enough to sustain us, presently the three of us and soon to be the four of us? The presence of Bob did not relieve me of the pressure of paying the mortgage on Mother's house, which at this time had not been sold, nor would it be sold for several years yet. I did my sums, worked out how much I would have to make to keep a roof over our heads. Maybe I should have kept the JP&S job. Only time would tell.

CHAPTER 19

NO PROBLEM WITH SNAKES, SIGNOR; THE WILD BOAR EAT THEM

A Freelance Life (September 1974 – April 1976)

I should love to be able to describe that man in Nottingham in September 1974, who faced an imminent future living off his wits, that married man whose wife stood by his stumbling attempts to find a way in the world, who was the father of one son and soon to be the father of two, who had a big mortgage to pay on the house he lived in and a smaller one to pay on the house his Mother lived in. I should love to be able to describe him in other than material terms and to get close to his spiritual side but I cannot see that side of him although I know it must have been there. He seems two dimensional now but surely he cannot have been so.

It would be too easy to say that this fellow was going through a mid-life crisis but he was surely not. Facing a watershed, perhaps. (I have saved my mid-life crisis until now, which is my sixtieth year – this is my sneaky way of grabbing a little longevity. This book is part of my mid-life crisis.) At 36, going on 37, I was just trying to find myself, that's all.

~

I dived into the freelance life. I wrote my first pieces for BBC Radio Nottingham and the county glossy, *Nottingham Life;* neither paid me. I drove over to Norwich to interview the Manager of the Theatre Royal, Dick Condon, whose innovative approach to theatre marketing had attracted my attention, and wrote a long piece with *The Guardian* in mind – and they took it, *they took it!* – and I achieved my first complete half page in that paper. I suggested that the newspaper ran an advertising supplement on arts sponsorship and landed the job of generating all the editorial for around four broadsheet pages. Then the paper called and commissioned me to interview the jazz composer Neil Ardley – a wonderful boost to my ambitions and my morale.

Finding that local radio had no potential for me I called the BBC Radio 4 arts programme, Kaleidoscope, and suggested a feature on arts sponsorship; to my surprise they welcomed the idea and within a day or so I was trying to pretend that I knew all the techniques of radio work whilst doing my damnedest to learn them. I discovered that while the writer has only to put words on paper for them to be saleable the radio journalist has to do the acoustic equivalent of laying out and typesetting the item to produce one spool of tape on which is recorded the finished 'article'; this finished piece would almost certainly be edited by someone else but the contributor was expected to produce a pretty good attempt at a final version.

My arts sponsorship piece consisted of several interviews which I had to edit and make up into one item complete with linking material. The BBC in London loaned me the portable tape recorder but I had to rely upon the studios of BBC Radio Nottingham for editing. Editing consists of running tape, listening, deciding what has to be cut out, stopping the tape, running it through by hand whilst listening for the redundant sentence (or something as short as an Um or an Ah or even a cough) which at slow speed sounds nothing like the original, cutting out that section of tape and sticking the tape together again. My task was made no easier by the presence of a local freelance radio journalist who saw me as a threat and made sure that he occupied the editing suite whenever I needed it. It seemed like a lot of work for three minutes of radio time and quite a small fee.

The arts sponsorship piece got me into the BBC in Portland Place and I began to talk to the Kaleidoscope people; this could well become one of my markets, I thought. Then I received a telephone call from the programme's producer, Rosemary Hill. Would I like to present Kaleidoscope on 16 November?

I shall never forget this experience – which left me devoid of all hope for a career in broadcasting. The programme sounded fine enough but the time, effort and nervous strain that went into its preparation pushed me to my limits. I had to make several visits to London to see a photographic exhibition in the Photographers Gallery, the premiere of a film of Frederick Forsyth's *The Dogs of War,* a performance of the opera *La Rondine* at Sadler's Wells and talks with the producer for this particular broadcast, John Powell. During the afternoon of the programme I interviewed the choreographer Christopher Bruce together with dance expert, Peter Brinson. The programme goes out live with taped items interspersed with live interviews and live links; all this preparation was for the pre-recorded material and to enable me to talk knowingly during the live parts.

My producer seemed happy with the programme. I had written my script and as the hour of transmission approached I felt reasonably confident. Then a few minutes before we went on the air John Powell announced that he was not happy with the Bruce/Brinson interview; their answers to my questions were fine, he did not like the questions. What he proposed was to wait until the interview's transmission time and as soon as I had read my introduction I would read one of his questions; he would then play the appropriate answer from the taped interview. Thereafter he would give me 'a green' (a flash on the green light at my desk) and I would read the next question. He would then respond with the next recorded answer and so on.

I got through it without any serious fluff but I decided then and there that this would be the end of my radio broadcasting career.

~

I also started my weekly visits to London for the Arts Marketing lectures I was giving at The City University for the post-graduate diploma course in arts management. This was the first time I had ever been asked to prepare and present a course spanning two terms and to set and mark the examination at the end of the course. I am sure I was unaware of it at the time but this was a most significant part of my career; here I was, an almost completely unqualified person teaching to graduates a subject that I had invented from scratch. In the country of the blind the one-eyed man is indeed king but I do believe that however blind were my students, I had both my eyes and my vision was pretty good. I had developed the subject to the point where it could stand the intellectual scrutiny of anyone and now it was to become one of the foundations of my new independent life.

~

I started to write a book, called *Marketing the Arts*. It was the first book that attempted to offer a theoretical basis to the subject of finding and keeping audiences and although it was hardly more than a transcription of the lectures that I customarily improvised, it was to make a serious contribution to the profession of arts management during its lifespan. There had been one other book on the subject of audience development, published in the USA some years before, but it did not attempt the fundamental analysis that mine did, nor did it contain the original thought that made mine unique. For practitioners in the UK this was the first.

A year later I talked The City University into publishing the book; its agreement was obtained in return for an undertaking that I would take full responsibility for every aspect of its production. I thus wrote it, arranged for typesetting, commissioned the cover design, placed the print order and planned and executed the marketing. We agreed to produce 2000 copies and eventually, *eventually*, we sold out.

~

During one of my earlier visits to London I looked in to see the freelance consultant, Bill Kallaway, the man who had masterminded the John Player International Conductors Award, and we struck up . . . not exactly a friendship . . . we struck up an acquaintanceship that we both could see had business potential. Bill certainly knew the ways of the larger companies and was making great strides in the development of arts sponsorship amongst such companies but he lacked credibility with the arts organisations that he needed to complete the equations. I could obviously provide this credibility. My knowledge of the arts world was also useful. It was not long before we found projects to work on together and I started to combine my visits to The City University with time spent working with him.

~

Meanwhile, back in Nottingham, a former JP&S colleague, Martin Rowland, the man in charge of Press Relations, saw that I was beginning to develop a journalism portfolio and asked if I would be interested in working with him on a freelance basis. He was particularly interested in developing media coverage of two JP&S sponsored activities, the company's power boat racing team and the World Speed Sailing event held in Portland harbour. My part was to sell the idea of articles written by me on these topics to magazines. I set to work on the telephone and after the usual series of 'No thanks' I placed an article on power boat racing with a magazine called *Game* and one on speed sailing with *Mayfair*. Both publications were then known as 'men's magazines' which meant that they contained pictures of girls and the substantial acreage of naked female flesh shown in their pages was leavened with articles about other masculine interests such as sport and motor cars. (Over time I came to know the editors of both magazines quite well and found them excellent company and not at all the depraved creatures one might imagine them to be. *Game* sadly folded after a couple of years and later on *Mayfair*, whose editor Kenneth Bound was a particular favourite of mine, a wealthy bon-viveur with a strongly developed sense of hospitality, was sold to the soft-pornographer Paul Raymond, who quickly brought the magazine down to the level of his other trash.)

~

Julian Caedmon Diggle was born on 14 November 1974, a delightful brother to Marcus Charles Winfield who was by now a cherubic figure with an aurora of blonde hair and an irrepressible personality and who was thrilled to pieces at the prospect of having a brother. Julian was simply wonderful. Noisy at first, very noisy at first, but simply wonderful. There were now four of us and it felt pretty good.

~

In Spring of 1975 Heather and I left our boys at home with their grandparents, Charles and Cathie, who were always willing to help us in this way, and set off to Domfront in Normandy. This led to a rediscovery of St. Cast and a return visit with the boys two months later. You may read all about this in the central section of this book called *A Resort Runs Through It*.

~

This period of freelance activity lasted for about a year before I stopped and took a look at what was happening to me and to us. It was an exciting time and it was a nerve-wracking time. Put all together, my various activities were paying the bills. In my first year I had been able to afford two holidays in France. I felt strangely secure now that I had no employer but life still did not feel right. There was that old nagging feeling telling me that this was still not what I really wanted to be doing.

The new academic year of 1975/76 saw me starting with a new group of arts management students at The City University and thus a weekly commitment to travel to London. Bill Kallaway and I were now doing so many things together I was often spending three or four days a week away from home. This was far from ideal.

Things came to a head for me when I went to Portland with *Mayfair* photographer Andrew Morland to cover the John Player World Speed Sailing Competition. We were booked into a good hotel as guests of my ex-employer and were to spend five days watching the fastest sailing craft ever invented screeching down a course of one nautical mile, to see which could cover it in the shortest time. It was truly fascinating to watch and Andrew and I produced a fine piece of work for *Mayfair*.

I had been in Portland for three days and in spite of all the jollification that characterised any evening spent in the company of JP&S people I awoke the next morning feeling very depressed. I lay in bed and pondered my life. Then I suddenly realised what I wanted to do next. I breakfasted thoughtfully and then I telephoned Heather. 'I'm not happy with this life we're living', I told her, 'How would you feel about going to live in Italy?'.

Heather thought about this for a second or two and replied, 'Why not? Why not, indeed?'.

~

In early December 1975 Heather and I left our boys behind with Charles and Cathie once more and flew to Pisa. We collected a hired car and drove to Castellina-in-Chianti. We were to stay for a week with Graham Fawcett and his wife Bodie, who had moved there from England a year or so earlier. Graham had been deputy director of Southern Arts Association and so was an ex-colleague. I had telephoned him, told him that we had Italy in mind, and asked if we could visit, discuss the idea, travel around and see how the idea felt when brought close to reality. Graham and Bodie agreed and so for one splendid week we lived with them in the middle of a stripped-bare vineyard in the middle of an Italian Winter. They were wonderful hosts and understood the feelings that had brought us to Italy for they had experienced them too.

Graham and Bodie saw their principal task as being to make an assessment of our ability to survive in such an alien environment and as the week progressed our rating was increased to the point where they announced that they thought we could handle it. Heather and I took this as the deciding factor and pledged there and then that we would do it.

There were a couple of days before we flew back home. Hadn't we better start looking for a place to live?

In those days Chianti was not the Chiantishire of John Mortimer and there were no estate agents with windows full of colour photographs. There was instead an elderly gent, with cloak and staff who quoted Dante; Signor Virgilio sat with us in our car while we followed his directions. He showed us roofless barns and barns without walls and rough outlines on bare land where once a barn might have stood. There were houses with no water supply and houses with no kitchens. In the short dim days of Winter the business of house hunting became depressing to us but Signor Virgilio was undaunted; he was having a smashing time. Then he seemed to have a new idea and purposefully directed us to a town called Greve-in-Chianti. Through the town, up that hill, miles and miles going upwards at an angle of about 45 degrees and there is *Canonica!*

Canonica is nothing more than a few houses, five or six, clustered around a desanctified church. There is a big house (is there not always a big house in our lives?), which is *the* Canonica in that it goes by the name of 'The Canonica', which is where the priest once lived. There is a house and yard where the gamekeeper of the estate (the Caprolla estate which encompasses Canonica) Signor Lelli, his wife and children live. Around the corner of the dirt track which the upward road soon becomes there are a few more houses and a barn. I groan at the sight of the barn.

Signor Virgilio indicates with his staff a house set at right angles to the track, almost opposite The Canonica. Number two. *Numero due.* It is presently occupied but soon it will not be and then we may rent it (since we are clearly not in the market for buying barns). The present tenants, a family from Florence, welcome us and show us this, their weekend retreat.

Outside the house looks gloomy, all stone with tiny, shuttered windows and a red-tiled roof with large stones holding down the bits that might blow off on a stormy night. Steps lead up to a door that provides the entrance to the house's single floor that is built at first floor level above a *cantina,* a cellar that is at ground level. Within, the main living room is vast with a roaring open fire in one corner; the floor is well worn terracotta tiles and the ceiling . . . there is no ceiling, above us there is only the underside of the tiles that can be seen from outside; liberally distributed amongst the roof tiles that separate the house's occupants from the Winter sky are large, white balls of cobwebs, like birds' nests stuck there.

There is a bedroom as large as the living room and two more, smaller bedrooms. A tiny kitchen and a bathroom with a short bath and a water heater that employs either electricity or burning sticks (one has the choice) to do its job.

Oh but it would suit us very well!

We have been told by Graham and Bodie that before we commit ourselves to any habitation in this part of the world we ask three questions and this we do, although we are by now so excited at the prospect of living here that we scarcely listen to the answers provided by Signor Virgilio.

'Is there a supply of water all the year round?' we ask. 'Yes, of course', comes the reply. (He lies.)

'Has the *fossa biologica* (septic tank – but it sounds so much better in Italian) been emptied recently?' 'Why, only last month I do believe.' (He lies.)

Now comes the big one. 'Are there *viperi* (vipers – a creature indigenous to Chianti and as poisonous there as they are anywhere else) in the vicinity?'

Signor Virgilio's reply came smoothly as though with practice. 'No problem with snakes, Signor; the wild boar eat them.' (It was to transpire that he was not lying – or not lying very much, anyway.)

Chapter 20

We Ate A Lot Of *Questo* In Those Early Days

Life in Italy (April 1976 – August 1976)

From the time of our return to Nottingham after the Italian exploratory visit everything in our lives was focused on our removal to Italy. A friend put us in touch with a man who would organise one of those long, long intercontinental trailer lorries into which all our furniture and other possessions would go. We sold masses of things in order to reduce the amount of material to be transported and to raise money. We would sell the house and the tax-free profit therefrom would be our nest egg, our insurance policy against disaster, our sinking fund. There was something of psychological importance to us in this process of stripping ourselves down to the bare essentials, something that may well have been connected with the experience of working with JP&S. Whatever the reason, the less clutter there was in our lives the better it felt to me. The Lit continues to reserve her position on this matter.

I had one term of teaching to go as 1976 began. I would set the examination and bring the papers with me to Italy; marking them would be my first job as an expatriate. Our removal date was set for April. I started to run everything else down.

~

I did start one·new project in the period between deciding to move to Tuscany and the removal; it may well strike you as foolhardy. It certainly strikes me now as foolhardy. I decided that if we were to play fast and loose with our future we might as well go the whole hog. To be living within a couple of hours drive of the Mediterranean Sea and not to have a boat seemed an awful waste of an opportunity. So we had better have a boat.

Eros was no longer with me. She had been left on her mooring in the Helford River after the famous adventure with Roger Wilby. The Lit, baby son Marcus and I had spent the Whitsun week of 1974 staying at the Pons-A-Verron Guest House using the boat almost every day and had then left her there. Roger had offered to sail her around the coast to the River Medway from where I could collect her later in the year but he had fallen in love with her and bought her from me once he had made the voyage. So at the time we were planning our Italian adventure we were boatless.

My journalistic work had kept me in touch with every possible source of income and I had never lost touch with *Practical Boat Owner,* having had several articles published in the magazine since the days of 'Single Handed To Rhyl'. One of my writing projects introduced me to the company that made 'Kingfisher' yachts who had recently put onto the market a junk-rigged version of their 20 Plus model. The firm had involved a marvellous man called 'Blondie' Hassler, an ex-commando, a war hero of considerable valour and a famous single-handed sailor with a couple of transatlantic crossings to his credit. Those crossings had been made with a junk-rigged boat and Hassler had been consulted on the design of the new boat. I had gone down to Poole to sail it with Hassler and had written articles about it for *Practical Boat Owner* and *The Guardian.*

Junk-rigging would suit me very well, I thought. Its advantage is that the boat has only one sail and that can be handled from within the cockpit. The sail has battens from luff to leech (front bit to back bit) and is furled by simply lowering the sail onto itself whereupon it makes a rigid bundle in special rope slings. One never needs to make those terrifying scrambles to the sharp end to haul down the foresail when the wind is howling, the boat is pitching and rolling and it is the middle of the night. With junk-rigging one can shorten sail in a trice and stay safe. This boat that I had sailed with Hassler was too small. Could a junk-rig be fitted to the larger, 26-foot version of the Kingfisher?

Yes, it could and 'Blondie' Hassler would supervise the design. I commissioned the boat. I paid the deposit.

The boat would not be ready until August and we would be living in Italy by April. No problem. We would, the four of us, fly back to England in August, go down to Poole, take possession of the boat and . . . wait for it . . .

Sail it to Italy! To Lerici, near La Spezia, in the Gulf of Genoa, the place we had discovered in 1973 when we took baby Marcus, in his Abel Magwitch days, for his first holiday ever.

We would cheat a little. The route across the Bay of Biscay, down the coast of Spain and Portugal and around through the Straits of Gibraltar would take too much time (and who knows, it might have been somewhat beyond my competence – what would happen if I missed Gibraltar the way I had missed the Cotentin peninsula?). We would go across the English Channel to Le Havre, up the River Seine and work our way through the French inland waterway system to emerge at the southern end of the River Rhône and then into the Mediterranean Sea. A quick sail over the top bit and . . . there you are. A piece of cake. The journey did not look too long on my AA Book of Europe.

This plan was firmly in place when the lorry, loaded with everything we had not sold and, most carefully packed, the entire Keith and Heather Diggle Collection of Liverpool Paintings, set off. Our dark blue Renault 16 and trailer loaded with camping equipment for overnight stays *en route* and for holidays in Italy, was packed with us and a few hours later we left behind the nice house in Villiers Road, Woodthorpe for Portsmouth and the ferry to Le Havre – and the Italian Adventure (not to mention the Third Great Sea Adventure – Rhyl and Cherbourg counting as numbers One and Two) was before us.

~

The intercontinental trailer lorry could not make it up the final dirt track leading to Canonica. It made it bravely up the 45 degree road out of Greve, past the grand mansion of our landlord, the Florentine lawyer who owned the Caprolla estate, past the small quarry where there lived a pair of the most exotic birds, hoopoes, called by the Italians *upupe,* and up, higher and higher, until Greve, now far away and in the valley, looked very small indeed – but when it came to the left hand turn with the badly hand-painted sign nailed to the oak tree its length proved to be too much and it could go no farther. Everything we needed for life in an unfurnished three-bedroomed house was stuck about 100 yards from where it had to be. There was just the driver, Heather and me – and two very small boys who wanted either to eat, drink, play or pee. I nervously approached the door of the only other apparently inhabited house in Canonica, that of the estate owner's gamekeeper, the *guardia di caccia,* Signor Lelli.

Signor Lelli, a small, stocky man in his early forties, took in the situation calmly. 'Attenda', he said. During the next half an hour we unloaded the Keith and Heather Diggle Collection of Liverpool Paintings onto the grassy side of the road and waited – whatever the gamekeeper's solution we thought it wiser to take personal charge of our only treasures. Signor Lelli then appeared driving a tiny two-wheeled tractor that was nothing more than an engine, two wheels and a seat, towing a two-wheeled trailer that made the device stable. The trailer had an area about the size of a large dining table. The whole thing was like a toy. Walking beside the tractor were two men, labourers from the estate. They started to unload the lorry and piled our furniture onto the tiny trailer – higher and higher it went. When it had reached a positively dangerous height, so that whole was swaying and about, it seemed, to fall, Signor Lelli chugged it up the bumpy dirt track with the two labourers holding the load steady.

They continued all day stopping but once for their midday meal; for the labourers cold pasta with no sauce and red wine taken while sitting on the low wall outside our house and for Signor Lelli the considerable gastronomic delights prepared by the Signora Lelli at the family table. At 6pm most of our things were in the house, the remainder piled outside. Signor Lelli approached me as I stood before the house, the two labourers standing several feet behind him. They were beyond exhaustion. Signor Lelli smiled weakly. 'Basta', he said. The bill for their collective services was modest and I paid in cash there and then. My gratitude was immeasurable.

~

On our second evening, when we had cooked and eaten a simple meal and the boys were tucked up in bed, Heather and I took a stroll along the dirt track and down a pathway into the trees, the *quercie,* the oaks, that grew on all sides of the huge hill upon which perched Canonica. There were other trees, of course, sweet chestnut and acacia, but the oak is the tree that stays in the mind as being typical of the Tuscan landscape – and the tree whose wood would be our main source of fuel when winter came. This was the *bosco,* the deep and dark wood that was to become one of our favourite walks.

As we returned we passed a thick hedge and from behind it we heard strange snuffling, grunting noises. What could it be? Speaking against the impression that was forming in my mind I said I thought it must be a dog. Strange though, a dog being out here, by itself. Heather thought it was probably a dog. The light was disappearing fast. We found ourselves walking a little bit faster. When we were safe inside the house Heather said, 'You don't think it was a . . . ?' and paused. 'Well', I said, 'We didn't see any snakes, did we?'.

~

Of the few houses in Canonica only two were occupied as far as we could see, that of the Lelli family and ours. No-one had yet been seen in The Canonica itself and the two or three houses (it is strange but we never actually counted them) around the far corner of The Canonica showed no signs of life. No cars or motorbikes went past our house. So it was just the Lellis, Mr and Mrs, and daughters, Laura aged 15, Barbara aged 12 and son Fabrizio aged 10 years – and the Diggles.

A few days later Signor Lelli cut the grass outside our house so that we would have a play area for the boys and a place for open-air eating. It was evening, the light just beginning to fall, and the atmosphere sultry, hot and damp, with rain in the air. I was looking through the small window that faced the front of the house when three young women walked around the corner of the road from the direction of the 'two or three houses' and came over to the recently mowed grassy area. They were in their very early twenties and all wore long dresses made from a thin material, cotton or muslin, of a kind I had never seen before. They were chattering to each other animatedly and it seemed that they had come out of one of the houses to take the air whilst taking an undemanding stroll. One of them stooped and took up a handful of recently cut grass and threw it at the others with a loud laugh.

At this point Heather came over to see what I was looking at and we stood side by side. The game started. Grass was thrown back and soon the three were screaming with laughter as grass cuttings flew. Then the weather broke and large drops of rain started to fall. The atmosphere had become even heavier and warmer and the rain was clearly welcomed by the girls who then linked hands and danced around as it drenched them. The dresses became completely transparent and it became very apparent that the dresses were all they wore as they laughed and gambolled, the grass cuttings now sticking to their bodies, their faces and their hair.

For a few minutes the scene created before our eyes had an unreal quality as though an event from a different century was being replayed before our eyes. Were the girls aware that the house that had been empty for a few months was now occupied? Were they doing what they were doing in the belief that they would be unobserved because there was no-one in *Numero due?* There was plenty of evidence of occupation on the piece of land that was obviously ours in front of the house; the car, a children's swing, various boxes and so on. Was it a rather unusual and impromptu welcoming ceremony?

Strangely, we never saw the young women again; never semi-naked outside our house but also never fully clad, going to work or to college, or anywhere else. Perhaps they were weekend visitors of the people who rented one of the two or three houses around the corner – or perhaps not.

Several months later one of that little clutch of houses was to be the centre of a most amazing drama that is as vivid in my mind today as is the memory of those Three Graces.

~

All too soon after our arrival I had to go back to the United Kingdom to give a lecture tour on Arts Marketing and, while there, to pass back the examination papers that I had marked during our first couple of days in Canonica, sitting outside in the sunshine, with the view of snow-capped mountains miles and miles and miles away and the cypresses of Canonica beside me with their rarely seen but constantly heard goldfinches. It gave me no small pleasure to sit there knowing that this unique work of mine had developed to the point where it could support us in a significant way; this was the end of the subject's second academic year with two full terms of weekly three-hour lectures followed by an examination, the results from which would count in the final assessment of each student. Now I was to tour the one-day seminar I had developed during Merseyside days, three hours in the morning and three in the afternoon – and total exhaustion every evening. I had ten engagements to fulfil, the tour including Southampton, Manchester, Liverpool and Canterbury. I hated the thought of leaving this wonderful place so soon after our arrival but it would soon be over and we could start enjoying the place and getting to know it better. I felt fairly buoyant about my situation.

That was my view. Heather's was somewhat different. She was being left with two tiny boys, Marcus was but three and a half and Julian one and a half. She had virtually no Italian. She would have to shop, make arrangements for Marcus to go to the *scuola materna,* the infant school, down the hill in Greve, and all the other things that have to be done when setting up a life in a new place. As I left Greve on the bus for Florence (and from thence to Pisa airport) she stood on the pavement holding little Julian in one arm with Marcus standing beside her holding her hand, smiling while the boys waved. It was most definitely a brave smile for she has told me since on many occasions how alone and frightened she felt at that moment.

~

Greve was a good town and in spite of the frightening challenge of being left to fend for herself there Heather found the people helpful and friendly. She had to remember, however, never to let the children be seen without shoes or she would be damned forever. Julian, still in a pushchair, must nevertheless wear shoes no matter how warm the weather; this was the rule amongst decent Italian folk and our understanding and ready acceptance of it lay at the heart of the ease with which we settled into the community. We learned that the trick is to go with whatever the flow happens to be and to show respect for local customs. Shoes for children, whether they needed them or not, was just one of many tiny but vital ways in which we showed our neighbours that we too were decent folk and wanted to be part of the life there.

~

So Marcus was enrolled in the *asilo,* or *scuola materna,* because that was what happened to little boys and girls of his age. The school was maintained both by church and the local communist government in most amicable co-operation. The teachers were either nuns or civilians. They were all dedicated, kind, good-humoured and professional. Very early on Heather attended a Parent Teacher Association meeting that was chaired by the communist mayor, a man of about 26 years, and although she understood little of the discussion it did strike her that most of it concerned the vitally important issue of the quality of the school lunches which, according to Marcus, were already superb.

Marcus was dressed just as any other little boy going to the *asilo* was dressed, in a *grembiule,* a smock with little white collar that covered him from neck to wrist and knee; a garment of quaint turn of the century appearance that covered his shirt and shorts but left his excellent shoes fully exposed for general inspection. He carried his mid-morning snack, his *merenda,* in a little blue and yellow bag that said upon it *Io vado al asilo.*

~

In my absence Heather got to know who was the superior butcher in the town; Signor Falorni who, when Autumn and the hunting season came around, would have a freshly killed wild boar hanging outside his shop in the shadows of the cloisters that protected all the shops around the main piazza (no place for squeamishness here). He, Falorni, was a master craftsman in the trade of wild boar and pig exploitation and the fruits of his genius, in the form of myriads of different sized and shaped sausages and meat preserved in all manner of ways, were displayed everywhere in his shop. I was always intrigued by the dry cured *prosciutto* made from the wild boar; large chunks of the stuff with the hairy pelt left on one side were presented temptingly, but we could never afford it.

In her first period of isolation Heather entered Falorni's in a paradoxical state of excitement at all these wonderful things combined with terror at the thought of having to ask for some. She found that the most readily available meat for us was *Questo*. She would point to a piece of meat and say *Questo*, which means 'This'. We ate a lot of *Questo* in those early days.

She also learned how to cope with the inevitable question involving the amount of *Questo* she wanted. Kilos could be handled by Heather but in this part of Chianti they employed a unit of weight that was obviously related but sounded different; it was something called a 'heelo', that commenced with an aspirant 'k' from the back of the throat sounding as though it was being cleared so that when the sound emerged it had become an 'h'. This was the local sound of the 'ch' as in *chilo*, the Italians having no 'k' in their alphabet. To get the full effect of the Greve 'ch' sound one has to say in Italian, 'A kilo of apricots and a Coca-Cola' which translates as 'Un heelo di albihocky e un Hoca-Hola'.

~

The town of Greve was a pleasant place and daily visits to take Marcus to and from *asilo* gave us plenty of opportunities to get to know it. The central piazza was triangular with the church at one apex; outside the church the road was cunningly marked with a sign that was the 'Ki-Ro' (we must settle for phonetics as I don't believe my typesetter can handle Greek characters) sign of the Christian church, where the 'Ro' looked like a 'P' and the 'Ki' looked like a superimposed 'X' – so the message delivered was 'No Parking'.

Looking down on us all as we walked around and across the piazza was the statue of Giovanni de Verrazano, the Italian explorer on the payroll of France's King Francis I, who ventured to North America some 30 years after Columbus landed at San Salvador and is claimed by Greve as its most famous son.

Around a substantial part of the triangle there were the cloisters that sheltered and shaded shops like that of Signor Falorni. There was the greengrocer who, when you had made your purchase, would give you *odoro*, a small gift of herbs, a carrot and a small onion, to be used when making your *sugo*, your sauce for your pasta which, naturally, you would be making every day. There was a baker whose white bread looked wonderful but tasted awful as it contained no salt at all and lasted about four hours before it went rock hard – the wholemeal bread, *pane integrale*, was fine but was only available a couple of times a week (not a hint of today's highly popular *ciabatta* which seems to have been invented quite recently). There were all the other little shops providing the necessities of a community that was not yet familiar with the large supermarket that has as its aim the destruction of town centres the civilised world over.

Along one narrow street leading down towards the church were the premises of the man I mentally labelled 'the rabbit strangler'. His trade was rearing rabbits for sale as food and his shop, very dark and very smelly, was lined with cages containing rabbits of a wide variety of colours. One went to the shop, picked a rabbit which was then strangled and put into a bag to take home. We never took advantage of this service and allowed the boys to think of the shop as a sort of miniature zoo into which they were allowed to peer from time to time. On the occasion of one of Italy's many general strikes all the butchers went on strike too (even the beatific Signor Falorni closed his doors and shuttered his windows) and there was no meat to be had. Walking down the street of the rabbit strangler, slightly ahead of Heather and the boys, I saw that the man was obviously expecting a major increase in demand. He had taken all the rabbits from the shop, strangled them, and had laid them out on the pavement for all to see. There were about a hundred of the poor creatures, black ones, brown ones, marmalade ones, white ones. I managed to head off my family before the rabbits came into sight and turned them around towards less distressing sights.

The town had a couple of cinemas and a couple of bars, and in the way of normal life in a small town one had one's preferences (there was also a butcher other than Signor Falorni but he scarcely entered one's thoughts). There was one bar that I detested and another – the one where our postman drank and played bar billiards with a local lawyer – that I adored. There was a cinema that looked appealing and another that did not so we favoured one and not the other. There was a *gelatteria,* an ice-cream serving cafe where one could sit quietly, read a paper with a cup of coffee after having dropped Marcus off at *asilo* and occasionally marvel at the beauty of the proprietor's daughter who wore jeans that were too tight (not too tight for me, perhaps) and smoked her cigarettes in such a way that the smoke drifted upwards from her slightly sullen mouth into her nostrils.

The clockwork-operated spit in the window of the ironmonger gave us our first spendthrift temptation and we gave in to the lure of a device that would enable us to roast food in front of our wonderful open fire that measured some one and a half metres across. Everyone seemed to have one of these gadgets that held a spit horizontally and rotated it before the glowing heat of burning *quercia*. You wound it up and your pieces of chicken, quail, or whatever it was your pleasure to roast, roasted. When the clockwork spring wound down a bell pinged and one returned to the winding handle. We carried it home proudly and never regretted our extravagance.

There was a dress shop in town and it took no time at all before Heather became firm friends with Marizza, the lady who ran it. Marizza spoke little or no English but as she and Heather were *simpatico* communication proved no problem. Marizza not only sold rather good clothes, she was also the town's 'injector' – she administered injections for those too squeamish to do it themselves. Italian doctors, it must be explained, frequently prescribe drugs that must be administered by injection – but they do not inject. Patients must thus do it themselves or go to Marizza. Heather became quite used to having her chats with Marizza being interrupted by men, women and children who would enter the shop, greet the proprietress and go to sit quietly in the changing booth. Marizza would then excuse herself from Heather, disappear behind the curtain for a few minutes and then return to resume the conversation.

Very close to the church was one of the glories of Greve, the *Enoteca,* the wine shop that contained a vast manifest of wines from virtually every *fattoria,* or wine producer, in this king of wine producing areas. Greve was the heart of the region producing Chianti Classico and this wine was at the heart of the culture of the place. One went into the *Enoteca* much as one might enter a museum, not with the intention of buying (for, as you will learn, one bought one's wine in a different way, from a different source) but in order to inspect, to wonder, to absorb the atmosphere.

~

The Saturday morning market in Greve was one of its great glories. As good markets do, and most often do in continental Europe, it bustled with good-natured crowds. One would meet friends and stop for a chat. One would perhaps see the local policeman, the one in the grey uniform, smile a greeting and offer a *Buon Giorno* that would be reciprocated. One might offer a similar greeting to the black and red clad *caribiniero* from Sicily, known to us as 'Ratface', in the firm knowledge that he would not reciprocate (these chaps are unpopular throughout the length and breadth of Italy I am told, for they are the rotweillers of the police system).

The whole piazza was filled with stalls: the run-of-the-mill clothes stalls, tool stalls, music stalls, vegetable stalls, the fishmonger whose very visible advertisement was the head of a swordfish on his stall with the sword pointing skywards, the *parmeggiano* cheese salesman with half a dozen new cheeses that would be chiselled open one at a time, with small slivers of cheese for tasting and the whetting of appetites being passed down the queue of customers that would start to form as soon as he showed his face – this cheese was one of the staples of life and today, living in England, I sometimes wonder how I manage to survive without my daily fix of this fabulous food.

Our favourite was the *porchetta* man, an old fellow whose stock consisted simply of one whole roasted pig. It had been stuffed with a variety of materials, herbs and garlic featuring prominently in the mix. The beast lay out on the wooden stalls, a golden shiny brown, with the canvas covering flapping above it; the proprietor would approach knife in hand and a queue, if one had not already formed, would form now. To hand there would be an assistant, a female relative invariably, with piles of *panini,* bread rolls. Pork could then be bought by weight or by the filled *panino.* Buying one's pork involved answering a series of questions from the old man to ascertain from which portion of the pig your slices would be taken and also your preference for the type of stuffing. It was always worth the wait.

Heather and I returned to Greve several years ago, on market day, and found the old *porchetta* man, now very frail, still at his craft. We bought two *panini* for lunch and to complement them, a bottle of *Nozzole,* our favourite Chianti Classico, from the *Enoteca*. Outside Pisa airport, just before we returned our hire car, we drank from plastic cups and ate our *panini*. It was one of the finest meals we have ever eaten for one of its principal ingredients was nostalgia and in our memory now it excels many, many others far more lavish and expensive.

~

Back up the hill we were settling down very nicely in *Numero due* now that I had returned from the UK tour. It was Spring and just to the left of our front door there was a lilac bush bursting forth with sweet-smelling flowers. The flowers attracted a large and lovely swallow-tailed butterfly that had within its overall design an eye, an imitation eye, at the end of each of its two tails; the eyes were decoys so that hungry birds spotting a tasty morsel at rest would peck at the wrong end and so be confounded by prey that would suddenly take off in the wrong direction. These butterflies awoke in me those feelings for small and beautiful things that I had possessed when a small child and I watched them blissfully.

~

Now, what was to be done about wine? Here we were living in the centre of the Caprolla estate that was known to produce some of the best wine around; where was it? It was not in the *Enoteca* and it was most definitely not in the Co-op (our nearest equivalent to a supermarket). I enquired of Signor Lelli who explained that the wine of Caprolla was not bottled for commercial sale. It was available to tenants of the estate but only by special arrangement and by the *demigianno,* a glass carboy containing 54 litres of wine. A bit of a struggle lifting this to one's glass, one might think. Indeed. I asked Graham Fawcett, our former host in Castellina-in-Chianti, who often visited with his wife, Bodie. Graham explained all.

First one needed to acquire 27 two-litre *fiasci,* flasks of the kind that are generally available with a rush or straw jacket (the kind that students in the Fifties and Sixties would make into table lamps). No, they could not be purchased – unless one wanted to buy and drink 27 very large bottles of wine in order to acquire the empties; they had to be *acquired*. I looked into the dark recesses of our *cantina,* our above-the-ground cellar and there, under piles of cardboard boxes, were the required number of two-litre bottles, the jackets slightly the worse for wear from the depredations of the cockroaches that lived there. The bottles were washed out very carefully and then sterilised.

Then one went down to the ironmonger and bought a bottle of *olio minerale* and a packet of corks.

Having first made the arrangement to buy the wine at a certain time on a certain day through Signor Lelli, one drove down to the grand house, the very, very big house, of the Florentine lawyer who was one's landlord. There, Signor Lelli would meet one outside a stone building beyond the sight of the inhabitants of the grand house and the two of you would carefully lift one of the huge glass jars that occupied the building's floor into the back of the Renault 16. The weight of 54 litres of wine is almost exactly 54 kilograms; add the weight of the demijohn and there is a substantial piece of avoirdupois to manoevre in and out of the back of a car.

The wine is paid for in cash and the receipt shows that one has not bought 54 litres of wine, but 54 *chili* for the wine is traditionally sold by weight and this adds to the impression of heaviness.

The demijohn is sealed with a loose cork. The wine within has floating on top of it an unpleasant slurpy sort of liquid. What is to be done now?

The demijohn is placed on a box, or table, or anything to raise it above the level of the ground, and left to recover from its journey up the 45 degree hill and along the dirt track. Then, when it is calm, the 27 *fiasci* are brought out. One has borrowed from Graham and Bodie a large polythene syphoning device and one end of this is placed carefully down the narrow neck, through the layer of slurpy liquid and down to the very bottom of the jar. A *fiasco* is placed to receive the wine that will soon flow. One then sucks on one piece of pipe and the wine starts to course through another, the outlet pipe. There is a tap at the end of the outlet pipe and when the wine has reached halfway up the neck of the *fiasco* the tap is turned off.

The full *fiasco* then has approximately one eighth of an inch of the *olio minerale* added to it, the bottle is loosely corked and placed on the shelf in the cantina that a former occupant of *Numero due* has provided for your use. The process is repeated 27 times until one has a shelf full of wine and a demijohn that has slurping around in the bottom the thick liquid that was formerly floating on top of the wine (which you pour out discreetly behind a bush somewhere prior to returning the container to Signor Lelli).

What is this thick liquid? It is the same stuff that one puts into the *fiasci* when filled with wine. It is oil that is put there to stop the wine from oxidising. It is exactly the same method that the Romans used but they, of course, used olive oil. The corks cannot be relied upon to keep out air so the oil is used to do this and the cork is present to keep out anything more solid, dust, dirt, cobwebs and small insects. Why Italian corks cannot be relied upon to do what French corks do perfectly well I cannot say. Why mineral oil is used rather than the more palatable olive oil I cannot say; I just followed orders.

When your two-litre bottle of Caprolla Chianti Classico is brought to the table you will need one more thing, a *tir'olio*, an ugly polythene bottle with sucking device that is used to remove the oil which floats on top of the wine and would go straight into the first glass if you did not. You never get rid of all the oil and get used to having tiny little scintillae of oil glistening in one's glass.

But it doesn't matter because the wine is gorgeous, gorgeous, gorgeous!!!

~

As Spring progressed into Summer Heather and I rose earlier and earlier and I developed the habit of taking a walk in the cool air touched by the smell of the wild thyme. One morning, not long after our arrival I decided to investigate the ruin of a tiny chapel at the place where the 45 degree road was joined by our dirt track, just opposite the badly hand-painted notice to Canonica. There was the smallest of graveyards, only about five yards by six, with vestigial tombstones, and a roofless building that was far smaller in area than that. It was but four walls with an open doorway. I walked through the brambles that overran the graveyard and entered. In the middle of the paved floor there was a circular stone with a metal ring in it as a handle, set into a hole. What could be beneath that stone?

It weighed very little and as I moved it away from the hole I could see below me a substantial void. I moved so that my shadow did not fall over the aperture, so the sun would perhaps show me what lay within. The beams of light, made visible by motes of dust, shone onto a jumble of human ribcages and other bones. I felt very strange as I replaced the stone and retreated back to the road.

~

During the days that passed it was as though we were catching up on all the days of rest and recreation that we had missed in the activity of just trying to get ourselves started in life. Not that we idled – with two young sons there was little chance of that – but we used our time in a way very different from how we had spent it in Nottingham, Heswall, Corby and London. I wrote in the morning, after my walk, and in the afternoon after our siesta (a habit we quickly took up as the weather became hotter). We made much of lunch, sitting out at an old table we found in the *cantina* and eating our pasta (with *sugo* made using the complimentary *odoro*) with grated fresh *parmeggiano* cheese, followed by the wholemeal bread and an assortment of cold meats and sausage. The wine was, needless to say, gorgeous and plentiful. The need for a siesta may well have stemmed from these generous lunches.

~

During the weekdays those lunches were spent with the rapidly growing Julian who continued to delight us. He was 17 months old when we came to Italy and was now walking and talking and bubbling over with the joy of being. He had then as he has now such a distinct sense of who was was and what he did. It was always perfectly clear that there was no-one in the world he wanted to be more than Julian Caedmon Diggle.

Marcus, three years and four months old when we arrived, was happy beyond words at the *asilo*. He loved the nuns and the pretty young secular teachers and they lavished attention upon him. He learned to speak Italian very quickly and was soon as fluent as he was in English. I remember in particular a little show put on by the chidren for parents in which Marcus danced and sang and only his blonde curly hair and blue eyes showed that he was not Italian. He was as blissfully contented as his younger brother.

Heather and I were happy too. We worried about money, but we had always worried about money. Our life in Italy could have been more lavish, we could have travelled more, we could have bought more clothes and gone out more frequently to restaurants, but we did not make our move for these reasons. Moving to Italy was, for me at least, a reaction to the JP&S days as much as it stemmed from a desire to spend some time with myself and some time with my family. So it was a simple life but, within the standards that were appropriate to Canonica and Greve and Tuscany and Italy, it was very rich in the things that mattered.

~

As the Summer wore on we became increasingly aware that there was an adventure on our schedule. There was a boat being built for us in Poole, back home in England and that boat had to be brought to Italy. I had maintained contact with the builders, paid the agreed sums on the due dates as building progressed and by mid-July I knew that we should be ready for the 'off' in about one month's time.

We locked up *Numero due* and paid a local man to drive us to Pisa airport in our car and then to take it back to Canonica to await our eventual return. On 26 July we flew back to England and stayed with Roger and Heather Wilby while we awaited the news that our junk-rigged Kingfisher 26 was ready for us to . . . occupy. I am sure that there is a more correct nautical term for taking over a new boat but as it was to be our home for a long time we tended to think of the business as being, initially at least, rather like moving into a new house. It was the roof over our heads.

On 14 August in 1976 we found ourselves sitting in *Lorcha,* a bright and shiny new boat that smelled strongly of resinglass and wood, surrounded by cardboard boxes most of which had contained various bits and pieces for the boat that I had ordered and had rather hoped would be fitted for me by the boat builder. Chaos overtook us for a day or so as we wrestled with the problems of making *Lorcha* ready for the trip while keeping two active boys from falling into the murky and moving waters of the sea that flowed around our pontoon mooring in a dingy backwater of Poole Harbour. Then we were ready; I started the diesel engine and with huge junk sail most definitely furled and securely lashed, we motored out of our backwater into the main harbour and tied up against the sea wall in full view of the world.

There were formalities to complete: a visit to Customs and Excise to fill in forms showing that we were exporting the boat and so would not be required to pay Value Added Tax on the purchase price – a huge amount for at that time the VAT on luxury items was 25%. There were also strict currency export regulations that held the overseas traveller to a limit on how much money could be taken abroad. A formal visit from the Customs and Excise man was then needed and we sat in our new boat patiently until he called, asked how much sterling we had on us (his face remained impassive as I admitted to carrying an embarrassingly small amount and he did not offer to make a donation), and then he saw us off the premises, as it were. In his words, we were about 'to go foreign'.

The engine took us clear of other boats and then we sailed out to Studland Bay, a short hop, to spend our first night at sea, just the four of us, all alone. It was 19 August. Tomorrow we would set off for Italy.

Chapter 21

It Was The Great Disappearing And Diving Light Show Being Played In Reverse

The Third Great Sea Adventure (August 1976 – October 1976)

Early next morning, after a good night's sleep (there's nothing so relaxing as a snug berth in a boat on gentle water) I pulled up the anchor, pointed the boat at Le Havre and sailed away. She sailed well. She was heavy on the tiller (rather like a front wheel drive car without power steering) but the sun was rising, the wind was in a convenient quarter, Heather was able to prepare breakfast without being thrown about, and it all felt rather good. I knew the course to sail, I had a grown-up compass, an echo-sounder to tell me the depth of the water we were sailing in – and I had my own Radio Direction Finder which, unlike the rented one that came on the Shoreham–Cherbourg–Pons-A-Verron trip with Roger Wilby, worked.

I tried out the RDF, pointing it vaguely towards Le Havre, listening out for the characteristic morse code sounds of 'L' and 'H'. There was nothing but crackle but we were miles away. I'd get an accurate position after we had been sailing for a few more hours.

At some time in the morning, without any warning, there was a bang. It was so loud a bang that I could not believe I had heard such a bang. We all froze. Then overhead I saw Concorde. It had been a sonic boom, not a collision with a submarine, not an exploding gas cylinder, not the end of the world.

I shall avoid any attempt to avoid the embarrassment of confessing what happened next. I cannot continue until I get this part of the story off my chest. We were going to Le Havre. We had read books about taking boats through France and we knew that one entered Le Havre, proceeded to a certain quayside and there, on payment of a small fee, a crane would remove one's mast. The removal of the mast was a *sine qua non* for successful travelling down the rivers and canals of France – because there are, along the way, lots of things for an upright mast to hit. I had stacked on board, lashed to the deck, lengths of timber from which to make cross-trees that would support the mast when it was horizontal, at a height that would not impede our free and easy movement about the boat. I had planned everything most carefully – but everything started with our going to Le Havre.

As the day proceeded, lunch was prepared and eaten, and as the afternoon, not quite so sunny now with water just a little choppier (but nothing to worry about), wore on, I tried my RDF equipment again. Nothing from Le Havre. I could get another bearing from another beacon but you do need two bearings to get a fix, really you do. Eventually land came in sight and I was perplexed to find that through the misty daylight of early evening there was nothing I could see that looked remotely like Le Havre – which is a pretty big place, after all. It should have been . . . over there. It was not.

I sailed up the coast and down the coast and, as the sea grew less and less friendly (to the extent that it was splashing my nice new Admiralty chart – I had been forced to overcome my distaste for the austere approach to colour) I made myself confront the truth of the situation. Just as with Cherbourg, I had bloody well missed Le Havre as well! Once again the tidal streams had failed to cancel each other out and while I had been chasing apparently non-existent radio signals I had been swept far away from my destination.

Then I saw some lights on shore and on approaching them (not a moment too soon for the evening light was fading fast) I found a lock gate leading to . . . I did not know where but it was *inland* and that is where I wanted to be just then. A few boats were gathering, awaiting the opening and when the gates parted in we slipped. Within a few minutes we found ourselves in Paradise.

～

We had entered the spanking new marina at Deauville. These days it looks rather shabby but then all the paintwork was bright and shiny, the concrete was fresh, the lights were shining and all around there were places to eat and drink, there were toilets and showers and it was as safe as houses. If I had not already learned it I learned it then, that the real pleasure of sailing lies in stopping, tying up somewhere safe, eating and drinking lovely things and then going to sleep secure in the knowledge that nothing ugly can happen to you.

Having admitted this let me underscore one fact that may have gone unnoticed while I was making these confessions about missing Le Havre and preferring safe harbours to open sea: *the Diggle family had just sailed the English Channel.* Even if you do it badly this ranks as an achievement.

～

In conversation with other sailors in the marina we discovered the reason why there had been no detectable radio signal from Le Havre. The transmitter was, they told me, on a light vessel and it had been taken away for servicing or repainting or something.

～

Next morning the sun shone and we enjoyed ourselves. I inflated our new dinghy, attached the new Seagull engine, and gave Marcus a trip around the marina while Heather gave Julian a bath in the tiny galley sink. Outside a restaurant a guitarist was playing. We held the dinghy close to the quayside and listened for a while. It was all rather lovely, I recollect.

~

I must now relate the marine toilet anecdote. Everyone who sails has a marine toilet anecdote but mine, I believe, outranks them all. On our second day in Deauville Heather said that she thought that there was something wrong with our 'Lavac' marine toilet which seemed not to be evacuating its contents. This type of toilet requires the lid to be closed after use and then a handle of about one foot in length to be pumped to-and-fro rather like the handle of the old-fashioned beer engine. This action builds up pressure and at a certain point the contents are expelled from an outlet located beneath the waterline. The unfortunate result of this whole approach to sewage disposal is that one did not lightly enter the waters of a typical marina. (These days, I am told, boat owners are exhorted not to use such toilets when in harbour, less ecologically harmful – and more spacious – toilets being provided on shore.)

I determined that there must be a blockage. It was a very hot day and so I was wearing only my bathing slip when I entered the marine toilet compartment carrying my toolbox. I knelt beside the basin and studied the bulge behind it that obviously contained the pumping apparatus; there were various rubber pipes going here and there attached to the device by means of jubilee clips. I tried the handle a few times and although it could be moved there was considerable resistance. I took my screwdriver and, picking a likely looking jubilee clip, started to undo it.

There was a bang. Not a bang to compare with the sound of Concorde breaking the sound barrier, but a very loud bang. There was more than a bang. Our marine toilet had been converted into an explosive device that propelled outwards, in an instant, everything that it had been keeping to itself for the past couple of days. Most of it hit me for I was in the direct line of fire.

Heather, who had been sitting in the cockpit taking the sun and keeping an eye on the boys, saw me emerge from the toilet compartment and make my way up the companionway. She says I was speechless (I dared not open my mouth) and looked like some creature from a horror movie. I edged my way past them and walked onto the pontoon. I considered the waters below and realising that there could be nothing beneath me that could compare in awfulness with the thing that I then was, I plunged in. After much splashing about I was deemed by Heather to be fit to visit the marina's splendid new showers and so, with towel in hand, I went off to make myself fit to take my place in human society once more.

There is a rule about the use of the marine toilet that says one should only put into it what one has first eaten; I have seen notices on sale in chandlers' shops offering this maxim to the intending user that one may affix to the wall of the toilet compartment. When I returned smelling of soap I told Heather about this notice that I should have bought and said how much I regretted not having attached one to the wall of our toilet compartment.

~

We sailed over to Honfleur on the bright morning of 22 August. It was the kind of sail that we liked – short, with the sea calm, the wind favourable and the sun shining. We tied up alongside the outer part of the harbour so that we would be ready for the off first thing next morning.

The range of the tide at Honfleur – the difference between the height of the high tide and the depth of the low tide – is, or was on this occasion, remarkable. We tied up at high tide and, with low tide in mind, I allowed plenty, *plenty,* of rope on the moorings. We dined in style, in the cockpit, while the sea supported us at a level with the evening passersby, and then we went to bed.

At about 2am, when profoundly asleep, I heard a deeply disturbing moan, an eldritch groan, the sound of soul tortured in hell. It proved to be the sound the mooring ropes of a boat make when they are being stretched to their absolute limit – stretched by the weight of the boat they are trying to support. We strangers in paradise were about to be suspended somewhere in space. I rushed up onto deck and managed to unwind enough rope to allow us discreetly to follow the downward path of the receding sea. Then back to bed I went, quietly, hoping not to awake Heather who was, by then, lying in her bunk quietly quaking with fear.

~

Early next morning we slipped our moorings – oh, so easy now that the sea was back in its proper place – and we sailed out until we were poised to ride the flood of the Seine. We positioned ourselves absolutely in the centre at absolutely the right moment, at sea but with the mouth of the Seine before us and beyond that, just visible in the misty light, the great bridge of Tancarville, the bridge we had driven over countless times on our trips down to Brittany.

As the flood tide bore us forward we, with sail furled and under the power of our diesel engine, charged on into the wide mouth of the great river at a fine old pace. We rode the tide, past the small towns that line the river's banks, past the high white cliffs and on and on to Rouen. Now, look at your maps and you will see that Rouen is some fair way along the Seine on the riverway to Paris. A tidy step. Yet, while the tide still had its forward urge and with our engine roaring away, we found ourselves on the outskirts of that city within five hours of our entering the stream. By that time the surge had lost most of its power and was preparing to take the little rest that slack water brings but there was just enough life in it to cause us trouble.

~

That fine, unstayed mast of ours still rode proudly vertical as we galloped our way down the river and it remained so as we approached the first bridge of Rouen. We first perceived the possibility of a problem when we saw a small crowd gather before and above us on that bridge. Their eyes appeared to be focused on the top of our mast. I slewed the boat around so that the engine was driving us away from the bridge, against what remained of the tidal thrust of the water. Was there room for us? By a whisker, I concluded. I turned the boat around again and this time, with engine only idling, I aimed us for the yellow diamond that marked the central and highest part of the bridge. As we passed safely below the span did I hear applause from the crowd or does my memory add that bit of gloss to reinforce my feeling of achievement?

There are several bridges in Rouen and after our success (or near miss) with number one and with the tide still rising I knew that we would never pass under the others. We tied up alongside a moored *peniche,* a barge, and waited out the flood and the beginning of the ebb until the water level had fallen sufficiently to allow us to proceed on to the *port de plaisance* where we could tie up safely. This was the first time we had ever approached a barge and we had done so nervously, not knowing the etiquette. It proved to be a simple matter. We would approach the barge with Heather holding a mooring rope hopefully and we would nudge up alongside with our nice, white, new fenders protecting us from the black mess that usually coated barges. Someone would emerge, usually with a friendly smile, and would take the rope from Heather and then a rope from me. Once secured the rules of behaviour were simple. One did nothing antisocial. When one's window happened to come alongside the window of the next craft one either did not look or one drew one's curtains. One did not play loud music when sitting out in the cockpit – but then one never did, did one? Going ashore was a matter of climbing on to the next craft and walking over it. If there were several boats and barges all moored alongside one another, then one walked over all of them, but carefully, not to make a loud noise and not to break things.

~

A couple of mornings later found us circling around a remote and deserted harbour somewhere in the industrial zone of Rouen. We were waiting to be dismasted. The process called for a crane and a crane operator and both had been booked the day before. We discovered why the facilities at Le Havre were preferred when we were told that the harbour authorities here saw no distinction between lifting a mast from our boat and lifting a 50-ton boiler from the deck of a cargo vessel. Whatever the task it required a crane and a man and the price was around 250 francs, or £25. A month's rent in *Numero due* was £45 so you can see that we found the price steep. It was far cheaper in Le Havre.

I cleared away all the rigging and lowered the sail and batten bundle on to the deck, lashing it securely. I assembled the cross trees I had made in Poole and tied them in place. The mast was lifted from its bed in the base of the boat, through the hole in the cabin roof and was gently persuaded to lie horizontally across the supports at the front and rear of the boat where it was secured with ropes. A special plate was screwed on to cover the hole where the mast had been. The long and heavy mast looked secure; surely nothing could shift it (Oh no? Wait and see). Then, there we were, ready to go.

~

Now dismasted we set off for Paris immediately. It was 26 August. The weather was balmy and we enjoyed every second of the three and a half days we spent chugging quite gently through lovely countryside, mooring at night wherever we chose. One blissful evening we passed a house where the family was dining in the garden; I stopped, walked up their little jetty and asked if we might spend our evening and night as their waterfront guests. They welcomed us and so we two families shared that evening, quite separately, with no more passing between us than friendly waves.

~

On this stretch of the river we learned to be wary of barges. Although the *penichiers* were friendly folk and would never do anything consciously to put at risk a small boat like ours, the huge beasts they rode brought threats of damage to any craft in their immediate vicinity. Their large propellers sucked immense volumes of water from the area in front of them and pushed it violently behind them; the result was a momentary decrease in the depth of the water beside the barge. If a twin keel boat such as ours was hugging the river bank to keep as far away from the barge as possible the sudden decrease in depth would cause one keel to stick into the mud and the smaller craft would then pivot around so that one end would come perilously close to the juggernaut that charged on relentlessly. Our very long mast overhung the stern of the boat so when the stern was pulled out the mast would scrape along the barge noisily and dangerously – and, it always occurred to me, potentially expensively. I quickly developed a technique that enabled me to avoid these near collisions.

~

The *écluses,* the locks, began to make themselves known to us and, as with the barges, there were tricks to be learned. The lock is, without doubt, the site of more domestic rows than any other place. Men stand in cockpits, tillers in one hand and ropes in the other; women climb nervously up slippery steel ladders set in the walls of the lock, then wait for the ropes to be hurled up to them and fail to catch them. The men, trying to persuade their craft to stay in one place while other craft manoevre themselves around them, while trying to put fenders here, there and everywhere to protect them, become embarrassed, red in the face and angry. Voices become curt. Ropes are hurled up more aggressively. Eventually the mooring ropes are caught and slipped around bollards to be taken up as the water level rises. This applies to the 'up' lock, of course. The 'down' lock, where the boat starts at the same level as the lock gates, is easier as there is no need to climb ladders and hurl ropes. But locks are never easy places because there is always someone there to witness one's stupidity and, by their presence, to guarantee that it will manifest itself.

~

Somewhere along the way from Rouen to Paris we stopped for the night by a tiny and almost deserted jetty at the edge of a town. Another boat had chosen this spot and in the way of travellers we quickly made contact with its occupants. The boat was an 'Eventide', a classic design, and was called *Bokky*, a derivative of Springbok. It was occupied by a small, tanned, South African man of 40 or more, his wife, who was in her twenties and a baby, who was the result of their combined labours.

We got to know this couple almost as soon as we stopped for they observed the convention that had them as occupiers of the place coming out to take the ropes of the newcomers and help us in to a mooring. They had been there some time and looked likely to stay for a good deal longer. They had, they explained, set out from England not so very long ago but their destination had been the West Indies; an ugly cut with a carving knife while trying to prepare a meal in the galley during rough weather had put the wife out of commission and they had decided to try Europe instead. The engine of their boat had since broken down and one could see parts of it around the boat where the man had dismantled it and failed to put it together again. They had been in this spot for many weeks and, in the manner of my Father during his Bath bachelor days, were to a degree living off the land and, in particular, the gardens of the houses nearby.

They appeared glad to see us and sorry when we left the next morning *en route* for Paris. They had already visited Paris but only by bus from the nearby town. It seemed unlikely that they would ever reach Paris by boat.

~

We entered the environs of Paris on 29 August, motoring our way slowly through the outskirts until more familiar sights came into view. The *carte de navigation fluviale* we had bought told us that the *port de plaisance* of Paris lay at the Pont de la Concorde and that is where we headed. It was not the brightest of days as we moved slowly up the line of moored boats looking for a little space where we could snug in; the rain started to drizzle and our earlier euphoria brought on by a few days of good weather, pleasant scenery and relaxed travelling, soon disappeared. Oh, where were we going to moor our boat so that we could settle down for a few hours, eat and rest?

As though following the example of *Bokky,* a healthy-looking man with grey hair appeared on the deck of a very beautiful motor sailer, a 'Fisher' of 32 feet, that was flying the British ensign. He beckoned us over and invited us to lay alongside, which offer we accepted promptly. Within a few minutes the man invited us all to join them down below for a welcoming drink. He was an Englishman, Arthur, and he was travelling with his American wife, Esther, their teenage son Robin and eleven-year-old daughter, Mimi. They lived in Puerto Rico and had come to England to buy a boat suitable for a trip to Spain via the French waterway system and the Mediterranean. When this, their long-planned extended holiday was over, they planned to sail the boat back to the USA, across the Atlantic.

This couple, in their forties, with their two children, were to become our travelling companions for almost the whole of our trip through France. Arthur was an almost exact double of my old sailing companion from Heswall, Ken Stubbs, with his prematurely grey hair, calm manner, ready smile and complete mastery of sailing and anything to do with boats; he had sailed the Atlantic three times. Esther's place in life was to have as little as possible to do with boats apart from being in them with Ken and making sure that the gin stocks were kept high. Robin was good looking, cheerful and sufficiently strong and agile to run up those dreadful steel ladders at the locks, catch mooring ropes first time and then to secure their boat, *Lady Tina of Kilburn,* but also, after a day or so, to perform this service for us as well. Mimi just sort of hung around here and there being extremely pleasant to everyone.

We spent a couple of days in Paris, which was largely closed due to *fermature annuelle.* The shut-up shops sent us walking for miles while we tried to stock up with all the provisions needed by a family that includes two very young children. I will always associate this expedition with long, long walks with arms aching from the weight of plastic bags stuffed full with not only food but the milk, juice, bottled water, wine and beer – Oh yes, and gin *and* tonic – needed to support all our lives afloat. We were to find that most towns turned their backs on their canals, keeping them as far away as possible from decent folk and when they had to make contact then they kept the shops as far away as possible. We could see why most of the barges had on their decks push bikes and trailers, motorbikes and even, in several cases we observed, a small car that could be winched off and on when provender was needed.

Lorcha and *Lady Tina* moved off together, the Jardin des Tuilleries and the Musée du Louvre quickly coming up on our left and the Ile de la Cité straight ahead. We passed to the left of the great island in the heart of the city and then beneath the Pont St. Louis that links it with the Ile Saint Louis so that the great Cathedral of Notre Dame towered above us to our right. Bridge then followed bridge until we arrived at the point where the River Marne joined the River Seine.

~

The very hot weather of 1976 had reduced the level of water in the rivers and canals to the extent that the normal route down to the South was unavailable to us. Arthur and I had discussed the waterways that we might use and settled on a plan to go out of Paris and to take the easterly route offered by the River Marne and then to join the Canal latèrale à la Marne which would bring us down in a south easterly direction until, at Vitry-le-François, we could go onto the Canal de la Marne à la Saône which would take us south down to a point that was close to Dijon. At a place called Heuilley we would enter the River Saône and stay on this route until we came to the great Southern city of Lyon. Then there would only be the River Rhône to navigate and we noted from our charts and guides that the use of a pilot out of Lyon going south was obligatory.

Lady Tina would stay with us all the way down the River Rhône until just after Avignon, when at Beaucaire they would go right into the Canal du Rhône à Sète and on to the port of Sète where they would enter the Mediterranean Sea and go on to Spain. We would continue with the Rhône through Arles and down to Port St. Louis where we too would meet the sea and make the eastward journey over to Italy.

We entered the River Marne and another stage of our journey began.

~

On our second night out of Paris, on 1 September, we moored near a restaurant and with Robin and Mimi babysitting there we celebrated our fifteenth wedding anniversary in as much style as we thought we could afford. The restaurant food gave us mild food poisoning. It was to be a fairly common experience during this trip. Food that we cooked for ourselves on board often made us ill. Food served to us in restaurants also often made us ill. It is something that happens on boats, I think.

~

Cruising deeper and deeper into France we became aware of the degree of planning that had been brought to bear on this waterway system during Napoleonic times when it was made to be a highly efficient means of conveying goods throughout the country. The only power then was the horse but one horse could pull a huge load if the weight was carried by water. As the centre of France rises so the canal system had to be raised and the path we travelled followed this steady elevation as locks, first occurring only now and then and later one following hot on the heels of the other, held the water level and moved us upwards, step by step.

In those Napoleonic days every lock had to have its lock-keeper and every lock-keeper had to have a house in which to live. The bureaucracy of the times obviously established the French Standard Lock-keeper's Cottage and with it the French Standard Lock-keeper's Garden, for by many of the locks we found derelict cottages, all following the same or very similar plan, with one pear tree, one plum tree and one apple tree all similarly gone over to sourness after decades of neglect. I do not claim that these sad trees were the ones planted when the cottages were built but bureaucracy being the way it is there is every likelihood that the earlier model of an official lock-keeper's garden would go on being followed until someone realised that the days of the French Standard Lock-keeper were over and he would no longer need his Cottage and his Garden.

Those folk who dream of the little place in the French countryside to do up and turn into a place for dreamy holidays probably need look no further than the banks of a remote canal.

Not that they were all gone, these lock-keepers. In many places they were much in evidence but where the locks are scrambling over themselves to give you a leg up as the high central area of France is approached, the water traveller is pretty much left to his own efforts to get those gates shut and opened and shut once more. Our lot was not too hard here for we had Robin and often we needed Robin, for whenever we approached a lock it seemed that both our sons needed to take a pee. It became an almost magical phenomenon; a lock would be about to come into view and, just as a dog will get excited about going for a walk before its owner has even reached for its lead, those boys would start calling for attention as a matter of urgency.

~

In between locks the trip quickly took on its own leisurely pace. Little skill was called for; only the most basic commonsense and patience. One motored steadily onwards, only taking particular care when a barge came into view ahead or, if one was wanting to pass, when it forced its way into one's attention with an ear-shattering blast on its immense hooter. There was plenty of time to look at the scenery and dream. Mostly we travelled in the wake of *Lady Tina* and when she stopped for lunch or at the end of the day, we did too. The two parties of travellers usually met when the boats were moored for a pre-prandial drink. We had discovered that French supermarkets sold a brand of French manufactured gin that had an English name; the label bore the words 'Old Lady's Gin', and this was adopted as the official team tipple by Esther and Heather.

Sundays were always, perforce, a day of rest for by law all river traffic halted on that day. What a good idea the Sabbath is!

Autumn was beginning to show itself in the French countryside and we began to find 'food for free' along the way. There was one stretch that seemed to go on, day after day, where there were heavily laden walnut trees along the canal banks. Blackberries were everywhere. Not all the fruit trees in the deserted lock-keepers' cottages were barren and pears and plums could be found. Mushrooms started to be visible here and there in the fields that we passed. I developed a technique for mushroom picking; when they were spied I called Heather's attention and then gently put the boat into the mud of the bank nose first; she would then skip over the sharp end with plastic bag in hand and pick the large field mushrooms of the kind we used to call 'horse mushrooms' when I was a child. On her return I would reverse out of the temporary mud berth and then it would be full steam ahead to catch up with *Lady Tina*.

Robin, who had only ever before seen mushrooms in the shops of Puerto Rico, a country where it seems they do not grow wild, was fascinated by the lovely specimens I would bring over to them for their own table and determined to go find some for himself. Early one evening, while the Old Lady's Gin was being circulated, he went out with Mimi on the hunt. Ten minutes later he returned with a handful of excellent mushrooms asking if these were all right to eat. They were indeed and I commended him on them. He took me over to the field where he had found them and there I saw a sight only ever before seen in my childhood dreams when sometimes happiness meant nothing more than finding lots of lovely mushrooms; the field was full of them. It was almost entirely white with mushrooms. Beginner's luck, all right.

~

The up locks on the Canal de la Marne à la Saône, the increasing frequency of which each day made me think of a gigantic set of steps carrying us up higher and higher, eventually achieved their objective at Balesmes, near Langres, where we arrived at the great tunnel that would take us 4,820 metres through a very large hill (indeed, it might even have qualified for the title 'mountain' but we never saw it from the outside and could not pass comment on this). Courtesy of the engineers of Napoleon we had been elevated to 1,115 feet above sea level. From Vitry-le-François, where we left the Canal latèrale à la Marne, we had passed through 71 locks in 155 kilometres – about one lock every two kilometres or so. From Balesmes we would pass through 42 locks in the 69 kilometres to Heuilley where we would join the River Saône – about one lock every one and a half kilometres.

4,820 metres is, in British currency, three miles and that is a long way to travel through an unlit tunnel that was built nearly 200 years ago, on water that cannot even be seen in the blackness.

This tunnel was wide enough only to permit the passage of barges and boats in one direction at a time and access was governed by the slowest set of traffic lights in the world. While we waited moored behind *Lady Tina* we watched one or two of the *penichiers* cut branches from a nearby wood and then lash them across their vessels so that the leafy ends protruded sufficiently far to brush the wall near to their steering position. This was the traditional thing to do when horses pulled the barges, the sound of the twigs brushing against the wall providing some idea of how straight the boat was travelling along a canal the walls of which simply could not be seen. These days the bargees did the same thing although their craft were powered by engine, had spotlights and they could see their way perfectly well – but they were French and so respected their traditions. As the red light refused to change to green Arthur took some rope and taught me how to splice.

Eventually we entered, motoring slowly, keeping a safe distance behind *Lady Tina*. There was light behind us from the entrance but ahead there was only our companion vessel. I switched on our cabin lights and they threw some illumination on the circular walls that contained the canal and us. To our right there was the towpath for horses. One had the impression of dark, cool – verging on cold – moistness. The sort of place where there might be rats. Heather drew the boys into the cabin, closed the curtains and the hatch cover; she would feed them and so take their minds off where we were and what we were doing as well as hers.

The tunnel at Balesmes is absolutely straight but when you look ahead in perfect blackness, no matter how good your eyesight, you will not see the light at the end of the tunnel. Light will not penetrate so far; it cannot make the distance; according to their individual wavelengths the constituent colours that we see in a rainbow fall away and die. Do they drop into the dark water, I wonder, do they momentarily give it a hint of indigo, say, before being extinguished? Whatever the dying lights do, ahead is blackness.

The hole behind you gets smaller, as you would imagine it would, but it is still there providing you with a link to the outside world; as long as it is there you could always walk back to it along the old horses' towpath, or swim if you had a mind to.

After a surprisingly short time you turn and look for that reassuring spot of light and find that something very odd has happened to it; it has turned green. The light of shorter wavelength has already plopped into the water leaving only enough to make a strange sort of green – but there is still light enough to give you confidence. Then it goes red, just like that. No-one has thrown a switch, it is just following a natural law. More plops in the water. It may be small, it may only be red but it is still there, a link with the real world. Then it goes out; the final dive into the canal. Complete blackness now.

You motor on and on. There is no reason to be frightened but you are certainly not at ease. How long does it take to travel three miles in pitch blackness? I kept no record of how long it took us but it surely took more than two hours before I saw, there ahead of us, a tiny red light. It was not an electric light. It was not the other half of the slowest traffic lights in the world. It was the great disappearing and diving light show being played in reverse; the first wavelength to be visible is the red which pulls itself from the water, then it is joined by others, still dripping no doubt, to make a green light of distinctly wider diameter, and then, the grand finale, the whole ensemble appears to make good old-fashioned daylight shining through a hole that enlarges with every minute of motoring that passes. We emerge into the sunshine.

Having crossed the subterranean plateau we prepared for the downward *whoosh* through the 42 locks in the next 69 kilometres. Would that it had been so swift and easy. We became very weary of locks.

~

At Heuilley we joined the River Saône, broad, calm and positively restful after the canal and all its exertions. We spent our first night at Chalons sur Saône.

The next morning was to produce an incident that was so terrible in what might have happened, what very, very nearly happened, that in the years following Heather and I could not bring ourselves to discuss it and even now, as I prepare to describe it, I feel myself go cold at the horror of . . . what might have happened.

I was in my customary place at the tiller and Heather was in the cabin making breakfast. It was a bright clear morning and it felt wonderful to be moving along almost in the wake of *Lady Tina,* making good progress towards the South. The boys climbed up from the cabin into the cockpit and took up their favourite position on either side of the tiller, kneeling on the seat and looking over the stern. Whenever the boys were out of the cabin they wore lifejackets and safety harnesses, *always.*

I leaned forward to look into the cabin to speak to Heather and when I looked back Marcus told me, very calmly, that Julian had gone. I did not take this in. How could he have gone back into the cabin when I had been standing in front of it?

As what must have happened struck me like a blow to the head I leaned on the tiller and pushed the boat into the tightest, fastest 180 degree turn imaginable. I yelled at Heather to get out of the cabin fast, to grab Marcus and hold him tight and to look out *there,* in the water, for Julian.

We saw him. Thank God, we saw him. He was lying in the water absolutely motionless, facing upwards, his body supported by the tiny blue kapok-filled anorak he had been wearing. He had on neither lifejacket nor harness. I slowed the boat right down and drew alongside our little boy. He still did not move, yet his face was fully out of the water. I took the boat hook from Heather and made ready to pull him in.

At this point, Heather, fully clad and wearing the heaviest of sweaters and her glasses, simply jumped off the boat and grabbed him tight. She fixed his anorak onto the boat hook and I pulled him in to safety. He was fine. He was breathing. He was not even spluttering. It was as though he had been gently placed on the water with the anorak carefully arranged to keep his mouth and nostrils clear. He was all right. I shouted it. He was all right.

Holding Julian in my arms and with Marcus clutching my legs I then had to face the rather more daunting problem of pulling a thoroughly sodden Heather from the river. She was very heavy and almost hysterical with fear and shock. I pulled and she scrambled and eventually I landed her.

By this time Arthur had realised that something had gone wrong and had returned to join us. With our boats alongside we spilled out the story of our near tragedy. Arthur lashed our two boats together, side by side, so that *Lorcha* needed no-one on board and we four transferred ourselves to the relative luxury of *Lady Tina* with its large cabin and, most important of all, its lovely hot shower. Heather took Julian into the shower compartment and spent a long time with our son allowing the warm water to splash over them, to bring their body temperatures back to normal and to wash away the memory of what had just occurred – something which worked for Julian but failed completely for Heather who, to this day still shudders visibly when she is reminded of the incident.

As Arthur took both boats down the river we then sat and tried to work out how the accident had happened. We had never consciously broken our rule about life jackets and safety harnesses and yet both boys had been allowed into the cockpit without either. Perhaps each of us had assumed the other had seen to it. I know that I had looked at the boys as they came up onto deck but I had not noticed the absences of safety equipment. Why had I not? I do not know. I feel that I was like the perfectly safe car driver who sees the red stop sign at traffic lights tens of thousands of times in his life and always obeys the signal, year after year, and then one day sees it as green with disastrous results. However I may explain it, I know that what happened was my fault and I thank . . . God? . . . for having saved Julian's life.

It is strange how we, Heather and I, both atheists, find ourselves using the word God in times of agony. It is no more than a way of expressing extremes of feeling. If it was God who saved Julian's life then it was God who took our son Piers' life; we hold no God responsible for either. We learn to live with the responsibility of our lives.

~

When the trauma of the near-tragedy had gone we separated our boats and continued our way down this most lovely of rivers and shortly found ourselves in Macon. There we met *Brave Bull.*

Travelling the way we did we formed distinct impressions about the people who made the boat trip through France, why they did it, what they were searching for and how they responded to the – occasionally severe – stress of it all. We had seen plenty of evidence to prove that many never completed the journey for there were abandoned boats littering boatyards and moorings throughout the country. I imagined that the couple, perhaps recently retired, would set out to make their dream come true by taking a boat through the French waterway system, and as week followed week and lock followed lock they would slowly lose their zest for it all. They would leave the boat there, wherever there happened to be and you can bet that it was raining there, and they would 'just pop back to England for a few weeks and then continue the journey later, maybe in the Spring'. The boat would be left mouldering until the months of absence ran into years and no-one locally would know what to do about it. We saw plenty of craft like this, some still with yellowed magazines resting on bleached cushions, curtains hanging in tatters, glasses containing the corpses of flies on shelves, varnish peeling off like sunburned skin. (Just as anyone looking for a dream cottage in France should look at those lock-keepers' cottages so anyone looking for a bargain boat should pop into the many *ports de plaisances* along the rivers and canals and see what can be picked up for a relatively small sum.)

Arthur, Esther, Robin and Mimi knew why they were doing what they were doing; they had a plan and they had the money, the experience and the gumption to stick to it. We Diggles were not in the same class but we would last the course, we never doubted it. We all shared the same basic motive – to spend some time away from day-to-day life, to see new places, to have new experiences, to have an extended holiday, to *see what it felt like*. Neither party was going to drop out at this stage of the game.

Arthur and I met the skipper of *Brave Bull* in the shower room at the Macon *port de plaisance*. He was in his fifties, was short, incredibly broad and looked strong, his body covered in curly black hair. When I think of him today I remember him as *Brave Bull* rather than his boat.

Len was taking no simple holiday; he was *escaping*. Escaping lawyers, a wife and, but for a stroke of good luck, the British Customs and Excise. Oh, and probably the Inland Revenue as well. Lou's name was once plastered on posters in every London underground station as the proprietor of a chain of fitness studios. His marriage started to founder and, I believe, the Inland Revenue were closing in on him. He had a girl friend, an employee at one of his studios, Julie, and he decided that it would be a good thing to do the classic bunk with her. They would go away to start a new life in Spain.

He sold his share in the fitness studios and with some of the money bought the shell of a new boat, a large and beamy motor cruiser, put it in a boatyard in London and there started to fit it out. No-one knew except Julie. Eventually, with the secret still kept, he finished the boat, named it *Brave Bull* and, with Julie safely stowed away, sailed down the Thames and into one of the English Channel ports. His wife, who would surely have been entitled to some of the cash from the sale of the studios, knew nothing of all this and neither did her lawyers who had been leaning heavily on him.

He told us all this story as we sat in the cabin of *Lady Tina* knocking back the Old Lady's Gin. He told us how they came alongside at Dover and the inevitable visit from the Customs man took place. The officer saw Len in the cockpit and asked the customary, 'Going foreign, are we then?'. Len said that they were. 'Got any English currency on you?' Len most certainly had. There was a suitcase of the stuff down below; about £25,000. Now the maximum amount of British currency that could be taken abroad in cash was £25. If you wanted to take more it had to be in the form of travellers' cheques and it had to be declared by having the amount noted in one's passport. Undeclared cash in excess of the limit found in one's possession was customarily (as it were) confiscated.

The customs man asked Len if he would show him the money and, of course, Len did not have it on him. His 'declarable currency' was in his wallet on the cabin table – £50 for the two of them. Len called down, 'Pass up the cash, will you Julie?' and as he did so he realised that the suitcase was on the floor next to the table and, as far as he was aware, Julie did not know who their visitor was. What would she do? Len confessed to a slight shakiness in his hand as the wallet was passed up for inspection.

Len and Julie showed us around their purpose-built boat. Its most distinctive feature was the aft cabin that contained a very large double bed. It was not a bunk, it was a bed. I remember it as being circular but if my memory plays me false it is because the whole style of this room – not cabin at all – this *boudoir* – with a lot of black fake fur used in its decoration, really demanded a circular bed. The boat was painted black and during the daytime it was usually gaily decorated with Julie's rather amazing underwear hanging out to dry.

The two of them were good fun to be with and by acclamation they were elected to be part of our southward-bound convoy.

~

At Macon Marcus decided to emulate Julian and walked off the pontoon where we were moored. He chose a time when Robin (by now well established as his hero) was nearby and he was wearing his lifejacket, so that was all right.

~

The River Saône ends at Lyon and within a couple of days our three boats were tied up in the centre of the city on the bank of the River Rhône about which we had by now heard many horrific stories. The level of water in all the French waterways was by now very low after such a hot Summer and this had the effect of making the rivers run faster. I could never see why but that was the received wisdom of the day and the place. The normal speed of the river was about six knots and it was said now to be running even faster. There were many sandbanks, sharp rocks and obstructions in the river too; lower water level meant, not surprisingly, that they would be closer to the bottoms of our boats. A pilot for the first day's run was a requirement of the French authorities and also seemed to me to be very wise indeed.

But we delayed our departure. Lyon was a comfortable and interesting place to be and the stories of what lay ahead made it seem even more so. Near our three boats there was another, a Dutch boat, whose three occupants were in a state of shock; somewhere *down there* one of their original party had gone overboard and had had been swept away. His body had not yet been recovered. Lyon began to assume the characteristics of a womb.

I made it a little custom to take my sons to the *boulangerie* each morning to buy our breakfast. Our route took us through what must have been a red light sector (unless the whole of Lyon is like this) and we exchanged greetings with the ladies of the ... morning. If they had been hanging around all night then they did look remarkably fresh but maybe in Lyon they run a shift system and do mornings. One bright and beautiful young thing made a lamp-post her own, standing by it in thigh-length boots, ten-centimetre skirt, leather coat draped over her shoulders and, with fingers entwined behind the post, swinging from side to side. There are times in life when it does feel as though one has walked into a film set for these girls, the lamp-post girl in particular, looked nothing like the drab old tarts one usually sees and then rapidly looks away from. That whole street scene was reminiscent of Hollywood-director-doing-a-life-in-France-is-romantic-and-wonderful movie.

~

The consensus of the convoy was that it was time to get cracking. This was spurred by the arrival of the pilot who said that he could handle all three boats if we followed his instructions very carefully. He would travel in *Lady Tina* which would be followed by *Brave Bull;* we would be attached by a line to *Brave Bull.*

We travelled in Indian file for one whole day, sweeping from one side of the river to the other to avoid underwater obstructions and as we did we could see disturbing whorls and swirls in the dark waters where lurked danger. At one point we came across a large inflatable craft with a massive outboard engine occupied by three men accoutred in waterproofs and lifejackets; they were circling around and appeared to be trailing a light rope in the water. Our pilot waved us to slow down and there was a brief shouted conversation before we were waved on again. When we stopped for a break the story of the men was explained.

The week before a large German yacht had attempted to make the Rhône passage without a pilot and had gone aground on a sandbank. Somehow or other they had attracted the attention of nearby villagers who had, on promise of a generous payment, said they would help get them off. The local fire engine, which had a winch and cable, was stationed on the river bank and as a precaution, was placed behind a low stone wall. A cable was got on board the yacht and fastened. The fire engine started its winch rolling and the craft was dragged off the sandbank; as soon as it was clear it was taken by the current and swept downstream rapidly. As the yacht moved downstream it pulled so hard on the cable that the fire engine was pulled through the wall and into the river. After having dragged the fire engine well into the course of the river the German crew, seeing the dilemma they faced (and, no doubt, not wanting to face an even larger bill than they had negotiated) cut free the cable and hot-keeled it down the river. The strong current then rolled the fire engine downstream and its location had been unknown until the time we saw the men who were the local, no doubt embarrassed, fire brigade. Their machine, which they had just located, had rolled no less than three kilometres downstream. A powerful river indeed was the Rhône.

~

The pilot left us at St. Vallier and we tied up alongside the concrete quayside. The wind blew all night, long and strong, and *Lorcha* bounced up and down all night most uncomfortably. In the morning I found that our ropes had been almost completely worn through by the abrasions of the night and would surely have snapped had we not awakened early. We continued our southerly course with some apprehension.

~

As we travelled the Rhône became wider and wider. The wind was blowing from the south against the current which was, of course, travelling from the north. The result was an uncomfortable chop against which it was increasingly difficult to motor. The sun hardly shone through the clouds and rain threatened constantly. I was very glad that we had the company of our friends in the other two boats, if only for the reassuring waves we gave each other from time to time.

After another night's rest we arrived at Avignon where we were able to turn out of the main stream of the great river and into the calm of the branch upon which is the famous half bridge. We gave ourselves a day off and explored this fine old city. Then, next day, we set off knowing that soon, just as the waterways would divide, so we should be parted from our friends as they set off westwards to the port of Sète along the Canal du Rhône à Sète.

They left us at Beaucaire and as they did we felt remarkably alone on that wide and increasingly unfriendly river with its cold wind in our faces and its uncomfortable short, sharp waves. Arles gave us another opportunity to escape as we entered the Canal Arles à Bauc in order to find a spot for mooring that was free of the constant bounce of the waves of the river – but we knew that we could not escape the inevitable, the passage down the even wider final stretch of the river leading to Port St. Louis where we could eventually escape into the Mediterranean Sea. Next day we set out alone for the first time in many weeks. Oh, how we missed *Lady Tina* and *Brave Bull* and their friendly, ever-helpful crews.

The passage down from Arles quickly became horrid. The southerly wind blew up and created even deeper and steeper waves that we punched into wetly. The shores (they had somehow ceased to be 'banks') became more and more distant. Heather and the boys wisely stayed below and endured the increasing discomfort. Across the river there ran small, powerful ferry boats and one passed in front of us so closely that we ran into its wake with an almighty crash so strong that the wooden cross-trees supporting the rear end of our mast were shattered and the mast crashed down onto the cockpit where I laboured over the tiller. As the mast started to slip sideways I had a vision of the whole thing sliding into the murky depths of the Rhône. I made a wild grab at it and held it down onto my shoulder so that, with the forward cross-trees still intact, some security was achieved.

The next four hours or so were a nightmare as I fought to control the boat while clinging on to that damned mast to stop it sliding away from us. Our destination was the final place on our itinerary before we entered the Mediterranean, Port St. Louis. Where was it? Was it to follow Cherbourg and Le Havre in my list of ports that just disappeared?

~

With rain by now pouring down and wind lashing us we eventually turned off the main river and saw a miserable little quayside with a few dejected boats tied up. There were enough boats, however, to occupy every foot of mooring space. Which one should we lie alongside? The decision was made for us by the sight of a man and a woman who appeared on the deck of a yacht and waved us over. As we approached their hands were extended to take our ropes – the traditional sign of welcome. We secured ourselves and breathed sighs of relief. The couple, Tony and Nancy, Americans, proud possessors of a fine wooden boat, a 'Golden Hind', immediately invited us to come aboard and take a drink with them and warned us not to spend any more time than we had to in the open air. Why? Mosquitoes.

We were in that low-lying, marshy area of France, the Camargue, and in those days there was no eradication programme for the monstrous mosquito that infested the place. They bit everything they saw, including the old dog that lived in the boatyard whose eyelids were horribly swollen from their assaults. We rubbed ourselves with repellent and we bought remedies to rub in after the beasts had taken their blood samples from us but we still suffered. We tried to keep them out of the boat and were even reduced to taping plastic saucers over the air vents to prevent their entry. On one occasion I had to walk over to the lock gates to enquire as to opening times and in that brief walk I took seven bites to my scalp and face, including one on the eye.

~

On the second day a large, wooden boat flying the British ensign turned the corner and approached the quayside. In spite of drizzle and mosquitoes I did the honorable thing and turned out to take their ropes and help them in. The occupants, two couples in their late middle age, ignored me. It was remarkable to think that these four had presumably travelled all the way through France and had not picked up this vitally important piece of boating etiquette. Feeling slightly stupid I returned to *Lorcha* and battened down the hatches against the mosquitoes. Later that evening the rain cleared and we saw the newcomers setting out a table in their cockpit for dinner *al fresco*. I wondered if I should go and warn them about the mosquitoes – but not for long.

~

The main task was to refit the mast, and the reason why we could not just get out of the place with the haste that circumstances warranted was that we had to wait on the pleasure of the elderly owner of the boatyard until we might use his crane to lift the mast sufficiently high for its base to be lowered through the hole in the cabin top and then secured. When, after a couple of days of idleness, the old fellow turned up to do the job, I had collected my clutch of mosquito bites and my right eye was completely closed. In order to sort out the rigging I had to be lifted up to the top of the now vertical mast by the crane while sitting in a loop of rope; this, for a man who suffers from vertigo, was exquisite agony.

Then it was all done. The rigging and the sail were all set to go and it needed only the opening of a lock gate to get us out of this grim little place and into the Mediterranean. Tony and Nancy, who proved to be most interesting people pursuing their own dream of a life outside the normal mainstream, took our address in Italy and made a promise to visit in the Spring of 1977 (which they kept).

In no time at all we were sailing out into the Golfe de Fos whose water bore small relation to the bright blue our expectations promised us. It was murky gray and on our right there was an extended sandbank upon which there rested the rotting skeletons of boats and barges that had gone aground there. But this was soon left behind and with a sea that began to look more and more like the Mediterranean of our dreams, we set course for Marseilles.

~

It took but a few hours of sailing to reach the great port of Marseilles. The weather became appropriate to the South of France and after so many days of feeling cooped up by the confines of the boat and by the weather we began to remember why we had started out on this trip in the first place. The first sight of the city and the entrance to the harbour is magnificent – huge, beautiful buildings in shimmering white stone – and we thrilled at the thought that we had brought ourselves so far to experience this. We made our way to the Yacht Club moorings, right in the centre of the old port, in the heart of the city, and there, with the minimum of bureaucratic difficulty we took up our place on a pontoon, in front of the Hôtel de Ville where marriages were performed. During our stay we must have provided the backdrop to a dozen wedding photographs.

~

After a couple of days we started out on what Heather and I both regarded as being the really testing time for us and probably more so than the trip across the English Channel. We were to traverse the Mediterranean Sea from Marseilles to Lerici near La Spezia and this we saw as being fairly awe-inspiring stuff for a couple of beginners. Our route would take us to the island of Porquerolles, then either Cannes or Nice, then Monaco and finally, in one long leg (take a deep breath) right across the Gulf of Genoa and into the harbour of Lerici.

~

The sail to Porquerolles, a journey of some 70 nautical miles, was a day's delight, with a perfect wind and glorious sunshine. The island, hitherto to us just a small area marked on the austere Admiralty chart (but known to me as the location of one of George Simenon's Maigret stories) was a wonderful surprise, reinforcing our impression that this experience was beginning to open out like a flower, getting more beautiful as each day passed. We moored stern first on a pontoon in water that was quite clear and in which could be seen myriads of colourful fish. It was quite tropical in its character.

(The method of mooring that is virtually insisted upon in these waters is a way of cramming more boats onto a pontoon. One lines the boat up so that the blunt end is pointing at the mooring position, an anchor is dropped from the sharp end and, when secured in the sand or mud, the boat is reversed into place before being tied up at right angles to the pontoon. It is a good way of making mooring space stretch further but, as we were to discover, not a secure system if there is a serious blow.)

For the first time Marcus and Julian were able to enjoy life off the boat. Hitherto one of their principal diversions had been when we created a paddling pool out of the cockpit by sticking corks into the drainage holes and filling it up with good water from the nearest mains supply. They always loved this treat and we were able to keep a close watch on them while they played. They had had plenty of walks in lovely countryside as we passed through France and shopping excursions into villages and towns *en route* had exercised their legs (as well as my arms). Here in Porquerolles there was a *beach*. We walked through a wood of immense trees and there was an almost deserted stretch of white sand with clear, clear water gently lapping. Oh, boys, was that not a lovely afternoon we spent there?

I suppose it was on this leg of the journey that our relative lack of wealth started to impact upon us. There were aspects of Marseilles that we could have enjoyed had we more money and here on Porquerolles the temptation to go into a restaurant, to sample one of the many advertised versions of *bouillebaise*, was hard to resist – but afford it we could not for this was an expensive place to be. We contented ourselves with the natural glories of the place and ate in the boat.

~

And so to Cannes, or Nice; whichever struck us as being most convenient at the time, we thought. We sailed in the morning with no particular sense of urgency, aiming to cover about the same distance as the Marseilles to Porquerolles leg. During the afternoon I noticed that the sky had changed and that there were cloud formations that looked oddly ominous; they made up a banded pattern – it had to be the 'mackeral' sky I had read about, but what did that mean? Was this good or bad? A book told me that this configuration of clouds, at a very high altitude, presaged bad weather.

After 45 nautical miles of sailing I took us in to St. Tropez as light began to fail. I took us right into the inner harbour and moored alongside the restaurants that faced the water, the places where people gathered at the end of the day to see the strange and wondrous orange-red light of the setting sun that suffuses everything for a few precious moments of the early evening. I did not moor stern first as did every other boat I could see; I tied us up securely the good old-fashioned British way. Why? Those clouds and my instinct told me that there was a mistral on the way. I had never experienced a mistral before but something told me to expect one now. As I added ropes to the mooring there was not the slightest hint that anything would happen to change the calm, balmy mood of the day's end with people sitting quietly chatting, drinking, smoking – enjoying themselves.

I think that our presence embarrassed the port officials of the *capitainerie* for one came and told me that I should not moor where I was but should go into the outer harbour and pick up a buoy mooring. I can sympathise with the fellow now for we were by then very slightly gypsylike – although, be assured, we maintained normal standards of dress and hygiene throughout. I think it was the recently washed clothing and nappies hanging from every possible place that looked odd next to the very long and lovely Italian sailing yacht moored stern first next to us on one side and the glittering white gin-palace the height of a two-storey building on the other. I told him in a friendly but firm way that we would stay where we were, thank you very much.

Apart from protection offered by our location we were very near to a nice-looking restaurant where we could eat and keep a close watch on our sons who by seven o'clock were deeply asleep – just over *there,* some 15 feet away. We decided to cast financial prudence to the winds (or threat of mistral, if you prefer) and gave in to the temptation. We were halfway through the meal when the scalloped edge of the restaurant's awning started to flutter in a very positive sort of way. When we had paid the bill the blow had started with considerable energy. We checked our ropes and headed for our berths.

At about 2am the mistral was giving of its best and we were awakened by its screaming through halyards, masts, furled sails – and by the sound of some very energised people who turned out to be the crew of the Italian yacht next to us. We donned waterproofs and crawled out into the buffeting wind. The Italian yacht had dragged its anchor and its bow was coming round with the stern mooring acting as a pivot. We were in its path and already it was uncomfortably close to us. Italians were running here and there, throwing ropes and pulling on them and trying to prevent our being crushed. They seemed to be succeeding.

On the other side I watched in some awe as a door slid open many feet above my head. A man emerged clad in a dressing gown. He looked quite unruffled. Elegantly he walked down an open stairway and approached the stern of his boat where thick white ropes held it to the quayside. They were immaculate ropes. How did they remain as white as this? How was it that when everyone else was being buffeted by this wind, when hair was streaming, when eyes were being shielded by hands, when people had to shout to be heard over the racket, how was it that this fellow remained untouched by it all? It had to be *class,* it had to be *wealth.* He touched the ropes and, apparently satisfied that they would hold (how would they dare not to hold?), the Master of the Universe elegantly retraced his steps and went back to his quiet retreat up *there.*

We slept well enough after all the commotion had passed and spent the next day enjoying being in a boat in the centre of a mistral-free St. Tropez. We, sitting in the cockpit with the boys, were at a conversational level with passersby and were engaged in countless impromptu exchanges with English speaking people who saw our tattered red ensign and stopped for a chat.

~

Our destination on the morrow was Monaco, a distance of 60 nautical miles, and we made it in plenty of time to pick up a mooring amongst all the gin palaces. We needed fresh water so I brought us alongside a tap which had what looked like a meter attached to it. Water was only to be had by inserting a small metal token, a *jeton*. I obtained a token from the *capitainerie* and brought out the four 20 litre plastic containers that held our water supply (did you imagine that we had such luxuries as a water tank and taps?). In went the *jeton* and out from the hose gushed water, and gushed, and gushed. The plastic containers were soon filled but on it gushed, this water that we had paid for and Monaco was going to be quite sure that we had. Gin palaces need a lot more water than 26 foot 'Kingfisher' sailing yachts and so on it gushed. I gave the boat a well needed wash down, twice, and then Heather put the corks in and I filled up the cockpit so the boys would have a paddling pool.

A walk around the part of the city that was nearest to us, the customary indrawn breaths at restaurant prices, and then back to bed ready for an early start next day. Tomorrow was going to be the big one, the longest non-stop sail I had ever attempted. We were going to sail from Monaco to Lerici in one leg, a distance of 150 nautical miles, straight over the Gulf of Genoa, into the Gulf of La Spezia and into that pretty little harbour that we had set our hearts upon as a home for our boat.

~

Oh, but it was a glorious morning when we left Monaco behind us! It stayed glorious all through the day. We were to experience the most relaxing, happiest day on a boat anyone could imagine. This flower of experience was opening wide for us.

Everyone has heard of the continental shelf, I suppose, but very few have looked for it on a nautical chart. It is not marked as such on the Admiralty chart but depths are given and if one looks at the depths of the sea off the south coast of France one see that within a few miles of the coastline the depths are roughly as they are in the English Channel, varying around 50 fathoms or 300 feet. In our passage over to Monaco, coast hopping, I doubt if we had sailed in water much deeper than this. Our course to Italy took us well away from the coast. When we were about ten miles out of Monaco Heather called my attention to the colour of the water ahead which appeared to be of a different colour, a much deeper shade of blue. There was a distinct line separating the light blue water on which we had been sailing from the deep blue water which we were about to enter. It was not a straight line, it was extremely jagged but, as we passed over it, looking from left to right there was the line with light blue water behind us and deep blue ahead. I consulted the chart and at the point where we were the depth fell away from about 50 fathoms to 1,400; the sea bed was now 8,400 feet beneath us. We were sailing over a clifftop and, although there was no sense in it, we both confessed to a flutter of nervousness as we sailed over the abyss.

The wind then soon fell away to nothing and we downed sail and went under power, as we would for the rest of the journey.

There were dolphins out there (does one ever successfully photograph a dolphin? I tried, oh how I tried!) and shoals of tuna, making the water boil with their frantic motions. The water was clean and clear and even then, 21 years ago, we were surprised to find it so, for we had read much about the pollution of this sea and half expected to be making our way through a slurry of sewage. Indeed, the water close to shore in the tideless Mediterranean was often disturbingly cloudy, and made so by what seemed to be the fibres of toilet tissue, but out where we were it seemed perfect.

We came across an Italian fishing boat towards the middle of the day when the sun was at its hottest and on a whim I motored over and asked if they had any fish to sell. They were line fishing, their nylon filaments hanging down who knows how many hundreds of feet into the dark interior of the sea. The fish they caught, and gave us in exchange for a couple of plastic bottles of mineral water, had lived their lives adjusted to the high pressure of the deep water and, when they were brought to the surface, partly exploded, their eyes popping and their guts protruding from their mouths. Heather cooked them for supper as we motored on.

So relaxed were we at this easy form of transport (motoring is so much more comfortable than sailing – why can't we all admit this?) that I was able to read a book as we travelled. It was a true story about a man and woman who took a boat along more or less the same route that we had followed so far and, by coincidence, I was reading about their voyage across the Gulf of Genoa as we motored. They were off Bordighera when their engine stopped and the cause was found to be a plastic sack caught in their propellor; the author had to go overboard to cut the wretched thing away before they could continue. I was commenting to myself on the coincidence that we were off Bordighera when our engine stopped. This author then had to go overboard to cut another wretched thing – a plastic sack – away before we could continue. Odd that, I thought.

But it was a long trip and soon the day gave way to night. We decided not to run for a port but to keep on; the weather was good, the visibility excellent and we were not at all tired. We reached the Isola del Tino and Isola Palmaria, the islands that marked the southern limit of the Gulf of La Spezia at around 4am next morning. Over there was Lerici, just a few miles away, but, according to the chart, between where we were and Lerici there was a Torpedo Range and a Submarine Exercise Area. I decided to just keep on going.

On the Isola del Tino there was some kind of observation post, either naval or coastguard, and whoever was there was definitely observing anyone entering the gulf. We were about half a mile across when a beam of light burst from the

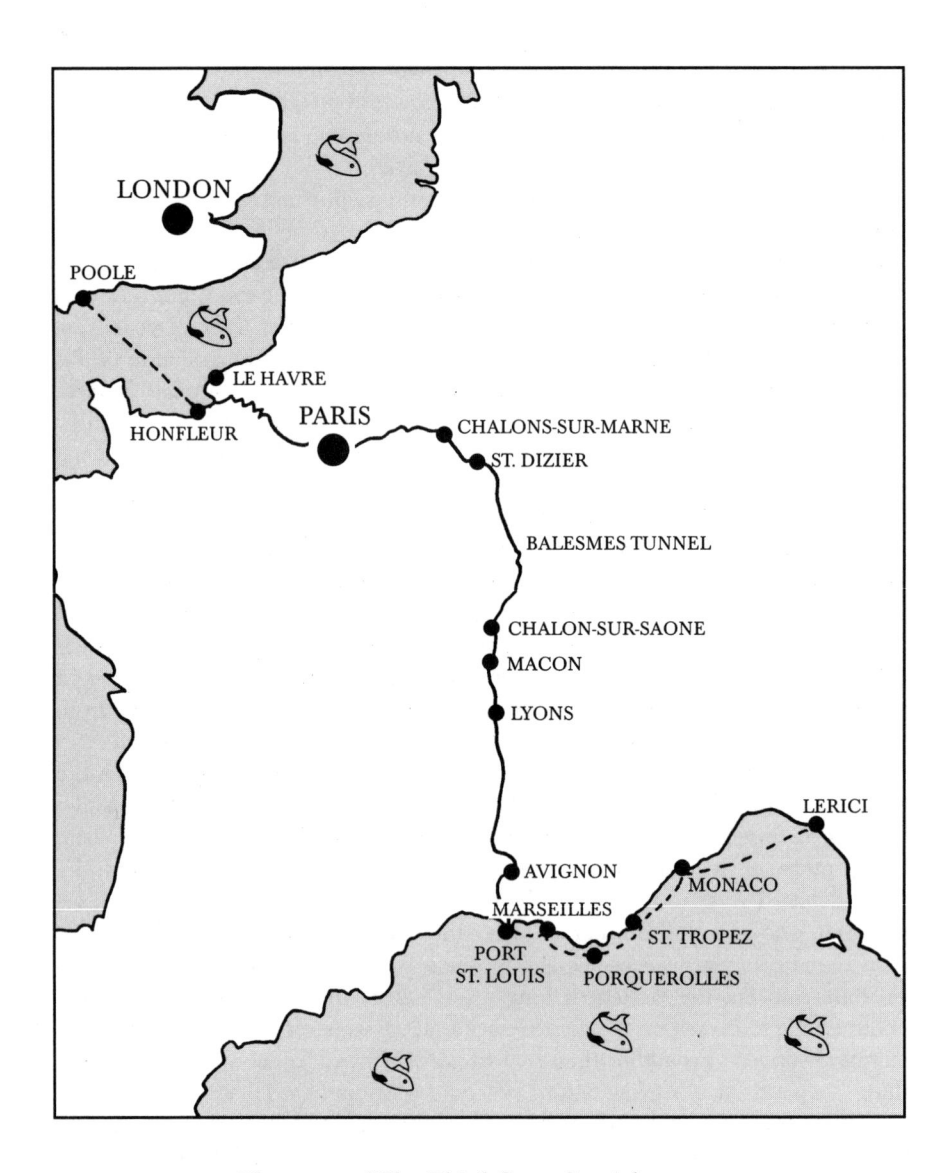

The route of The Third Great Sea Adventure

top of the island and started to flash what appeared to be extremely angry morse code messages at us. We couldn't read morse code but, from its intensity and its state of agitation, I could tell it was saying something like, 'What the bloody hell do you think you are doing? Get out of my torpedo range or I'll start shooting'.

Eventually the demon flasher gave up and we were left to continue in peace. As dawn was breaking we nosed our way gingerly through the moored boats in Lerici harbour and in the middle of them we found an unoccupied buoy. By now tired and ready for a good long rest we wearily grabbed the rope with the boat hook and within five minutes were secured. Deep, deep sleep followed.

When we awoke it was 7 October and our 50th day in the boat. The Third Great Sea Adventure was over and it was time to return to *Numero due* at Canonica.

Chapter 22

They Were, It Transpired, Members Of The Red Brigade, Urban Terrorists

(October 1976 – July 1977)

I found the Renault 16 where it had been left when our driver returned it after taking us to Pisa. I poured tap water into the bone-dry battery and bump-started it down the dirt track road. A couple of hours later I was in Lerici; I collected Heather and the boys from the boat and soon we were on the way back to resume our Canonical life. Oh, but it was good to be back on dry land once more!

~

Before the great adventure on water we had seen Tuscany in the Spring and for part of the Summer. Now we were to face Autumn and Winter. Although life was to go on very much as it had before, the character of the place and of our lives slowly began to change; the darkness of Winter would cast its shadow over our self-confidence and morale.

~

While we had been on our long boat trip, Graham and Bodie Fawcett, now with baby son Gabriel who had been born a few weeks before we moved to Italy, took themselves to live in Céret in the Pyrennées Orientale region of southern France. These good people had hosted us and introduced us to Italy in the December of 1975 and had assessed our capability to survive in Tuscany; it had been their vote of confidence in us that had given us the faith to make the break with life in England and their advice that had helped us to settle in to our new life. We shall always owe them a debt of gratitude for all they did for us.

~

Darker evenings made us aware of the need for entertainment and the record player and radio became more important. There was no television for us but occasionally the boys would go in to the Lellis' house to watch programmes such as *Tarzan*, which was required to be pronounced, in the Italian version, as 'Tartzan'. Although most Italian radio programmes were meaningless to us (our Italian never became so good that we could follow broadcast speech), we discovered a record programme presented by one Franco Nebbia (which, in translation, seems to mean Frank Fog), called *Pranzo Alle Otto,* Dinner At Eight, which was transmitted from Monday to Friday. The man's choice of music was broad and deep, from very early Louis Armstrong to Shostakovich quartets, and his programme became an integral part of our weekday evening meals. We listened to our records and developed a romantic affection for the songs of Paul Simon and Carly Simon (no relation).

As evenings became cooler the fireplace, the stone dais that invited logs of *quercia* one metre in length, with its canopy of thick, black timber and terracotta tiles, became the focal point. We would spit-roast meat and sit warming ourselves, with beakers of Chianti Classico to hand, while it cooked. Wine glasses were generally scorned. Amongst Italians and the English people we knew who lived locally the glass that once contained the chocolate and nut spread called Nutella was used for drinking wine and we went along with the fashion. Even today, when I am alone in the house, I favour the Nutella *bicchiera* over the stemmed wineglass.

~

Down in the *bosco* the *fungi* were flourishing and we would make forays into its dark depths to find the wild edible varieties that the Italians adored; Signora Lelli would pickle those her husband brought home by the basketful and use them in her home cooking.

The Lellis were almost self-sufficient in food. There were pigeons by the dozen that lived around their house and our house (they roosted in our outside bread oven that was no longer in use) and when pigeon was required for the pot Signor Lelli would walk out of his front door bearing a shotgun; there would be two blasts and tonight's dinner was secured. The same method applied to the wild rabbits whose warrens surrounded Canonica; *bang, bang* and there is dinner. Chickens were everywhere; nests were made in our *cantina* and eggs appeared in the most unlikely places (we were tempted to take them but never once gave in). Signora Lelli made her own pasta with durum wheat flour and the fresh eggs from her free-range chickens and the thin paste that she rolled out on her marble table-top was orange from the rich colour of the yolks.

Occasionally the Signora would bring us a share of some delicacy she had made: pasta with a special sauce or, on one occasion, a wild boar casserole that was incomparably delicious. (Signor Lelli, the gamekeeper, organised shooting parties to go hunt the wild boar and large pieces of the catch seemed inevitably to go to him as one of the perquisites of the job.) On one occasion Signor Lelli gave us a bottle of the estate's own *Vin Santo,* a sweet wine to rival anything (well, almost anything) from Bordeaux.

~

A pig appeared on the scene. It was the Lellis' extra Winter food supply and it was given free range of the place. Pigs are friendly looking creatures but, as in the case of that genial looking Oundle schoolmaster who had me beaten, appearances can be deceptive. As the *suino* grew it started to show a very particular interest in Julian and one day I watched it trail the boy as he was playing and then launch itself in his direction. This pig saw Julian as *food,* of that I had no doubt. A bell was tied to the beast's neck and from then until the day of its death (Oh Happy Day!) Julian's life was marked by sporadic leaps to the safety of the house when the sound became dangerously loud. Occasionally the bell came loose and then it was rather like the sound of the drums in a film about Red Indians – when they stop it means they are preparing to attack.

We were invited to attend the slaughter but we declined. It was something of a social occasion for the Lellis'. The butcher (the wonderful artist-butcher, Signor Falorni) attended in a white van and when we left, rather hurriedly, the pig was being brought to the front of the Lelli house and ropes were being prepared so that it could be hauled up by its rear legs. When we returned the animal was just so many joints and a massive pile of sausages of many different kinds.

~

The *bosco* also yielded sweet chestnuts at this time of the year. A ten-minute walk would result in bags full. We bought a steel pan with holes in so that we could roast them on our lovely fire.

Outside the Lellis' house there were two fine almond trees and when the winds of Autumn blew strongly down would come cascades of nuts. The boys would gather them up and, sitting on the ground outside the house would, armed with a stone apiece, crack them open in traditional style.

~

The Case of the Vapourised Diggle Family is one of the anecdotes from that period of our lives. We, all four, were driving down the dirt track out of Canonica one heavy day when there were storm clouds threatening. Within sight of the house of the Lellis there was a sharp bend in the road. As we passed the Lellis' house we waved to the Signora and Signor and drove on towards the bend. As we went into the bend there was a great flash of lightning that almost blinded me but I drove on and soon we were in Greve. On our return we were greeted with extraordinary warmth by the Lellis who seemed very, very pleased to see us. The Signor took me by the arm and led me to the bend in the road where it could clearly be seen that there had been a huge conflagration. The hedge and all the surrounding grass and other vegetation was burned black. It seemed that the lightning had struck the wire fence just beside the car as we passed by and had created a vast soaring flame within an instant of our turning the bend. What the Lellis' thought they had seen had been our car being hit by lightning and then disappearing in a flash of flame and a cloud of smoke. By the time they arrived to inspect the scene we were down the hill and out of sight.

∼

Thoughts, and later on evidence, of cooler weather made us consider the matter of fuel. The main fireplace, the principal source of heat, consumed wood voraciously. There were woodburning stoves in the bedrooms and we bought a mobile gas fire that was fuelled by bottled gas. Gas was easily purchased but what about wood?

Wood for the fire was ordered by volume from a woodcutter and merchant in Greve and delivered by lorry. The unit of volume was not, as in England, the conveniently imprecise 'load' or 'half-load' or 'sack'; it was the *quintalia,* a pile of logs each one metre long, stacked in a pile one metre high that was five metres long. One thus had five cubic metres of wood – a *quintalia.* The wood was, of course, *quercia,* that burned with a good clear flame, sparked only a little, lasted a long time and produced hard, bright embers that were perfect for grilling (one had a wire stand to place over them), roasting – and warming one's bed.

We had found a strange device in the *cantina.* It was a curved wooden frame that had within it a tin suspended by its handle from a hook. I never discovered its Italian name but it was a Tuscan bedwarmer. An hour or so before one turned in, some of those hard, bright embers were placed in the tin and the tin was hung from the hook. The covers of the bed were turned right back and the wooden framework with its heart of fire was placed on the mattress. The covers were then (very carefully!) replaced and tucked in. This device created a cocoon of such warmth that after removing it and getting into bed one was protected from the very worst of weather all night long.

Lighting fires required kindling and it became a fundamental fact of everyday life that when the Diggle family went for a walk on the hills or in the *bosco* the boys collected twigs for the fires and they would always return laden; it was their job.

We bought our first *quintalia* almost as soon as we had returned from the great boat trip. Until then we had used what had been left in the *cantina* and odd bits of wood that lay around the place. When it started to get really cold our rate of consumption increased and I anticipated our running out in mid-Winter. I paid another visit to the wood merchant and was told that he had no wood left – a patent nonsense as he had mountains of the stuff. It was, I think, the only case of discrimination against *stranieri,* strangers or foreigners, that we ever came across during our time there. The wood merchant could see that it was going to be a hard Winter and he was reserving his stocks for his local, long-term, regular and *Italian* customers.

One side of the hill on which perched Canonica, the side closest to *Numero due*, at the end of the land we thought of as ours (there were no fences so any sense of possession was illusory), fell away very steeply right down to the valley hundreds of feet below. It was not a sheer fall but it was sufficiently steep to make walking almost impossible. Several years before, the electricity for Canonica had been brought up this hillside, the cable being carried on posts that had been dug into and concreted into the surface, and in order to make way for these a swathe of cleared land had been made through the scrub oak and the acacia trees that clustered on the slope. The fallen trees still lay there, all of them about the right size around the trunk for our main fireplace.

With another lecture tour of two weeks due in early December it became imperative that I lay in a stock of wood that would last Heather for that period. I bought a rip saw and a small axe in the market and started work on the fallen trees nearest the top. First I cleared the trunks of boughs and then I cut them into two-metre lengths; these I pitched up the slope so that they landed at the top. When I had exhausted myself I climbed back up, took some refreshment in the form of a healthy swig of Chianti Classico and then performed the final cut into one-metre lengths ready for storage in the *cantina*.

As the Winter progressed I worked my way down an increasingly slippery hillside and eventually had to cling to a dangling rope to reach the timber. Logs were tied to the rope and Heather had to pull them up one at a time from her superior position on the hilltop. The nadir of the season, in terms of the downwards distance I had to travel as well as my level of energy when I had finished cutting a week's supply of wood in extremely chilly conditions, required a good half of a *fiasco* of chilling cold wine taken in an almost continuous swallow to bring me back to normal; the Caprolla wine never tasted better.

~

Those concrete columns running up the hill brought only a small amount of electricity to our home. One fairly slender cable brought the supply for the whole of Canonica and a system of circuit breakers in each house rationed out the supply; try to draw off too much and the supply was automatically closed down. Our share was a niggardly 1.9 kilowatts; this meant that at no time could the combined total power requirement of our electrical appliances exceed this figure – this included lights which, naturally, became more necessary as the days drew in. The immersion heater (1.5kw) could thus not operate at the same time as the toaster (0.75kw) and careful calculations were needed before almost any switch was turned on.

I reasoned that the electricity allocations must have been made on the basis that all houses in Canonica were occupied; that would have been the only sure way of protecting the supply from overloading. The houses in Canonica were never all occupied at the same time so I thought it might be possible to squeeze a little more from the system. I investigated the distribution box containing the circuit breaker and saw that it would be possible to attack it from the rear.

So, one morning, wearing wellington boots and standing on a pile of dry newspapers I unscrewed the box and gained access to the back of the circuit breaker. Ignoring the sign saying that tampering with the device was strictly forbidden and with heavily insulated screwdriver in rubber-gloved hands I carefully inserted a thick piece of copper wire into the terminals behind the circuit breaker that would cause the electricity to bypass it. The deed was done. The box went back onto the wall and I stepped down from my little pile of insulating newsprint. Heather looked visibly relieved. I took a large glass of wine. Heather started doing the ironing with the radio playing while the washing machine churned away.

What I had done had no effect on the price we paid for our extra electricity; the meter ran a little faster and, no doubt, if some clerk had done the sums the bill would have revealed our little deception but no-one did and we paid up happily for the luxury my few minutes of nervousness had brought us.

~

As the end of the year approached it was first Julian's birthday (14 November) and then Marcus's (15 December). By this time we were so much part of the local life that it was easy to bring together enough children to make up two decent parties for our sons. Signora Lelli brought her three children and produced cakes she had made with her eldest daughter Laura, that bore the birthday greeting *Auguri!* Heather did her stuff with all the other usual party food. In spite of language difficulties games were played and a jolly time was had by all. Marcus was by this time fluent in Italian and Julian, although only two years old by now, was communicating easily with the Italian children.

~

I returned from my lecture tour in early December with so many boxes of good things for Christmas (including a massive vacuum sealed pack of *real* bacon, immense jar of Marmite and boxes of Scott's Porage Oats – the three items missed most by British expatriates the world over) that Alitalia tried to surcharge me for excess baggage (and failed) and we all had a jolly, jolly Christmas.

~

As 1977 dawned the darkness of Winter turned our thoughts to England and there was sown in our minds the beginning of the realisation that one day we should have to go back to face the music (an apt choice of phrase as it was to turn out). At this stage there was only the seed of the idea and this took the form of our thinking that perhaps we could find an English family with whom we could occasionally exchange homes – so that instead of my returning to England alone for my work I could bring us all back and we could stay in London all together.

More than me, Heather, with her passion for theatre, was pining for some time in London where she could get back in touch with life. Tuscany was lovely but it was not London; the cold and dark climate in which we were by now living was the antithesis of what we wanted from Italy and emphasised how different was our life from the life we aspired to. By being grim and unfriendly, Italy was letting us down, breaking the pact we thought we had made with it.

~

There was also the loneliness to contend with. Heather may have focused on the theatre when she thought of England but what she really needed was more contact with people who spoke our language. We made the most of those who lived nearby. The Canonica itself, the large and lovely building over the way from us, was owned by an American Italian Jewish family, the most prominent of which was Leo Levi whose wife Terri and small daughter Karma often spent weekends there. Terri, of Irish American stock, was young and bore a striking resemblance to Jackie Kennedy; she was great fun to be with but she was not there to be with in the Winter when she was needed most by us.

Down the road into Greve there was a cluster of houses that had been developed for letting; they were classic old Tuscan on the outside but modern and centrally heated on the inside. The place, Melazzano, housed an English oil roustabout, Al, who flew out to work in Abu Dhabi for alternate fortnights, and his American wife, Abi, but we had little in common with them and so social life between us was sparce. In Melazzano there also stayed, for all too short a time, the Irish painter, Carey Clarke, his wife Hilda and his two young daughters. Carey was on sabbatical from the Dublin College of Art and he and his wife were most congenial and interesting companions. One day in the very early Spring of 1977 he put his easel outside our house and, wearing my anorak against a biting wind, he painted The Canonica, the view we had whenever we opened our front door. Nearly two years later, after we had returned to England, I bought that picture from him as a Christmas present from us to us and it remains one of our most treasured works of art.

Graham and Bodie may have moved away but they left us the legacy of a friendship with their friends, the poet Patrick Creagh, wife Ursula, son Jake and daughter Katia. Patrick was, and still is as far as I know, a fine poet (in recent years I have managed to get hold of a couple of his books, now long out of print, and they fill me with admiration) and a man of intellectual depth and wisdom. Ursula, the great grand-daughter of Freida Lawrence, the lady who left her husband to live with and then marry D. H. Lawrence, was a warm and generous hostess who laughed her way through problems that would have brought us to our knees.

The Creaghs lived in a crumbling farmhouse in the centre of a vineyard at the bottom of the deepest valley imaginable, in Radda-in-Chianti, about ten miles away. Ten miles in Tuscany is about 30 miles anywhere else as the roads wind around the hills, up and down, and simply prevaricate over the business of getting you anywhere – great views but an impediment to easy access. So we did not see these fascinating people as often as we should have liked, although the fairly primitive conditions in which they lived were sometimes hard to take and occasionally we did have to suppress our more delicate instincts when we were in their house. There was a free-range goat; free-range in that it had the run of the house and defecated wherever it pleased – mostly it chose the fireplace but often it did not and that, of course, was where you then chose to stand. There were mice everywhere and after one night staying there Heather drew the line at repeating the experience. There were hints of rats, too; the idea of rats is sufficient to repel Heather forever and even tough old me is not too happy about the beasts.

~

We could not overcome the growing feeling that we could not stay in Tuscany full-time. On 14 January 1977 *The Times* carried the advertisement which was intended to bring us into contact with a London-based family who were attracted by the idea of occasional house exchanges with an English family living in Tuscany. A few replies were received and, as a result, I travelled back to England to meet two families who seemed to fit the bill. In Herne Hill I met Steve and Buffy Fender, he a lecturer in English at University College, London and she a doctor, a GP, with two small children. We struck a bargain in outline; they were very interested in such an arrangement and their house and its location precisely suited our needs.

~

Towards the end of January the climate was beginning to create a noticeable depression in us. Nowadays what we suffered would be called 'Seasonally Affective Disorder'. To be added to this SAD situation was a form of influenza that gripped me and held me in its grasp for weeks. I managed to fight it to a draw for a while but one morning I got up and looked in the mirror and saw an old, haggard man, a man of 70 at least, with bloodshot eyes looking back at me. We called the doctor and he, seeing my situation as being most serious, not to say life-threatening, prescribed antibiotics administered via injection.

My whole state of mind at that time was summed up in a letter I wrote to Graham and Bodie Fawcett in France on 14 March. I said:

We are in bad need of stimulation and that means people. It has been wickedly cold up here, very dark in the house, and very lonely. If I were an outsider looking in I might even say that the Diggles were more than a trifle bored. There's an admission for you!

They have done strange things to the cost of living here. I am now coming around to the belief that, taking everything into account, it is costing me about £60 to £75 a month more to live here than it did in England. Of course UK prices have risen too but when we were first here it was cheaper. (This was not true: what we have here is SAD talking.)

Of course, my view is somewhat jaundiced – or rather 'influenza-ed'. I'm still in the grip of a bug that smote me two weeks ago. After three days of lying back waiting for it to go away it suddenly occurred to me that it wasn't going to go away – and it was winning! The doctor took the proverbial one look and prescribed shots in the bum very quickly. The Guardia's wife – a lovely lady with a velvet touch – appeared at six-hour intervals to stab me with syringes (including visits at two in the morning). So I lived but now, after nearly a week of coughing and spluttering, my sinuses have started to explode and I think the bug has opened a second front.

~

It was one Sunday morning soon after my illness, when Heather and the boys seemed to have picked up a variant of the bug and we were all feeling groggy, that we did not rise as early as we normally did. Quite uncharacteristically we felt unwilling to face that particular day. At about nine o'clock I stumbled from the bedroom into the living room which, with shutters closed, was still dark. I opened the shutter of the window that faced out on to the front of the house, the window from which we had seen the 'Three Graces' dancing half naked in the rain almost a year before. I could just see the end of a dark blue car by the steps leading down from our front door. I went into the small bedroom whose window faced directly out onto the dirt track running alongside the house, opened the shutter and looked out. I could see three dark blue cars and a jeep of the same colour. They all bore the word *CARABINIERI.*

Puzzled I opened the door and looked out. A policeman appeared and urgently waved me back inside without any attempt at explanation. Before I closed the door I saw other policemen – who were bearing rifles and sub-machine guns.

We were prisoners in our house and knew nothing of what was going on beyond what we could see through the partly open shutters. After half an hour, there was a flurry of activity with armed men positioning themselves at the corner of The Canonica with rifles aimed. Policemen had obtained the key of The Canonica from Signor Lelli and had gone upstairs to take up places in the windows that overlooked the area where were the 'two or three houses'. Then the policemen moved around the corner out of our sight. A few minutes later a small group of young people with their hands above their heads was escorted by armed policemen around the corner from the 'two or three houses' and were put into the cars. The cars and the jeep drove off and we were free to venture out.

Had there been more inhabitants of Canonica we should have generated a fine old babble of excited chatter but we had only the Lellis to chatter with and chatter we did.

Since October of the year before there had been in residence around the corner a group of young people who were simply referred to as *gli studenti*. We saw little of them beyond their occasional trips in and out by car and motorcycle. They kept to themselves and we knew them not at all. They were, it transpired, members of the Red Brigade, urban terrorists. They had, we were told, a cache of weapons and explosives hidden in the *bosco;* we were also told that the police had found a death list on them. This was around the time that a group of terrorists had kidnapped and murdered the Italian Prime Minister, Aldo Moro, so such tales were quite believable.

Since that strange day, when Fate had kept us all indoors, we have often wondered what might have happened if our sons had been playing just outside the house of the students as they often did, and the presence of the police had been detected by the students in time to take some form of protective action. Could Marcus and Julian have been taken hostage? It must have been a possibility.

~

When Spring came we looked around us and we were struck by how gloomy our house looked. It seemed that Winter had left its dark mark upon the very walls of our living room. This made a most unhappy contrast with the bright light outside that seemed to have to fight its way through the small windows of our three feet thick walls before it died in the murk within. Over the long Winter period those one-metre logs of oak and acacia to which our fireplace had played host had put into the air a rich smoke, heavy with tar that had condensed onto what was once bright whitewash. As each cold day progressed so the walls grew darker. By March they were the colour of the ceiling of a public bar in an English pub.

More than this, the tar had laid a patina of a tobacco hue on the exposed surfaces of books on our shelves and upon the surfaces of the Keith and Heather Diggle Collection of Liverpool Paintings. The canvases were later cleaned successfully but to this day books may be found in our bookcases that bear a brown stain on the upper surface of the pages and on the spines.

Out came the whitewash and with all furniture pushed to the centre of the living room we painted energetically to transform it into a place that was fit to accept the clear bright light of Spring. The wild irises and broom were growing now and so was the lilac with its attendant butterflies. The house was brought back to life with the whitened walls and jars of wild flowers.

We took photographs of the transformed house to send to the Fender family in Herne Hill who were by now absolutely confirmed in their desire to exchange homes because Steve had been granted a sabbatical three months at the end of the year and they wanted to spend this time in Canonica.

~

The Fenders' letter bearing this news made us focus more clearly on our present situation and the future. We had never envisaged house exchange periods of three months but now the proposition was before us and a decision had to be made.

We had one son who would be five years old at the end of this year of 1977 and another who would be three. It was time to consider their education seriously. Julian could, of course, go to *asilo;* his Italian was now excellent for his age and he could have fitted in easily, but what of Marcus? If we put him into the post-*asilo* Italian education system now we should have to make a commitment to stay here for years more. Were we able to sustain ourselves in Italy for several years? Did we want to?

Even more significant to me than the ages of my sons was the thought that at the end of this year of 1977 I would be 40 years old and this gave me some pause for thought. To be 40 is to be very grown up indeed and I began to wonder if what I was – we were – presently doing was at all grown up.

What Heather and I were doing was taking a break from the routine of everyday life at the one time we could do so without jeopardising the futures of our sons. There was some slight financial risk in the venture but I had had sufficient experience of the freelance life in Nottingham to have confidence in my ability to sustain us. In the ruled school notebook in which I kept note of our financial position it showed that when we arrived in Italy we had around £2,500 in the bank; at this time, with mid-Summer approaching, after some 14 months away from England (including the 50 days in *Lorcha)* we still had about the same amount. So, whatever money I had earned it had been enough to keep us.

Nevertheless, it was time to take stock of our position. The boys' education was of paramount importance but we were important too. Where stood we now? Where would we stand if we stayed in Italy? Where would we stand if we went back home?

Our conclusion was that we had 'done' Italy and it was time to stop eating lotuses and start building some foundations. There was no growth in my freelance work nor could there be while I was in Italy. Heather wanted to start teaching again as soon as possible now that both sons would soon be old enough to go to school.

We had no house to go to in England and so would have to buy one. Everything we owned was now in Italy and we would have to transport it back to England if we were to furnish the house that we would have to buy. Neither Heather nor I had secure employment to return to so whether we should be able to buy a house at all was problematic.

Three months in London, in the home of the Fenders, would give us the springboard we needed. Three months in which to find employment, or develop my freelance work, or both. Three months in which to find a house.

~

Where was *Lorcha* now? She was moored in Lerici harbour under the protective eye of Beppi, the man who owned the mooring. We paid her a couple of visits during the Winter. We stayed overnight but it was damp and really no place for active boys, much less inactively inclined parents. Then one day we made the trip and found the weather so appallingly windy that launching the dinghy to reach her was an impossibility. We left her to it and vowed to return when the weather was better.

Lorcha was due to be scraped and anti-fouled and our first trip to her in the Spring, as soon as we had brightened up *Numero due,* was to arrange this. We booked into a small hotel and had her hauled out onto the harbourside. We scraped her bottom, washed her down and painted on the anti-fouling paint that a friendly Italian chap who had taken a fancy to us obtained from the nearby Naval dockyard. We were anti-fouled with stolen anti-fouling paint. Now it can be told.

She then went back into the water ready to give us plenty of good times as Spring moved into Summer. The gloom of Winter was now far behind us. I wrote another letter to Graham and Bodie only 15 days after the earlier depressive one:

We've had some very successful days in Lerici preparing the boat and getting to know the Lericini. There's something about quaysides that agrees with us and the folk working on their boats – usually retired old codgers who like boats more than sailing – seem to like us. And Lerici is warmer. We had three evenings sitting in the cockpit at 8pm enjoying the warm air of a Sirocco – beautiful . . . so we feel better already.

I had had in mind to make some extra money by renting her out but it was a limp half-hearted scheme that I had not properly thought through and I had but one taker, an English father and his son, who took her to Corsica for a fortnight and came back full of complaints about the state of the diesel engine injectors and the overall standard of workmanship on the craft. She was, in truth, not the quality of boat that I had hoped for and I had some respect for the frank opinions of my one and only customer. The junk sail had worked well enough on the smaller model Kingfisher, the 20 plus, but in the larger form the furled sail, when lowered, made a huge and weighty bundle of sail and battens that was uncontrollable in a rolling sea or when the wind caught it. The result was that when the weather blew up to the extent that the sail had to come down the first thing I had to do was lash the whole thing to the cabin roof while runnning a grave risk of being knocked out of the cockpit by it.

I believe too that the position of the unstayed mast had been incorrectly calculated so that the centre of effort of the sail was too far to the rear with the result that there was always too much weatherhelm. So much weatherhelm was there that the ingeniously designed Hasler-Gibb Vane steering gear I had stumped up good money for could barely cope and in anything approaching a good blow gave up the ghost; under such conditions steering the boat was often very hard work.

Another disappointment came from the mounting of the propellor shaft which relied upon bearings that were 'glassed in' to the inside of the resinglass hull. On the way over to Italy the Autumn of the year before, one bearing had started to break loose so that the propeller shaft had started to rotate eccentrically and the whole assembly started to make horrid knocking noises. I had to spend a couple of days that Summer, on my knees in a hot cockpit with my head and hands in the bilge area, trying to build up the mounting support with resinglass. Later it was to be revealed that either I had not made a sufficiently good job of it or the propeller shaft had gone out of true and would have smashed its way out of any mounting no matter how well repaired it was.

~

Lorcha was mainly used for weekend pottering. Lerici was a delightful place, very popular with Italians and less so with *stranieri,* which made it fine with us; to be moored within a hundred feet or so of the harbour wall right in the heart of the town was very pleasant. Apart from the atmosphere of the busy streets and the sheer 'Italian-ness' of it all, the view of the town from the boat, with big palm trees in the foreground and the terracotta roofs rising up behind them was beautiful. It was here that we had taken the baby Marcus in the Spring of 1973 when he was in his Abel Magwitch days and we had been welcomed enthusiastically then because babies are always welcomed in Italy. Now, with two small boys, both blonde and looking very English, shop-keepers and restaurant proprietors welcomed us again.

We made only one longish voyage and that was a coast-hop down to Viareggio but we did not like the place very much so we came home promptly. It was a great luxury having a boat to use on the Mediterranean but what I remember and value most about owning *Lorcha* was the trip to Italy and then getting her home to England again.

~

Our thoughts kept returning to the future; how we were to manage the process of getting back to England and then sustaining ourselves. The Fender arrangement would give us three months in which to lay down some foundation but what of *Numero due?* What of our possessions? What were we going to do after the three-month period had expired?

The difficult decision we made was that we should leave behind in Italy almost all of our furniture, for the cost of bringing it back to England would be too much for us and we did not then even know if we should have a house to put it in. Encouraged by my success in finding the Fenders through newspaper advertising I would see if I could find someone who would take over the lease of *Numero due* and who would buy our furniture. If I could pull this off and time the arrangement to start in January 1978, immediately after the Fender exchange finished, we should be free and clear of obligations in Italy and ready to start a full life in England. Our only remaining problem would be to bring back to England our personal possessions and the Keith and Heather Diggle Collection of Liverpool Paintings.

A certain amount of optimism was called for at this stage of the planning process.

~

My advertisement in the *Sunday Times* produced a man, Kenyon Roth, and we struck a bargain. I would introduce the man to the Fiorentine lawyer, our landlord, and arrange for the transfer of the rental agreement to Ken Roth; no money would change hands for this. We would be paid £2,250 for the contents of the house – all the furniture, pots and pans and utensils, everything except linen, books, personal effects and the Keith and Heather Diggle Collection of Liverpool Paintings. This arrangement would save us having to organise and pay for the removal of our possessions back to England and the price we would receive would be higher than the intrinsic value of the goods. Ken Roth would take over *Numero due* from January 1978.

Heather was far from happy about parting with things for which we had laboured so long to be able to buy (and she still is not – the matter of the handbuilt kitchen dresser is a recurring topic) but accepted it as being part of the price we had to pay for our extended sojourn in Italy.

~

I also wrote to Bill Kallaway, the consultant whom I had first met during my JP&S days and with whom I had worked during my Nottingham freelance days. Bill had kept in touch and he had made it clear that he was interested in forming some sort of association with me when I returned to England. Working with Bill was not my preference. His field was business sponsorship of the arts – not something that interested me greatly – and he took a very cool, disinterested and essentially selfish view of the activity; Bill did what he did for his sake – his family crest might well have carried the motto *Ars Gratia Gulielmi*. In his favour, he was extremely hard-working and clear thinking – and he was an achiever. To his eternal credit he valued me and that, at such a worrying time, transcended whatever faults he may have had in my eyes.

Bill offered me a job to start on the day I managed to return to England. I took it. He was then working with one other person, a bright and charming young woman who acted as secretary and personal assistant. The two of them were working in a small room in William Blake House in Marshall Street, just off Carnaby Street in London but were just about to move to Marlborough Street and would be there when I eventually managed to pull us all out of Italy back into England. Bill's willingness to be flexible over my starting date enabled me to put together the final parts of my plan for our return. For his confidence in me and his open offer of employment I will always owe him a debt of gratitude.

~

Lorcha had always occupied two distinct rôles in our Italian adventure. The first was the obvious one; she was a boat and we used her as a boat. The second was as something that would hold our nest egg of capital intact, an asset that could be made liquid if I really worked at it but not so liquid that I could fritter the money away. It might even be, I thought, that she could become an appreciating asset for in those days it was by no means unknown for boats to be sold secondhand at prices higher than were originally paid for them. *Lorcha* could not be liquidated in Italy (I made a couple of half-hearted attempts but lumpy-looking *Lorcha* did not appeal to the Italian taste for *bella figura* – boats for Italians tended to be rather svelte, fast, powered by big engines and ornamented with a pretty girl or two).

We would take *Lorcha* back to England, just as we had brought her to Italy, across the Mediterranean Sea, through the French waterway system, across the Channel and back to Poole where she could lay until we found a buyer for her. There was time for this in our schedule if we acted promptly.

~

The plan then was to prepare *Numero due* for the arrival of the house-exchange couple, with all personal effects packed away safely, just as though we were renting out the place. We would then bring *Lorcha* back to England and move into the other couple's house in Herne Hill. We would leave the boys with Heather's parents and return to Italy to collect the car and trailer which would be loaded up with the minimum requirements for our new life in London. Once back in London we would have about three months in which to sell the boat and find a house that we could afford to buy, using the money from the boat as the deposit.

It did not quite work out like that but at least we started out with a rational plan.

Chapter 23

Large Wads Of Money Secured By Elastic Bands Are Passed Over To Disappear Into Capacious Pockets

The Fourth Great Sea Adventure (August 1977)

We left Lerici when darkness fell. The boys were snugged away in their bunks and Heather and I were wrapped up well against the elements. We motored out of the harbour and then, taking the official route out of the bay (the one that avoided violent language in morse code) we set out to cross the Bay of Genoa, the first leg of our trip back to England. Up went the brown sail, now somewhat bleached after the Summer sun of Italy, and we took the benefit of a comfortable following wind that suited us nicely. Heather took the helm and after determining the course to sail I went below for a sleep: I was awakened by her after about five hours with the information that the wind was now very much stronger and the boat was getting hard to handle. After lowering a couple of panels of the sail to reduce the strain we sailed more comfortably and Heather was able to get some rest. This had been her longest period of sole control of the boat, sailing in darkness, with only the compass to guide her, and a rising wind that was becoming altogether less comfortable as waves rose behind us threatening to wash over the stern – which they were to do before I was able to shorten the sail.

We sailed on throughout the day and the following night under uncomfortable but bearable conditions. Our destination had been Porquerolles, that lovely island we had visited on the outward trip, but as dawn broke we saw ahead of us not open sea, that our course marked on the chart indicated would be there, but the faint outlines of land. The weather was by then foul with rain lashing down, and the damned wind throwing tons of seawater over us from behind (making my chart all wet – oh how I *hate* that!). We were in another 'Where the hell are we?' situation.

Why had we gone so far off course? The explanation was simple enough. *Lorcha* had been moored in Lerici harbour for about ten months, in a constant position relative to the earth's magnetic field and the compass had deviated, its needle being persuaded to point just a tiny amount away from Magnetic North. It was a common phenomenon that I knew about and half expected but the problem for me had been that I could not think of a way of obtaining the help needed to correct the compass, a procedure involving another boat and an accurate compass.

To work out the reason for the cock-up was all very satisfying but... 'Where the hell are we?'.

Over to the right, through the sea mist and the raindrops pouring down the front of my glasses I could see what I thought must be a navigation buoy and I altered course to get close enough to inspect it. I also asked Heather to turn on the echo-sounder to check the depth of the sea at this place. Identifying a buoy is a good way of establishing one's position but matching depth with that shown on the chart is a good back-up. I asked Heather what the depth was (I could not see the damned dial for all the water in my face). She called back that it was 'Five or six feet'. Impossible! There is a device on the echo-sounder that one uses when the depth is great; it effectively divides the real depth by ten, so that 1,000 feet reads as 100 feet. She must have switched over to this. We were in 50 or 60 feet of water. We must be. We had to be for we drew three and a half feet. If Heather was right we had only a few inches below us and the rocky sea bed. 'I'm sure it is five or six feet', she said. Stupid woman! I dropped the sail and temporarily secured it before angrily passing the tiller over to Heather while I (the *man*) checked the depth. A few minutes later, with a red face and apologies tumbling from my lips, and scared out of my wits, I started the motor and put the boat about 180 degrees to get out of that danger zone just as fast as possible. It had not been a buoy that I had seen but a marker mounted on rock and we had been heading for it; the visible rock offered but a hint of the sharp and nasty rocks lying beneath the water that surrounded it.

This did not tell us precisely where we were but I was able to make a reasoned guess that we were to the east of the island of Saint Honorat, which, with the island of Sainte Marguerite, is just off Cannes. I took us around the southernmost tip of the island (giving rocky outcrops a very wide berth). As we passed into the lee of the island the wind and the sea took on an altogether friendlier attitude – the lashing rain stopped and the sun came out. It was by now the middle of the day. The boys were warmly dressed and equipped with waterproofs and life jackets. Heather and I were clad as we had been throughout the night and morning. The Diggle family looked altogether prepared for tempests.

Just a hundred yards or so away from us there was a gin palace at anchor, a large white motor cruiser. I took us over to it with the intention of checking our position with the skipper. I rehearsed my 'Where the hell are we?' speech in French. As we approached, the Diggle family all dressed up in its foul weather gear, about half a dozen people came to the side of the cruiser to take a look at us. They were all entirely naked and had, presumably, been sun bathing. Such is the nature of the Mediterranean Sea.

A couple of hours later, having decided to leave Porquerolles for the morrow, we were comfortably moored in Cannes.

~

The next day we sailed into the little harbour of Porquerolles. Now that we knew our compass was deranged we could make allowances for the poor creature and we did not miss our target this time. The weather was fine and the terrors of the rocks were almost forgotten. We swam and played on the beach.

~

Our plan was to sail over to the port of Sète and make our way up the canal system to Bordeaux, where we would enter the sea via the River Gironde. We would sail up the western coast until we could re-enter the canal system again at Trehiguier in the South of Brittany. Eventually we would travel along the River Rance and emerge at St. Malo. My plan was to leave *Lorcha* there and travel to England by ferry. The boys would be left with Grandparents, Cathie and Charles, and Heather and I would go back to Italy alone to make the final preparations for the arrival of the Fenders and then to bring the car and trailer back to London. We should then be set for three months in the Herne Hill house, I should have a job and we would be set fair for the start of a bright and happy future.

A hitch developed as we motored into Porquerolles; the propellor shaft mounting that was secured to the hull's interior with resinglass started to break free and a horrid knocking developed when we were under engine power. This was the fault I had attempted to repair in Lerici during the Summer and I realised now that the boat would need specialist attention. We decided to abort the trip to St. Malo. There was nothing for it but to hobble into Marseilles and investigate the possibility of getting *Lorcha* back to England mounted ignominiously on the back of a lorry.

The cost implications of this were frightening.

~

We were a week in the *Vieux Port* of Marseilles before I could sort out the boat transportation problem but during the time we enjoyed the city. This time we were moored very close to the Yachting Club of Marseilles, a wooden building that extended over the water and had an excellent restaurant. This was the very part of the quayside where Gene Hackman chases or is chased (I cannot remember which) in the film *The French Connection* and it was marvellously atmospheric with little restaurants, shops and chandleries just a few yards from us. On the way down the quayside there were half a dozen or so fresh fruit juice stalls and one of the ways in which we kept the boys amused was to make a visit to them part of each morning's activities.

Entertaining these growing boys became a principal occupation of ours during our stay in Marseilles. The cockpit would be filled with fresh water every day so that they could play. There was the regular fruit juice trip. There was feeding the fish that regularly fed from the detritus from the Yachting Club; these fish created a feeding frenzy whenever food was detected and the water boiled as these large and powerful creatures fought each other for scraps – most entertaining for Marcus and Julian (and for an ex-little boy who still loves aquaria).

We often walked in the city and once, when visiting the post office, we went through the Arab Quarter which was like a trip to the Middle East. Letter writers sat in shop doorways while men dictated letters home. Story tellers sat in shop doorways while a small crowd of men listened to them spin stories. Fortune tellers sat in shop doorways with their clients. The shops themselves, that supplied those extremely useful doorways, seemed largely devoted to the sale of massive trunks to be used, presumably, by Algerian residents of Marseilles wanting to go home (the trunks were certainly large enough to contain a medium-sized family). It was all fascinating and not at all threatening.

One morning, quite early, we were boarded by a team of uniformed officers (Customs or Police – they did not say who they were). There was a knock on the hatchcover and suddenly there was a large, armed man standing in our cabin. He was joined by a couple more large, armed men, and very courteously he explained that we were required to show our passports and submit to a search. It was inconvenient but, in our constant quest to find something to amuse the boys, we happily complied, tucking our legs beneath us on our bunks so that these chaps could more easily search through our tins of sugar and tea and the dirty linen bag. I was relieved to think that the evening before I had remembered to drain the cockpit of the water used to give the boys a paddling pool; those smart, shiny boots would not have benefited from total immersion I felt. We were, as you would expect, found to be entirely without evidence of sin and the uniformed gents left the premises.

~

As the week progressed I was making arrangements for the boat's transportation to England, back to the manufacturers so that they could repair the damage their inadequate design and insufficient building specification had brought about. I obtained a quotation from a transporter; the inclusive cost would be £1,000, to be paid in cash before departure. I did not have £1,000 so made a telephone call to my bank in Nottingham to ask if the equivalent in francs could be made available to me through the National Westminster International branch in Marseilles. 'Is this likely to put your account into overdraft?' the man asked. 'Very likely', I replied, 'But we can talk about this later, can't we?'. Bless them, they complied; the cash would be available the day after next.

~

The next day would be our last on *Lorcha*. The sun shone and the wind blew in a friendly manner. We made our farewell excursion out onto the bright blue sea – this time with no destination to reach by a certain time, just a gentle trip out to take the air, to savour the atmosphere, to delight in the view of Marseilles and to feel sad about what would inevitably be the end of a phase of our lives.

~

The currency notes given me were of such denominations that they completely filled the briefcase I took with me to the bank. I slept that night with the case under my pillow. I wondered what interpretation the official visitors of a couple of days earlier would have placed on my having enough money in my possession to buy (or to have sold) a considerable amount of heroin.

Very early next morning a scene was enacted that would have been truly worthy of *The French Connection*. A rendezvous with M Serge Brisset, the boat transporter, on the quayside at 6am with mist swirling about us. We kneel and a briefcase is opened. Large wads of money secured by elastic bands are passed over to disappear into capacious pockets. We look around us to see if we are being overlooked, to see if some waterfront thief is waiting to intercept the transaction, to see if a rival boat transporter is waiting to pounce.

Then, rather more mundanely, *Lorcha* is surrounded by immensely strong canvas straps and, once the mast is removed, she is hauled out of the water and deposited on the low loader that is to take her back to Poole.

Goodbye, *Lorcha*.

The Diggle family, with all its possessions in bags, remains on the quayside. I go to collect the rental car I have previously booked and then, with a stop for one more delicious, freshly-pressed grape juice drink from the friendliest of the stall holders, we drive back to Italy, to Greve and back to *Numero due*.

~

Within a few days we are all packed up and ready to go. Six cases of the best Chianti Classico available in the bottle, *Nozzole,* that we think we may need to help us through the culture shock of a new life in London, are in the trailer. Our possessions left in the house are put in the 'rental mode' and lists of instructions made out for the Fenders. The Fenders arrive and are our guests for a couple of days during which time we familiarise them with the house, Canonica and the town.

We drive to England.

Chapter 24

No More Would We Need To Ask 'Where The Hell Are We?'

Back to England (September 1977 – December 1978)

It is hard for me today, writing these words some 20 years after the event, to stop myself thinking that our return to England was accompanied by a feeling of failure and depression. That we were frightened and ill-at-ease is true for there was little on our horizon when we first arrived in London to give us cheer. One small incident at the time comes back to remind me of how I felt at the time but it was, I now tell myself, only one incident and it should not be elevated to symbolic status.

One of the last things I had done in Greve before we left, as we went around to say goodbye to our favourite shop-keepers, had been to buy a pair of shoes to make me a little smarter for my new London life and my job with Bill. By now worried about money (£1,000 lighter after having loaded *Lorcha* onto that lorry in Marseilles) I spent too little of it on the shoes. As I returned from my first day at work, walking from Victoria tube station on to my main line platform I found myself stumbling. One heel of my new shoes had fallen off. I picked it up and looked at it. It was made of hardboard and had been attached with a small dab of adhesive. It depressed me terribly. Was my future life going to consist of cheap shoes, cheap everything?

Well, it wasn't. We were living in a delightful house in a pleasant part of London. It was mid-September. We had capital in the form of a boat. We had the money from Kenyon Roth for our furniture and effects left behind in Italy. I had a job and I was scheduled to start a new Arts Marketing course at The City University that I could run alongside my job. Within a very short time, a matter of a few weeks, we were taking a very positive view of our life . . . because *Classical Music Weekly* came along.

~

Work with Bill consisted of my taking responsibility for a number of projects and, naturally enough, when I started I had only a few bits and pieces to handle, nothing substantial, nothing to get my teeth into. I handled the launch of a new product: the first range of recorded books produced on cassette in this country, on the 'Listen for Pleasure' label, and found this fairly interesting but there was nothing really *meaty*. Then a telephone call came in from a magazine called *Classical Music Weekly* asking if the Kallaway organisation would be interested in advising on a relaunch.

I knew the magazine. It had been launched the year before, in September 1976. I remembered it because I had bought a copy of the first issue during a visit to London. It had the look of *Private Eye* (it was produced by the same printer) and had a grainy picture of André Previn on the front; it was printed in black with the title in red.

The magazine had struggled through its first year against all odds, run by a brave little team of talented young men, but it was failing. At some time in its first year it had attracted the financial support of a couple of investors, Tony Gamble and Colin Wills, who, with the editor, Robert Maycock, now owned it. Tony and Colin, long time friends and former colleagues at Rediffusion Television, had formed an investment partnership and had been looking for something to back and to 'bring on'; the two of them had realised that their new project would fail unless some new thought was brought to bear on the matter and they would lose their investment. So Kallaway Limited was telephoned and, as a result, Bill and I went to meet Colin, Tony and Robert. It was agreed that Kallaway Limited would put forward plans for a relaunch and it was agreed between Bill and myself that this would be my project.

There are times in one's life when luck plays an important part. The arrival of the *Classical Music Weekly* project was one such case; it came along just when it was needed. Then another stroke of luck: Heather, now looking after our two little boys in Herne Hill, taking them to nursery schools every day and waiting for husband to get home from work every evening, made contact with some friends the Fender family had recommended to us. The couple who lived over the road, the Lanes, were friendly and communicative – and the man, Mark, was the editor of a magazine called *Community Care*.

One evening, in response to my invitation to take a drink or two with me, Mark Lane came over and chatted about his magazine; it was the evening before the day when I was next due to meet Tony, Colin and Robert and put forward my outline plan for *Classical Music Weekly's* relaunch. Until that time my mind was a blank. (Indeed, after my return from the Italian sojourn I frequently found my mind to be a complete blank; it happens when your mind is left for long periods with not very much to do. 'Use it or lose it' is the motto of my life these days.) I found the conversation with Mark extremely informative and stimulating: my brain became less blank as the evening wore on. My bottle of whiskey became less full.

Community Care was a magazine for community workers, a discrete group of professionals which needed, as do most groups of people sharing common activities, interests and needs, a medium of communication. Mark told me that the magazine was *given* to this readership. My ears pricked up at this. By giving the publication away, to specific people who at some time or other had positively stated that they wanted it, what was called a 'controlled circulation' was obtained. This meant we had a circulation figure that could be audited and would therefore be convincing to potential advertisers. From the conversation I extracted three key elements about *Community Care* that seemed to be applicable to the project I hoped to secure: it was a magazine aimed at a profession rather than the 'man in the street'; a magazine that was given away; a magazine that based its income on revenue from display advertising and recruitment advertising rather than from sales in the news agent.

Classical Music Weekly was then aimed at that rather indistinct group of people known as 'music lovers', it was not given away and relied as much upon income from sales as it did from advertising and the two sources combined yielded little more than £600 an issue. Not many people bought it. Not many advertised in it. It cost about £600 per issue to produce. As it stood it was doomed.

My plan had at its heart the production of a magazine not for music lovers but for the music industry; the large number of organisations and individuals involved in making, composing, arranging, publishing, playing, recording, promoting, marketing and all the other activities involved in bringing classical music before the public. A lot of people were involved in the industry and most of them were contactable, most of them could be added to a mailing list. The new magazine would initially be given to these people.

The new magazine would thus have a large circulation at a stroke and this would give the advertising people a story to tell, a story that should be irresistible to those with something to sell to them or to someone seeking to recruit personnel from that readership.

The main question was whether or not this advertising strategy would generate enough money, quickly enough, to pay for the greatly increased print run and to make a profit.

Tony, Colin and Robert saw the sense of my plan and accepted it. My major task then became to manage the relaunch, to build up the free circulation list, to have the magazine redesigned, to find a printer capable of producing a better quality magazine at the lowest possible price – and all the other activities that publishing involves. I was now enjoying myself hugely.

The change did not produce immediate results in terms of profits but we all felt we were on the right track. The magazine was losing money but the losses were being reduced slowly and surely. It was only many, many months later when Colin Wills, who had hitherto played a passive part in the transformation, said that the change was not happening fast enough and something would have to be done. 'Why don't we go fortnightly?' he asked. The reduction in publishing frequency of *Classical Music,* as it was now called, was in substantial part responsible for the change in its fortunes. I do wish that I had thought of it.

Later I was to launch for *Classical Music* what I called 'Operation St. Paul', a campaign to persuade those who had been receiving the magazine free of charge that it was now worth paying for, a notoriously difficult task. We succeeded well enough and today this fortnightly magazine is the flagship of our little fleet of publications deriving its income from both advertising, subscriptions and sales at the newsagents.

~

Our first three months moved on quickly and my 40th birthday drew near. Our agreement with the Fenders had been to stay in each other's houses until after Christmas (1977) and Heather had planned a surprise birthday party for me on 19th December in the Herne Hill house. Sadly for us the Fenders decided to break the agreement and announced that they wanted to come home in time for Christmas and we should simply have to get out well before we had planned. It was not very kind of them but maybe, I thought, they had suffered from the same kind of depression that had affected us.

Bill had found premises in Holland Park and a few weeks before Christmas we moved the company there. Above the office there was a two bedroomed flat and Bill offered it to us. We took it without hesitation and with no small measure of gratitude to him and to the Fates that were guiding our fortunes at that time. We moved in the day before my birthday. Next day I accepted an invitation to go out for a drink with Roger Wilby and when he drove me back to the flat I walked into a gathering of most of our dearest friends whom Heather had miraculously persuaded first to come to a birthday party for me in Herne Hill and then, with only a few hours notice, to one in Holland Park.

I was 40 years old.

~

I have one particular recollection of that Winter, after we had moved into the flat, when the four of us had as our home a place that could not have been more of a contrast with *Numero due.* It was tiny and there was no garden. There was nowhere for two little boys to play. We took them out to the parks whenever we could and Green Park became our favourite. The first time we went there it was very cold and the boys were wrapped up well against it. Walking along we came conscious that Julian, still a tiny lad, only three years old, was lagging behind. We turned and saw that he had filled his arms with twigs fallen from trees, filled them so high that he could barely see over the pile he held before him. He was gathering kindling for a fire that was now many hundreds of miles away in a very different place.

~

Marcus and Julian were left with Charles and Cathie for Christmas of that year of 1977 and Heather and I, in rented Ford Transit van, set off for the saddest journey of all, the trip back to Canonica to collect all our bits and pieces and the Keith and Heather Diggle Collection of Liverpool Paintings. In January 1978 Kenyon Roth would take over the tenancy. Our task of clearing out and preparation would be short and doleful.

We threw ourselves into the task on our arrival and soon all was loaded and ready. I observed with sorrow the cereal that had been splashed from the plate of the youngest Fender onto our painting 'Girl and Garage' by John Baum, where it had congealed and hardened to cementlike consistency but weighed this against the advantage to us of having had a good house in Herne Hill from which to venture out into a different world. After a quiet Christmas, some of which was spent with the delightful Creagh family, we said our goodbyes and started our mournful trek back. Heather has said of that time that she has never felt more like a gypsy as we trundled through Europe with our pitifully small collection of belongings and a very tatty child's high chair strapped on top for all the world to see. When the normally rose-tinted glasses that we use for retrospection turn dark then Heather remembers that trip and I remember my disengaged hardboard heel.

That was the end, the absolute end, of the Italian experience and it ended with much more of a whimper than a bang.

~

In the Spring a man telephoned me from Australia, said he was coming to London the following week and asked if he might come in to see me to discuss my making a lecture tour of Australia and New Zealand. I later had a discreet meeting with him (I was still employed by Kallaway Limited) and we pencilled a lengthy period in the Spring of the following year when I would visit the two countries. My first book on Arts Marketing, published in the Spring of 1976, was continuing to act as my ambassador and was still bringing in the work. I found the prospect of this trip very exciting and kept the thought of it close to me throughout the year.

~

We found a buyer for *Lorcha* and so our capital was released. We started house hunting.

Our friends the Wilbys, who lived in Gravesend, reported that the very pleasant house next to theirs was about to come on the market and suggested that we might like to meet their neighbours and look the place over. We loved it on sight and bought it. We moved to Gravesend and I became a commuter.

Once in Gravesend the boys, who had already had to adjust to two different homes in London in the space of a few months, were able to be placed in schools where there was every chance of their being settled. Over the next few years they would attend the Bronte School, a small independent school in Gravesend and then, immediately before the time for the serious stuff of secondary education, would travel by train to Rochester in order to attend St. Andrew's School.

~

Towards the end of the year I had what I shall always remember as an historic meeting with Tony Gamble. We had lunch together and I told him that I was thinking of going it alone once more. My Australia and New Zealand plans were taking on a firm outline and it looked as though the tour would definitely take place. I had also been in touch with the Hong Kong Arts Centre with a view to stopping off on either the outward or return part of my trip and the director was interested in having me conduct a seminar there. This trip, scheduled to last six weeks in April 1979, would provide me with a good boost to my finances (and would do no end of good to both my reputation not to say my morale) but I would have to build for the long term. Would he be interested in being my first client? He said he would. He would settle up with Kallaway Limited and I would be consultant to Rhinegold Publishing, the publisher of *Classical Music*. The deal would provide me with an office and the freedom to develop my other consultancy work as I chose; there would also be a fee and this, combined with the fee to come from the lecture tour, would be the financial foundation of my future independence.

The magazine had by then moved itself to 52 Floral Street, immediately across the narrow thoroughfare from the Royal Opera House. On the ground floor there was a greasy spoon sandwich bar run by Signor Santucci, the magazine renting the three floors above. It was here, working closely with Tony Gamble, that my new life was to blossom and bear fruit. I have worked with Tony ever since, our wholly different personalities, talents and interests meshing in together to make a remarkably effective complementary relationship.

~

The party held to celebrate my 41st birthday in December 1978 was held in the Gravesend house, 104 Darnley Road, a spacious Edwardian house with a large garden that was perfect for us and our two rapidly growing sons. Not only were our dear friends Roger and Heather Wilby present and many other old friends but also a lot of new ones, made in Gravesend. We were, we felt, established at last. There was in us, the Lit and I, a feeling of enormous self confidence and as we talked and laughed with our friends that evening it felt as though a new life was beginning; having been through so many experiences together we were now ready to take on the challenge of the future. No more would we need to ask 'Where the hell are we?'.

Chapter 25

A Whistle-Stop Tour Of The Past 20 Years Or So

*Life in Gravesend and Oundle and the Growth of Rhinegold
(1978 – Present Day)*

My sons, when I started this book my intention was to write about that time of my life before you were born and that time of your lives before your minds began to hold memories that were meaningful. I know that neither of you have any significant recollection of our lives before we moved to Gravesend in 1978 but I also know that your knowledge of what happened in the early years that followed is sketchy. You were, after all, very small boys when it all started. So I thought I should end this book with a sort of whistle-stop tour of the highlights of the past 20 years or so and this would complete the picture for you.

Remember as you read this chapter that all of the activities and incidents that I recount here took place against a background of our life together as a very happy family and that the real thrill for your parents lay in watching you both grow and become distinct personalities, slowly leaving childhood behind you. When children are at school and parents are at work the really good times are usually holidays and when it came to making sure that we made the most of those times together I do believe that the Lit and I may hold up our heads with pride. Not only did we have the annual delights of St. Cast that I have described in the 'book within the book', *A Resort Runs Through It,* but there were many other excursions to places like Thailand, Turkey, Bavaria, Crete and Switzerland, where we had good times together.

~

At the same time the Lit and I had to build a present and a future for you and we both worked hard at it. We knew that the time for taking risks was over; you both needed stability and support and we took no action that would threaten this. We were also beginning to have an eye on our own, later future, the time when you were grown up and we would be facing the prospect of old age. The spectre of my parents scrabbling around taking job after job, desperately trying to keep their heads above water, has always haunted me and to this day one of my deepest fears is of seeing what I have built crumble away leaving us with nothing and leaving you both with the sense of obligation towards us that I felt towards my parents – so we have taken life after Italy very seriously.

~

Heather was now free to resume her teaching career. It took her a long time to find the right job but eventually she joined the English Department of Gravesend Grammar School for Girls where she was a huge success and loved it, staying there until many years later when we moved away to live in Oundle.

~

My Arts Marketing lecture tour of New Zealand, Australia and Hong Kong took place in early 1979. I was away from home for six weeks. I returned to England with some money in my pocket and started to work hard for *Classical Music* magazine and to develop further my Arts Marketing work in lecturing and consultancy.

~

Tony Gamble and I thought it might be interesting to see if the well known annual work of reference that Arthur Jacobs had started, *British Music Yearbook*, was available for sale. It was making no money for its publisher, A & C Black, and so it was for sale. We bought the title for £500. We now had a classical music magazine and a reference book to go with it. Both were intended for the classical music industry. They went well together as the readership of the first was contained within the lists of the second.

~

Classical Music Weekly had always been published by the limited partnership known as Rhinegold Publishing although we made little of the name. With a magazine and a book to publish we stopped thinking of ourselves as *Classical Music* and started to refer to ourselves more and more as Rhinegold Publishing to reflect our wider ambitions. We later became a limited company of which Tony, Colin and I were shareholders.

~

I became aware of an American consultant in the marketing of the arts who specialised in what was called 'Dynamic Subscription Promotion'. His book *Subscribe Now!* had been published two years after mine. I sent away for a copy from the American publishers and found its contents to be revelatory. I was so impressed by the man's ideas and the evidence of his successes in implementing those ideas that I wrote to him immediately. In Autumn 1979 Tony and I went over to Chicago to meet the man, Danny Newman. Then, with the backing of Colin Wills, we decided to set up an Arts Marketing consultancy service to promulgate the Newman approach in Great Britain and 'Subscribe Now (UK) Limited' was born. We took on a former colleague of mine from Kallaway, Hugh Barton, and in 1980 launched the consultancy with a series of seminars conducted by Danny Newman whom we invited to come over to our country.

The seminars were highly successful and many senior arts managers, energised by the concepts and the passion of the ebullient Mr Newman, approached us to carry out feasibility studies with a view to longer term relationships. We found ourselves working on major projects for the Philharmonia Orchestra, the Churchill Theatre in Bromley, the Old Vic, English National Opera, Everyman Theatre in Liverpool and a host of other smaller clients. Everyone in the arts world was talking about Dynamic Subscription Promotion and our press cuttings book became very fat.

~

The money I earned from the consultancy business working with projects outside Rhinegold was vital. Although Rhinegold was looking promising Tony and I took out only a very small amount of money (he £5,000 and I £4,000 each year – an arrangement that continued for about ten years) and my fee income from clients combined with my lecturing work and the Lit's earnings kept the Diggle family solvent. This low level of drawing from Rhinegold was what enabled the business to grow and our practice of restraint was in no small way responsible for our growth over the company's first ten years of life.

~

Every other Tuesday we held a *Classical Music* lunch on the top floor of our offices in Floral Street. We invited four guests from the outside world, people involved with music and entertainment, and a young woman would come in to cook and present the meal. Two successive Ministers for the Arts, Richard Luce MP and Lord Gowrie were guests. TV personalities Richard Baker and Johnny Morris, singers Felicity Lott and Marion Montgomery, cartoonist Barry Fantoni, the present Minister for Sport (then a leading light in the old Greater London Council) Tony Banks, Arts Council Secretary General Sir Hugh Willatt and future holders of that position Luke Rittner and Mary Allen, and American organist Carlo Curley were amongst those who joined us on those delightful occasions. All male visitors were presented with a *Classical Music* tie and females with a black and silver scarf. Our little lunches became well known and did much to establish our central rôle in the classical music industry.

~

Later in the eighties Tony and I were tipped that the monthly magazine *Music Teacher* was for sale and we made an approach. Soon afterwards we paid £70,000 to the owner, Scholastic Publications, and it was ours. How did we pay for it? Out of its own earnings which, under our management, rapidly increased. By this time we had realised that in our sort of business one ignored advertising sales at one's peril and the growth in profitability of *Classical Music* and *British Music Yearbook* derived from concentrating upon building up income from advertisers. The early expansion of Rhinegold owed as much to its first two advertising managers, Tom Cornwall and Martin Huber, as to its editorial staff (talented and handsome as they were). Within a very short time we had discovered that the advertising potential of *British Music Yearbook* was not only substantial but we had a team capable of realising it. Today this annual reference book has an income from advertising of over £200,000.

~

With two magazines and one book in what people were beginning to call the Rhinegold 'stable', Tony thought it might be a good idea to create another book, an annual reference book as a companion to *Music Teacher;* we called it *British Music Education Yearbook* and it worked quite well. It still works well.

~

There was a period in the very early Eighties when Subscribe Now! (UK) Limited was creating or assisting in the launching and managing of subscription schemes for many national arts organisations and I was directly involved in all of them. It struck me that in addition to the quality of the performances they presented and the substantial benefits to customers offered by their discounted subscription packages conveyed via highly attractive sales brochures something else was needed to add a little *zing*.

At about this time I had been invited to visit the Philippines to conduct a three-day seminar in Manila. My host was to be the Cultural Center of the Philippines, known as CCP. Resources there were limited so a fee was out of the question but I thought that a public appearance in Manila would help my professional reputation so I accepted. CCP would provide five-star hotel accommodation but air travel posed a problem; the organisers asked, would I see if I could persuade Philippine Airlines in London to provide me with a free return flight?

At this point the Lit invoked what is known as the 'Mabel Clause' which requires me to find a way to have Heather accompany me on any trip that looks as if it might be fun. It derives from the custom of the late actor and radio presenter, Wilfred Pickles, whom we both had the pleasure of meeting in the Sixties, who told us that he never travelled anywhere without his wife, Mabel, and if anyone wanted to book him they had to pay for Mabel to accompany him.

I made contact with PAL's senior man in London, an Australian, Henry Arnott, who turned out to be an enthusiast for the arts and opera in particular, and

I asked for *a pair* of return tickets to Manila. He agreed. The Lit and I went to Manila. We stayed at the Philippine Plaza. I gave my three-day seminar in the grand cultural centre (built on Roxas Boulevard on the initiative of President Marcos' wife, Imelda) at which I addressed an audience of some two hundred. Following local custom every attender was awarded a certificate of attendance; I received one as well.

While we were in Manila the Lit gave a splendid recital of English Love Poetry in CCP's studio theatre and attracted a full house drawn from young students to elderly academics. She remembers one elderly man, a professor of English of Chinese birth who approached her after her performance, 'I have taught English Literature all my life', said he, 'But I have never known precisely what is a *dell*. Could you explain?'.

We made a lot of friends including the awe-inspiring *grande dame* of CCP, Lucretia Kasilag, known as 'King' Kasilag, who terrified me at first but later revealed herself to be a closet pussycat.

Henry Arnott was fascinated by what we were doing with Subscribe Now! (UK) Limited and he and I started to discuss ways of involving the airline with our projects with a view to adding that element of *zing* I had been looking for. I came up with the idea of offering all subscribers to the subscription schemes the chance of entering simple competitions, the prize for which would be a pair of First Class return tickets to Manila. The colourful brochures each carried a generous section which made much of the prize, the competition and, not unreasonably, the airline. We ran these competitions for English National Opera, Old Vic, Philharmonia, Churchill Theatre in Bromley, the Palace Theatre in Westgate and several others.

At about that time PAL opened up its first direct route from London to Manila; hitherto flights had gone via Paris. It was decided to celebrate what the airline people insisted on calling an 'inaugural' flight (theoretically the first flight on this route, although this was a PR fiction for there had been many flights before) by organising a visit to Manila by some of the great and good. Henry put me on the PAL payroll as a consultant and asked me to help put together a party. We looked around our many contacts in the arts and started to make telephone calls.

Lord Ted Willis, the playwright, was on the board of the Bromley Churchill Theatre; I invited him. Actor Timothy West was at the time joint director of the Old Vic; I invited him. General Manager of the Philharmonia, Christopher Bishop, was an all round good egg so he was asked to join us. Marion Tait, prima ballerina with the Royal Ballet said she would come along. Paul Findlay, of the Royal Opera House management team said he would join us provided he could pop off after a few days to go to Korea to fix up a company tour. Others in the party were Lord and Lady Kenilworth (we had Lord Willis but it was felt that a few more titles were needed to show our Philippine hosts that they were entertaining the cream of British society), grand daughter of Sir Winston Churchill and journalist, Emma Soames, and a young man of uncertain background, a friend of someone important in PAL, who later revealed that he was writing a book on brothels of the world. Our party was now heavy on Lords but of Sirs there was not one; I remedied this by inviting Sir Hugh Willatt, now retired. Sadly the Mabel Clause could not be invoked on this occasion.

Our party took off from Gatwick. We occupied almost all of the First Class cabin at the front of the PAL Boeing 747. Upstairs there were the airline's new sleeper beds all of which had been allocated to its guests of honour. It was a very sybaritic experience.

Our visit had many highlights. We spent an hour with President Ferdinand Marcos at the Macalañang Palace and returned two days later to meet his wife Imelda. At the meeting with Mr Marcos, Emma Soames expressed interest in a Vietnamese refugee camp being run in the Bataan region by his government; he responded immediately by laying on two helicopters to take us there next morning. This was a fascinating experience and we all left the little community with its small huts, spontaneously created market and even – Vietnamese initiative at its best – a tiny restaurant, feeling very moved. We were flown to Baguio City, traditionally the Summer location for government, and were met off the plane by a group of Igorot tribesmen who were so tiny that the Lit would have towered over them. After a week of luxury we flew back and made maximum use of those PAL beds on the way.

A few months later Andy Morland and I went back to Manila to do a five-page piece for my old friend Kenneth Bound of *Mayfair* magazine on the 'Jeepney', the whimsically decorated form of public transport that is to be seen in Manila by the thousand.

Later, long after the bloodless revolution that put Ferdinand and Imelda Marcos out of power, I received another invitation to lecture at CCP – on this occasion via the British Council – and I was able to apply the Mabel Clause. In 1984 I gave three days of seminars with CCP staff and Heather conducted some very successful drama workshop sessions with teachers and gave another poetry recital in the CCP studio theatre. We met many of our old friends but the place did not feel quite the same. It is strange but when President Marcos was in power the outside world saw the country as being in the hands of a wicked despot yet within the country it felt quite free and open and the atmosphere was rather jolly. Now, after a revolution had purged the place of its tyrant, it felt depressed and looked distinctly shabby. Our Philippino friends had a term that discreetly put a marker on when the country's fortunes had changed; they used the word 'since'. 'Things have not been so pleasant *since*' they would say.

~

Sadness entered this phase of our lives when your maternal Grandfather, Charles Henry Ellis, who adored you both with equal fervour, died on 14 November 1984, the date of your tenth birthday, Julian. He had had a cruel beginning to his adult life having been taken into the Army at the age of 20 years at the start of the Second World War, within weeks of his marriage to Catherine, your Grandmother. He was part of the force that tried unsuccessfully to defend Crete against the Germans, was wounded and taken prisoner there. When recovered he was sent to a Prisoner of War camp in Poland – he was marched for most of the way, an experience that he could never be drawn to talk about – and put to work in an iron foundry. There he was given to wear for protection an asbestos hood and it was this that was eventually to kill him. So many years later, having coped bravely with the psychological damage done to him by inhuman treatment during the War, he developed cancer of the lining of the lung, which is now known to be caused by the inhalation of asbestos fibres, and after suffering much pain he died. Amongst the pictures I have chosen to be included in this book you will find one of Charles carrying you, Julian, upon his back. At the time this photograph was taken he was in the throes of the disease that was to kill him and so it has a particular poignancy for us.

~

In 1984 I produced another book, *Guide to Arts Marketing*. My first, *Marketing the Arts*, a slender work it seemed by now, was sold out and I could not bring myself to take the easy way out and simply reprint it. I had sold 2,000 copies of that work. So I set to produce another, better, book. I found that I could not work at home in the evenings and weekends and I could not work in the office during the day for there were too many distractions. I bought a chair/bed and tackled the task in the office in the evenings, working until late and sleeping over.

I produced 3,500 copies in paperback and 500 in hardback. This was ambitious and it took two or three years to sell out, but sell out it did and it made Rhinegold quite a lot of money (for we published the book under that imprint) and it even made me a few thousand pounds.

It was a book that was most carefully planned in its production. Knowing that it would be sold by us direct to its readers rather than via bookshops I calculated carefully the cost implications of postage and saw that there would be considerable savings for us if the paperback edition of the book weighed under 500 grammes. Then, knowing the weight of the paper to be used and the number of pages likely to be involved I was able to juggle the length of my text and the typography to bring the number of pages and hence the weight down so that when wrapped for posting the overall weight fell below the critical 500 gramme level. This relatively simple exercise increased the book's profit by some £1,250.

I learned something of the way the world is when the time of publication approached. I attended a meeting of the London Society of Arts Publicists, of which I was a member and before everyone sat down, I put a leaflet advertising the book on the table before each place. Everyone present was responsible for building audiences for the arts; they were my market. No-one said a word to me.

The leaflet seemed to embarrass them. Most people left the leaflet behind when the meeting was over.

As I write this I find myself wondering how people will react to this book which, now that I am nearly at its end, I have thought to produce for a market slightly larger than you two young men who are my sons. It was strange then how people whom I knew seemed to have a 'who does he think he is?' reaction and I suppose that I had better prepare myself for some disappointment on this front now.

However, many who lived in this country and throughout the world, did buy the book and I was thrilled when I saw the orders, accompanied by cheques, money orders and credit card authorisations, coming in from every corner it seemed. No sophisticate me, I would sort the mail first thing every morning and dig out every likely envelope, opening it instantly. How could the author of a book on marketing not want to see the results of his marketing of his own book?

~

During this time you boys were growing and growing and the time drew near when your secondary education had to be considered. In 1985 you, Marcus, were 12 and you, Julian, were 10. We were still living in Gravesend, in the same house that we had bought in 1978. One day, at work, I was indulging my passion for tearing open envelopes that might contain orders for *Guide to Arts Marketing* and I opened one from Oundle. It was an order for one copy and it came from the Music Department of Oundle School. When the book was dispatched I took care to ensure that the title page was signed and I put after my name, in brackets, 'Laxton School: 1951-56'. Soon after I had a telephone call from the Deputy Head of Music, James Parsons, who, in the course of our chat, asked if we would like to attend the Laxton School Speech Day that was due to take place within a few weeks. A few days later an invitation arrived; on a whim I accepted and so it happened that the Lit and I found ourselves walking the familiar streets of Oundle on a seductively warm September day. The Speech Day ceremony and Prize Giving awoke all kinds of nostalgia in me (including the keen recollection that I had never proved heavy enough to win one of those prizes) and, in conversation with the then Headmaster (the title 'Master-in-Charge had long gone), David Richardson, the matter of my sons' future education came up. We soon agreed that you should both sit entrance examinations to attend the school.

~

So it was that almost a year later the Gravesend house was sold and we four moved to a tiny, rented house in a small estate on the outskirts of Oundle; it was an interim measure, taken to give us time to discover a house that had qualities similar to our Gravesend house while you boys started your careers at Laxton School. The fact that the school which I had attended for no payment was now almost fully integrated into Oundle School and was the day school of the boarding school for which substantial fees were charged had a bearing on the type of house we could afford to buy. With fees to find for two sons our choice was restricted. We bought an inadequate house in Cotterstock Road and have been bolting bits on to it ever since in the hope of transforming the pig's ear into a silken purse. Another 20 or 30 years and it should be quite nice.

~

My Mother had married Bob and had gone to live with him in a tied cottage near Wells. There was a time in your lives, my sons, when your paternal Grandmother and her husband were able to give you country holidays and although you appeared to find little in her husband to interest you, she ('Who's she? The cat's mother?') was adored by you both. All the cuddly, warm qualities that she had lavished on me she lavished on you, and you loved your 'Other Momma', as you called her, very much. As they grew older he retired and they were allocated a smart new little house in a sheltered estate administered by the local authority. They still had the caravan my Mother had bought with the money from the sale of her Nottingham house that had not yet been swallowed up by Bob's passion for new cars and they were able to live a modest life together.

One day Bob telephoned me to say that my Mother had begun to act strangely and from what he said it seemed that she was hallucinating, as though her dream world was entering her conscious world and she could not tell the difference between them. Her doctor seemed unable to find what was wrong and she went into the local hospital for a brain scan and other tests. The diagnosis was multi-infarct dementia, a progressively degenerative brain disease quite similar in its effects to Alzheimer's Disease. Mother was taken into a local home for the round-the-clock care she needed and her husband could not provide.

She had been in the home for just a few months when her husband had a heart attack and died very suddenly. After arranging his funeral I brought your Grandmother to our home while we sought a suitable place for her nearby. During those few days we became familiar with the strange ideas that occupied her mind – for example, the notion that there was a sort of parallel world where there was another house identical to her little house in Wells in which a large number of people lived that she had to cook and care for. She had moments of lucidity and during one of those spells I sat her down and took a photograph of her that has the same status in my closest thoughts that the one of your Grandfather, Charles, has. I have put it in the collection of photographs I have chosen for you in this book. It shows your Grandmother as she was before the disease took final hold of her and made us strangers to her. Does she not look wonderful?

We found a comfortable place for her in nearby Polebrook but it could not hold your Grandmother who constantly had it in mind to 'go home'. Home was a place of many decades ago, a place where a young country girl played with her brothers and sisters in the meadows of Gloucestershire and she tried so hard to go back there. So many times was she found wandering along the road that once she had bicycled along on her daily trip from Polebrook Aerodrome to the home of the Watts-Russell family on the road to Benefield at the time of our great family crisis, that we had to take her away and put her in a home in Irthlingborough where doors were locked.

On 5 March 1994 my Mother, your Grandmother, died.

~

About the time we moved to Oundle Rhinegold moved out of its Floral Street offices to occupy four floors of a large red brick turn-of-the-century building at the junction of Shaftesbury Avenue and New Oxford Street, almost on top of what was once the old Museum underground station. We thought at first that we would rattle around in the place like peas in a pod but we expanded to fill the place and now there are 33 of us sharing its four floors. Rhinegold has grown so that now it not only publishes those titles upon which its fortunes were founded – *Classical Music, British Music Yearbook, Music Teacher* and *British Music Education Yearbook* – but also *Opera Now, The Singer, Early Music Today, Piano* and *British Performing Arts Yearbook*. We have also published the quarterly magazine *Musician* for the Musicians' Union for many years and, from time to time, we venture out on the publication of books such as *The Musician's Handbook, The Art of Auditioning* and even (could I possibly be accused of milking my subject?) another book from me, *Arts Marketing*, published in 1994.

~

Inevitably my concentration on Rhinegold has led me to devote less and less time to the activity that once supported the Diggle family when it lived in Italy and for the ten years or so after it returned to England. Since my spate of visits to the Philippines I have lectured in Spain on three occasions and I have made two lengthy visits to Hungary to conduct courses. I maintained a constant outpouring of articles in the magazine *Arts Management Weekly* for well over two years but, in the end, I had to make my book, *Arts Marketing*, my swansong. I have said my say on the subject of how the arts may most effectively be marketed and while doing so I, with my co-director Tony Gamble, have demonstrated how publications for the arts world may most effectively be marketed.

~

Ever since choosing the title of this book I have lived with the thought that it demands of me some sort of conclusive response to the implicit questions it poses with the reader, if not fatigued by now; wanting to know if, after nearly sixty years of living, I think I have deserved a prize and, if I do, whether I feel bad about never having been given one.

Prizes are nice things to have; they are tangible evidence that other people have judged you to be a success and they go on to form part of your personal memorabilia. They live on after you have gone. There can be few people who genuinely disdain prizes.

There have been a few times in my life when a prize would have been nice to have. One of those lovely Laxton School leather-bound, gold-embossed books would have been treasured for its own intrinsic beauty as well as showing me that the school did not take me for a complete fool.

The metaphor I saw in that newspaper report of my Father's angling achievement was that of *nearly* achieving a prize. Its impact on me was enhanced by the humour of someone having their failure to win a prize made into a news item. This book is a sort of equivalent to that newspaper cutting.

It would be too banal of me to say that life itself has been the prize but . . . well, what is wrong with a little banality at this stage? Life itself *has* been the prize; so far, at least. You, my sons, and anyone else who reads this book, may judge from its contents whether you think it has been a prize worth having but I know that it is all I'm going to get and I feel genuinely satisfied. The Lit, you my sons, my Father and Mother, are my prizes. This book is our memory.

~

A final word. Many years ago you two boys, on different occasions, tried to find ways of expressing your love for your parents. Marcus, you said you would love us 'For all the days' and you, Julian, said you would love us 'To the end of the counting'. These are good words and I offer them back to you and to the Lit with all my heart.

POEMS

Unserious Poems

For Julian After A Creative Dream

Beware of the pink silly things.
With their delicate voices and idiot grins,
Their long golden tresses and sparkling rings,
Their gossamer clothing that glitters and clings
But hides from your view their leathery wings
And long scaly tail that whips out and stings.
Beware, oh beware, of the pink silly things!

Anagrammatic Poem For Peter Palumbo

Pelt opera bum
Probe pale tum
Pump beer a lot
Blame pure pot

Christmas Time In The West Indies

I got a lovely necklace for my wife
And for my eldest son a Swiss Army knife.
My youngest boy gets rugby boots
And for myself I got a box of nice cheroots.
Of my Christmas list I've now given you de essence
And what I'm doing now is rapping de presents.

Religious Experience
(In the style of Roger McGough)

Yesterday, on the Tube
Between Russell Square and Covent Garden
I met God.
Now I'm a Holborn Again Christian.

The Black Death
(In 1625 the Head Master of Laxton School, Oundle, Anthony Death, was dismissed for showing too great an interest in his male pupils.)

Watch out, young men, for Anthony Death
With his gentle ways and bait-ed breath
What he has in mind you may only . . . gueth.

Those who know are wont to say
That his name should be said in a different way
To record that he favours an alternative path;
So, not down with Death but up De'ath.

The Gypsy's Warning
(On renting a room in Liverpool in 1969)

What a place!
A palace, Mr Diggle
A palace fit for, fit for
Fit for you, Mr Diggle.

Eight by Twelve, room for me or eight coffins
(Six by two approximately, work it out)
One small window, very dark
(No patch of blue to call the sky)
And Uncle Nathaniel's Cooking Corner
(Bijou kitchenette, Mr Diggle, bijou)
Shelves lined with Echoes of 1963
(Will Khruschev back down over Cuba?)
And a truckle bed called Smokey Joe
(Broke and all its junk ran out).

Wee Baby Belling
Mother's run off yelling
She put the Vesta curry on
And now the hotplate's smelling.

As we parted, My good friend Rose-in-Bloom
Crossed my palm with silver as he took his three pounds ten commission.
A silvery book of paper matches with his name embossed.
Inside a message . . .

HEED THE GYPSY'S WARNING
LOOK TO THE FUTURE
BUY YOUR OWN HOME

I should be so lucky.

Three Found Poems

Exercise 94
(Translate into Latin)

If you provide the lamp, I shall provide the oil.
I am rich enough, if I have a friend to love me.
If a storm were to arise, this ship would soon sink.
The old man would have died, if I had not come to his aid.
If anyone pulls the lion's tail, he is exposed to great danger.
If you walk up and down in silence, how can I ascertain your desires?
If the young men were not foolish, they would not be drinking so much wine.
If the city falls into the power of the tyrant, the citizens will be deprived of their liberty.
If the philosopher had not reduced himself to poverty, he would not have needed the help of friends.
I should have esteemed you more highly, if you had allowed me to consult the interests of my parents.

Welsh Mantra
(Taken from a shop in Abersoch)

Grocer Abel William Draper
Grocer Abel William Draper
Grocer Abel William Draper
Grocer Abel William Draper

For Adrian Henri
(A label from a package containing copies of his book of verse Tonight At Noon*)*

20 Copies
Tonight At Noon
Limp Edition

Not Dorking Dworkin

Andrea Dworkin's
Always torkin
About forkin.
Myself, I'd rather stick a cork in
Or a leg of pork in
Than my dork in.

News Report

"The snow-plough is broken",
Said the mayor of Hoboken.
"I can offer you shovels, but they're only a token.
So light up your stoves and git stuck in to stokin'
Else the sick and the old will soon start in a croakin'.
So shovel that snow. Your Leader has spoken!".
They thought he was foolin' – but he meant it – snow jokin'.

Pillow Talk

"I'm a very selfish sleeper",
To Veronica I said;
"So duvet up your chances,
If you want to go to bed".

The Arts Manager's Prayer
(Written for Arts Management Weekly Christmas edition 1992)

Oh Lord*

Protect me from my Chair and my Committee
Who do not understand the way the business works,
Who pay me peanuts and who think I am a monkey.
Who are themselves a pretty hopeless bunch of jerks.

Guide me in my search for better artists,
Who'll fill my seats and charge me fees I can afford,
Who won't throw tantrums at my cleaning lady;
For this guidance I will thank you, Lord.

Forgive me if I moan about the money,
How tight things are and all the strings that are attached,
But I can't afford to pay the printer's invoice
And the auditorium roof is badly patched.

Grant me . . . that's all I ever wanted,
A grant to meet the losses that we make,
A grant to keep the show in motion,
A grant, a grant, a grant for Heaven's sake.

* Lord Palumbo: once Chairman of the Arts Council of Great Britain

Changing My Mind

I'm changing my mind.
This one's no good.
I can't understand things with it.
I can't recall faces.
I don't remember names.
I couldn't tell you where I was last week
Much less what I was doing.
And it wanders.

It's your fault.
You've been there for years,
Upsetting all my normal functions.
And now you're going,
The baby with the bathwater.
I can't get you out of it, so I'm changing it.
I'll do a trade-in, a fair deal
And I'll get me a new one.

Holiday Advice

Benidorm
Do as the Dormans do

Serious Poems

Watch Your Language
(For Heather – The Lit)

Watch your language.
I am watching your language.
I can see it now.
It leaps up and down
Then fades when you are lost for words.
I watch it fatten sometimes when you've had too much to drink
And form itself into silly little pointed bubbles.
The colour is remarkable.
When you talk non-stop it's kaleidoscopic –
A rainbow of phrases!
And when you stub your toe or bite your tongue
Sharp stellated icosohedra of purple tinged with angry pink
Hang in the air for ages.

Dreaming Of Illegal Elderberries

Gather illegal elderberries
Step through the misty frame
Into the new land
Where black pearls grow
That you must not touch.

The long toothed tiger leaps
To defend the tumid fruit
Roaring his warning –
And you can't move;
Your legs are jelly.

Fly up until you soar
Above the map of London.
Hold up by virtue of your will
And feel the power,
Until it starts to ebb.
Then fall until you wake.

The Overclass

We are the overclass.
We know the rules of the game.
We call the shots.
We give you freedom
And know how you'll use it.

In the old days we used power
To control you. Made you
Do what we wanted.
Passed laws to make you.
Killed you if you didn't.

Religion came in handy.
Worked with most.
Made you respect – even love – us.
And you did what you knew you should – obey us.
You even thought we spoke for God.

Those days are past.
We don't need to fool you.
We don't need to bully or break you.
We don't need to keep you in the battery house.
You can go free-range.

Wander where you will.
We still control you.
We feed your bellies and your minds
And know that with all the freedom in the world
You'll do our bidding.

Dresden
(It has been recorded that towards the end of the Second World War rescue workers in Dresden who refused to enter cellars after bombs had killed those sheltering within were summarily shot.)

People jam is mainly red.
I will not wade in it.
I will not enter the dark caves
Where the sticky stuff lies
To scoop it up by the bucketful.
I should rather die than do that.

Ancient Dosser

He's bent half-double
The old guy outside the Fox and Goose.
All you can see is the wild halo of his hair,
The colour of fag ash,
And the sodden raincoat hanging low on one side
From the weight of Rich Australian Ruby Wine.
Around him and between his legs
An ecstatic mongrel dog sniffs
And savours the dark, warm, exotic places of his body.

The Earth Loves You
(Another dream)

Somehow you are lying on your back,
Knees slightly bent and arms spread out
And raised as though resting in a deep armchair.
You hair streams past your eyes Ophelia-like.
The earth loves you.

Reach and pull a shoe away
And watch it dawdle before making off.
Then the other, taking care not to disturb
The precious equilibrium.
The earth loves you.

You strip yourself birth naked
And watch the garments drift away.
You turn your eyes back to the sky
And close them.
The earth loves you.

To move requires much effort
But move against the chilling pressure
And break the balance. Turn now, turn
As though the solid air were water and see;
The earth loves you.

Take up the final posture,
Arms outstretched and legs forced wide,
Eagle-spread as though to swoop and stop and then
Appear again, pulsating, bloody, satisfied.
The earth loves you.

Transfixed and screaming you achieve
Your terminal velocity.
The earth loves you.

Souvenir Of War

Geoff dropped him.
Nice clean shot.
Straight through the eye.
Never felt a thing.

Not going to waste it,
Are we? Said Geoff
Opening his knife.
He won't need it now.

Now, when I drive,
Tearing through the gears.
I have the enemy
In the palm of my hand.

Don't I?

Sniper

They have no sophistication, that mortar mob.
A basic grasp of Newton's laws of motion
And a sense of direction
Is all they have.

They stuff their ugly faces 'til they bulge
And grease runs down their chins.
They swill it down with slivovich
Then fall asleep.

From time to time they amble to their sandbagged pit.
One scans with glasses the field of opportunities
And belches out an elevation
And a range.

The others hold their ears and giggle
While the least drunk one drops in a shell.
When it bangs they yell
Like silly boys.

Somewhere it falls; it makes a noise and, if they're lucky,
Blows off a head or arm or leg – or two, or three,
Or breaks a window.
How very crude.

I stand tall, a man of honour and iron discipline.
Lightly camouflaged against a non-contrasting background,
With a wall on which to rest
And to protect me.

My near friend, my dear friend, my companion in arms
Lies close to my face and I survey the other world like God,
Ready to – how shall I put it?
Take what I like.

How can I convey to you the elegant sublimity of what I do?
It is pure, honest, dignified, and, above all, free of malice.
I have no hatred for those who come within
My magic circle.

I do not kill for pleasure, indeed I often do not kill at all.
I choose my target within my target – such is my skill, my artistry.
Such is my power that I can be generous,
Almost kind.

The left knee of a moving target, a young boy who knows I'm here
And runs to challenge me then lies jerking (and screaming, no doubt).
He's learned his lesson all right.
He'll show respect.

Snap! Old woman through the head, dead before she hits the street.
Snap! The babe in arms, the mother – not a scratch on her.
Snap! An irritating little dog
Just for fun.

I have gained so much from this experience, this mystical experience.
I have become a man at one with the verities of life.
Ignore those scum in the mortar mob.
They are mere thugs.

Nursing Home

I watched my Mother hold me tenderly
Into her once full breasts,
Murmuring syllables of comfort
While she snugged me down for sleep.
One arm of mine stuck awkwardly up
And would not go down
Until she grasped the simplicity of the joint
And brought the limb beneath the blanket
So that all of me was warm and cuddled.
As she looked lovingly upon her baby son,
I watched her in her play
Of fifty years or so ago.
I watched her live again that time
And wept to see that only this remained.

Reasons Why We Killed You

Having written this it occurred to me that it had no beginning and no end that could be described as such by virtue of meaning. The poem ends because I had run out of Reasons but there are, I know, many, many more Reasons – the human race invents a few more every day. The poem begins where it does because, well, one has to start somewhere. The verses fall in no particular order, which is as it should be for no one Reason is more important than any other and the only relationship they have with one another is their common contempt for the value of life. I suppose that one way of printing this poem is on cards, one Reason to a card, that are thrown into the air and allowed to fall as they will – or perhaps written on a long thin strip of paper, twisted half a turn and then joined at its ends, to make what is called a 'Möbius Strip', a paradoxical piece of origami that has no beginning and no end.

We killed you
Because you were the enemy
Because you looked like the enemy
Because you were not our friend.

We killed you
Because you were our friend
But you did not kill our enemy
So you ceased to be our friend.

We killed you
Because you were our friend
But you killed our enemy too well and became a threat
So we had to kill you.

We killed you
Because you were the wife of our enemy
And the child of our enemy
And the wife and child of our friend who became our enemy.

We killed you
Because everyone else was killing you
And we did not want to attract attention to ourselves
By not killing you.

We killed you
Because you had what we wanted
Or because we had what you wanted
It didn't matter what it was.

We killed you
Because you were a symbol of something
It is easier to kill a symbol than a person
The killing was symbolic don't you see?

We killed you
Because we believed in God
And you believed in God as well
So you didn't really die when we killed you.

We killed you
Because after the torture
Which we enjoyed although you did not
Your anguished face embarrassed us.

We killed you
Because it was necessary
To show others that we had the moral strength
And courage necessary to kill you.

We killed you
As a simple rite of passage
From innocent childhood to responsible adulthood
And we wore part of you as a sign.

We killed you
Because we were very angry.
Not with you but you were there and you would do.
We were both quite calm afterwards.

We killed you
For fun. The lump of concrete was not dropped
Onto people. It grew smaller as it fell into the dots.
Like a video game without the sound.

We killed you
Because you were in the way.
You were in the fucking way you fucking fuck, you.
Why didn't you fucking move, you fuck?

We killed you
Because you were so beautiful
That it made the beast within us rage with hunger
And we had to feed it on you.

We killed you
Because although your need was pressing
Our need was far, far greater
And we had to, had to, let you die.

We killed you
Because we had far more than we needed
And sold the surplus to you at a very fair price.
We regret that it was less than wholesome.

We killed you
Because there were so many other demands on us.
So many hands held out in supplication.
We did not have the time to save you.

We killed you
Because you were not wanted.
You were hardly bigger than an apple and it didn't matter
We would have killed you later, anyway.

NAMES DROPPED

NAMES DROPPED

Members of the Author's immediate family are not included in this index

A

Alford, Canon Leslie, 124-125, 127
Alfred the gorilla, 24
Allan, Mary, 294
Alric, Colette, 173, 176
Ardley, Neil, 219
Arnison, Geoffrey, 88
Arnott, Henry, 295, 296
Ashcroft, Dame Peggy, 206
Atcherly, Air Marshal Sir William, 67
Ayshford Sandford, David, 34, 41

B

Baker, Richard, 294
Banks, Tony, 294
Barber, Ralph, 78, 80
Barton, Hugh, 294
Bass, Doris, 130
Baum, John, 207
Bell, Trevor, 125
Bevan, Peter, 163, 197
Bill the disposal system, 14
Bishop, Christopher, 296
Boot, Wendy, 125
Bound, Kenneth, 222, 297
Brain, Bernard, 32
Brinson, Peter, 220
Brisset, Monsieur Serge, 285
Brubeck, Darius, 89, 104
Bruce, Christopher, 220
Brudenell, Mr, 70
Bunning, Derek, 78
Burton, Lynne, 163, 200

C

Canard, Bertrand, 173, 176
Carss, Eileen, 113-114, 116
Carver, Mr, 47-48, 50
Case, John, 63-64, 68

Churchill, Winston, 24, 26-27
Clarke, Carey, 272
Clarke, Hilda, 272
Clarke, Jeremy, 84
Clayton, Peter, 125, 127
Clews, Tony, 207
Coates, Roy, 139
Cockrill, Maurice, 207
Collins, Anne, 44
Condon, Dick, 219
Cooke, Pat, 207
Coombes, Farmer, 152, 153, 157, 158, 160
Cornwall, Tom, 295
Cound, David, 145, 185
Cound, Margaret, 185
Course, John, 201
Creagh, The family, 272-273, 290
Cruft, John, 187
Cuff, Arthur, 91, 92
Curley, Carlo, 294
Cutler, 'Butch', 57

D

Dakstins, Mikki, 53, 54
Delage, Jean-Louis, 172, 173, 174
Delage, Josse & Simon, 172
Delage, Sybil, 172, 173, 174
Desoutter, Denny, 205
Diggle, Albert, 8, 9
Diggle, Alice *(wife of Harold Diggle)*, 9
Diggle, Dora, 8
Diggle, Harold, 8, 9, 138
Diggle, Hilda, 8
Diggle, Isabella Winfield *(author's paternal grandmother)*, 7-8, 9, 12
Diggle, Marjorie *(married Richard Isherwood)*, 8, 9, 58
Diggle, Monica *(married Albert Poolman)*, see Poolman, Monica

Diggle, Samuel *(author's paternal grandfather)*, 8, 9
Diggle, Samuel *(son of Samuel)*, 8, 9
Dilkes, Neville, 140, 141, 142, 147, 185, 189
Dilkes, Pamela, 185
Dunham, Leo, 131
Dunn, Philip, 109-110, 112
Durkin, Mr & Mrs, 44

E
Ellis, Aunt Janet, 77, 81
Ellis, Jenny *(married Richard)*, 82
Ellis, Richard *(known as 'Dearie')*, 77, 81, 82, 83, 88
Evans, Mike, 116, 118, 119

F
Falorni, Signor, 231-232, 233, 268
Fantoni, Barry, 294
Fawcett, Bodie, 223, 224, 235, 236, 266, 272, 273-274, 277
Fawcett, Gabriel, 266
Fawcett, Graham, 223, 224, 235, 236, 266, 272, 273-274, 277
Fender, The family, 273, 275, 276, 278, 283, 285, 287, 288, 289
Fennell, John, 190
Findlay, Paul, 296
Flapdoodle, Willy *(a toy)*, 2, 61
Flattum, Jack *(married Hilda Diggle)*, 8
Forman, Dennis, 205, 206
Foyle, Christina, 93

G
Gable, Clark, 61, 69
Gamble, Tony, 287, 288, 291, 293, 294, 295, 301
Garrett, Tony, 187, 188
Gasqueton, Colette, 171, 175
Gasqueton, Martial, 171, 175
Gasqueton, Martin, 166, 171, 173
Getz, Stan, 88-89, 104
Goodman, Lord, 198

Gowrie, Lord, 294
Grayson, Barrie, 112
Green, Audrey, 68
Green, Joyce *(married Tom Lane)*, 68
Greenwood, Ken, 116, 118, 119-120
Griffith, Anne, 68, 69

H
Hadman, Derek, 68, 78
Hagan, Gerry, 205, 206
Haggart, Richard, 52
Hamon, Monsieur & Wife Annie, 166, 167
Harrold, Cynthia, 60
Hassler, 'Blondie', 227
Haw Haw, Lord, 29
Hayes, Tubby, 104, 135
Heaton, Danny, 44
Henri, Adrian, 201
Hepple, Peter, 218
Hill, Rosemary, 220
Hitler, Adolf, 15, 26, 40
Hodson, Ron, 190, 191, 192
Huber, Martin, 295
Huggins, Mr, 52

I
Irvine, Jane, 34
Isherwood, Richard *(married Marjorie Diggle)*, 58
Isherwood, Sheila, 9
Iturbi, José, 60

J
Jacobs, Dick, 97-98, 115, 131, 145
Jardine, George Wallace, 207
Jewell, Derek, 137
Joe the grey tom cat, 17

K
Kallaway, Bill, 209, 217, 221-222, 223, 279, 286, 287, 288, 289, 290, 291, 294
Kasilag, Lucretia, 296
Kempe, John, 138, 139

Kenilworth, Lord & Lady, 296
Kentner, Louis, 185
King, Pete, 135

L

Lane, Edward, 68
Lane, Mark, 287-288
Lane, Tom, 68
Laxton, Sir William, 62
Le Sage, Bill, 137
Leach, Alan George, 116, 118, 119
Lee, Jennie, 60
Leech, S. J. J. *(known as 'Quack')*, 62, 63, 64
Lelli, Barbara, 229
Lelli, Fabrizio, 229
Lelli, Laura, 229
Lelli, Signor, 224, 228, 235, 236, 274
Lelli, Signora, 229, 271
Little, George, 73
Livermore, Sir Harry, 195, 197-198, 207
Lott, Felicity, 294
Lowden, George, 34-35
Lucas, Bernard, 145
Luce, Richard, 294

M

Mack, Margaret Ann Devereux *(always referred to as 'Ann')*, 94, 95, 96, 98, 102, 103-104, 105, 106, 107, 109, 112, 113, 114, 115, 116, 117, 118
Marcos, Imelda 296, 297
Marcos, President Ferdinand 296, 297
Marshall, C. A. B., *(known as Arthur Marshall)*, 83
Mash, Bob, 68, 69
Mason, Daphne, 77
Matisse, Madame, 164-165
Maude-Roxby, The family, 138
Maxted, James, 7
Maxwell, Mr & Mrs, 125, 126, 127
Maycock, Robert, 287, 288
McClean, Sheila, 125
Misery, A desiccated old, 126, 127

Moene, Ivar, 58
Montgomery, Field Marshal, 24
Montgomery, Marion, 294
Montier, 'Mami', 172, 175
Montier, Catherine, 172
Montier, Henriette, 172, 176
Montier, Jean-Pierre, 166, 171, 172, 174
Morgan, Maggie, 125, 210
Morland, Andrew, 223, 297
Morris, Johnny, 294
Morrissey, Dick, 137
Murphy, Mark, 137, 143, 148
Mussolini, Benito, 40

N

Nanna *(Heather's maternal grandmother)*, 121, 128
Neville, John, 144, 145
Newman, Danny, 294
Newman, Yvonne, 89

O

Oughton, Mrs, 74, 75, 82-83, 86
Oughton, Yvonne, 75, 82-83
Over, Malcolm & Janet, 128, 129

P

Palmer, *(Oundle School chemistry teacher)*, 64
Parsons, James, 299
Pat on the Mat, 38
Peach, Mr & Mrs, 69
Pelham, Roger, 88
Peron-Lambert, Monique, 172
Pershing, General, 8
Pickles, Mabel, 295
Pickles, Wilfred, 295
Plough, Joppa, 51, 55, 57
Pontin, Fred, 73
Poolman, Kenneth, 7, 8, 125, 151
Poolman, Monica *(Mona, formerly Monica Diggle)*, 7, 8, 125, 151
Powell, John, 220-221

R

Rattle, Simon, 217
Rhodes, Cecil, 8
Richardson, David, 299
Rittner, Luke, 294
Rosie the elephant, 23-24
Roth, Kenyon, 279, 286, 290
Rouxel, Madame, 164
Rowland, Martin, 222

S

Savill, Jennifer, 68, 78
Scott, Ronnie, 89, 104, 135, 137
Seager, Godfrey, 187, 188
Selby, Mrs, 68, 77
Semprini, 147
Shaw, Margaret, 113-114, 116
Short, 'Fearless Frankie', 135
Sinclair, Geoffrey, 88
Smith, Maurice, 125
Smith, Roy, 20, 71
Soames, Emma, 297
Staddon, 'Gran' *(author's maternal grandmother)*, 9, 14, 75, 125
Staddon, Benjamin, 9
Staddon, Florence, 9
Staddon, James, 9
Staddon, John *(author's maternal grandfather)*, 9
Staddon, Marie, 9
Staddon, Thomas, 9
Stainforth, G. H., 63
Stalin, Joseph, 17, 32, 53
Steinbeck, John, 111, 115
Stewart, Jim, 139
Stoneley, Dick, 115
Stretton, T. A., 64, 76, 78
Stubbs, Ken, 203, 205, 247

T

Tait, Marion, 296
Thomas, Ronald, 141
Thor, That bloody Great Dane, 84, 91, 117, 138, 160, 183
Tom Call Me Harry, 38
Trevellick, Tom, 210
Turner, Bruce, 143
Turner, David, 109-110, 112
Turner, Robin, 88

V

Vine, Phillip, 144
Virgilio, Signor, 224, 225

W

Wakeley, Bob, 87, 90
Walsh, Sam, 207
Watts-Russell, The family, 72, 73, 91, 160
Way, David, 209, 217
Webster, Ben, 143-144, 147
Weeitch, Mr, 93-94, 95
Wellins, Bobby, 148
Wesker, Arnolf, 102
West, Timothy, 296
Whittington, Dick, 32, 37
Wilby, Heather, 182, 194, 195, 210, 238, 290, 291
Wilby, Roger 182, 194, 195, 203, 210, 211-216, 226-227, 238, 240, 289, 290, 291
Wilby, Sarah, 182, 195
Wilde, Sergeant, 69
Willatt, Sir Hugh, 294, 297
Williams, Margaret *(author's cousin)*, 126
Willis, Lord Ted, 296
Wills, Colin, 287, 288-289, 293, 294